PEREGRINE BOOKS

THE MAN ON HORSEBACK

The Man on Horseback received wide acclaim when it was first published and has proved itself as the definitive work on the role of the military in politics. Now brought up to date with a new chapter, a revised bibliography and tables setting out the number, distribution and provenence of military *coups* in the last fifteen years, it provides a lucid and coherent summary of one of the key political phenomena of our time.

Professor Finer examines 'political colonels' as a type, generalizing from numerous examples about the military as a political force and the factors which promote or inhibit the intervention of the armed forces in politics. As the discussion develops, a clear pattern emerges from which the author draws the conclusion that military *coups* are likely to increase in the future, as the new nations of Africa and Asia develop.

'The writer's discussion of the motives and situations which precipitate military intervention is as thorough as his examination of the historical reasons which make it possible in the first place' – David Rees in the *Spectator*

Professor Samuel E. Finer has been Gladstone Professor of Government and Public Administration at All Souls College, University of Oxford, since 1974. He has written numerous articles and published a large number of books. Among them are *The Life and Times of Sir Edwin Chadwick* (1952), *Anonymous Empire: a study of the Lobby in Britain* (1966) and *Comparative Government* (Pelican, 1974).

D1577800

S. E. FINER

The Man on Horseback

THE ROLE OF THE MILITARY
IN POLITICS

Second, enlarged edition

PENGUIN BOOKS

Penguin Books Ltd, Harmondsworth, Middlesex, England
Penguin Books Inc., 7110 Ambassador Road, Baltimore, Maryland 21207, U.S.A.
Penguin Books Australia Ltd, Ringwood, Victoria, Australia
Penguin Books Canada Ltd, 41 Steelcase Road West, Markham, Ontario, Canada
Penguin Books (N.Z.) Ltd, 182–190 Wairau Road, Auckland 10, New Zealand

—

First published by Pall Mall Press 1962
Revised edition published in Peregrine Books 1976
Copyright © S. E. Finer, 1962, 1975

—

Filmset in 'Monophoto' Times by
Richard Clay (The Chaucer Press) Ltd, Bungay, Suffolk
and printed in Great Britain by
Fletcher & Son Ltd, Norwich

In recognition,
gratitude and love to
my great teacher and
constant guide

my brother
HERMAN

CONTENTS

ACKNOWLEDGEMENTS

THIS essay grew out of a short paper I presented to the British Political Studies Association. The more I thought about the subject, the more important it seemed to me. Since nobody else seemed to have examined it – at least, in the way I thought it ought to be examined – I felt compelled to do so myself. I hope I have done so competently enough not to have spoiled the field for others better qualified. I by no means offer the book as the last word – for this will not be written for a long time to come – but as a first one. I shall be disappointed if it does not lead to further research in this field, however critical of my own standpoint it may prove to be.

I have written it for the general reader rather than for my professional colleagues, though I trust the scholarship will not prove any the worse for that; but this explains why I have cut down the usual apparatus of citations and references, and limited the bibliography.

Colleagues have given me great help and encouragement. I would particularly thank Mr F. G. Carnell of the Institute of Commonwealth Studies, Oxford; Professor George Fischer of Cornell University; Professor John Lewis, also of Cornell University; my friend, Professor W. J. M. MacKenzie of Manchester University; my old colleague, Mr A. P. V. Rolo, Senior Lecturer in History at the University of Keele; and, finally, my crony of undergraduate days at Trinity College, Oxford, Brigadier Peter Young, D.S.O., M.C., M.A., of the Royal Military Academy, Sandhurst, who used to beat me in a fascinating *kriegspiel* which we invented together. All these colleagues read my typescript and offered valuable comments and corrections which have much improved the book.

I must also thank Mr S. O. Stewart, the Librarian of the University of Keele, and his staff, for the help they have given me in obtaining the very wide range of books and other materials that was necessary to carry out my research.

PREFACE TO THE PEREGRINE EDITION

THIS appearance of *The Man on Horseback* in a Peregrine edition provides me with a happy challenge and opportunity to do something that I have long wished to do: that is, to take account of the accumulating number and variety of military interventions – and the equally increasing number of books and papers written about them – since the book made its first appearance.

After reflection, it seemed to me to be unwise to proceed by way of footnotes and interpolations of new material. I am sure this would have proved more confusing than enlightening. It would certainly have unbalanced the original presentation, on which I spent some care. And in any case, though it is presumptuous for me to say it, the text itself has by now acquired a certain authority: while, as far as I myself am concerned, the main lines of its argument still stand.

I have therefore revised this text by way of supplementing it. The original twelve chapters are presented intact and as they were written. But to them I have added a revised bibliography; a number of tables which set out, in various ways, the number, the distribution and the provenance of military interventions over the last fifteen years; and, above all, a long supplementary Chapter 13. Taken together, these will, I hope, provide a coherent review of what has been happening over the last twelve years, what has been said about it, and the modification these events call for in my original formulation.

All Souls College, Oxford   S.E.F.
18 July 1975

In tes - ta egli ha un cap - - pel - - lo con can - di - di pen - nac - chi, ad -dos - so un gran man - tel - lo, e spa - da al fian - co egli ha.

CHAPTER ONE

THE MILITARY IN THE POLITICS OF TODAY

THE year 1962 opened with brisk outbursts of military revolt. Four risings – those in the Lebanon, Portugal, Turkey and Venezuela – were unsuccessful, but the month of March witnessed three victorious revolts in quick succession. In Burma, General Ne Win deposed the government and established direct military rule. In Argentina, the armed forces removed President Frondizi and set up a Provisional President in his place. In Syria, exactly six months after the 1961 coup, military factions first swept away the civilian régime and then, quarrelling among themselves, restored it.

The date of the unsuccessful Lebanon rising, between the last day of the old year and the first day of the new, was symbolical: in all this military activity, 1962 was but continuing where 1961 had left off. For 1961 was also a busy one for the armed forces. They overthrew the provisional government in El Salvador in January. In April the 'Four Generals' staged their unsuccessful coup in Algeria. In May it was the turn of the South Korean army; it overthrew its government and established a thorough-going military dictatorship. In August the Brazilian armed forces strove to prevent Vice-President Senhor Goulart's accession to the Presidency (which had been vacated by the resignation of President Quadros). In September the army of the Syrian province of the U.A.R. revolted, drove the Egyptian officials out, and established a government for an independent Syria. In November Ecuador's army and air forces clashed as to who was to succeed the President – who had himself resigned as the result of a military revolt.

Nor was 1961 very different from 1960. That year had seen the Turkish army revolt of May, and the establishment of General Gürsel's dictatorship; the mutiny of the Congolese Force Publique in July and the subsequent rapine and carnage throughout the newborn Republic; the Laotian coup of Captain Kong Lee in August – the move that sparked off the civil war; the bloodless coup by which Colonel Osorio ousted President Lemus of El Salvador in October; and finally, the revolt of the Palace Guard against the Emperor of Ethiopia in December.

In every case the armed forces had defied or indeed used violence against the government of the state. In May 1960 on the occasion of General Gürsel's revolt, *The Times* commented: 'It has been a good year for

Generals'; but this was not only belated but quite misleading. For 1959 had witnessed an unsuccessful rising in Iraq, an unsuccessful military plot in Cambodia and a successful coup in the Sudan, while 1958 was – for the military – an *annus mirabilis*. That was the year when Marshal Sarit abrogated the constitution of Thailand and made himself dictator; in which Generals Ayub Khan, Kassim and Abboud seized power in Pakistan, Iraq and the Sudan respectively; in which, also, General Ne Win was raised to power in Burma and General de Gaulle in France.

Yet perhaps this period 1958–61 is exceptional? Hardly so. Consider the sovereign states that are at least seven years old, i.e. those created in or before 1955. Leaving aside small states of nominal sovereign status such as Liechtenstein, San Marino or the Trucial States, 79[1] sovereign states existed in or before 1955: 15 came into being between 1945 and 1955, and of these 9 have suffered from military coups (including the Lebanon). Another 13 states came into being between 1918 and 1944 (including the 3 Baltic States, now absorbed into the Soviet Union). Of these, 6 experiences military coups, and one of them (Jordan) may fairly be said to be a royal military dictatorship. The three states created between 1900 and 1917, i.e. Albania, Cuba and Panama, have all witnessed military revolt and dictatorship since 1918; and so likewise have the two – Bulgaria and Serbia – which became fully independent between 1861 and 1899. 46 states have been independent for more than a century. Since 1918 no less than 26 of these have suffered from some form or other of military intervention in their politics, usually of a violent kind.[2]

Thus the military coups of 1958–61 were certainly not exceptional. Of the 51 states existing in or before 1917, all but 19 have experienced such coups since 1917; while of the 28 created between 1917 and 1955, all but 15 have done so. Independent political activity by the armed forces is therefore frequent, widespread and of long standing.

Nor are its effects transitory. On the contrary. At the moment of writing some 11 states are military dictatorships: Thailand, Pakistan, Egypt, the Sudan, Iraq, Spain, Portugal, South Korea, El Salvador, Paraguay and Nicaragua. In addition, in a large number of countries the army alone guarantees the régime: e.g. in Jordan, the Congo, Persia, Honduras. In many other countries, e.g. Indonesia, Argentina, Brazil, Venezuela, Peru, Ecuador and Guatemala, the régimes must needs court the armed

1. Properly, 76. The figure of 79 includes Esthonia, Lithuania and Latvia, now absorbed into the U.S.S.R., but independent from 1918 to 1940.

2. China falls outside this classification. It was a prey to incessant civil war and military turbulence until 1949.

forces' goodwill – a favour which may be suddenly withdrawn, as in the past.

Finally, this political activity of the military is *persistent*. In certain areas of South America, earthquakes are so frequent that the people date great events from the years when by rare chance no earthquake has occurred. Likewise with the political activity of the military; there are areas where it can fairly be described – by virtue of its recurrent and its widespread nature – as endemic. Such an area is Latin America, where the phenomenon has persisted for a century and a half; the Middle East; and likewise South East Asia. A fourth such area lay in Europe (up to the communization of most of its countries) in the strip connecting the Baltic, the Balkans and Turkey.[3]

From what has been said so far we may draw two conclusions. In the first place there is a distinct class of countries where governments have been repeatedly subjected to the interference of their armed forces. They are certainly not liberal democracies of the British or American kind wherein the military are strictly subordinated to the civilians. Nor are they despotisms or autocracies of a totalitarian type, where, we must emphasize, the military are subordinated to the civilians as much as or even more than in the liberal-democratic régimes. These régimes of military provenance or military rule are *sui generis*. They constitute a large proportion of those sovereign states which are neither communist nor liberal-democratic, and will soon comprise most of them; for the two other main types of government in the world, the colonial oligarchies (like Angola or Kenya) are disappearing, and so likewise are the proto-dynastic régimes like those of Nepal or Arabia or the Yemen. The régimes where the military are the decisive political factor form a distinct class which we may call the *empirical autocracies and oligarchies*. 'Empirical' distinguishes them from the ideological autocracies and oligarchies of the Soviet type; 'autocracies and oligarchies' distinguishes them from the democracies.

Secondly, the military as an independent political force constitutes a distinct and peculiar political phenomenon. Consider that the armed forces have intervened in the politics of many and widely diverse countries; that they have done so continually in the past, and are doing so today; that their intervention is usually politically decisive; and that, above all, they tend to intervene persistently, over and over again, in the same countries. None of this suggests that we are observing a mere set of ephemeral, exceptional and isolated adventures. On the contrary, it does emphatically suggest that we are in the presence of a peculiar political phenomenon: one that is abiding, deep-seated and distinctive.

3. For the significance of this geographical spread see Chapter Twelve.

The régime of military provenance or direct military rule is, in short, a distinctive kind of régime; and the military as an independent political force is a distinctive political phenomenon.

Little attention has been given to either. For one thing, few have tried to distinguish between the forms that military intervention takes; or the depth to which it is pressed. At first glance the characteristic mode of military intervention is the violent overturn of a government and the characteristic 'level' is the establishment of overt military rule. Yet the military often work on governments from behind the scenes; and even when they do establish a military dictatorship they usually fabricate some quasi-civilian façade of government behind which they retire as fast as possible. Overt military rule is therefore comparatively rare, and, apparently, short-lived. It is this that gives the appearance of transience to military régimes. But the modes of military intervention are as often latent or indirect as they are overt or direct. Likewise the 'level' to which the military press their intervention varies; they do not always supplant the civilian régime. Often they merely substitute one cabinet for another, or again simply subject a cabinet to blackmail. When all these varied modes of military intervention in politics are examined and the 'levels' to which the military press such intervention are recognized, the phenomenon appears in its true light – distinctive, persistent and widespread.

Secondly, there is a common assumption, an unreflecting belief, that it is somehow 'natural' for the armed forces to obey the civil power. Therefore instances which show civilian control to have broken down are regarded, if at all, as isolated disturbances, after which matters will again return to 'normal'. But no reason is adduced for showing that civilian control of the armed forces is, in fact, 'natural'. Is it? Instead of asking why the military engage in politics, we ought surely to ask why they ever do otherwise. For at first sight the political advantages of the military *vis-à-vis* other and civilian groupings are overwhelming. The military possess vastly superior organization. And they possess *arms*.

CHAPTER TWO

THE POLITICAL STRENGTHS OF THE MILITARY

THE armed forces have three massive political advantages over civilian organizations: a marked superiority in organization, a highly emotionalized symbolic status, and a monopoly of arms. They form a prestigious corporation or Order, enjoying overwhelming superiority in the means of applying force. The wonder, therefore, is not why this rebels against its civilian masters, but why it ever obeys them.

The modern army [1]

In practically every country of the world today, except possibly in one or two of the proto-dynastic survivals such as the Yemen, the army is marked by the superior quality of its organization. Even the most poorly organized or maintained of such armies is far more highly and tightly structured than any civilian group.

The fact that not all armies were highly organized in the past, or that they need not necessarily be so, is irrelevant here. Modern armies are *cohesive* and *hierarchical*. Some armies of the past have not been cohesive but have consisted of a mere multitude of men independent of one another and maintaining little contact between themselves. Others have not been hierarchical, but almost republican in their relations to their chiefs. The Spartan host and the Cossack settlements were cohesive enough, but republican as to command. The *voortrekkers* and the American frontiersmen were neither cohesive nor hierarchical formations. In the early stages of their development, some revolutionary armies (e.g. Fidel Castro's, or Pancho Villa's or Zapata's) resemble these primitive prototypes of the modern armies, and to that extent we still have some occasion to deal with them in this book; but for the most part, and certainly for the time being, we are concerned only with the modern type of army, characterized by its uniquely high level of organization.

Organization and coherence

'*Non est potestas super terram quae comparetur*' runs the quotation on the title page of Hobbes's *Leviathan*. May we not think likewise of the modern army?

1. What is said of the army here is to be taken also to apply, *mutatis mutandis*, to the air force and the navy.

The army is a *purposive* instrument. It is not a crescive institution like the church; it comes into being by fiat. It is rationally conceived to fulfil certain objects. One may be to assist the civil power, but the principal object is to fight and win wars. The highly peculiar features of its organization flow from this central purpose, not from the secondary one, and find in it their supreme justification. These features are (1) centralized command, (2) hierarchy, (3) discipline, (4) intercommunication, (5) *esprit de corps* and a corresponding isolation and self-sufficiency.

Military command is centralized. In practice, much is delegated to units in the field, but always within the supreme command's general directives and always subject to be resumed by it should occasion arise. A continuous chain of command links the very lowest echelons with the supreme H.Q. This centralization of authority derives from the basic object of the army – in military parlance it exists 'to be fought' by its commanders and for this it must respond to their commands as a single unit.

The army is arranged in a pyramid of authority, a hierarchy, each echelon owing explicit and peremptory obedience to the orders of its superior. The army is therefore very highly stratified. Further to this, each echelon in the hierarchy is immediately and objectively identifiable by named rank and distinctive insignia. Authority is depersonalized; it is owed to the rank, not to the man, and it exactly corresponds to the rank, and the rank to the insignia. The importance of subordination and superordination is further enhanced by social practices prescribing a social distance between the superior and the inferior ranks. The hierarchical structure, like centralization, derives from the army's basic imperative – to fight as a unit; it must have a supreme directing command – hence centralization; the command must transmit its orders from highest to lowest – hence hierarchy.

From high to low, each member is subject to discipline. The army is difficult to leave – desertion is punished heavily, and desertion on active service might even incur the death penalty. The chain of command is sacrosanct; everything is supposed to 'go through the channels'. In practice, this often is offset by the 'Old Boy Network', whereby one can speed up the 'usual channels'. This is true of most large-scale organizations. It only thrives, however, where the organization has developed an *esprit de corps* (for which see below). Each echelon is subject to the orders of its superiors; failure to obey carries penalties, some exceedingly heavy. This obligation to unquestioning and prompt obedience is enhanced by the depersonalization of the soldier. The army is too big a machine to reck of individuals, and the soldier becomes a number. Extraneous considerations are thereby thrust aside, and obedience to superiors, recognized by their rank and insignia, becomes the dominant or sole criterion of action. This rule of obedience also springs from the army's primary purpose, i.e. successful combat. Unless it existed, the behaviour of the units that are being 'fought' would not be calculable. It must be calculable and predictable if the battle plan is to be executed.

Centralization of command, the hierarchical arrangement of authority and the rule of obedience – all are necessary to make the army respond as a unity to the word of command; but they in turn demand a nervous system, a network of communication. Armies have developed elaborate signal systems independent of the civil authorities. The most modern methods of telephone, wireless and teleprinter are supplemented by the older systems of physical communication – the despatch rider, and this in turn by the primitive methods of semaphore and the runner. For so important are communications that there must always be methods available, even the most clumsy. By these means the nervous articulation of every unit in the country and the combination of all arms and services is rendered *physically* possible. By the same token, the territorial dispersion of units, their geographical separation offers no impediment to their unity of decision and of action.

But any army which possessed only these characteristics and none other would hardly win a battle. Its unity would be entirely mechanical, wholly compulsive, singularly lifeless, and not very bellicose. An army must in addition be animated by consciousness of its martial purpose and inspired by a corporate spirit of unity and solidarity. What Durkheim called *organic* solidarity, namely a 'system of different and special functions united by definite relationships', has to be supplemented by his (strangely named) *mechanical* solidarity, i.e. 'a more or less organized *ensemble* of the beliefs and the sentiments common to all the members of the group'. This can only be, as Durkheim says, 'in proportion as the ideas and inclinations common to all the members ... exceed in number and intensity those personal to each of them ...' [2]

This 'more or less organized *ensemble* of the beliefs and sentiments common to all members of the group' is deliberately inculcated in armies and constitutes their vital spark – their *esprit de corps*. It is grounded on service to a cause – as with Cromwell's Ironsides or Trotsky's Red Army – but, much more commonly, on service to the nation. The inculcation of an extreme nationalism, often of the most rabid or it may be vulgar sort, is universal in the training of all but the very few ideological or religious armies. This is accompanied by the systematic disparagement of the

2. E. Durkheim, *La Division du travail social*, Paris, 1960, p. 99.

foreigner, and the channelling of all aggressive tendencies into hatred of the enemy.

Such indoctrination is supplemented by measures to inculcate a sense of solidarity. The newcomer is instructed in the history and traditions of his regiment. He is taught to respect its insignia and its colours. And all this is enhanced by some of the physical arrangements of the military life. The army differs in function from the society that surrounds it and this function requires that it be separate and segregated. It requires a common uniform, and this immediately distinguishes it from the civilian masses. It requires separate housing, in purely military quarters, the barracks. It demands a systematized nomadism moving from one garrison town to another. It demands a separate code of morals and manners from that of the civilian population, so that the normal freedom of life – to take leave, to change one's employment, in some cases even to marry – are exercised only under surveillance and tutelage, and by permission. All this tends to enhance military solidarity by making the military life self-centred. It is easy, even, to inspire contempt for one's own nationals – the 'civvies', '*les pékins*', '*les bourgeois*' – and so forth. The barracks becomes the world.[3]

Thus because of their centralization, hierarchy, discipline, intercommunication and *esprit de corps*, armies are much more highly organized than any civilian bodies. Few of these attain to the degree of organization obtained by even the most primitive of modern armies. The Roman Catholic Church certainly displays these five features; but it is a voluntary organization which the member may enter or leave as he thinks fit; for those of tepid faith the penalties for disobedience are feeble; its segregation from the laity is much less extreme than that of officer-corps from civilians. Firms and bureaucracies may possess these five characteristics too, but, once again, they are voluntary bodies, the sanctions for indiscipline are feeble and there is no segregation, no very special code of manners or rules that have to be obeyed, and no tutelage. Of political parties only the communist parties of the 'popular democracies' resemble the armed forces. Not for nothing have they been described as 'lay armies'. Their high degree of organization and their formidably energetic *esprit de corps* are, as we shall see, of the highest importance to the question of civilian control of the armed forces;[4] yet here again, they are neither as hierarchical, as severely disciplined, as physically interconnected, as armies, nor are they physically and psychologically separated from the rest of the population.

3. For proof, if it be needed, witness the plots and escapades that make up the tale of such television programmes as *Sergeant Bilko*.

4. See p. 88 *et seq.*

Modern armies, then, are usually far more highly organized than any other association within a state. This is not the only political advantage they possess. The military profession often – though not always – carries with it certain emotional associations. In so far as this is so, the army may enjoy a politically important moral prestige.

The military virtues

'Their sons,' wrote Herodotus of the Persians, 'are carefully instructed from their fifth to their twentieth year in three things alone – to ride, to draw the bow and to speak the truth.'[5] Herein we see the prototype of the famed military virtues. These virtues – bravery, discipline, obedience, self-abnegation, poverty, patriotism, and the like – are associated, by long standing, with the soldier's choice of career. They are values which all esteem. Where they are identified with the military, these acquire a moral halo which is politically of profound importance.

Yet we must be cautious. The military are *not* universally well regarded. In Germany or Japan, up to 1945, their prestige was preternaturally high. In Egypt, during the same period and up to 1952, the profession of arms was despised; likewise, the Chinese soldier was despised until 1949. *Autres pays, autres moeurs.* Furthermore, in any one country, public opinion may be quite different at one period from what it is at another. This has been elegantly demonstrated for the French army by Girardet.[6] After 1815 there was a reaction against all things military. The soldier was regarded as vulgar, uncouth, brutal. 'These soldiers,' writes Girardet (echoing the sentiments of that time), 'who take up the middle of the pavement, noisy and arrogant; who often behave as in a conquered town, pursuing the women with their gross assiduities ...' Yet fifty years later general sentiment favoured the soldier. The social prestige of the officer was very high and to marry a daughter to one became an object of middle-class ambition. Instead of stressing their stupidity or their unproductiveness, society sentimentalized over the 'life of order, hierarchy, obedience and poverty'.[7] Not very much later, after Sedan, the army became *'l'arche sainte'*, its hierarchical nature rendering it the darling of the Right, and its democratic mass basis the favourite of the Left.

Yet, at most times and in most countries, traits like courage and discipline and self-sacrifice and patriotism, traits which seem almost characteristically to inhere in 'the soldier', are esteemed and cherished. From this

5. Herodotus, *History*. Everyman ed., vol. 1, p. 72.
6. R. Girardet, *La Societé militaire dans la France contemporaine.*
7. ibid., Chapter 1.

there arises, at the lowest, a sympathy for the armed forces; at its highest a veritable mystique.

... That it may become as it ought to be, the career of arms requires from those who seek or are called on to pursue it, certain specific qualities which we call the military virtues: valour, fidelity, patriotism. The exercise of these virtues to a very high degree is so essential to the career of arms that they constitute its characteristic feature, define its own peculiar spirit. They are the necessary conditions of the existence of the career, and if they disappeared it would disappear also. How can one conceive of a cowardly soldier, an unfaithful comrade, a warrior who betrays his country? No! To the extent that cowardice, disloyalty and treason arise, there is no force, there are no troops, there is no army. There is only a multitude in arms – and for that very reason more dangerous than any other ...

In internal structure, the army is not simply a collection of men: it is an organism to which union, collaboration and solidarity are indispensable. Fidelity in the army is necessary to make sure that at all times all organs will carry out their duty. For this reason there must be no plots, no disunity, no mutual distrust; watchful of itself the army must expel from its midst, like dead bodies, those elements which do not belong to it in spirit, and whose hearts do not beat in unison with its own ...

For the soldier ... there exists neither the hamlet, nor the region, nor the province, nor the colony: there is for him nothing but the national territory. He has no family, no relatives, no friends, no neighbours: only the people who live and work in the national territory. He has only – in a word – the fatherland; the fatherland in all its material expressions, in the totality of its sentiments and traditions, in all the beauty of its historical evolution and its future ideal. To it he must surrender all; safety, peace, family and life itself.[8]

Sentiments such as these would be re-echoed today in Cairo, Baghdad, Khartoum; in Madrid or in Karachi; and wherever they are harboured they help lift the military to power. But even in London, or Washington, or Stockholm, an atmosphere of candour, self-sacrifice and vigour clings to the armed forces, and of all among the 'powers that be' there is a tendency to esteem them as the most noble. Where and in so far as this happens, it constitutes a second political strength of the military.

The armed forces then are not only the most highly organized association in the state. They are a continuing corporation with an intense sentiment of solidarity, enjoying, in many cases, considerable favour. This formidable corporate body is more lethally and heavily armed than any other organization in the state, and indeed enjoys a near-monopoly of all effective weapons.

Since this is so, why is military intervention in politics, or military

8. Oliveira Salazar, *El Pensamiento de la Revolucion Nacional*, Buenos Aires, 1938, Chapter V, pp. 118–22, 'Elogio de las Virtudes Militares'.

government, the exception rather than the rule? Why and how do civilian forms of rule persist?

The rest of this book sets out some of the factors which are relevant to answering these questions. Two of these, however, are sufficiently general – and indeed fundamental to all that follows – to be noticed immediately. They constitute the basic *weaknesses* in the political position of the military.

CHAPTER THREE

THE POLITICAL WEAKNESSES OF THE MILITARY

POLITICALLY the armed forces suffer from two crippling weaknesses. These preclude them, save in exceptional cases and for brief periods of time, from ruling without civilian collaboration and openly in their own name. Soldiers must either rule through civilian cabinets or else pretend to be something other than they are.

One weakness is the armed forces' technical inability to administer any but the most primitive community. The second is their lack of legitimacy: that is to say, their lack of a moral title to rule.

The technical inadequacy of the armed forces

Even in those states commonly described as 'military dictatorships', the ruling body, junta or cabinet, will be found not to consist exclusively of military men. In Iraq, for instance (in March 1961), only 7 out of the 16 cabinet members were soldiers; in Pakistan, only 3 out of 14; in Spain, only 6 out of 18. There have been few exceptions to this rule, and those have been shortlived. Primo de Rivera's first government, 1923, was called a 'Military Directorate' and consisted entirely of military, but in 1925 he changed to a largely civilian cabinet. In the first phase of the Argentine military régime in 1943, nearly all the cabinet posts and top administrative positions at federal and provincial level were manned by soldiers, but after 1944 civilians replaced them. In Peru, in 1948, General Odría formed an all-military cabinet in which colonels headed the ministries of public health, education, labour, the interior, the treasury and justice, while a rear-admiral conducted foreign relations; but this stage lasted only until 1950, after which the cabinet was composed of six officers and six civilians.

The more primitive the economy, the easier it is for the armed forces to administer it by purely military men and measures. Modern armies are a microcosm of the state; they possess their own separate and self-contained systems of provisioning, supply, engineering, communications, even of education. In primitive economies they may therefore be even better technically equipped than the civil sector, and it is not surprising that even in comparatively advanced societies like Brazil or Argentina the armed forces are used for promoting economic developments. In Brazil, for instance, the army has explored the interior, set up telegraph and wireless stations, developed agricultural colonies and helped educate the Indians. The army did likewise in Peru in the 1940s and in Bolivia in the 1950s. In Argentina it has opened new roads, constructed schools and hospitals[1] and carries some responsibility for the development of the domestic oil industry.

As societies become more complicated, however, so the technical skills of the armed forces lag further and further behind them. Laos, for instance, is a primitive state of $1\frac{1}{2}$ million inhabitants, one third of whom – the autochthonous Kha tribesmen – are primitive in the extreme. The administrative capital of Vientiane is a tiny town of brick and wood. Apart from the tin mines of Phôn Tiu, the economy is almost entirely subsistence agriculture, employing archaic techniques. Other than the Mekong river, there are few communications. Argentina, one hundred years ago, was not much more developed. The most advanced area was the town of Buenos Aires, and before 1870 this had no artificial drainage, but depended on scouring by the heavy rains; its water supply was carted in from the river; and its population was tiny. As for the rest of the country (the Campo), except for a few mines in the north-west it was pastoral. There was no industry, and only 800 miles of railroad.

Armies could – or do – easily dominate such primitive societies. All they have to provide is law and order, and communications. Even the educational, social and economic development of such countries would be well within their capabilities, if they chose to undertake it; though, since the armies of these countries are not usually much more enlightened than the societies they serve, they do not in fact usually try to do so.

Compare the task of administering such societies with that of ruling, say, Great Britain or the United States, or, for that matter, even Detroit or Chicago or London! How very very much more is required can be seen from Allied experiences in military government in Italy and Germany after 1945. It must be remembered that in both cases the occupying powers were dealing with compliant and cooperative populations, anxious to ingratiate themselves with the victors and eager to restore their shattered economies; whereas in most (or at least many) military dictatorships the armed forces have to face a mutinously sullen or openly hostile people. Yet the occupying powers were only able to carry out their task by heavily reinforcing their military personnel with specially trained civilian administrators. In the U.S. Control Council for Germany 'a roster of the names and business associations of the economic advisors and division heads' reads, we are

1. R. Lieuwen, *Arms and Politics in Latin America*, pp. 137 *et seq*.

told, 'like a *Who's Who* of American industry and finance'.[2] The United States army also had to recruit civilian technicians to supplement its very limited supply of specialists in the fields of 'administration, law, finance, economics, public works, public health, public relations, public safety, public welfare, transportation, communications.'[3]

Secondly, the administration was successful only in repairing material breakdowns. 'Later,' runs the account, 'as problems of security, sanitation and restoration of public utilities faded into the background, their inadequacy in such fields as denazification, political revival and re-education became apparent. It was far more simple for them to replace a broken water main, since both ruler and ruled could appreciate the service of a good one, than it was to select a suitable burgomaster on the definition of which they might differ.'[4]

Thirdly, the military proved incapable, by their training, of ruling in any sense wider than putting the economy of the country on a 'care and maintenance' basis. Theirs, says a critic, 'was a narrow emphasis on the maintenance of law and order ... extreme reluctance to disturb existing institutions, suspicion of politics and politicians and distrust of trade unionists ...'[5]

In short, in Germany, the professional military men conceived their task as putting the country on 'a fodder basis' – and little more; and even for this their forces' own resources of technicians and administrators was entirely inadequate. Indeed, the military had to lay down their previous jobs and become policy makers, and turn over the doing of things to their own civilian staffs and to the civilians of the subject population.

Thus as an economy advances, as the division of labour becomes more and more extensive, as the secondary and then the tertiary services expand, and as the society requires the existence of a trained professional bureaucracy, of technicians, labour organizations, and the like – so the army ceases to be able to rule by its own resources alone. Its aim must be to cajole or to coerce the civilians and their organizations into collaboration. And to the extent that it has to depend on them, so to that extent is it weakened.[6]

The right to govern

Now in an advanced society, i.e. just where the military's technical inability to rule is at its greatest, its moral inadequacy hampers it still further, by

2. 'Military Government', *Annals of the American Academy of Political and Social Science*, vol. 267, 1950, pp. 78–80. 3. ibid. 4. ibid. 5. ibid.
6. See below, the cases of Japan, Germany, France, Chapter Seven.

denying it the civilian collaboration it must secure. For the second and cardinal weakness of the military as a political force is its lack of title to govern.

Rule by force alone, or the threat of such force, is inadequate; in addition, government must possess *authority*. It must be widely recognized not only as the government but as the lawful, the rightful government. A government that based its rule on the fact that it was materially stronger than any other force or forces in society would prove both shortlived and ineffective.

This is not 'moralizing'. It is a generalization based on experience, and is capable of simple explanation. First of all, such government would be impermanent. The reason is simply that the claim to rule by virtue of superior force invites challenge; indeed it is itself a tacit challenge, to any contender who thinks he is strong enough to chance his arm.

> The same Arts that did gain
> A pow'r, must it maintain

wrote Marvell. 'If force creates right,' wrote Rousseau, 'the effect changes with the cause. Every force that is greater than the first succeeds to its right. As soon as it is possible to disobey with impunity disobedience is legitimate; and the strongest being always in the right, the only thing that matters is to act so as to become the strongest.'[7] It is indeed! And this succinctly explains one of the most usual consequences of a military coup, namely a succession of further coups by which new contenders aim to displace the firstcomers. '*Quitate tu, para ponerme yo,*' runs the appropriately Spanish proverb. We shall meet many examples later; here let one suffice – Iraq, where six successive coups were carried out between 1936 and 1941.[8]

> Force should be right; or rather, right and wrong,
> Between whose endless jars justice resides,
> Should lose their names and so should justice, too.
> Then everything includes itself in power,
> Power into will, will into appetite;
> And appetite, an universal wolf,
> So doubly seconded with will and power
> Must make perforce an universal prey,
> And last eat up himself.[9]

Thus governments that have achieved power by force have to defend it against one challenge after another. Such governments, therefore, either

7. J. J. Rousseau, *The Social Contract*, Book I, Chapter 3.
8. See pp. 121–2.
9. *Troilus and Cressida*, Act 1, Scene III.

fall to further coups or hasten to convert themselves into something else: that is to say, to ground their claim to govern on something other than their successful seizure of power. They seek, in short, to exercise a *right* to govern; or, as the expression goes, to *legitimize* themselves. Some do this (e.g. General Gürsel in Turkey) by claiming to be on a 'caretaker' basis preparing the way for a legal government, perhaps on the basis of elections. Others take the plunge by organizing a plebiscite (like Colonel Nasser or Primo de Rivera or General Franco) to vote them into the power they seized by force of arms.

> Treason doth never prosper: what's the reason?
> For if it prosper, none dare call it treason.

A military junta legitimizes itself in order to slam the door of morality in its challengers' faces. Until it has done so, it bears the mark of Cain. It is outlaw. Let it once be legitimized, and it is entitled to hunt down the new contenders for power as rebels or mutineers. As Victor Hugo put it, after Louis-Napoleon had legitimized himself by the plebiscite of 1852:

Mr Bonaparte's crime is not a crime, it is called a necessity; Mr Bonaparte's ambuscade is not an ambuscade, it is called defence of order; Mr Bonaparte's robberies are not robberies, they are called measures of state; Mr Bonaparte's murders are not murders, they are called public safety; Mr. Bonaparte's accomplices are not called malefactors, they are called magistrates, senators, and councillors of state; Mr. Bonaparte's adversaries are not the soldiers of the law and right, they are Jack Cades, demogogues, communists . . .[10]

There is, however, a second reason which drives governments to seek authority rather than to rely on the prowess of their arms alone; namely that the threat of physical compulsion is not an efficient, i.e. an economical, way of securing obedience. Suppose, for instance, a village schoolmaster. Suppose that his only means for getting his charges to school, keeping them there, making them regular attenders and – presumably – trying to teach them something, were by physical force alone. Imagine him motoring to the houses of the children; dragging them protesting and arguing from their houses; beating one or two to make the others more compliant; forcing them to sit, to exercise, to learn – all by threat and physical violence. We must suppose, too, for the sake of the example, that the children are determined, as ever expediency allows, to defy him, disobey him and if possible get rid of him. In these circumstances, calculate how much more of the schoolmaster's time would be spent in rounding

10. Victor Hugo, *Napoleon the Little*, London, 1852, pp. 21–2.

them up, punishing them and devising schemes to beat down their opposition than would be spent in teaching them.

Contrast this with the other more common possibility, that his authority as 'the schoolmaster' is recognized. By this we mean simply that he claims the right to the children's attendance and attention at school; and they for their part recognize it as their duty to get to school, attend regularly and behave themselves in class. In these circumstances, he can spend almost the whole of his time on his primary function – teaching. Physical compulsion will emerge only as a sanction in marginal cases.

It is recognition of his authority that works the miraculous difference. This simple psychological bond between ruler and ruled does all the work of securing school attendance and discipline for him. In this sense, then, *authority is the mother of power*. Authority comprises a double relationship. On the one side goes society's recognition that in certain matters a person or body of persons has the moral right to demand obedience and on the other goes society's recognition that in these matters it has the moral duty to obey such persons. It is for this reason that Rousseau's words are so significant for armies that desire to rule: 'The strongest is never strong enough to be always the master unless he transforms might into right and obedience into duty.'[11]

The moral inadequacy of military intervention

Thus, when the military breaches the existing political order, it will be forced to claim a moral authority for its actions. Now in certain societies the public are most unlikely to recognize any such claim; and will indeed resist it.

Whether and how far a people will recognize or resist it, depends on the *political formula* current among them. This political formula is that widespread sentiment or belief on which the title to govern is grounded. Such are, or have been, the 'will of the people', 'the divine right of the monarch', the consciousness of forming a distinct nation, fidelity to a dynasty and so forth. Thus in the Middle Ages, where it was widely taught and believed that kings ruled by divine appointment, the contender for power had to demonstrate that he himself was really the 'king' and that the reigning king was not; and this was done by elaborate argument about and among genealogies. (That interminable and boring speech by the Archbishop of Canterbury, in Act I, Scene II, of *Henry V* exactly illustrates this point. King Henry finally asks: 'May I *with right and conscience* make this claim?' and is answered: 'The sin upon my head dread sovereign.') Once he had

11. Rousseau, op. cit., Book I, Chapter 3.

proved he was the king, i.e. the real king, he was entitled to command his subjects and they in turn duly bound to obey him.

These formulae change with time. Then the title by virtue of which the ruling group claim to govern becomes obsolete. It was no use Louis XVI claiming the right to rule by divine appointment when his subjects no longer believed a word of this rigmarole. As long as the rulers base their claim on a formula which is unacceptable to their subjects, these will regard them as illegitimate, as usurpers. That being so, the rulers will be able to maintain themselves only by increasing reliance on coercion.

The form that military intervention takes (e.g. violent or non-violent) and whether or not the military entertain the wish to intervene at all, both vary from society to society according to the political formulae current therein and their compatibility with such military intervention.

Where public attachment to civilian institutions is strong, military intervention in politics will be weak. It will take the form, if it occurs at all, of working upon or from behind these institutions – be they throne or parliament – according to the political formula current. By the same token, where public attachment to civilian institutions is weak or non-existent, military intervention in politics will find wide scope – both in manner and in substance.

These 'civil institutions' are a complex of procedures and organs, recognized as duty-worthy by a wide consensus in the society.[12] Where civilian associations and parties are strong and numerous, where the procedures for the transfer of power are orderly, and where the location of supreme authority is not seriously challenged: the political ambit of the military will be circumscribed. Where the parties or trade unions are feeble and few, where the procedure for the transfer of power is irregular or even non-existent, where the location of supreme authority is a matter of acute disagreement or else of unconcern and indifference: there the military's political scope will be very wide.

We can therefore think of societies as being at different levels of political culture according to their observed degree of attachment to civil institutions. At the highest political-culture levels will be countries like Britain or the United States, where attachment to civilian institutions is very strong. At the lowest level will be those countries like, perhaps, Haiti or the Congo today, or Argentina, Mexico and Venezuela a hundred years ago, where a conscious attachment to civilian institutions does not exist at all. Now it is a striking fact that people may have a high level of artistic or material

12. This crucial topic is further treated and explained in Chapter Seven where the concept of 'civil institutions' and 'political culture' is defined.

culture but a very low level of political culture. 'Many people have had periods of material and intellectual splendour and yet, as it were by a sort of fatal curse, have never been able to rid themselves of certain types of political organization that seem to be utterly unsuited to ensuring any real progress in the morality of their governing classes.'[13]

In lands of a low political culture the need for legitimacy will not, and indeed has not, proved a serious handicap to the military. But in countries of mature or advanced political culture it will prove crippling. In such countries, countries where attachment to civilian institutions is strong and pervasive, the attempts of the military to coerce the lawful government, let alone supplant it, would be universally regarded as usurpation. This, the moral barrier, is what has prevented the military, for all its organization, prestige and power, from establishing its rule throughout the globe.

13. G. Mosca (ed. A. Livingston), *The Ruling Class*, p. 133.

CHAPTER FOUR

THE DISPOSITION TO INTERVENE
(1) MOTIVE

WE HAVE been using the expression 'military intervention in politics'. By this we mean: *The armed forces' constrained substitution of their own policies and/or their persons, for those of the recognized civilian authorities.*

The military may pursue such intervention by acts of commission but also by acts of omission. It may act against the wishes of its government; or it may refuse to act when called on by its government. In either case it brings constraint to bear.

Now to intervene the military must have both occasion and disposition. By a 'disposition' we mean a combination of conscious motive and of a will or desire to act. It is this disposition that forms the subject of this chapter.

However, just as there are factors disposing the military to intervene, so there may be factors inhibiting them from such action. This is too easily lost sight of. In the nature of the case, armed forces that have intervened in politics are more vocal in explaining and justifying their action than are the numerous bodies of troops that have remained faithful to their obedience. We shall deal with them first.

Motives Inhibiting the Military from Intervention

The most obvious of such factors is, of course, the lack of motive. The military must not be conceived as everywhere simmering with discontent. We can therefore leave motives and turn to the second aspect of the disposition to intervene – i.e. desire or will. An important factor inhibiting a desire to intervene is military professionalism.

1. *Professionalism and its consequences*

'Professionalism' forms the central concept of a most important study of military intervention, Professor Huntington's *The Soldier and the State*.[1] For Huntington, it is the decisive factor in keeping the soldier out of politics, and the whole of his argument is made to hang on this.

For him 'professionalism' comprises three ingredients. They are expertness; social responsibility; and corporate loyalty to fellow-practitioners. Modern armed forces may therefore be described as a profession. They are

---

1. S. P. Huntington, *The Soldier and the State*, Harvard, 1957.

technicians in the management and organization of violence; they feel a responsibility to their client (i.e. the state); and they have a powerful corporate tradition and organization. But this professionalism, as he says truly, is of recent date. Before the French Revolution the various officer corps were either mercenaries who followed the paymaster, or noblemen who followed their king – even when he went into exile. Whereas the beginning of the nineteenth century knew no professional armies, the beginning of the twentieth century saw few armies that were not.

Professionalization makes the armed forces, as it were, self-centred. Like other professions they develop a sense of corporate unity *vis-à-vis* the layman – those 'civvies', 'frocks', or '*pékins*' of soldier slang. Their task – organizing and equipping a force, training it, planning its activities, let alone 'fighting it' in combat against the enemy – is a full-time one. It calls for special skill and demands long training. Thus, the greater the professionalism, the more immersed does the officer become in his own technical tasks, and the less involved in any policy issues that do not affect them. Huntington maintains that the logical consequence is for the officer corps to leave politics to the politicians. The officers' own responsibility becomes increasingly confined to representing the requirements of the military to the civilian authorities, giving advice to them, and, finally, when so charged, executing their decisions.

Having defined 'professionalism' as strictly as this, it is not surprising that Huntington should argue that the surest way to insulate the military from politics is to encourage them to be *fully* professional. In this way the military would be made 'politically sterile and neutral ... A highly professional officer corps stands ready to carry out the wishes of any civilian group which secures legitimate authority within the state.'[2] 'An officer corps is professional only to the extent to which its loyalty is to the military ideal ... Only if they are motivated by military ideals will the armed forces be the obedient servants of the state and will civilian control be assured ...'[3]

In so far as professionalism makes the military look on their task as different from that of the politicians, and as self-sufficient and full-time, it ought, logically, to inhibit the army from wishing to intervene. Yet it is observable that many highly professional officer corps have intervened in politics – the German and Japanese cases are notorious. It is of no use to retort that in such cases these armies cannot be described as 'fully' professional. This is the whole weakness of Huntington's thesis. All is made to hang upon a very special definition of professionalism, and by pure

2. ibid., p. 84.   3. ibid., p. 74.

deduction from this, of a so-called 'military mind'. The argument then becomes 'essentialist'. If soldiers are observed to act in ways inconsistent with these concepts of 'professionalism' and the 'military mind', so much the worse for the soldiers; they are not completely 'professional', not purely 'military'.[4] The fact is, however, that, if the armed forces are not to intervene, they must believe in an *explicit* principle – the principle of civil supremacy.

2. *The principle of civil supremacy*

The reason is that the very nature of the professionalism by which Huntington sets such store and which he regards as 'politically sterile', in fact often thrusts the military into collision with the civil authorities.

In the first place, the military's consciousness of themselves as a profession may lead them to see themselves as the servants of the state rather than of the government in power. They may contrast the national community as a continuing corporation with the temporary incumbents of office. It is this that explains the mystical concept of 'The Reich' in the attitudes of von Seeckt and Gröner under the Weimar Republic.

'The role of the Reichswehr,' said Seeckt, 'is to maintain the unity of the Reich and those who compromise this are its enemies from whichsoever side they come.'[5] 'To serve the State – far from all party politics, to save and maintain it against the terrible pressure from without and the insane strife at home – this,' said Gröner, 'is our only goal.'[6] Exactly the same attitude is implied in the famous interview between Sir Arthur Paget, Commander-in-Chief of the troops in Ireland, and the recalcitrant cavalry officers, at the time of the Curragh 'mutiny'. According to Gough's account, General Paget 'said that no resignations would be accepted, etc. etc. . . . He said that we must clearly understand that this was *the direct order of* "*the Sovereign*", *and asked us* "*if we thought he would obey the orders of those dirty swine of politicians*".'[7] Here Paget makes an implicit distinction between the community or state (symbolized by the Sovereign) and the government of the day. General MacArthur was to make this distinction explicit when he said in 1952: 'I find in existence a new and heretofore

4. Another way of looking at it would be to argue that Huntington's concepts or definitions are purely abstract, and have little relation to the facts of the case. For a thorough analysis of Huntington's book along these lines – with which, I completely agree – see Professor Morris-Jones's review article, 'Armed Forces and the State', in *Public Administration*, vol. 35, pp. 411–16.

5. Quoted, J. Wheeler-Bennett, *The Nemesis of Power*, pp. 108–9.

6. ibid., p. 213.

7. A. P. Ryan, *Mutiny at the Curragh*, p. 142. (My italics.)

unknown and dangerous concept that the members of our armed forces owe primary allegiance or loyalty to those who temporarily exercise the authority of the Executive Branch of Government rather than to the country and its constitution which they are sworn to defend.'[8]

'No proposition,' added General MacArthur, 'could be more dangerous.' On the contrary, it is General MacArthur's view which opens Pandora's box. The moment the military draw this distinction between nation and the government in power, they begin to invent their own private notion of the national interest, and from this it is only a skip to the constrained substitution of this view for that of the civilian government; and this is precisely what we have defined as the very meaning of 'military intervention'. This purported care for the national interest as defined by the military is indeed one of their main reasons for intervening, as we shall see. The point here is that it flows inexorably from one particular facet of military professionalism.

A second motive for intervention also flows from professionalism. We may describe it almost as military syndicalism. As specialists in their field, the military leaders may feel that they alone are competent to judge on such matters as size, organization, recruitment and equipment of the forces. Yet on every one of these points they may find themselves in collision with the civilian government. In their professional capacity they may be impelled still further into trying to establish the security as they see it – both economically and socially – of what, as professional fighters, they regard as their civilian base. To them, the community is precisely this – a reserve of manpower and materials on which they can draw. They may also seek to press on the civilian authorities that only in certain international conjunctures can they guarantee victory. Such views are all consequences of professionalism, yet they have often led the military to try to establish itself as an autonomous body. Such was the attitude of the German and the Japanese armies up to the outbreak of the Second World War, and of the French army during the Dreyfus period.

There is yet a third reason why professionalism may give rise to intervention. This is the military's reluctance to be used to coerce the government's domestic opponents. The professional army sees itself as the nation's custodian against foreign foes; the foreigner is the enemy, not a fellow national. It also sees itself as a fighting force, not as a body of policemen. It often vents its discomfort at having to act against its own nationals by blaming the 'politicians', and by thinking of itself as being 'used' by these for their own sordid purposes. The strain which such duties put on the loyalty of the

8. Quoted, Telford Taylor, *Sword and Swastika*, p. 354.

23

armed forces is often too great and impels them to disobey or even to act against their government. The only serious clash between soldiers and the government in recent British history, the so-called 'mutiny' at the Curragh, was provoked by precisely this kind of situation. Again, it was by playing on the Reichswehr's reluctance to act as a police force that Hitler and Himmler were able to persuade it not to oppose the creation of the S.S. – which in other respects the generals distrusted as military rivals. Disgust at the use made of Turkish forces in a succession of political clashes was one important reason for General Gürsel's coup of May 1960 in Turkey.[9] Significantly the rebels' song on that occasion was an old soldiers' ballad, dating from the siege of Plevna, which ran: 'Shall brother strike brother?'[10]

Thus three tendencies all push the military towards collision with the civilian authorities; and each one grows out of professionalism. Professionalism is not, therefore, what Huntington says it is – the sole or even the principal force inhibiting the military's desire to intervene. To inhibit such a desire the military must also have absorbed the principle of the supremacy of the civil power. For this is *not* part of the definition of 'professionalism'. It is a separate and distinct matter. By it we mean, to quote a recent and convenient definition, that, 'both formally and effectively, the major policies and programmes of government . . . should be decided by the nation's politically responsible civilian leaders.'[11]

In certain countries with highly professional forces this principle was by no means always unequivocally expressed – even by constitutional law. The German army under the Empire owed allegiance to the Kaiser as its *Kriegesherr*, and its relationship to the popularly elected Reichstag was ambiguous. While the parliamentary opposition and especially the Social Democrats argued that it was responsible to the Minister of War and through him to the Reichstag, the parties of the Right and the armed forces themselves maintained that it was responsible only to the Emperor. The Japanese armed forces, from the Meiji restoration in 1868 to the defeat of 1945, claimed a similar position with similar justification.

Against this view stands the military's quite clear understanding, in modern Britain, for instance, or in the United States, that the civil power is paramount and must be obeyed. Before the war, 'American officers of both services typically referred to the armed forces as "instruments" on the dictum that national policy dictated military policy'.[12] This simple dichotomy between national and military policy has nowadays become com-

9. *The Times*, 30 May 1960.   10. *The Times*, 16 June 1960.

11. B. M. Sapin and R. C. Snyder, *The Role of the Military in American Foreign Policy*, p. 52.

12. Huntington, op. cit., p. 307.

plicated and blurred, but the fundamental axiom of civilian supremacy has not been blown upon. 'Economically, politically and militarily,' declared General Omar Bradley, chairman of the Joint Chiefs of Staff, in a famous controversy with Justice Douglas, 'the control of our country resides with the civilian executive and legislative agencies.'[13] President Kennedy has made the position quite clear: 'Our arms must be subject to ultimate civilian control at all times. The basic decisions on our participation in any conflict and our response to any threat ... will be made by the regularly constituted civilian authorities.'[14] In Britain also the axiom is unequivocal. There the classic illustration derives from the Curragh incident of 1914, as this is the only British case since General Monk's time (1659–60) to raise the question of the limits of the soldier's loyalty. In 1914 it was well known to the cabinet and the War Office that many officers serving in Ireland would be most reluctant to fight against the Ulster civilians in order to enforce the government's Home Rule policy. Unwisely the Commander-in-Chief of the troops in Ireland provided a loophole for such officers by holding out to them a rather ambiguous opportunity to resign their commissions, and the bulk of the cavalry officers, commanded by and including General Gough, took advantage of this and resigned. Now two points ought to be noticed here. The first is that General Gough's colleague, General Fergusson, who commanded the 5th Division, rallied his own doubtful officers in the following way.

I told them that the first duty of soldiers was to obey the orders of their King and of constituted authority ... I pointed out the responsibility of influencing those under us. Personal considerations must give way to the duties of our respective positions as commanders of troops. I would be no party to anything that tended to weaken discipline. Logically, we officers could not refuse to obey the present orders and yet expect our men to obey orders when they, on strike duty, for instance, were placed in difficulties similar to those now confronting us.[15]

The second point is that even General Gough himself was not disobeying the civil power. He had been offered the opportunity to resign and had taken it. He had *not* disobeyed a formal order, and when questioned on his conduct at the War Office, a dialogue like this took place:

General Ewart [the Adjutant-General] asked me if I thought any officer had any right to question when he should go, or should not go, in support of the civil power

13. Quoted, Millis, Mansfield and Stein, *Arms and the State*, p. 363. For the situation prevailing in the United States, between the military and the civilian authorities, see pp. 127–31.

14. President Kennedy, Special Message to Congress on the Defence Budget, 28 March, 1961 (United States Information Service).   15. Ryan, op. cit., p. 145.

to maintain law and order. I said: 'None whatever'; and I added if Sir A[rthur] P[aget] had ordered my Brigade to Belfast, we would have gone without demur, although I could not think why we should be wanted there.[16]

In British military history soldiers like Lord Wolseley, Sir William Robertson and, more recently, Lord Montgomery have had occasion to criticize the civil power and to contest its policies; but all this has always been subject to the overriding maxim that in the last resort the civil power is paramount; and since 1660 it always has been.

Firm acceptance of civilian supremacy, not just professionalism, is the truly effective check. In 1873 the Duke of Chambord (the pretender to the French throne) came secretly to Versailles to win over Marshal Macmahon to his cause. In vain. 'I supposed I would be addressing a Constable of France,' the Duke is reported to have cried. 'The person I met was a colonel of the gendarmerie!' It is to this pass that the doctrine of civilian supremacy brings the armed forces: 'To support the laws of the country. This means to sustain, protect and defend the institutions in force and the current form of the State.'[17]

3. Other inhibiting factors

In addition to professionalism *plus* the tradition of civilian supremacy other factors serve from time to time to deter the military from intervention.

One of these is fear for the fighting capacity of the armed forces. If these became highly politicized with their members taking opposite sides, their value as a fighting force could be seriously undermined. Fears of this kind drove von Seeckt to base salvation for both Reichswehr and Reich on *Überparteilichkeit*. 'The task of the Commander-in-Chief,' runs his Order of the Day when the army was ruling Germany under the State of Emergency in 1923, 'is to recognize the vital interests of the State and to see that they are respected. As for the soldier, it is not for him to seek to know more or to do better than his commanders; his duty consists in obedience. A Reichswehr united in obedience will always be invincible and will remain the most powerful factor in the State. A Reichswehr into which the cancer of political discord has entered will be shattered in the hour of danger.'[18]

Mustafa Kemal had reached a similar conclusion early in his career, in 1909 during the heyday of the Committee of Union and Progress: and he never swerved from it throughout the rest of his life. The firmness of this

16. ibid., p. 150.   17. Girardet, op. cit., p. 119.
18. Wheeler-Bennett, op. cit., pp. 115–16.

belief is what accounts for the fact that the Turkish Republic which he founded subordinated the military to the civilian power. At the annual party meeting in Salonika, in 1909, Mustafa Kemal is quoted as saying:

> As long as officers remain in the Party we shall build neither a strong Party nor a strong Army. In the 3rd Army most of the officers are also members of the Party and the 3rd Army cannot be called first-class. Furthermore [he added] the party, receiving its strength from the Army, will never appeal to the nation. Let us resolve here and now that all officers wishing to remain in the Party must resign from the Army. We must also adopt a law forbidding all future officers having political affiliations.[19]

Another factor is the generals' fear of a civil war in which comrade will have to fire on comrade. This too was potent in inducing von Seeckt to keep the Reichswehr out of politics. In the same Order of the Day quoted above he also said:

> As long as I remain at my post I shall not cease to repeat that salvation cannot come from one extreme or the other, neither through foreign aid nor through internal revolution – whether from the Right or Left – and that only by hard work, silent and persistent, can we survive. This can only be accomplished on the basis of the laws of the Constitution. To abandon this principle is to unleash civil war. Not a civil war in which one of the parties will succeed in winning, but a conflict which will only terminate in their mutual destruction, a conflict similar to that of which the Thirty Years' War has given us so ghastly an example.

Finally the military may fear that if they intervene and are vanquished not only their lives but the army itself will be forfeit. Such things can happen. In Costa Rica, in 1948, Colonel Figueres led a popular revolt against the government which had just tried to set aside the results of the election. He dissolved the army and replaced it with a police force of 1,000 men. 'Why,' he asked, 'should a group of professional men assume the right to annul the popular will as expressed at the polls?'[20] A similar threat faced the defeated German army in November 1918. It was threatened by the lack of supplies, and also by the spread of the Soldiers' Councils, abetted by the left-wing socialists who were the dedicated foes of the military. The apparently unnatural alliance of the monarchist General Staff with the socialist Provisional Government, which they detested with all their heart, was a shot-gun marriage based on their fear that otherwise the extreme left might seize control and make away with the army altogether.

19. Quoted, D. Lerner and R. R. Richardson, 'Swords and Ploughshares: the Turkish Army as a Modernizing Force', *World Politics*, vol. 13, no. 1, 1960, pp. 19–20. For effects of Mustafa Kemal's doctrine on the Turkish republic, see pp. 184–5.

20. Lieuwen, op. cit., pp. 96–7.

Thus certain forces may inhibit the military desire to intervene. Professionalism may work that way, though it sometimes actually drives the military into intervention rather than inhibits it; fear for the fighting capacity of the armed forces, or of a civil war tearing them in two, or even for their future as a force of any kind may also turn the military's thoughts from intervention. The most important factor however is the armed forces' acceptance of the principle of civil supremacy.

Motives Disposing the Military to Intervene

1. The 'Manifest Destiny of the Soldiers'

Describing the army coup of 1948, President Bétancourt of Venezuela has written that from the office of the Chief of Staff there went 'a message of Messianic intent – the "*manifest destiny*", *the providential mission of the soldiers as saviours of their countries.*'[21]

An elegant expression of such a belief is to be found in a speech by Dr Salazar, five years after the establishment of his dictatorship.

It will not offend anyone to recognize that the material and moral disasters of the last decades brought the decay of the Portuguese nation to its final term. In politics, in administration, in the public and the private sectors of the economy, the same spectacle of permanent disorder was displayed, with its natural consequence in the collapse of the prestige of the State at home and overseas . . .

In such circumstances, with all the forces of society disorganized and in peril of dissolution, the chief problem was to find the fulcrum for the reaction of redemption . . .

The Army, neglected in the intemperate climate of recent years – wars, revolutions and reforms – is not, despite all, what we would like it to be; by the very nature of its peculiar constitution, it lives apart from politics, subjected to a hierarchy and discipline, serene and firm as a guarantee of public order and national security. This very superiority of discipline, existing in a body organized in the name of the honour and the destiny of the country, was the sole factor capable of surmounting, with the minimum of dislocation and danger, the obstacles created by the empty rigmaroles then in being; and to support the New Authority, pledged to work for the salvation and resurgence of the country . . .[22]

Sectional bodies all plead the national interest when making claims for their own benefit, but the military are specially well placed to do so. In the first place, they are, purportedly, outside party politics; their charge is the state; and they exist, unlike churches and the like, by a deliberate fiat for

21. Romulo Bétancourt, *Venezuela: Política y Petroleo*, Mexico, 1956, pp. 468–70. (My italics.)

22. Dr Salazar, op. cit., pp. 147–8.

the sole purpose of defending this state. Secondly, their claim is more plausible than that of most other sectional bodies. Quite apart from the public's approval of 'the military virtues' no other national institution so symbolizes independence, sovereignty, or equality with other peoples as a country's armed forces. The first thing a new nation creates is a national army. The army symbolizes, as well as makes effective, its distinctive identity. Thirdly, by the very nature of its appointed task, i.e. national defence, the military is and indeed has to be indoctrinated with nationalism. This forms its distinctive ideology. Its whole *esprit de corps* without which it would have no fighting spirit is founded on the supposed national values and virtues. All military training lays heavy emphasis on the national identity, and whips up patriotism and nationalism in its recruits, and by contrast hatred and contempt for the enemy. Where all nations are enemies, one's own nation is the focus of loyalty; and all military training presupposes an 'enemy'. The combined effect of all these sentiments – recognition of its unique mission in society, complacency with its self-sacrificial virtues and consciousness of its power – provides the basis for its belief in its ' "sacred trust" . . . The duty of the Army to intervene and "save the nation".'[23]

Such sentiments form the necessary condition for the belief in a 'manifest destiny', but are not in themselves sufficient. This would have to be sought in such factors as the social composition and status of the military, its public standing, and the ideologies current in its ranks; and also in more specific circumstances such as its success or otherwise in war and the international situation of the time.

We know little or nothing about the mechanism by which rival political ideologies are transmitted into and throughout the armed forces. On the whole, the military are effectively prevented from participating in civilian party activities: and it is not through such participation that political ideologies are usually transmitted to and through them.[24]

23. *The Times*, 6 April 1961.

24. In most countries (outside the ideological dictatorships) the military authorities strive to prevent their forces from joining political parties. The reasons are obvious: the armed forces have to serve a succession of ministers and governments, and official neutrality is a precondition of their being able to do so; the party-affiliated members might be dismissed by a hostile party in power, with serious effects on discipline and training; party disputes in the force could impair its fighting efficiency by breaking up its carefully fostered *esprit de corps*; and in any case the military's moral authority is maximized by the argument (put by Dr Salazar in his speech quoted above) that 'it lives aloof from politics . . . as a guarantee of public order and national security'. For all this, the military authorities have sometimes been hard put to it to prevent their forces dickering with political parties. The Japanese High Command tried vainly to prevent the junior

What are the ideologies, who bears them into the armed forces, who spreads them there? We are largely ignorant, but two remarks are relevant. First, ideas do not transmit themselves; people and books carry them. Second, the armed forces have always been – by the closed and intimate nature of the personal relations they foster – peculiarly susceptible to infiltration and the establishment of networks of conspiracy. Of these we have, every so often, fascinating glimpses which attest to their existence but do little more: the Freemason network in the Spanish army of 1820; the secret patriotic societies that began to honeycomb the Japanese army after 1930; the Grupo de Officiales Unidos in Argentina in 1943; likewise the military leagues in the pre-1939 Balkans, such as the 'Black Hand' and the 'White Hand' in Serbia, the officers' leagues in Bulgaria (1922), and in Greece (1909 and later).[25]

Recent studies of Egypt since 1952 show how the intense chauvinism of the high schools was carried forward into the Military Academy, and how the like-minded nationalist officers, known as the 'Free Officers', came together and carried on their clandestine propaganda.[26]

2. The motive of the 'national interest'

All armed forces which have become politicized as described hold in some form or another a similar belief: that they have some special and indeed unique identification with the 'national interest'. We have already seen how Dr Salazar expresses this view. It is to be found elsewhere too. 'The Army,' said General von Seeckt, 'should become a State within a State, but it should be merged in the State through service; in fact it should become the purest image of the State.'[27] The Spanish *Enciclopedia Universel* speaks of the Spanish army after 1931 as 'the last bastion of

officers joining patriotic societies; the German High Command, as the Ulm trial of 1930 showed, could not resist Nazi infiltration; the Syrian army officers were connected with the Ba'ath party by 1957; the Iraqi officers in the 1936–41 period were consistently intriguing with the political parties – if one can so call the cliques of politicians that formed and reformed around certain dominant personalities in the Iraqi Parliament.

25. For France, see Girardet, op. cit., *passim*. Also his article, 'Pouvoir civil et pouvoir militaire dans la france contemporaine', in the *Revue Française de Science Politique*, March 1960, pp. 5–38. This explains the politicization of the French army since 1940, a process which culminated in the *Treize Mai* of 1958. This is the best account we know of both the why and the how of politicization; brilliantly accomplished, it is indispensable to the study of military intervention in politics. For Japan, the relations between the patriotic societies and the army have been explored by R. Storry, *The Double Patriots*, pp. 42–95 and *passim*.

26. J. and S. Lacouture, *Egypt in Transition*, p. 128. Also Anwar el Sadat, *Revolt on the Nile*, *passim*.

27. Quoted Wheeler-Bennett, op. cit., p. 87.

Spanish nationhood'.[28] 'The Armed Forces,' said Perón, 'are the synthesis of the nation. They do not belong to specific parties or sectors. They belong to the nation.'[29]

However, the military's conception of custodianship is not uniform; no more is its substantive definition of 'national interest'.

Some armed forces conceive of 'custodianship' as meaning their overt rulership of the nation and the establishment of a more or less complete political programme under their authority. One example of this was the wholly military directorate (1923–5) of Primo de Rivera in Spain. Another example comes from the notions of certain members of the army faction in Japan (1930–36) which went under the name of the Kodo-Ha. It contained some officers who had come to believe in what was called the 'Showa Restoration', under which the capitalists were to surrender their privileges to the *Tenno* (Emperor). The political parties of the Diet (identified in the military mind with the hated *zaibitsu*, the industrialist clique) were to do likewise. And the military were then to rule the country in the name of the Sacred Emperor of the Showa period. (Hence the expression, 'the Showa Restoration'.)

Other armed forces, however, look on their role of custodianship differently. They see it as a duty to arbitrate or veto. They feel authorized to exercise it when some convulsion or decision of the civil authorities seems to them to threaten what they think are the permanent interests of the nation. In this conception the armed forces are not to merge into the public authorities but to remain distinct and outside them but with the power to intervene against them.

Such a role is similar to what in Spanish public law is termed the *poder moderador*, the 'moderating power'. The concept is one of a head of state (as in a constitutional monarchy) who acts as a balance wheel to the constitution, intervening when the political authorities or forces seem to be out of alignment with one another.[30] True cases of this belief are difficult to distinguish from bogus ones because nearly all military seizures of power are accompanied by the statement that the movement is purely temporary, designed to cleanse public life and to permit the nation to choose its own rulers freely. As countries in which the people have been freely choosing their own rulers are very few, the claim is often made with the greatest plausibility and amid transport of public enthusiasm. The

28. *Enciclopedia Universel (Supplement 1936–9)*, p. 1444.

29. Quoted, Blanksten, *Perón's Argentina*, p. 307.

30. See article *'Poder Moderador'* in the *Enciclopedia Universel* (Madrid, 1923). Compare the situation of the President of the French Republic under Article 5 of the 1958 Constitution.

number of times the claim has been made in Latin America is so great that it would be tedious to particularize them. Elsewhere, however, we may note similar claims made by Neguib (1952), Kassim (1958) and General Gürsel of Turkey in 1960. In all these cases the plea had considerable justifications. Egypt had been under martial law since 1939 and its elections were notoriously 'made'; in Iraq the elections were, even more than in Egypt, a mere façade, and power resided in the hands of a tight oligarchy; while in Turkey the Menderes government had moved appreciably close to suppression of the opposition and had, just before the coup, put an embargo on all political activities. But though most military seizures of power introduce themselves as interim measures designed to restore the freedom of elections, singularly few have that result. Whether the military are sincere or not when making the claim, it is almost common form for them to fall in love with the power that has come so easily, and to convert their 'interim' régime into full-blooded rule by the army.

This for instance is what happened in Egypt. Neguib declared, on the very day of the coup (23 July, 1952), that his first measure would have to be 'to recall the previous parliament and make sure the proceedings are constitutional'.[31] On 8 August, he postponed the elections from October 1952 to February 1953. On 10 December, he declared that the constitution was abrogated and that power resided in a 'transitional government'; that for the time 'the leader of the Revolution will exercise the power of supreme sovereignty'.[32] On 18 June 1953, Colonel Nasser declared that this transitional régime would last for three years, though the people would be permitted to decide whether it was to be a parliamentary or a presidential republic, and also to elect their President. On 28 February 1954, the great Nasser–Neguib battle began. On 27 March, Nasser successfully struck at Neguib and a previous decision to hold elections and return to civilian rule was abrogated till the end of the three-year 'transitional period', i.e. till 1956.

Most military claims to be acting to restore public liberties have a similar outcome, but some armies have honourably fulfilled their promises. As examples we might mention the Brazilian and the Turkish.

In Brazil, the 1955 elections had resulted in the victory of Senhor Kubitschek for President and Senhor Goulart as Vice-President. Thereupon a section of the military, led by a Colonel Mamede, called for a military rising to prevent their installation. The Minister of War, General Texeira Lott, was, however, determined to see the constitution observed.

31. Lacouture, op. cit., p. 150.
32. *Keesing's Contemporary Archives* (1953), 12846A.

He demanded of the Acting-President (Senhor da Luz) that Colonel Mamede be transferred to another post. Since the Acting-President refused, General Lott resigned his post, seized Rio de Janeiro and deposed the Acting-President. The President of the Senate, Senhor Ramos, was elected in his place by the two Houses of Parliament, until Senhor Kubitschek was duly installed. General Lott declared that the Presidents of the Supreme Court and of Parliament had supported his actions 'as tending to return the situation to a normal constitutional régime'. Shortly afterwards all arrested persons were released and even the unhappy ex-Acting-President da Luz was permitted not only to return but to take up his seat in Congress.

In Turkey, where the Menderes government had harassed the opposition and fettered the press, the Commander-in-Chief, General Gürsel, seized power in May 1960. Arresting President Bayar, Mr Menderes and a large number of deputies of the ruling Democratic party, he set up a provisional government and issued his *pronunciamento*. It stated that the army had acted to depose a small group who had acted against the constitution and repressed civil liberties. The new administration was to be temporary, it would restore rights and freedoms, draw up a new constitution, and bring it into being by free election.[33] October 1961 was later fixed as the date for return to elections, and this promise was kept.

Just as the military may regard their 'custodianship of the national interest' either as a duty to rule or as a duty to arbitrate, so they have no uniform notion of what constitutes the 'national interest'. For it is quite incorrect to suppose that the armed forces are always on the side of landed or industrial oligarchies; as often as not they oppose such groups. It is equally erroneous to suppose they are always anti-democratic, or to be more exact, anti-parliamentary. Armed forces that have supported landed and industrial oligarchies include those of Portugal and Spain, of Guatemala, El Salvador, Dominica and Honduras. Armed forces that have attacked such oligarchies include the Egyptian and Iraqi under Nasser and Kassim, and the military of Guatemala at the time of Arévolo and Arbenz (1944–54). Some armed forces are bitterly opposed to civil liberties and the parliamentary régime: e.g. the Peruvian army under General Odría or the Venezuelan under Jiménez, not to speak, again, of those of Spain and Portugal. The military of Pakistan, the Sudan, Egypt and South Korea are likewise authoritarian in outlook. But with these must be contrasted the armed forces of Brazil and (latterly) of Argentina. We have already noted the events in 1955 in Brazil. Of the Argentinian army, it must be

33. *The Times*, 30 May 1960.

remembered that it was responsible for the rise of Perón in 1943, repented briefly in 1945, then supported him fairly consistently for ten years; but that in 1955 it revolted, chased him into exile and broke up his party. The army today lives for the destruction of Peronism; this may be due to its leaders' fear of the consequences should he return; nevertheless the Argentine armed forces are now the devoted supporter of the parliamentary régime.[34]

They believe 'that the army has a sacred trust – that of supervising the democratic structure of the republic, of ensuring that its destiny shall never fall into the hands of totalitarians – and especially of Peronists and Communists. When the electorate is seduced from the path of rectitude, or when democratically-elected authorities betray their trust, it becomes the duty of the army to intervene and "save the nation".'[35]

'It is difficult [continued *The Times*, rather mordantly] to envisage some thirty or forty generals and a smaller number of admirals and airforce commanders appointed solely by providence to be the sole judges of what the nation needs.'[36] A comment of this kind is only too necessary at this stage, to recall to us implications of what is implied in this notion of the 'manifest destiny of the armed forces'.

This is not all, however. On closer examination, much of the military's enthusiasm for playing a political role is seen to spring from circumstances which either pander to or injure its pride as a peculiar corporation. Furthermore, its substantive conception of the national interest is often rooted in – even if it transcends – its interests or emotions as a peculiar corporation. And, finally, very often it acts primarily if not wholly not for the national interest at all, but out of a desire to protect or extend its privileges as a peculiar corporation.

3. *Another kind of motivation – the sectional interest*

The plea of 'national interest' is often hypocritical. It becomes more and more suspect as the interests of the military shift from the more general to the particular – from the defence of a region to the defence of a class, from the defence of a class to the defence of the army as an institution, until it reaches its ultimate degradation in those cases – and there are very many – where officers intervene in order (even among other things) to improve their own personal careers.

The complex motivations of the military vary with each particular case. The Egyptian army for instance acted from rage and humiliation at its

34. For the Argentine army after 1955, see pp. 167–71.
35. *The Times*, 6 April 1961.   36. ibid.

ignominious defeat in Palestine, from rabid nationalism, and from social resentment at the effendi class. The Spanish army displayed an explosive mixture of arrogance and boredom, regionalist hostility to Catalonian separatism, all formidably laced with individual careerism. To picture the motivations of the military it would be necessary to describe each individual case. But each is blended of such a mixture of mood and objectives that it is best to precede any such descriptions by first listing the commonest of these motives impelling the armed forces to intervene.

(a) *Class interest.* The most facile of all the theories of military intervention seeks to explain everything in terms of class interest. According to this theory the military support the civil power when this is drawn from a similar social class, and overthrow it when it is drawn from a different and hostile class. If this is to be taken as a general rule, it makes most of the political activities of military forces totally incomprehensible. Venezuela's armed forces, for example, have intervened three times since 1945 – in favour of Accion Democratica in 1945, against it in 1948, in favour of it again in 1958; is it to be therefore argued that the ruling classes of Venezuela had altered three times in that interval of twelve years? The Iraqi army intervened six times between 1936 and 1941; the Syrian army seven times between 1949 and 1962; the Thai army on eight occasions since 1932. Class interest is not a negligible factor; but it is only one of several factors influencing the military.

In certain instances, however, it is of great and sometimes decisive importance. The German Reichswehr after 1918, for example, was deliberately drawn from a narrow class, and this influenced its political attitude decisively. Its original 4,000 officers were meticulously selected, and its N.C.O.s, from whom officer-cadets were drawn, were also chosen as far as possible from the sons of the aristocracy and the former military class. The result was that in 1921, 23 per cent of the officer corps were members of the aristocracy, an even higher percentage than in 1913; and in 1930, it is estimated, 95 per cent of the officers were still being drawn from strata which would have been considered 'eligible' under the Kaiser, and only 5 per cent – a mere 200 in all – from the previously ineligible groups. This reformed military caste simply carried on the tradition and attitude of its pre-war predecessor. At home it aspired to be once again the unchallengeably superior social 'Order', and abroad once more the unchallengeably superior army. It was bitterly anti-socialist and anti-democratic. At its best, under von Seeckt and Gröner, it cooperated with the Republic. At its worst, from 1930 onwards, under von Schleicher, it sought to eradicate Social Democracy from the national life: the plan was to get the aged

President Hindenburg to prorogue the Reichstag and institute personal government under Article 48 of the Constitution, pending a constitution which would guarantee the victory of the nationalistic and right-wing elements of the nation. Its attitudes, too, made its junior officers a ready prey to Nazi propaganda, and induced Schleicher and his immediate successors to dicker and collude with the Nazis, for all their aristocratic contempt for them.

Class interest also supplied an important motive to the Japanese army in the inter-war period. By the 1920s, officers were increasingly drawn from the middle and lower classes and from the peasantry, while the other ranks were almost entirely peasant. While the most senior ranks were conservative and often (still) from the samurai clan of Choshu, and the middle grade generally had a samurai background also, the junior ranks contained an ever-growing proportion of these lower middle-class elements. By 1927, it is estimated, about a third of the junior officers were the sons of petty landowners and small shopkeepers. This made them particularly sympathetic to the social conditions of the shopkeeper, the farmer and the peasant. Politically, the opponents of the army were the parties, and these were financed by and acted in the interests of the *zaibitsu* – the industrialists –notably the two great houses of Mitsui and Mitsubishi. The class interest of the army exacerbated this quarrel. During the Great Depression the officers were outraged at the hardships of their own kin, or at the plight of their men's families, often forced to sell a daughter to the city brokers who touted for girls for the tea rooms and brothels. The middle and above all the junior ranks of the army therefore became bitterly hostile to the *zaibitsu* whom they blamed for their misfortunes, and by the same token to the political parties and the Diet itself which served as its instruments. For these reasons the Japanese army quickly absorbed the anti-parliamentary, anti-political party and anti-capitalist views of such people as Ikki Kita, the propounder of a Japanese kind of national socialism.

The Egyptian army's political attitudes are also largely influenced by its class structure. When the Wafd party opened the Military Academy to lower-class recruits in 1936, the Egyptian army had neither tradition nor prestige. Indeed it has been described as a 'mediocre hotch-potch of parade units, forces used as police for hunting smugglers, and cavalry squadrons for the sons of Pashas intent on playing polo'.[37] With the exception of the decorative cavalry, the army officer was socially despised, and no self-respecting bourgeois would dream of allowing his daughter to marry one. After 1936 the recruits who came into the Academy were often drawn from

37. Lacouture, op. cit., p. 130.

the petty landowners. Some were the sons of fellahin who had made good, some of lower-grade civil servants (Nasser's father was a postmaster). These cadets had no reason to love the effendi class – socially and politically their masters – and good reason to return their contempt with hatred. The sufferings of the fellahin in the inflation of the war years further inflamed this class resentment; and Nasser and his cronies, from the day they passed out in 1938, set a 'purge of the state' as one of their objectives by the side of ridding the country of foreign troops and reforming the army. It was natural for them, therefore, to blame the effendis and the political parties for their defeat in Palestine. It was equally natural for them to press on, once they had seized power in 1952, to smash the parties, sweep the old ruling class clear out of political influence and power, and cripple it economically by land laws in favour of the fellahin. The abrupt turn to 'Arab socialism' in 1961, and the confiscation or sequestration of what industry remained in private possession, is merely the latest manifestation of this class interest.

The class interest of the junior officers is of importance also in Latin American republics like Argentina and Brazil, which are experiencing the growth of a middle class. Before the First World War the officers came mostly from the rural oligarchies, and when they intervened they did so in support of their economic and political position. Nowadays officers are drawn increasingly from the families of industrialists, civil servants and professional people. This partly explains the increased radicalism of junior-officer revolts in such countries. The Argentine army in 1943, for instance (the year of the first coup), was not connected with 'the Oligarchy': 'The army officers, generally speaking, had no place in society and did not come from the governing class of *estancieros*, successful professional men and big merchants.'[38] The naval officers did, and throughout the period of Perón's rule never gave loyal support to the régime, and in 1955 played the decisive role in his overthrow. In Brazil, the young officers (the *tenentes*) staged uprisings in the twenties, and they became the instrument of Getulio Vargas's accession in 1930 over the opposition of the old 'coffee oligarchs' of Saõ Paulo.

This lower middle-class make-up partly accounts also for the counter-revolutionary activities of these same officers. The dictators they hoist to power, e.g. Perón in Argentina, Vargas in Brazil, Rojas Pinilla in Colombia, have often tried to become independent of the army by courting labour, in countries (moreover) where labour organizations are dependent on, and largely an organ of, the government in power. In these

38. Sir David Kelly, *The Ruling Few*, p. 296.

circumstances the officer corps becomes worried on two accounts – their diminishing influence on the dictator, and their bias against labour. Sections of the Argentinian army, not to speak of the navy, tried to get rid of Perón in 1945 while he was still Vice-President, on account of his courting of labour. In 1955, sections of the army, powerfully supported by the navy, brought him down, and since that date Presidents Aramburu and Frondizi both had to face continual pressure from the armed forces to toughen up their social policies. In Brazil, again, sections of the army had had enough of Vargas's pro-labour policy by 1945, and made him resign; after his sweeping electoral victory in 1950 which they could not prevent, their pressure forced him to his dramatic suicide in 1954; and those sections of the army which had been most prominently against him tried, in 1955, to set aside the election of President Kubitschek, which represented a triumph for the old Vargas alliance.[39]

(b) *The regional interest.* It sometimes happens that the officer corps is predominantly drawn from one particular region of the country or develops special ties with it; and this too can act as a motive for military intervention. The modern British example of military politics, the Curragh 'mutiny', is an instance in point. General Gough was himself an Irishman, and his cavalry officers, who preferred to resign their commissions rather than coerce Ulster, were connected with the Ulster gentry by birth or ties of friendship and domicile. The Spanish army's cruel and persistent hatred of Catalonian separatism was partly due to the fact that almost all its officers came from Andalusia or Castile – and Castile, pre-eminently, was the heartland of Spanish centralism (in the labour movement no less than in the army). Again, the army of pre-war Yugoslavia was the instrument of King Alexander's illegal abrogation of the Constitution in 1929 and formed the essential prop to his centralizing and anti-Croat policy – and to that of Prince Paul, his successor. Of the 165 generals in active service in 1938 no less than 161 were Serbs. The army movement in Pakistan has also been influenced by regionalism. All the Pakistani officers came from West Pakistan, the traditional recruiting ground of the Indian army. Largely Punjabi landlord types, they have tended to regard the Bengalis as disloyal autonomists and separatists. They have tended to regard East Pakistan as almost a 'colonial' area, needing 'strong' government.

Regionalism seems also to have played a part in the Venezuelan army's counter-revolution of 1948, and the subsequent rise of Jiménez to power in

39. Colonel Mamede and his group. See pp. 32–3. Their intervention in 1961 was for the same reason – to prevent Goulart (very left wing and pro-labour and running-mate to Kubitschek in 1955) from acceding to the Presidency.

1950. In Venezuela, Andean provincialism is still strong, though weakening. The Andino thinks of his region as the cradle of the state. From 1889 to the accession of Accion Democratica to power in 1945, not a single President of Venezuela had been anything but an Andino – all, Castro, Gomez, Contreras and Angarita had been men of the Andes. The majority of the officers were also Andeans. Their local patriotism played its part therefore in the 1948 coup which ejected the Accion Democratica government and established the military junta of Chalbaud, Jiménez and Paez. Between Jiménez and Chalbaud there soon developed a rivalry for the Presidency and in the contest it was the army and its Andean particularism which won the day for Jiménez, himself an Andino. Chalbaud, aristocratic by temperament, sought to bolster his strength by alliances among the narrow circle of '*los grandes appellidos*'. Perez Jiménez, however, formed connections with a group of army officers. 'To back his appetite for more power,' says President Bétancourt, 'he formed a Praetorian *camarilla* with military elements. And all the time it was stimulated and advised by a civilian general staff, the so-called Uribante group, a kind of lodge of professional men and politicians of Tachira State, inbred with the notion that they had been born in Venezuela's Prussia.'[40]

The most recent and by far the most important instance of the regional motive is the French army's ill-starred attachment to Algeria. To keep *Algérie Française*, units of the French forces stationed there have on three separate and successive occasions refused to obey the civil power. The first occasion was the *Treize Mai* (1958) when the civilian *colons* of Algiers rose and were supported and then joined by the forces, led predominantly by Generals Massu and Salan, in Committees of Public Safety. The second occasion, prompted by General de Gaulle's gnomic speech on the future of Algeria and sparked off by his dismissal of General Massu, was in January 1960. Once again the *colons* rose and occupied the government buildings and the paratroop regiments made no move to interfere with them. The third and infinitely most serious of the acts of insubordination was the open mutiny and insurrection of the 'Four Generals', the affair of 22 April 1961.[41]

Why this firm, in some cases fanatical, resistance to the severance of Algeria from France? We must distinguish: the regulars felt more deeply than the conscripts, the paratroops much more fanatically than the rest,

---

40. Bétancourt, op. cit., pp. 462, 482–3. Chalbaud was assassinated in the open street on 13 November 1950 (it is said, by a member of the Uribante Group) and the succession went to Jiménez.

41. See below for these incidents, pp. 85–8.

the S.A.S. and S.A.U. detachments were different again. Nevertheless, in 1958 at least, one sentiment was widespread throughout all sections – the feeling that France must remain; and at the same time a relatively small number of officers, but ones who were highly or influentially placed, held extreme right-wing views and developed an active interventionist mood.

Only in a few cases was this due to the troops having families or relations in Algeria, or having been stationed there for a long period. (Massu's paratroopers, however, were partly recruited from Algiers and had been stationed there for three years; and two of the four rebel generals of 1961, Zeller and Jouhaud, had family ties with Algeria.) It was due, in chief, to two causes. The first was what has been called the 'emotional geography' of the French soldier, the second the consequences and implications of '*la guerre aux foules*', the new kind of warfare introduced from Indochina.

North Africa was peculiarly attractive to the French soldier. The memory of Lyautey, the virtual creator of Morocco, pervaded it. Also it was there that the liberation of France had begun. In addition it was a particularly 'good billet' – living was cheap and attractive. And, finally, the army had developed close contacts with the Muslim population; indeed, with some exceptions like Massu's paratroopers, it was pro-Muslim and rather anti-*colon*.

Secondly, however, these attachments to the Muslims had been fostered by the 'new' warfare. The experiences of the Indochina war turned military thinking to exploring the methods and theories of Mao Tse-tung. To win the 'revolutionary war' it was necessary to seize control of the popular mind, to marshal and then permeate the masses with a myth, an idea. These theoretical notions reinforced the answers to a purely practical problem – how to retain contact with and derive information and support from the sparse Algerian population who would otherwise harbour and succour the rebels, out of fear if not out of sympathy. Thus from 1956 the army branched out into being both an administrative agency and a propaganda factory. In the *bled*, the S.A.S. units were set up to administer and care for the Muslim population and to win them over. Meanwhile from the '*Xième* Military Region' there issued newspapers, schools for cadres, teams of social workers, youth clubs, women's clubs, so that in some regions the army held in fact almost a monopoly of public authority. Now this effort to win the minds of a whole population in a country at war could not be neutral. The operation had to be based on some social and political philosophy and in default of directions from Paris the army began to evolve its own. It was necessarily a flexible one but two of its principles were clear. One was that, come what may, '*La France restera*'. The friends of today were not going to be abandoned for the F.L.N. to massacre tomorrow. The slightest hint that the army might leave, and the Muslim masses would fall away immediately to mend their fences with the F.L.N. The second was the provision of some counter-faith to the independence cry of the F.L.N.; and this could be little else than the encouragement of the civic, political and social advance of the Muslims, the promise that 'you shall be like us'. These two principles, the permanence of the French presence and the equality of Muslims and Frenchmen, could be, as they were, subsumed under the slogan of *Algérie Française* – though this meant something different to the *colons*.

This rapidly fostered attachment to Algeria and the imperatives of the psychological war that was being attempted, created in the leading cadres of the French army the determination that Algeria must on no account be lost to France; from this the determination to resist any Paris politicians who decided to the contrary; and from this the acts of insubordination which culminated in the *débâcle* of the 'Four Generals' in April 1961.

(c) *The corporate self-interest of the armed forces.* The military is jealous of its corporate status and privileges. Anxiety to preserve its autonomy provides one of the most widespread and powerful of the motives for intervention. In its defensive form it can lead to something akin to military syndicalism – an insistence that the military and only the military are entitled to determine on such matters as recruitment, training, numbers and equipment. In its more aggressive form it can lead to the military demand to be the ultimate judge on all other matters affecting the armed forces. As these certainly include foreign policy, and invariably include domestic economic policy and may well include all the factors making for morale, i.e. education and the mass media of communication, such claims are bound to bring the military into conflict with the civilian government which traditionally occupies itself with such matters.

We have already pointed out that such claims as these are an outcome of professionalism. A special body of persons, the military, are *functionally specialized*: designated, indoctrinated and trained to perform a special task, quite different from that of the rest of the community. The more specialized they are the more anxious to take the steps that will safeguard and guarantee their success.

The German army, both in the Imperial era (1871–1918) and under both Weimar and Hitler, was powerfully, indeed predominantly, driven by this corporate interest. Nationalism, arrogance, class bias, individual careerism all played their parts in determining its attitude; but most of what passes for a gratuitous itch for political power was due to its determination to safeguard, to win back, even partly extend its autonomous position in politics and society. Certainly the record looks extraordinary: in the period 1871–1914, two War Ministers (Kameke and von Schellendorff), a Minister of Foreign Affairs (von Bieberstein), a Minister of the Interior (Boetticher) and two Chancellors (General Caprivi and Prince Hohenlöhe) were made to resign by direct or indirect military pressure. Yet in so acting the military were all the time seeking to defend their autonomy. For the Imperial Constitution of 1871 was not unambiguous on the location of responsibility for the army. There was, indeed, a Minister of War, and the opposition in the Reichstag professed to believe that this meant that the army, through him, was responsible to the Reichstag (a similar view over a similar ambiguity had led to the celebrated crisis in the Prussian Diet in 1862). But the War Minister, like the other Ministers, was not constitutionally responsible to the Reichstag in any case; he was responsible to the Emperor, and the Emperor with his 'military cabinet' was the head of the armed forces, the *Kriegsheer*. The military (and the right-wing parties) therefore argued that the army was autonomous of the Reichstag, working in parallel with it directly to the Emperor. The military pressures of the Imperial period were chiefly devoted to making this true in fact.

The first conflict arose in 1874 over the size of the army. Since 1867, it had been provisionally fixed at 1 per cent of the population. In 1874, the army sought to perpetuate this arrangement, in which case the Reichstag would have had no control over the size, or, for the most part, of the cost of the army. It refused to agree, and the compromise Law of the Septennate (fixing army strength for seven years at a time) was the best the army could achieve. From that point therefore its fixed endeavour was to transfer powers from the War Minister (who had to answer to the Reichstag) to purely military bodies, e.g. the General Staff or the Emperor's 'military cabinet'. In this, Albedyll, Chief of the 'military cabinet', and Waldersee, Quartermaster General and later Chief of the General Staff, worked together. In 1883 they persuaded the Emperor to dismiss his War Minister, Kameke; and then, for the price of their support, got his successor Schellendorff to transfer the control of war personnel to the Emperor's 'military cabinet'. They also made him grant the Chief of the General Staff the right of personal access to the Emperor without the Minister's being present. From this time forward the Emperor's 'military cabinet' became a focus of intrigue. At first it welcomed General Caprivi's Chancellorship (1890); but Caprivi carried the Army Bill of 1894 in the Reichstag with the greatest difficulty and only after new elections, and even so had had to make compromises. Hahnke, Chief of the Emperor's 'military cabinet', and the rest of the *camarilla* were therefore unsatisfied, so that in 1894 William II replaced Caprivi by Prince Hohenlöhe. The civil–military quarrel then recommenced, this time over the question of military courts. The military code was being consolidated and revised, and in the course of this it was proposed that, conformably to what happened in other countries, trials for certain kinds of offences should be public. Egged on by his 'military cabinet', William II refused to contemplate this. Von Schellendorff, the War Minister, was dismissed, and General Gossler (the 'Emperor's General') put in his place. The parliamentary left and centre seethed with vexation but this merely persuaded William II that his policy was correct, and that the difficulties were due to the feebleness of his ministers. Accordingly he dismissed von Bieberstein and Boetticher, Ministers for Foreign Affairs and the Interior respectively, and in 1900 gratefully accepted Hohenlöhe's own resignation. Yet – and it is important, in order to maintain perspective – for all this bother, William II signed the new code after all. It should be noticed that the Reichstag had not completely lost control of the military budget and had been able to force the army to compromise both in 1874 and 1894; and that Waldersee's attempt to create his own foreign intelligence network, through the military attachés, had been decisively rebuffed by Bismarck and Caprivi.

The war period (1916–18) admittedly shows the powers of the General Staff at their height. This was the period of the so-called 'silent dictatorship' of Ludendorff and Hindenburg. In this period the military pressed to the limit their view that their task entitled them to decide on domestic and foreign policy; and such was the prestige of these two generals among the politicians and public opinion that a threat of resignation sufficed to let them get their way. The General Staff, therefore, concerned itself with press, films and general propaganda; it established complete control over the economy; and in the field of foreign policy it was the body responsible for the fatal decisions to create an independent kingdom of Poland and to introduce unrestricted submarine warfare, over-riding the opposition of the Foreign Office, and securing (on threat of resignation) the dismissal of the Chancellor, Bethmann-Hollweg. It can fairly be argued, however, that wartime is exceptional and that, in such circumstances, the military's claim to create the conditions for its own success is more plausible and likely to be acceded to with much less reluctance. Moreover, the Ludendorff–Hindenburg policy was not so much an aggression against the civilian authorities as an abdication by the latter to the technical claims of the military, now grossly expanded by the exigencies of total war.

In the inter-war period (1918–38) the army sought firmly and single-mindedly to restore its pre-war position in politics and society. But this brought it into collision with the Republic, for in the short term it entailed re-armament (forbidden by the Versailles Treaty) and in the longer term the restoration of authoritarian government and the creation of a war-minded nation, ready and able to provide conscripts for the new Wehrmacht and willing workers in the armament factories. Even the intrigues of Schleicher between 1928 and 1932, however much he enjoyed them for their own sake, had these objectives in view. His predecessor, Seeckt, however, had reasoned that they were best achieved by standing aloof from the party struggle rather than by dabbling in it like Schleicher. 'I have never had nor sought influence on economic matters,' he wrote in 1923, 'nor on the question of the Ruhr except with regard to those details directly affecting the military. Whether I agreed with the policy of the Reich is immaterial as I do not consider myself called upon to give my attitude public expression.' Yet he was furious when the government interfered with matters which he *did* think lay within the limits of military autonomy: when, for instance, the government made him revoke the measures he had taken against the insubordinate Bavarian military in October 1923, or when it appointed civilian commissioners to investigate how far the Reichswehr had participated in the Kapp putsch.[42]

The army's dickering and subsequent collaboration with the Nazis is also attributable to the same persistent motive – the return to the old Imperial status, size and situation. In the Nazis Schleicher saw a great civilian following which, with massive over-confidence, he thought he could harness to serve the army's aim. The result of his bungling intrigues was to bring the Nazis to power (and to prepare the way for his own subsequent murder). Yet the Nazi government was still so insecure that it had to share power with the army, and with von Blomberg the army reverted to its consistent pattern – a powerful and prickly autonomy *vis-à-vis* the civil power. Blomberg was prepared to cooperate with the Nazis because he thought them capable of identifying people and army, and of evoking such nationalism as to make conscription and re-armament possible. Among the first fruits of the relationship were the re-armament of Germany and the abolition of civil courts' jurisdiction over the military – thus returning to the Imperial situation in two major matters. The army took but would not give. It refused to accept the too radical von Reichenau as Commander-in-Chief and insisted on von Fritsch. It insisted on the elimination of the S.A. as a para-military force and so drove Hitler to the

42. H. J. Gordon, *The Reichswehr and the German Republic*, pp. 275–8.

murder of Roehm and his radicals in the 'night of the long knives'. It resisted party interference and Gestapo surveillance over its own members. The army was successful and could almost persuade itself that short of the Emperor it was back to 1914, when, with suddenness and finality, the end came. In 1938, Hitler dismissed Blomberg and Fritsch and effectively made himself the head of the armed forces. The autonomy of the army, the object of half-a-century of military resistance to the civil power, was over; and the civil power was henceforth supreme.

This German example illustrates the case of an army chiefly intent on securing or (after 1918) regaining its autonomy. Except for the special circumstances of 1916–18, it moved but fitfully beyond this into the realm of foreign affairs and domestic policy. We ought, therefore, parenthetically to note the case of the Japanese armed forces in the inter-war period: parenthetically, we say, because the Japanese armed forces do not properly fit here, and we shall be dealing with them more fully later.[43] But the Japanese armed forces illustrate the case of the military enjoying a secure autonomy, but using this to press forward into the civilian sphere to dominate foreign policy, economic policy and even education. This pressure was not motivated by a desire to defend its authority – this was secure enough – but to dominate the civil authorities. It is worthy of note, however, that it did not embark on its campaign until an incident occurred which it chose to interpret as civilian interference with its sister service, the navy. This was the ratification of the naval Treaty of London, 1930. The Treaty was accepted and sponsored by the civilian Prime Minister Hamaguchi who was not only Prime Minister but was temporarily heading the Ministry of the Navy as well. (Its chief, a serviceman, was at the London Conference.) Now the naval delegation at the Conference was divided in views on the Treaty; also Admiral Kato, Chief of the Naval General Staff, strongly opposed it. The services and the nationalist societies argued that the civilian Prime Minister and cabinet had no right to support a treaty and press for its acceptance, the supreme command being constitutionally responsible to the Emperor alone. Nevertheless, after much deliberation and delay the Privy Council ratified the Treaty. Thereupon the army began to fear that it too would be over-ridden by the civilians, the more so because they had already been made to accept reductions in the military budget and the size of the army in the twenties, as well as the conciliatory China policy of Shidehara. From this point on, therefore, the army began to invade the sphere of the civil branch until, by 1939, it effectively controlled national policy.

43. In Chapter Seven.

Corporate self-interest has also played a prominent part in the motivation of the Spanish army since, at the latest, 1890. Here, however, arrogance, class interest and regional interest were all powerful motives, too. In the earlier years of the nineteenth century the Spanish army had been involved in – and torn between – the contending factions of Liberalism and the Church. By the Restoration of 1874, these two forces had reached some kind of accommodation, and the régime of the landed oligarchy began. Its political system was underpinned by the army, which was not a fighting machine but, as Salvador de Madariaga puts it, a supine bureaucracy bent 'on the preservation of power and on the administration and enjoyment of a disproportionate amount of the budget'.[44] In 'the system', the monarch (as in Iraq, 1936–58, to which Spain of this period offers a striking parallel) could dispose of cabinets as he willed. Parliamentarism was a façade. The elections were 'made' by the party in power, even down to its arranging for the election of the members of the opposition. Given the weakness of the parties, Alfonso XIII was able to make and break cabinets at his pleasure. From his majority in 1902 he therefore claimed and exercised the right to communicate with his commanders directly over the heads of his cabinet, and he held *audiences militares*. In this way the King in effect reproduced a duality between civilians and army, each responsible to him but in parallel, as it were, and similar to that of Germany and Japan. As a result the army found itself both stronger *vis-à-vis* the cabinet, and also more likely to collide with it.

One or two incidents illustrate how the military, in pursuance of its corporate autonomy, interfered with the civilian government. The first is the passage of the notorious Law of Jurisdictions, 1905. A Barcelona newspaper, *Cut-Cut*, published a cartoon. The officers of the garrison found it offensive and wrecked its offices. For this they received congratulations from the commanders of the Madrid and Seville garrisons. The cabinet retaliated by removing the Captains-General of all three garrisons. The Minister of War, the sanguinary General Weyler, protested, and a military coup seemed so imminent that the deputies attended the Cortes in arms. The army now insisted that all attacks on the army and the nation should be tried by court martial. Since the King agreed, his Prime Minister resigned. In the new cabinet the Minister of Justice tried to compromise; he proposed to stiffen the penalties for defamers of the army, but insisted on their trial by the ordinary courts. At this, his cabinet colleague, the Minister of War, simply told the Senate: 'I reserve my opinion till [the Bill] has come to the cabinet. Then I will say whether the *army is satisfied or*

44. Salvador de Madariaga, *Spain* (2nd ed.), p. 136.

not.'* At this the Minister of Justice resigned. His more timid successor introduced a Bill by which, although defamation of flag and country were triable in the ordinary courts, defamation of the army was to be tried by courts martial, i.e. by the army itself.

A second instance of the Spanish army's corporate self-interest was the odd spectacle, in 1917, of the *Juntas de defensa*. Reacting against Alfonso's favouritism in awards and promotions and against the general decrepitude of the army, the officers set up trade-union committees to protect their privileges and better their conditions. These juntas demanded better pay, moderation in rewards, justice in promotions and respect for seniority. They demanded also that the medical corps and the commissariat should be reorganized; and, finally, they desired not to be used to quell civil disturbances.[45]

The great Dreyfus crisis in France was, essentially, an issue of the army's autonomy. At that period, as from the time of the Second Empire onwards, the army's viewpoint was a mystique of order, sympathy for authoritarianism and a violent hatred of parliamentary institutions. Nearly all its superior officers had been brought up under the Empire. Also the officer corps had become increasingly Catholic. In 1847 only two cadets out of a total of 306 promotions had come from the religious schools, but in 1886, 140 out of 410 did so. The social and political effect was even more marked than the religious, because the products of these schools formed a network of school and family relationships. These were the sons of the old families of France, who entered the army because the agricultural depression had made it hard for them to live off their estates, and also because the Republicans barred them from the high positions of state. Also, not a few of the old families saw in the manipulation of the army their sole avenue to regaining power.

Yet despite the officer corps' hostility to the Republic and to parliamentarism, it retained its cult of discipline and legality. Its hatred of democracy was a sentiment, not a programme. The officers did not conspire against the Republic. Much more important than the army's anti-Republicanism was its desire for isolation, for self-governing autonomy inside its sphere. It desired to be a privileged order distinct from the rest of society – not taking the place of the other institutions of government, but taking its own proud place among them. It did not matter if an officer were indifferent about politics, but it did matter if he mingled too freely with civilians. Conversely, the officer who held strong and anti-Republican convictions felt that his uniform protected or cut him off from the society of which he was a part.

* My italics.   45. For the subsequent history of the juntas, see p. 138.

And, indeed, by the end of the century the civil authorities had little grip on the army. Its promotions were governed by its own Classification Committees of generals (in which the Catholic 'old boy network' played an influential part) and was outside cabinet control. Most Ministers of War were generals selected from the active list, and those who were not tended (as under the Weimar Republic in Germany also) to act as the army's spokesmen.

The Dreyfus case, in its judicial and first phase, hardly affected military opinion.[46] It was when the civilian authorities began to question the authenticity of the military verdict that the army became excited. This was a civilian interference with their precious autonomy; and their view was, basically, that whether Dreyfus had been innocent or guilty was unimportant – the important thing was that the army had decided the issue, and the civilians should keep out of it. As the *affaire* built up, of course, all kinds of different arguments and emotions were introduced – anti-semitism, anti-Republicanism, the importance of not weakening the army's morale, the importance of not weakening the nation's confidence in its army; but the basic conflict arose from the interference (legitimate and belated) of the civilians with this proud and hostile autonomous corporation. With the triumph of the Dreyfusards in the Waldeck–Rousseau Cabinet (1899) that autonomy was destroyed. The Classification Committees were abolished and their functions transferred to the Ministry. The regulation dowry of 1,200 francs for an officer's wife was suppressed and one-tenth of the Second-Lieutenancies were reserved for 'adjutants' without their having to pass through a military college first. Later, the St Cyriens had to do one year in the ranks before proceeding to college. In 1906, civilian supremacy was symbolized by granting Sub-Prefects precedence over Colonels, and Prefects precedence over Generals.

The motive of corporate self-interest stands out boldly in those situations where the government is thought to be contemplating the establishment of some form of militia. The professionals react sharply to the joint threat to their pride and their careers. Latin America furnishes many examples, largely because civilian governments have been so harassed by the military there that they have despairingly turned to armed militias as a means of shaking off the military blackmail. When General Odría seized

46. Cf. G. Chapman, *The Dreyfus Case*, p. 200. 'As at the beginning of 1898,' he writes, 'all the soldiers desired was to be masters in their own house without interference from the politicians, to whip their own dogs, and for that they were ready to go to lengths but not to extremes, not to revolt. As isolated as monks from the main currents of civilian society, the generals did not know enough to decline the help of political charlatans who hoped to use them for their own purposes.'

power in Peru in 1948, he charged the ex-President Bustamente, among other things, with deliberately trying to weaken the power and prestige of the armed forces, reduce their numbers and disunite them. The 1948 Venezuelan coup of Colonel Chalbaud and Major Jiménez which followed a few days later made a similar charge against the Accion Democratica government. At a press conference Chalbaud declared that Accion Democratica had tried to introduce 'an armed militia in order to impose on the Venezuelans, by violence, a state of affairs inspired in the interests of faction' – a charge which, incidentally, Romulo Bétancourt has strenuously denied.[47] The Guatemalan army's disinclination to defend the Arbenz government in 1954 was partly due to a similar suspicion. In June 1954, there arrived in Guatemala the notorious shipload of arms from Poland (the incident that sparked off the United States protest, the armed incursion of Castillo Armas, and the fall of the régime). The purpose of these arms was unknown to the people but rumour had it, and the soldiers suspected, that President Arbenz intended it for a workers' militia. The army officers seem to have looked on this with hostility because it was communist-inspired, with indignation because it seemed as if one of their own men – Colonel Arbenz, the President – was betraying them, and with actual fear because they believed the communists were out to get rid of them physically. When Castillo Armas's rebel column invaded Guatemala on 18 June the communists strove to organize a para-military force among the labour unions and established committees to give this militia any weapons. Arbenz ordered Diaz, his Chief of Staff, to do so. The next day Diaz reported to him that the officers would not permit him to do so, and the next day the officers went further. They demanded Arbenz's resignation[48] – and soon received it.

(d) *The motive of individual self-interest.* The seismic zones of military intervention, the areas where it is or has been endemic, tend by and large to be regions where social stratification is marked, and where, by consequence, the army provides one of the few avenues for social advancement. It is so in most of the Latin American states, in the Middle East, and in contemporary South-east Asia, and was so in pre-war Eastern Europe. In most of the countries of these four regions the army provided a means by which boys of lower middle-class family, or even poor family, could rise to officer rank. Now there is no reason why the social aspirant, having come so far, should not wish to climb higher and to gatecrash into the circles reserved for the social set itself – i.e. the circles of government.

47. Bétancourt, op. cit., p. 473.
48. R. M. Schneider, *Communism in Guatemala, 1944–45,* p. 312.

To the extent that this is true of any particular state, it suggests self-interest as at least one of the motives for intervention.

It is also noticeable that in many if not most of the countries which have undergone a military coup, the military budget and the rewards and conditions of the military are sharply increased. The military receive a kind of donative akin to that of the Roman Praetorian Guard. Perhaps, therefore, their motives are influenced by the hope of such a reward, as were the Praetorians?

Examination of individual cases shows indeed that this is often so, and that a powerful motive in military intervention may be the material interest of the individual officers. In Venezuela, in Syria, in Greece, in Spain, even in the German Reichswehr one finds ample evidence and this list could be widely extended.

In Syria, for instance, after 1946, the armed forces were highly politicized – especially over issues of foreign policy – very self-conscious, and also highly self-interested. The Zaim coup of March 1949 was partly sparked off by mockery of the army after its *débâcle* in Palestine, but also by the rumour that President el Azm intended to cut military expenditure. The Shukayr coup of 1954 which brought down the dictatorship of General Shishakli was partly due to his colleagues' pure envy of Shishakli's newfound eminence, but also to resentment and fear over his purge of the officer corps.

The army group – the 'Patriotic Military Union' – which revolted in Venezuela in 1945 and brought the Accion Democratica to power were influenced by the stagnation of the army in which they found themselves; they 'painted a picture of an army', writes Bétancourt, 'where not even the superficial modifications introduced into the civil administration in 1936 had been realized, where the arbitrary methods of the days of Gomez for the conduct of the armed forces and the selection of commanders and officers still continued alive and active.'[49] Similar motives were and are current throughout Latin America. The armies there have no real fighting mission to perform; the officers and men are under-employed; the life is made up of routine peacetime manoeuvres. Revolutions mean opportunities for promotion and new and important jobs.[50]

The usual form that the material self-interest takes is simply ambition to

49. Bétancourt, op. cit., p. 160.

50. Cf. Lieuwen, op. cit., p. 127. 'Many officers in the lower ranks who talked of social reform really wanted increased pay and more rapid promotion.' For quite a different view, see T. Wyckoff, 'The role of the military in contemporary Latin American politics' (*Western Political Quarterly*, Vol. 13, No. 3).

play a part, or desire for better pay and easier promotion. And the classic example is the army of Spain. This army was grossly, almost unbelievably over-officered; in 1912, in peacetime, there were over 12,000 officers for 100,000 men; in 1931 there were 21,000 officers (as many as in the German army of 1939) for some 200,000 men. And of them, 690 were generals. This army was also very expensive, taking about one quarter of the budget. It was nevertheless grossly ill-equipped, since the bulk of its budget went on officers' pay, and yet this was not at all high because they were so numerous. The officers did not come from wealthy aristocratic families but from middle-class households and they had no private sources of income. As a single man the young officer could cut a dash, once married he found things difficult, and with a family he found them unmanageable. He took other, part-time jobs, he took bribes, in order to make ends meet. But promotion was slow. The army did not even offer the consolation of serious work, or of active service, only clerking, drill, garrison duty; even manoeuvres were rare, since money was short. 'The captain begins,' writes Brenan in his brilliant imaginary portrait of the Spanish officer, 'to think of all the nice jobs and of all the prestige that comes in Spain from government. No wonder that he is only waiting for one of those six hundred generals to give the word to rise.'[51]

It would be wrong to conclude without giving an example to show that this desire for promotion and betterment is met with in the military of advanced industrial societies as well as in the relatively underdeveloped states from which the illustrations have been drawn so far. The Ulm trial of 1930 shows that the same sort of restlessness that occurred in the Spanish army was also present in the Reichswehr. In 1930, two junior officers were found to be Nazis and engaged in spreading Nazi propaganda in the army. Such activities were strictly forbidden by the military code, and in any case General Gröner, the War Minister, who was still in effective control of the officer corps, was bitterly opposed to the Nazis. The officers were brought to trial at Ulm; and from his cell one of the accused, Scheringer, wrote and published this explanation of his motives:

The actual purpose of the Reichswehr as a citadel of the military idea, and the basic nucleus for the future war of independence, pales. The need for earning bread becomes all-important. Soldiers turn into officials, officers become candidates for pensions. What remains is a police troop. People know nothing of

51. G. Brenan, *The Spanish Labyrinth*, p. 62. The treatment above is based on this brilliant work. Compare a splendid passage in A. R. Vilaplana, *Burgos Justice*, pp. 204–11. It amplifies the point made in the text. Unfortunately, it is much too lengthy to quote.

the tragedy of the four words: 'Twelve years as subalterns' . . . Let the old men be silent.[52]

Hitler's public statement at the trial, 'We shall create for you a great army, much greater than you yourselves imagine today', had a profound effect on the attitude of the junior officers.

4. *The mixed motives of the military*

Such are the principal motives on which the military tend to act. They act from a mixture of them that varies from case to case. The Reichswehr's motives were very mixed. It wanted to have nothing to do with politicians partly because it disliked them, but more importantly because it feared that the introduction of politics into the army would lead to its destruction as an institution; and (its more far-sighted leaders like von Seeckt and Gröner would have added) to the destruction of its influence, since the Reichswehr was at its strongest when neutral, up for auction to all sides. On the other hand the romantic nostalgia for its heyday under the Empire, its desire to recapture its lost social status and to win back a complete autonomy, its desire too to realize the old Treitschkeian ideal of 'peace within and power without', all embittered it against the Republic; and its class composition led it to mortal hatred of the Social Democrats. It felt that it could never attain its ideal without first destroying the Republic, and indeed, even if it had been persuaded that this was unnecessary, it would have wished to destroy it nevertheless. These feelings were widespread among the senior officers. Their aristocratic background made them disdainful of the Nazis, but in the end they felt that they could climb back to power on their backs. And while the senior officers came hesitantly to tolerate dealings with Hitler, the junior officers came increasingly to see in him the opportunity for their own professional advancement.

The Egyptian army of 1952 affords sharp contrasts. It had never been esteemed. It had fought but once, and ignominiously. Its officers were of humble social origin. By 1952 the 'Free Officers' who made the coup were rabid with nationalism, furious with what they deemed to be corruption and nepotism in the matter of commands and equipment, seething with political and class resentment at the effendis who lorded it over them and over their families in the villages. The Egyptian army officers were in fact right-wing radicals, quite dissimilar from the caste-ridden Reichswehr and indeed with motivations much more akin to the Nazi storm-troopers whom the German officer corps despised.

52. Quoted, Wheeler-Bennett, op. cit., p. 216.

In the Japanese army in the 1930s the key motives were nationalism, class feeling and corporate pride. The army particularly was saturated with the samurai tradition of *bushido* and ferociously resisted any sign that the despised civilians were about to curtail their privileges. It was the more hostile to these despised civilians because they were the representatives of the capitalists, whom they hated for the hardships and servitudes of the farming people and small townsfolk from which the junior officers sprang. And they were fiercely nationalistic, believing in a sacred mission of Japan in Asia. They married this to their other motives by their programme of conquering living-space and raw materials on the Asian mainland.

The Spanish emphases were different. This was no fighting army but a bureaucratic machine. Its nationalism turned inwards not outwards. It did not yearn for expansion or power abroad but for unity and order in what Ortega y Gasset called 'invertebrate Spain'. Its ideal was of a timeless Spain, centralized, hierarchical, Castilian and Catholic. The ideal could indeed be partly defined in terms of its hatreds – for syndicalism and socialism, for freemasonry and for Catalan separatism and even – as its Foreign Legion put it – for 'intelligence' itself. The army was indeed completely shut off from the civilian currents of opinion that surged about it. Yet it was the traditional avenue to a career in a highly stratified society and so it attracted mediocrities who longed for a career; and when this did not arrive, they created it. Traditionally too – at least since the Restoration of 1874 – it was the police force of the ruling oligarchy. Thus its nationalism, its *Hispanidad*, was brutally laced with class hatred and with individual careerism.

So much for motives; but for motives to be translated into action, something more is required. This something is mood – the mood that nourishes the will.

CHAPTER FIVE

THE DISPOSITION TO INTERVENE
(2) MOOD

MOODS are more difficult to describe than motives. Psychologists have not yet established a recognized vocabulary for them, let alone a standard classification, and they say that the experimental material on which to base such a classification is still lacking. These difficulties are accentuated in the case of the military where evidence of mood is entirely lacking in all but a handful of cases.

In all instances, however, one element is always present – the consciousness of kind; the military is aware of its special and separate identity distinguishing it from civilian corporations. This self-consciousness, as we have seen, is rooted in and derives from the objective peculiarities of the military life.

In many cases all we can say is that to induce the mood to intervene, only two elements need be added to this self-awareness. The first is a sense of overwhelming power, the knowledge that, in the peculiar circumstances of that moment or that particular country, there is nothing that can prevent them having their own way. The second is some kind of grievance. These grievances or grudges may be some difference of opinion on political issues – for instance, the coups and counter-coups in Syria between 1949 and 1962 were partly due to differences of opinion on Syrian foreign policy. Equally, the grievances may be the emotional aspects of some or other of the motives we have listed – class resentment, regional grudges, ambition or pure predatoriness before a supine and helpless public. It is difficult to resist the conclusion that the Thailand experience (8 coups, 7 constitutions since 1932) or the Iraqi coups of 1936–41 and that of 1958,[1] or the history of many Latin American states,[2] or the recent coup (1961) in South Korea are not to be explained in these simple terms alone.

1. Cf. 'A Year of Republican Iraq' (*The World Today*, vol. 15, no. 7, July 1959), pp. 286–98. 'The Nuri-es-Said system would in time fail from lack of will: meanwhile national developments would undermine its economic and social basis. Its overthrow in July 1958 was, however, due to an accident: the fact that for reasons of internal rivalry, the efficient security system was extended too late to the army. Even so the conclusion was not foregone and was affected by the resource and courage of a handful of conspirators, and notably Colonel Arif when confronted with the irresolution of others.'

2. Peru (till 1956), Venezuela (till 1958), Ecuador (till 1948), Bolivia (till 1952), Paraguay and El Salvador to the time of writing.

54

In a narrow range of cases, the military's behaviour seems almost to follow the lines of a psychology textbook on 'Frustration'. Frustrated – no matter how or why – by their society or by the government of the day, the military react predictably (1) by the responses of anger and humiliation; (2) by 'projecting' the blame on the civilians and 'rationalizing' this reaction; and finally (3) by 'compensating' for the frustration and humiliation by 'taking it out' on these unfortunate objects of their censure. In this narrow range of cases it seems permissible to recognize a single basic mood which sparks off the revolt of the military and which may be summed up as a morbidly acute feeling of injured self-respect. To be sure, different armed forces have different 'flash-points', and some will tolerate what for others is quite insupportable. Furthermore, this sense of self-esteem, this sense of what is owing to one,varies from environment to environment. The matter becomes clearer if the two elements of this compound mood, viz. self-esteem and humiliation, are examined separately. The self-esteem may be a sense of self-importance, as in Turkey, or, say, old Serbia, where the army had really built up the state, or it may be a quite morbid sentiment of superiority to the whole genus of civilians. And the sense of injury, likewise, may range from anger at being rejected and despised by society as in Germany and Japan, or humiliation at being defeated in battle as in Greece and Spain in 1922. Or it may take a vicarious form; it may be humiliation at being identified with a régime which drags the army into contempt – Pakistan (1958) may serve as an example. Since this mood is so complex the best way to illustrate it is not to break it into components (as we did for motives) but to examine the total mood of a number of national forces.

(a) The 'self-important' armed forces

There are armed forces which have a good but not excessive opinion of themselves relative to the government or to civilians in general. In some cases, e.g. France or Pakistan, it would be hard to say that the sentiment went much beyond a professional pride in efficiency. In others, e.g. Turkey, or pre-war Bulgaria, Greece or Yugoslavia, it went beyond this, for these states were, in a very real sense, the endowment of the army. The Balkan countries had arisen from war against the Turk and were maintained by war among themselves. Turkey was the creation of Atatürk and his triumphant army. These armies had different 'flash-points' but all are grouped together here because, unlike the second group we shall discuss, they regarded themselves rather as the equals, not the superiors of the civilian population.

Pakistan serves to illustrate the mood of vicarious humiliation. The army felt outraged at being part of a régime which cut such a pitiable figure internationally. 'A perfectly sound country has been turned into a laughing stock,' said General Ayub Khan. 'Politicians have started a free-for-all type of fighting in which no holds are barred ... There has been no limit to the depth of their baseness, chicanery, deceit and degradation.' The army, he said, had 'kept severely aloof from politics. You may not know, but I refused on several occasions the late Ghulam Mohammed's offer to take over the country. I did so in the belief that I could serve the cause of Pakistan better from the place where I was and also had a faint hope that some politicians would rise to the occasion and lead the country to a better future.'[3]

The change of dynasty in Serbia in 1903 vividly illustrates this concept of a vicarious humiliation. From the first moments of its independence, Serbia had been divided between the protagonists of the Obrenovič and the Karageorgevič dynasties. In 1889, the young Prince Alexander Obrenovič succeeded his father Milan (who had abdicated), and in 1900 he married Madame Draga Mashin. This marriage was wildly unpopular. Not only did Queen Draga come of humble parentage, but her private life was extremely dubious. The marriage shocked the very touchy nationalism of the Serbs (only recently, in 1882, an independent kingdom), and made the little country the laughing stock of all Europe. The army was particularly affected. It was the very nucleus of the new country which had attained statehood only by continuous revolt and fighting. It felt bitterly humiliated at the contempt into which its creation had fallen. The 1903 conspiracy's horrible ending reflected this hatred of Queen Draga. The officers, having burst into the royal apartments and fired shots into the royal couple, frenziedly hacked the body of the Queen into pieces and threw her corpse with the King (who was still alive) into the courtyard below.[4]

The foregoing are examples of a vicarious humiliation. In other cases the armed forces are reacting to a direct blow to their pride. The two most important of the Greek revolts were both attributable to this. The 1909 revolution came about thus: following the Young Turk revolution of 1908, Crete revolted against Turkey and declared her *enosis* with Greece. But the feeble Greek government meekly complied with a succession of Turkish ultimata, even agreeing to refrain from any act prejudicial to Turkish sovereignty. This open confession of military weakness and subservience

3. 8 October 1958. *Keesing's Contemporary Archives* (1957–8), 16458.
4. The story is fully described in C. Mijatovich, *A Royal Tragedy*. This is a royalist account but it contains an appendix by one of the regicides. The mood of wounded pride stands out clearly, e.g. at pp. 221, 225 and 227.

proved too much for the Greek officers. They had already formed a Military League and they now compelled the Prime Minister to resign (August 1909). They then called in Venizelos as their political advisor and supported his convening the Constituent Assembly, which subsequently revised the constitution and regenerated the armed forces.

The military revolt of 1922 was a response to an even more humiliating situation. On 9 September the Turks rode triumphantly into Smyrna, driving the Greek troops into the sea, looting, raping and pillaging in the city, and then committing it to the flames. On the instant, those Greek officers who had got away to Chios constituted themselves a Revolutionary Committee, forced the King to abdicate, and then proceeded to try the ministers and generals responsible for the catastrophe. Accused and found guilty of sacrificing military interests to party considerations, six of these were put to death.

The Egyptian army's mood was more complex. As we have already seen, the Egyptian officer corps suffered throughout from a strong inferiority feeling. Far from being able to compensate for this by victory in the field or by ejecting the British garrisons, they were condemned to witness affronts to their King and their flag which deeply angered them (further instances of this vicarious humiliation which we have already described). An Egyptian historian of the 1952 revolution writes that the British *coup de force* against the King in 1942 was considered by the officers 'as an insult to the Egyptian people'[5] – not an act directed at the King but a slight upon the nation.[6] The British refusal to evacuate Egypt after 1945 was considered ingratitude and 'roused the resentment not only of the people but of the army'.[7] The army's pride therefore was already wounded when the great opportunity of 1948 arrived. The army burned to avenge its insults by massacring the Jews of Palestine. Instead it was defeated, and the government constrained to agree to an armistice. Here the generalizations of the psychologists hold true; far from the army blaming itself, it projected its chagrin on the government. The army had fought gallantly; but 'it soon transpired, however, that the brave men who were laying down their lives in the field had been the victims of a serious plot as a result of inefficiency and treachery'. The high-ranking officers of the General Staff, fighting the war from comfortable quarters in Cairo, were to blame. Worse still, the army had been provided with defective arms. They were defeated 'not because the enemy was braver or more efficient but because of better arms and equipment while they, almost unarmed, were engaged in an unequal

5. Rashed el-Barawy, *The Military Coup in Egypt*, Cairo, 1952, p. 190.   6. ibid., p. 190.
7. ibid., p. 190.

fight and were killed not by the enemy but by the traitors, crooks and corrupt persons of the Royal Court and of the Cairo senior officers.' The rank and file 'often bitterly remarked in reply to inquiries: "We have been betrayed, Sir." ' The dejection of the army was completed when, in returning, it was 'for the first time in the history of the army, taunted with reverses.'[8] It was then that the small group of military conspirators, the so-called 'Free Officers', which had preserved a tenuous existence during the war period, regrouped and decided to overthrow the régime, and paramountly the King who headed it.

There is a striking analogy between what overtook the Egyptian army and the *malaise* in the French army which culminated in the events of 13 May 1958. The original mood is vastly dissimilar; unlike the Egyptian army, the French has a long and most glorious history; it was respected and respectable, and suffered no such feelings of inferiority or hatred of the ruling class as possessed the younger Egyptian officers. But, from 1940, and especially after 1946, its junior officers suffered successive humiliations similar to the Egyptian, and they reacted in a similar way. To begin with, they also began to feel abandoned and rejected by the nation. Their pay and conditions had begun to lag behind comparable professions. Instead of spending most of their lives on garrison duty in France, from 1946 the regular officers spent most of it in the colonies, returning to France for only brief intervals. During the long years of the Indochina war these expatriate officers in the arduous terrain of Indochina read in their French newspapers of the domestic attacks on '*la sale guerre*'. They knew that reinforcements came out and casualties were repatriated in obscurity. And so they got the impression that they were carrying the burden alone. In these conditions, rejected by French society, they turned in upon themselves. Thus in its own way, quite different from that of the Egyptian army, the French officer corps also developed a sense of rejection and a corresponding grudge against civilians.

Secondly, the French officers too began to experience a sequence of disasters and in their humiliation they too projected the blame on the politicians. The critical moment was Dien Bien Phu, which led to the abandonment of Indochina: thereafter the civilian government was singled out as the cause of military humiliation. General Navarre, for instance, attributed the defeat to two reasons: that 'our rulers' never knew what they wanted in Indochina, or, if they did, lacked the courage to say so; and secondly, they 'permitted the Army to be stabbed in the back' by allowing the communists free rein for their 'permanent treason'. 'The accumulated

8. Rashed el-Baraway, op. cit., p. 193.

tergiversations, mistakes and poltrooneries,' he continued, 'are too numerous and continuous not to be imputable to the men and even to the governments which followed one another in office. They are the fruits of the régime. They proceed from the essential nature of the French political system.'[9] But hard on the heels of Indochina followed further reverses. Morocco and Tunis were abandoned, and then came the Suez expedition. Technically, this was brilliantly successful. All the more humiliating was the withdrawal. 'Two years after [Dien Bien Phu], pushed out of Morocco and Tunisia where we had lorded it for so long, made desperate by the Algerian problem, suddenly we were expected to fight a classical combat, without the disseverances of civil war, a military adventure with the clear order of command, "knock out a dictator". The disappointment over the Suez operation was as great as the enthusiasm it had roused. Nothing will ever describe the misery of the parachutists who, victorious, had to leave Egypt and turn their backs on victory.'[10]

From this moment disaffection multiplied among the junior officers, who had borne the heat of the day. It was these above all who felt angry and humiliated and, significantly, they not only turned their rage and contempt against the régime and the politicians but also against the senior officers and the High Command. This was the mood that provoked the events of 13 May and the downfall of the Fourth Republic.

(b) *Armies with a morbidly high self-esteem*

In the foregoing cases, none of the armies regarded themselves as inherently superior to civilians, and some, like the Egyptian, started off by feeling very inferior to them. Armies exist, or have existed, however, with a morbidly high opinion of themselves as compared with the rest of society. Affronts or imagined affronts to their pride tend to spark such armies into intervention more quickly than in the former class and for causes that are, objectively, much slighter.

Here again their self-esteem is nettled by vicarious humiliations as well as by direct ones or by society's rejection of their pretensions. The G.O.U.

9. For the treatment I have relied upon R. Girardet, 'Pouvoir civil et pouvoir militaire' (*Revue Française de Science Politique*, vol. X, no. 1, 1960). There have been subsequent treatments, e.g. R. and J. Brace, *Ordeal in Algeria* (New York, 1960), Chapter 6, but Girardet's is the most brilliant and best documented. The passage from General Navarre, quoted from his article, is to be found in *L'Agonie de L'Indo-chîne* (Paris, 1957), p. 319. (One of my military colleagues comments on General Navarre's remarks by writing that Navarre 'was outfought at his own game – strategy and tactics – and covered up by having a good whine at his political masters'. This makes my point.)

10. Quoted, Girardet, op. cit., from *Réalités*, May 1957.

(*Grupo de Officiales Unidos*) which seized power in Argentina in 1943 had the greatest contempt for civilians. 'Civilians will never understand the greatness of our ideal. We shall therefore have to eliminate them from the government and give them the only mission which corresponds to them: work and obedience.' So ran a G.O.U. manifesto circulated a month before the uprising of 1943. The Argentine public, however, regarded its army as·a jackbooted army of occupation. 'A non-militaristic people who avoid conscription like the plague, they sometimes feel their army's manoeuvring, posturing and bickering is either *opera bouffe* or the scrapping of a group of robber barons disputing their take.'[11] This attitude largely accounts for the tone of the G.O.U. pamphlet. In 1943, however, there were additional wounds to the officers' pride – their vicarious shame at the corruption of the government which abased them in the eyes of the world (a sentiment akin to the Pakistan army's in 1958), a vicarious shame too at knowing that their country was dependent on the United States and the immediate humiliation of knowing that the army was run-down and ill-equipped. The *coroneles* felt that for all these reasons the army had lost face.[12]

A similar mood was permeating the Japanese army by 1930. We have already had occasion to mention its great prestige. The military considered themselves the heirs of the Samurai, the traditional 'lords of the four classes', and adopted Bushido, its code of honour. The fact that officers were being drawn largely from middle- and lower-class families did not affect this Samurai tradition which was wholeheartedly adopted by the newcomers.[13] The military therefore continued to regard themselves as privileged. In the 1920s, however, the political parties successfully cut down the military budgets and boldly denounced the military in the Diet, and despite the patriotic secret societies, public opinion followed them. The soldiers became a target for mockery: 'What use are spurs in a tramcar?' ... 'Big swords are a nuisance to passengers.'[14] The military therefore considered the parties and the Diet as their enemies.

The German Reichswehr officers also regarded themselves as a privileged caste. Drawn from a narrow, aristocratic and reactionary social stratum, every effort had been made to link them with the pre-war Imperial army. The field-grey and the steel helmet were retained. Each new regiment

11. J. Bruce, *Those Perplexing Argentines*, pp. 302–3.

12. Cf. R. Josephs, *Argentine Diary*, pp. 155–8.

13. A common development. Parvenu British officers tend to become more regimental than those whose military roots lie far in the past, so keen are they to show their orthodoxy. Napoleon's Marshals became very noble indeed after Napoleon had made them Dukes of this or that – notwithstanding their humble origins. (Ney's father was a barrel-cooper.)

14. M. Shigemitsu, *Japan and Her Destiny*, pp. 28–9.

was made responsible for maintaining the tradition of one of the disbanded Imperial regiments, and allowed to keep its peculiar privileges and customs and to maintain contact with its former personnel. But its officers bewailed the still-departed glories – the pre-war immunity from the civil courts, the practice by which the individual officer might with impunity punish any civilian who insulted him, the deference paid him by the *Kapitulanten*, i.e. the postmen, customs officers, policemen who had taken up the civil service posts reserved for the ex-servicemen. Officers no longer held a legally privileged position and had to endure the strictures of the pacifistic public of the Weimar Republic. Internationally, far from being renowned as the strongest force in Europe, they were a mere shadow army, hard put to it to face up to the hated and despised Poles. Above all, the canker of defeat gnawed at them. This, psychologically, was too much to bear. They burned to fight the old war over again, this time to win it. Also, however, they eased the intolerable pain and humiliations of reality by the recourses of 'rationalization' and 'projection'. They maintained that they had not failed, and that the blame lay elsewhere; that they were as good and noble and worthy as ever they were; it was the others who were ignoble. The rationalization of their defeat was accomplished, of course, by the infamous *Dolchstoss*, 'stab-in-the-back', theory propounded by Ludendorff – that panic-stricken commander who had insisted on 29 September 1918 that 'the gravity of the military situation admits of no delay', and that 'a peace offer to our enemies must be issued at once'. The army, so ran this theory, had *never* been beaten; the home-front had cracked and had betrayed it. Thus all the obloquy was projected on to the unhappy socialists as the signers of the peace treaty, and on to the Republic which they were largely instrumental in establishing.

Finally one must notice the quite morbid superiority feeling of the army of Spain. We have already had occasion to remark how this army, from about 1900 onwards, had felt rejected by society and had drawn hermetic boundaries around itself, nourishing itself on its own values and hating without understanding the movements of separatism and socialism and syndicalism that were surging through Spain. After its decisive and humiliating defeat by the Moors at Anuel in 1921 the Spanish officers reacted like the Greek officers after Smyrna, or the German officers after 1918, or the Egyptian officers after 1948, or the French officers after Dien Bien Phu. The Spanish army never thought to blame itself but accused the civilians of betraying it. To this disastrous humiliation it responded, as commonly, by seeking psychological compensation elsewhere. If the Spanish army had not defeated the Rif, it would show that it could at least defeat its own civilians. Thus arose the dictatorship of Primo de Rivera in 1923.

This morbid preoccupation with its own precious self-esteem lay at the bottom of its fatal onslaught on the Spanish Republic in 1936. True, it suffered vicarious humiliations from the instability, the breakdown of law and order, and the separatist and pacifistic forces which had been unleashed by 1936; but it could have remedied these by placing itself at the disposition of the authorities rather than by conspiring against them. The key to its behaviour lies in its chronic mood of arrogance and disdain for civilians and its deep-rooted belief that unless it was everything, it was nothing. This monumental arrogance is well attested (because it is so completely unselfconscious) in the special *1936–9 Supplement* to the *Enciclopedia Universel.*[15]

The article says that the army received the proclamation of the Republic 'impassively'. It was accustomed to vicissitudes (it says) and was always unsuccessful in its 'longing to acquire the material and moral importance which was due to it as the national army, that is to say, the most important organ for the internal and external life of the Nation.' Hence (it continues) it received the new régime with cold scepticism. Some officers curried favour; others suspended judgement; the most adventurous however took part in the abortive rising of General Sanjurjo in August 1932. There followed 'a whole campaign of humiliation directed by the public authorities themselves'. These humiliations the army 'bore stoically'. Meanwhile the communist cells began to honeycomb the army, which was by now deprived of its most capable and influential leaders. Consequently its discipline was menaced. 'The idea stood out clearly – to bring about the disappearance of the last bulwark of Spanish nationhood: the army.' The officer corps realized then that they could not remain impassive any longer in face of such events, for these would bring about the disappearance of the nation itself. 'Then and only then', feeling it to be 'their sacred duty', did they begin to prepare for what later was to be called 'the Glorious National Uprising'. This is the official, Franco-ist account of the army's role.

The Disposition to Intervene

The disposition to intervene, then, is a skein of motives and mood. We have seen how various are its components and how differently they are combined in individual cases. Central to the disposition is one element which is the taproot alike of both the motives and the mood. That is the

15. *Enciclopedia Universel, Supplement, 1936–9*, pp. 1444 *et seq.* (Published 1943.)

military's consciousness of having an identity that is separate from, different from and yet juxtaposed with the civilians and the politicians. As we have pointed out, this derives from the objective characteristics of the professionalized standing army. It is this self-awareness that permits the military to conceive that they have a unique duty, a duty of supererogation, to watch over the national interest. This notion of the 'national interest' constitutes a motive; but it is coloured by sectional and regional interests, by the corporate self-interest of the military as such, and by the individual careerism, egotism and ambition of its members.

These motives provide a necessary but not a sufficient condition for intervention. To move the military to act, these motives have to be catalysed into an emotion. The realization – in certain instances – that there is nothing and nobody to stop the military taking what it desires, may convert these motives into the mood for action. Conversely, the frustration of its desires – some stinging rebuff to its pride or the indifference or derision of society – may provoke the familiar reactions of anger, the shifting of the blame to the civilians and, finally, the desire to vindicate itself by imposing its will upon them.

Even so, this is not quite all. The military may well be angry or humiliated, and disposed to intervene; but how they will do so, when they will do so and possibly whether they will in fact do so may and usually does depend on another factor. This factor is the *opportunity* to intervene. The disposition to intervene is an emotion; and though it is true that some armed forces, like some individuals, act blindly on their emotions, most people make some kind of rational calculation before doing so. Such calculation is based on the objective conditions in which the action will take place. There are some constantly recurring political situations in which the opportunities for an armed force to intervene successfully are maximized. These are what we must now describe.

63

CHAPTER SIX

THE OPPORTUNITY TO INTERVENE

CERTAIN situations make the civil power abnormally dependent on the military authorities. Others enhance the military's popularity while correspondingly depressing that of the civil authorities. The military's opportunities to intervene are maximized if both situations coincide.

I. (a) *Increased civilian dependence on the military*

'War is too important to be left to the generals.' Few civilians seem to have agreed with this and still fewer generals. War usually expands the influence of the military. The primacy of the civil power in Britain and in Germany during the Second World War does not invalidate the rather narrow proposition put forward here: that war conditions are among the circumstances that may provide the military with opportunities for intervention. In that same war, for instance, the civilian authorities of the United States handed the major decisions on policy and strategy to the Chiefs of Staff, and admitted them to a share in the mobilization of the civil economy. 'I have washed my hands of it,' said the Secretary of State to the service chiefs, 'and it is now in the hands of you and Knox – the Army and the Navy.'[1] In Japan too, from 1937 onwards, the military obtained the last word on all policy matters, including civilian ones. Ultimate power came to reside in the 'Liaison Committee'. Ostensibly, this brought the politicians and service chiefs together, but effectively it was controlled by its three-man secretariat in which the two service members were paramount. Thus the whole nation was harnessed to the military machine.[2]

In both instances the civilians had voluntarily surrendered to the military. How warfare expands the military's political powers is better demonstrated where the civilians have tried to resist. We have already mentioned the 'silent dictatorship' of Hindenburg and Ludendorff in Germany during the First World War. Where civilian resistance developed, e.g. when the Kaiser demurred to removing Bethman-Hollweg from the Chancellorship, the two generals relied on their indispensability to get their

1. Quoted, Huntington, op. cit., pp. 315–17.

2. Cf. Toshikazu Kase, *Eclipse of the Rising Sun*, pp. 87–9, and Mamoru Shigemitsu, *Japan and Her Destiny*, pp. 320–21. The most thorough treatment is to be found in Y. C. Maxon, *Control of Japanese Foreign Policy*.

own way; they threatened to resign. In Britain it was the other way round. The civil authorities had to use all their influence to make their generals resign. Kitchener was never overruled or even seriously challenged in the cabinet in the first six months of the war and even after his cabinet colleagues had lost confidence in him they had to leave him nominally in charge and simply whittle his functions away.[3] Lloyd George had to adopt similar tactics against Sir William Robertson. It speaks volumes for the increased wartime power of the military that Lloyd George should seriously have feared that the generals would 'form a cabal which would overthrow the existing war cabinet and especially its chief and enthrone a government which would be practically the nominee and menial of the military party'.[4]

Lord Beaverbrook aptly comments that 'people may wonder now at the absolute lack of self-assertiveness, amounting almost to a complete abdication of authority, which marked Asquith's attitude towards the High Command. It is only fair to recognize how widespread was the feeling of the inferiority of the highly placed civilian to the highly placed soldier both at the outbreak of war and for many months or years afterwards. In fact, in many cases it may be said to have lasted for the whole duration of hostilities.'[5] That these sentiments could arise in Britain of all countries affords the most impressive of all examples of the vast expansion of influence which accrues to the military in war.

Much the same occurs in 'cold war' conditions. Such conditions are not unique to the post-1945 period. The pre-1914 situation could equally well be described in such terms. In that period the French army, which half the population distrusted during the Second Empire, had become the 'sacred arch' of the entire population under the fear of renewed German invasion.

3. Cf. P. Magnus, *Kitchener* (Grey Arrow ed.), pp. 287 *et seq.*

4. Lord Beaverbrook, *Men and Power*, pp. 43–57, 186–216 and 408–14; D. Lloyd George, *War Memoirs* (2 vol. ed. Odhams), pp. 1668–9.

5. Lord Beaverbrook, *Politicians and the War*, pp. 237–8. Describing the superiority complex of G.H.Q. he continues: 'The picture of Ministers which the Generals drew to themselves and which was reflected to some extent to the public, was something like this. The Minister sat in a leather-bound armchair in a room where even the faintest hum of outside traffic was hushed, and pulled at a long cigar while he languidly superintended the activities of his secretaries. From this repose he would cheerfully give the order speeding "glum heroes up the line to death" by thousands – although he knew nothing of war. He then rose to go out to dinner with others of his colleagues who had been similarly employed. If the Minister ever did show any activity, it was of the inconvenient kind by which an ignorant civilian interfered with the superb expert efficiency exhibited by the General. And in the meantime, too, the General, instead of smoking a cigar, was daily qualifying for a V.C. by the hardships he endured and the dangers he ran,' (pp. 238–9).

Also, the military's involvement in foreign policy occurred in the pre-1914 period as well as today: for instance, the British agreement with the French on fleet dispositions played some part in convincing wavering cabinet members that Britain must enter the war against Germany.

Nowadays, deference to the military in the fields of foreign policy and even domestic policies is a commonplace. In the context of the 'cold war' it springs from the sheer size of national defence expenditure, which affects the whole national economy; from the increasing technicality of warfare, making much of it a matter for complicated specialisms; from the inability of civilian leaders any longer to assess military tactics and strategy as competently as in the past; from the fact that today's battlefields are entire countries or regions; and finally from the gruesome immediacy of the nuclear threat, which thrusts on some individual or individuals responsibility for a split-second military appreciation. That the expansion of military influence in the United States has attracted more attention than it has in other countries is easily explicable. It derives partly from the irrepressible garrulousness of American military men, as compared with the tortuous silence of their Russian counterparts; from the presence of a free and critical press in the United States; from a governmental system that has traditionally put a premium upon the virtues of publicity – again in contrast with the loud silences of Russia; and, finally, from a politically motivated criticism which sees in America the head and front of capitalist offence. Such cloudy indications as we have of civil–military relations in Russia – notably during the revolution in Hungary in 1956 and Mr Krushchev's reaction to the U2 incident in 1960 – suggest that the Russian military play a part not unlike that of the Pentagon.[6]

1. (b) *The effect of domestic circumstances*

In the foregoing examples the government depends on the military because this is indispensable to its foreign policy. Domestic circumstances may also produce this effect. The government may have to rely on the military as a police force. We can distinguish three kinds of situations in which this is likely to happen: situations of *overt* or *acute* crisis; situations of *latent* or *chronic* crisis; and finally *power-vacuum* situations.

(i) *Overt crisis.* Overt crises occur even in long-established states with well-developed civil institutions. The characteristic of such crises is that rival political forces have arisen willing and able to use violence, which are so equally matched that no government can rely on support from any single one without drawing on itself the full violence of the rest. Such a

6. See pp. 88–98.

country is effectively in a state of potential or even incipient civil war. The causes sometimes lie in the dislocations of some disastrous defeat; sometimes in the aftermath of a protracted and bitter war of political liberation; sometimes they spring from a vicious spiral of domestic events.

Overt crisis is well illustrated by the condition of Germany between 1918 and 1924. With the cease-fire of November 1918, all the old habits of political allegiance dissolved. The traditional political order had determined the goals of the pre-war political struggles, if only as the object of attack; once it was swept away, politics moved into uncharted seas. The familiar landmarks of legitimacy had been obliterated and thenceforth it was open to any group to steer by any means and for any horizon it fancied. The Provisional Government could not base itself on much public support, for political opinion had broken into mutually hostile groupings, each prepared to use violence. It had to contend simultaneously with mutinous units of the armed forces, with the ill-suppressed rage and humiliation of the monarchist and nationalist groups, with the pressure of the Independent Socialists and the Spartakists, and with the unpredictable Soldiers' and Workers' Councils. Possessing no authority it could rest only on force.[7] Hence the notorious 'pact' of 9 November between Gröner, representing the High Command, and Ebert, representing the Civil Power: the government would protect the army and the army would protect the government. The government would provision the army, bring it home and, by beguiling the Soldiers' and Workers' Councils, would discountenance indiscipline in the ranks. In return the army would defend the government. This pact was sealed in the blood of the Spartakists in January 1919; and when the National Assembly met it was under the protection of bayonets.

Succeeding governments were likewise 'couched between the fell contending points of mighty opposites'. By 1923 the cabinet was faced with separatist movements in the Rhineland, left-wing insurrections in Saxony, Thuringia and Hamburg, and military insubordination in Bavaria. Faced with the disintegration of the Reich and attacked by both left and right (because he had cancelled the civil disobedience campaign in the Ruhr) Chancellor Stresemann found the army his sole support. Under Article 48 of the Constitution a state of emergency was declared and the functions of government were transferred to the Minister of National Defence. In practice this meant to General von Seeckt, the Commander of the Reichswehr.

7. The situation in France in 1799, on the eve of Brumaire, was similar – and had similar results to those in Germany. See p. 214.

For the next nine months Germany was ruled by the army acting in support of the civil power.

A second example of 'overt crisis' is provided by Spain during the same period – 1916–23. Here the causes were internal. It would take us too far afield to explain the reasons for this. They lie in Spain's history and geography and in the temperament of her peoples. It must be enough to say that from the beginning of the twentieth century opinion in Spain was split along three lines of cleavage – separatism against centralism, church against state, capital against labour – and that these did *not* coincide but cut across one another. Thus, Catalan separatism could be pro-capitalist (e.g. the Lliga) or anti-clerical and anti-capitalist (e.g. the anarchists) – and so forth. The public was split into factions, none of which was capable of anything but the most hasty and fragile alliances with any other. 'Today', wrote Ortega y Gasset in 1917, 'Spain is not so much a nation as a set of watertight compartments.' These 'compartments' were not even concerned with trying to win allies. By a curse of Spanish cultural history, the Spanish 'True Believer' acted as though his private truth was shared by the rest of the population except the fools or the knaves; and therefore (again in Ortega y Gasset's words), 'The only form of public activity which, beneath all the conventional phrases, satisfies each class is the immediate imposition of its own peculiar will: in short, direct action.'[8]

Between 1916 and 1923 successive governments – purportedly cabinets dependent on parliamentary support – had to contend successively and often simultaneously with three major movements, each likely to shatter under the stress of their internal feuds. The anti-dynastic movement was fiercely divided between liberal-republicans, centralizing socialists and the separatist anarchists and syndicalists. The separatist movement (most important in Catalonia but linked with similar movements in Galicia and the Basque country) was split between capitalists and workers, pro-clericals and anti-clericals. Finally there were the military *Juntas de defensa*, the organs of officers' trade unionism.[9]

The murderous internecine hatreds of the political factions meant that no government could survive except with army support. The way was thereby opened for any amount of military pressure on the politicians. The *Juntas de defensa*, especially when the Moroccan disaster of 1921 embittered them against the civilians, behaved as blindly and selfishly as any of the elements they were busy repressing. Hence a succession of ever more ephemeral cabinets were formed by the favour and then overthrown by

8. Ortega y Gasset, *España Invertebrada*, p. 57.   9. ibid., p. 67.

the impatience of the army. The logical outcome was, as Prime Minister Maura despairingly cried: '*Que gobiernian los que no dejan gobernar*' – 'Let those who will not permit us to govern [i.e. the army] take over the government.' This is what finally happened by the *pronunciamento* of General Primo de Rivera in September 1923.

Thus the characteristic of overt crisis is a fragmentation of opinion into mutually hostile political movements of such pugnacity and power that the government is deprived of any coherent body of popular support, and to survive at all must turn to relying on overwhelming force: and this means relying on the armed forces.

(ii) *Latent crisis*. Much more common is the situation of latent crisis. This connotes a situation wherein a political or social minority rule in a way which the masses hate but which they are too weak to overthrow. Faced by a consensus of indifference or active hatred, often expressing itself in sporadic demonstrations, murders or *jacqueries*, the ruling oligarchy maintains itself by relying on the army, and, therefore, this becomes its master. A classically simple illustration of the effect of such a political situation is to be found in a telegram sent to Washington by the United States Chargé d'Affaires in Bolivia on 14 July 1937:

President Toro resigned last night after army withdrew its support.[10]

Most of the Balkan countries were in this state during the inter-war period. These countries – Rumania, Bulgaria, Yugoslavia, Greece and Albania – were predominantly agrarian. Yet except in Rumania and Bulgaria[11] the peasant was not represented by strong political parties and even they were too feeble to change the social order. All they did was needle the ruling clique into defending its privileges with greater violence. Apart from these two examples, the political parties both in Rumania and Bulgaria and throughout the rest of the Balkans were composed of the urban classes and represented the merchants, petty manufacturers, bankers and professionals. Their interests were hostile to those of the peasantry whom they despised, exploited – and feared. In such countries, the army was the only force to protect the régime against civil uprisings. The inter-war history of Greece, Bulgaria, Albania and Rumania was largely shaped by their soldiers. In Yugoslavia, where peasant unrest and Croat separatism coincided, the Serbian-officered army was the keystone of the régime.

10. *Foreign Relations of the United States* (Department of State, Washington, 1937), vol. V, p. 250. Bolivia was a country of which it used to be well said that 'what the army wants the country wants'.

11. And the Croat areas in Yugoslavia.

The world is still encumbered by similar régimes – Persia and South Vietnam, for instance. In such countries the army is the power on which the government relies. Therefore it has no difficulty in obtaining all it demands, and if it wants to govern in its own name it can and will do so.

Post-war Iraq may serve as a type-example of a condition of latent crisis. Before 1958 its ruling group was a narrow knot of sheikhs, landlords and politicians. This ruled by manipulating the forms of parliamentary democracy in a way identical with the Spanish 'Restoration' régime.[12] Before the war, government instability was due to rivalries within the ruling clique. After 1945, however, governments had to face a murderous but politically helpless hostility among the professional people, the students, the few workers and the declassed labourers of the towns. This opinion was known as 'the popular force'. It was powerfully imbued with pan-Arabism and embittered by the corruption and selfishness of the oligarchy and the lack of social reforms. The oligarchy met this opposition by delation, brutality and, in the last resort, martial law. The 'popular force' first showed its potential in 1948 on the occasion of the Portsmouth Treaty with Britain. The police were taken by surprise. The government fell and the Treaty had to be repudiated. On the next occasion, in 1952, when even more serious rioting occurred, the Regent entrusted the government to the Chief of the General Staff. Under martial law he dissolved the political parties, suppressed their newspapers and imprisoned their leaders. In 1956, when the 'popular force' was frenzied over the Suez campaign, the government took time by the forelock: it imposed martial law *before* the streets filled. In 1958, though opinion was again overwrought by events in the Lebanon, Prime Minister Nuri-es-Said was so confident that he ordered troops to march through Baghdad to Jordan, to be ready to intervene on the Syrian and Lebanese frontier. Unluckily for him, these troops happened to be led by officers who had been conspiring for three years past. They had no difficulty in seizing the key points in the capital, and in murdering the Regent, the King and Nuri-es-Said himself. With them gone, the régime collapsed. The army had simply taken the place of the ruling clique it had been upholding.

(iii) *The power vacuum.* There remain cases where there is, effectively, no organized political movement of any strength, and singularly little if any political opinion at all. These situations are rapidly passing away owing to the emergence of industry in hitherto medieval economies on the one hand and the impact of Western ideas on the other. Among such ideas, Marxism

12. See p. 45.

must be reckoned a powerful force, carried as it is with missionary zeal and the implicit or explicit backing of Russia and China. Hence the most typical examples lie in the past though this is not by any means a remote one: Peru, Venezuela, Ecuador, Bolivia up to about 1920, Guatemala, El Salvador, Honduras up to about 1930, Paraguay and Haiti to this day, may be said to be countries in which organized public opinion did not exist or was so weak as to be inconsiderable.[13]

In circumstances like these there is nothing to prevent the military from acting as it pleases. The six *coups d'état* which succeeded one another in Iraq from 1936 to 1941 were self-generating and would have gone on indefinitely but for the British intervention in 1941. The politics of Iraq from 1936 to 1941 resembled a game of 'change your partners' – a loose group of politicians rent by rivalries confronted a loose group of ambitious officers. From time to time a clique of politicians would link hands with a clique of officers and thereby get themselves installed in office. Then another clique from each side would momentarily combine to oust the first combination; and so forth.

2. *The popularity of the military*

The popularity or prestige of the armed forces is a second objective factor which may help them to intervene. Such popularity is very erratic and it fluctuates with time and circumstance. The initial popularity which so often accompanies a coup may wear off quite quickly. Thus the vocal public and the intelligentsia of Pakistan are today increasingly disenchanted with the Ayub Khan régime. Likewise in the Sudan.

In his study of the French army between 1815 and 1939, Girardet has shown how and why its popularity fluctuated so markedly during the course of the century. Tainted with Bonapartism and Jacobinism after 1815, it was coldly received by the wealthier classes, but by the same token was popular with the masses. A striking change began to occur after the events of 1848 when the army alone had stood between *La Grande Peur* of the Paris bourgeoisie and the insurrectionary workmen who invaded the streets. Under the Empire, the army became the darling of the upper classes, and it became increasingly clerical and aristocratic. For some twenty years after the shock of defeat in 1870, it was the idol of both conservatives and progressives alike; national humiliation had wiped out rancour. The army was the keystone. Then the Dreyfus affair revealed how sectional it had become – clerical, illiberal and anti-Republican.

13. This is further developed below, Chapter Nine.

Thenceforth till the outbreak of the war it was as fiercely hated in some quarters as it was adulated in others.

It is, therefore, impossible to generalize about the factors on which the popularity of the army depends. Nor is it necessary. One need note only that it is particularly helped, should it nourish any political ambitions, by any circumstances that tend to discredit the civilian régimes. Inefficiency, corruption and political intrigue appear to be the very reverse of that austerity, brisk authoritarianism, political neutrality and patriotism which pristine publics, unaccustomed to military rule, tend to attribute to the military. It is not surprising, therefore, that the military find in civilian mismanagement the opportunity, the motive and subsequently the pretext for their intervention.

Consider the case of Primo de Rivera. We have already mentioned that by 1923 Spain was deep in social crisis. The *Juntas de defensa* had contributed to this crisis and the principal reason for Primo de Rivera's coup, or at least the timing of it, was to suppress the parliamentary inquiry into the Moroccan disaster. Yet his coup was acclaimed with wild enthusiasm. The reason is quite simple: the politicians and the régime could not have been more unpopular. In his own words:

> We do not feel obliged to justify our action, which sensible public opinion demands and imposes. Murders of priests, ex-governors, public officials, employers, foremen and workers; audacious and unpunished hold-ups; depreciation of the value of money; the hogging of millions of concealed expenditures; a customs policy suspect for its tendencies but even more because whoever manages it boasts of impudent immorality; base political intrigues seizing on Morocco as their pretext; irresolution on this most serious national problem; social indiscipline which renders labour inefficient and of no account; agricultural and industrial production precarious and in a ruinous state; communist propaganda unpunished; impiety and barbarousness; justice influenced by politics; barefaced separatist propaganda; tendentious passions over the problem of responsibility [for Morocco].[14]

There is enough truth in this catalogue of woes to explain why the coup was widely popular and so easily successful.

Kassim's *plaidoyer* makes similar and equally valid play with the corruption and ineptitude of the politicians. 'The revolution has taken place to free the people of Iraq from tyranny and corruption in domestic affairs . . . Under the old régime there was no law or justice in Iraq. Only the interests of the governing classes were served by the administration of the law under that régime.'[15] The justification of the Pakistan coup was similar.

14. *Pronunciamento* of General Primo de Rivera, 13 September 1923.
15. *Keesing's Contemporary Archives* (1958), 16306 (b).

'Self-seeking leaders had ravaged the country or tried to barter it for personal gain.' – 'Weak and irresolute governments have looked on with masterly inactivity and cowardice and allowed things to drift and deteriorate and discipline to go to pieces.' – 'Politicians have started a free-for-all type of fighting in which no holds are barred. They have waged a ceaseless and bitter war against each other regardless of the ill effects on the country, just to whet their appetites and satisfy their base motives. There has been no limit to the depth of their baseness, chicanery, deceit and degradation . . .'[16]

The extent to which these remarks of General Ayub Khan hit off the popular mood can be gauged by Mr Wint's report on the '1958 Revolution', as he calls it. 'The government and politicians were despised,' he writes. 'In contrast, the army gained prestige. For the army was conspicuously efficient and conspicuously incorrupt. Thus an unbalance developed between the respected and capable army and the despised and incompetent politicians. The army might have moved into political control earlier but for one thing: its commanders had taken over the British military tradition that an army should keep aloof from politics. They had twice refused invitations to set up a dictatorship by the former Governor-General Ghulam Mohammed.'[17] Mr Wint then describes how the almost unbelievable scenes in the East Bengal Parliament finally impelled General Ayub Khan to act,[18] and he concludes: 'One result of these discreditable happenings was that none of the politicians whom the army despised was able to make a protest. They simply withdrew. There was no fight in them, and the reason was that they knew they could raise almost no public support if they opposed the army. After the first few days public opinion supported the Revolution.'[19]

Thus the decline of confidence in the politicians and civil processes is liable to enhance the popularity of the military. By the same token, it weakens the authority of the civilian régime and renders it an easier prey to the intervention of the army, which, in these circumstances, comes to be regarded as a deliverer.

16. Gen. Ayub Kahn, 10 October 1958: *Keesing's Contemporary Archives* (1958), 16458 (a).

17. Guy Wint, 'The 1958 Revolution in Pakistan', *St Antony's Papers*, no. 8, 1960, pp. 76–7.

18. There was to be a general election there in February 1959. Clearly the government in power would 'fix' it. Hence a fierce struggle to gain – or to maintain – power as between government and opposition. The opposition managed to get the Speaker certified as mad, the Deputy Speaker being one of theirs. In return, the government's supporters armed themselves at the next session with bits of wood and killed the Deputy Speaker.

19. Wint, op. cit.

Disposition and opportunity: the calculus of intervention

In the preceding chapters we discussed the military's *disposition* to intervene, and we have now reviewed its occasion or opportunity for doing so. These, the subjective and objective factors, are both relevant to the fact or likelihood of intervention.

It will be seen that there are four possible situations.

(a) *Neither disposition nor opportunity to intervene*. In this case no intervention will occur.

(b) *Both disposition and opportunity to intervene*. In this case intervention will occur.

(c) *No disposition to intervene but the opportunity for doing so*. An example of this kind of situation comes from Iraq, in 1952. General Mahmud, the Chief of the General Staff, was entrusted with the premiership to restore order, the police having failed. Two months later, order having been restored, General Mahmud resigned from the premiership. He had, one is told, 'no political ambitions'.

At first sight, then, one would say that the *disposition* to intervene is paramount – that if that is lacking, no intervention will take place. On the whole this is true. What might also happen, however, may be illustrated by three cases. First the army might after much prodding and pushing, reluctantly intervene after all. This is what, we are told, happened in Pakistan. In the first stage of the intervention the President, i.e. the civil power, abrogated the constitution, dissolved the Assemblies, abolished the parties and proclaimed martial law with General Ayub Khan as his chief martial law administrator. This was on 7 October 1958. But on 24 October the President appointed General Ayub Khan Prime Minister; and then, on 28 October, after swearing in the new Ministers on the previous day, the President resigned and handed over 'all powers' to the General.[20]

A second possibility is illustrated by the official version of the events in Burma on 26 September 1958. Premier U Nu announced that since his tour in Upper Burma, he was convinced that the forthcoming elections could not be fair and free and he had therefore invited the Chief of Staff, General Ne Win, to form a government which would make arrangements for free elections. He also arranged for the General to be legally invested by

20. This is the 'official version'. Pakistan circles have a different version in which General Ayub Khan was the importunate party and President Mirza the reluctant one. Some colour is given this by the General's statement on 10 October that whilst it was the President's constitutional duty to halt the disintegration of the country it would have been the army's responsibility to do so if the President had not acted.

the Parliament. If this version be the whole truth it would amount to intervention by invitation.[21]

A third possibility is that of a legal 'temporary dictatorship' of the military, like that of General von Seeckt, in 1923, under Article 48 of the Weimar Constitution – or the Iraq case (General Mahmud) already mentioned.

(d) *Disposition, but no opportunity*. This situation is not uncommon. It leads to abortive putsches. The Kapp putsch of 1920 was of this kind. So was that of General Sanjurjo in Spain in 1932 (Sanjurjo himself knew that his rising was bound to fail, but felt in honour bound to try). The abortive rebellion of the Four Generals in Algeria in April 1961 also falls into this category.

The opportunity to intervene, and the level of political culture

None of these opportunities for intervention arise at random, except for the ones occasioned by external circumstances. Wars or cold wars are indeed unpredictable. But those opportunities occasioned by domestic conditions are tied up with the nature of the society in which they occur. In what way?

As we have seen, *all* the opportunities of this kind arise through some weakening of the public support for the government, and thereby its increased dependence on the military. The less its authority the more it must rely on force. But this is simply to say that the greater the public attachment to civilian institutions' the less opportunity and the less likelihood of success will the military enjoy; and *vice versa*. And this brings us back to Chapter Three. There we coined a term to express this degree of attachment to civilian institutions. We called it the *level of political culture*. We suggested that one might conceive of societies as ranged at various levels of political culture according to the strength or the weakness of their attachment to their civilian institutions. We now see that the higher this level, the fewer are the objective opportunities open to the military; and that if it tries notwithstanding, the less support it will receive. The lower the

21. It is in fact most unlikely to be anything but a minimal part of the truth. There was at that time considerable friction between the army and U Nu's faction of the A.F.P.F.L. party. The army thought U Nu's A.F.P.F.L. too clement to the communist rebels. For their part the members of his party accused the army of interfering in several disputes in favour of the Opposition-A.F.P.F.L. The Home Minister certainly believed, on 22 September (i.e. four days before U Nu's announcement), that the army was preparing a coup. This General Ne Win denied. It ought to be noticed that General Ne Win did, two years later, turn the government back to the civilians, but also that in March 1962 he overthrew the civilian government and established a military dictatorship.

level, however, the more numerous the opportunities, and the greater the likelihood of public support.

The military's opportunity – and its public welcome – both derive from the level of political culture. The 'level' (i.e. the completeness) to which the military press their intervention also depends on this. This forms the subject of the next chapters.

CHAPTER SEVEN

THE LEVELS OF INTERVENTION
(1) COUNTRIES OF DEVELOPED POLITICAL CULTURE

'Levels' of intervention

INTERVENTION can be pushed to various levels of completeness. The activities of a von Seeckt are not different in kind from the activities of, say, a Kassim or Nasser, but differ in degree.

We can recognize four levels of military intervention. First we have the level of *influence* upon the civil authorities. By this is meant the effort to convince the civil authorities by appealing to their reason or their emotions. This level is the constitutional and legitimate one, entirely consistent with the supremacy of the civil power. The military authorities act in precisely the same way and with the same authority as any elements in the bureaucracy, though their influence may well be weightier and on occasion overriding, in view of the greater risks involved by the rejection of their advice.

The second level is to the level of *pressures*, or '*blackmail*'. Here the military seek to convince the civil power by the threat of some sanction. The span of such pressures is wide. It can range from hints or actions that are just barely constitutional at one end to intimidation and threats that are clearly unconstitutional at the other. It would be difficult to say that the Curragh 'mutiny' was downright unconstitutional, and it can even be argued that in strict legal terms it was not unconstitutional at all. Nevertheless, it constituted an effective exercise of pressure on the British government. In his *Memoirs*, Lord Montgomery says that he assembled the military members of the Army Council and got them to agree to resign in a body if the cabinet decided on anything less than 18 months' National Service, and that he notified the Secretary of State of this decision.[1] Mr Shinwell (the Secretary of State in question) has denied this. However, supposing it happened as described, again, it is doubtful whether the action was unconstitutional. It is on the margin. At the other extreme, threats to stage a coup, for example, are plainly unconstitutional.

At both the first and second levels, the military is working upon and through the civil authorities. Even in a complete form, its power is always

1. *The Memoirs of Field-Marshal Montgomery* (Fontana ed., 1960), pp. 486–7.

exercised behind the scenes. The military is, at most, a puppet-master. The third level, however, is that of *displacement*, i.e. the removal of one cabinet or ruler for another cabinet or ruler. This is achieved by violence or the threat of violence. The object is to replace one set of civilian politicians by another and more compliant set. However, the civilian régime as such is not overthrown – only one particular set of civilians.

The fourth level sweeps away the civilian régime and establishes the military in its place. This is the fourth and most complete level of intervention, the level of *supplantment*.

The parameters of the levels of intervention

The levels to which the military press their intervention are related to the *level of political culture* of their society. We must therefore look at this concept more closely.

The level of political culture is high, when

(1) the '*political formula*', i.e. the belief or emotion by virtue of which the rulers claim the moral right to govern and be obeyed, is generally accepted. Or, to say this in another way, where

(2) the complex of civil procedures and organs which jointly constitute the political system are recognized as authoritative, i.e. as duty-worthy, by a wide consensus. Or, again in other words, where

(3) public involvement in and attachment to these civil institutions is strong and widespread.

The criteria by which we can assess this attachment to and involvement in the institutions of the régime are three. We must ask:

(1) Does there exist a wide public approval of the procedures for transferring power, and a corresponding belief that no exercise of power in breach of these procedures is legitimate?

(2) Does there exist a wide public recognition as to who or what constitutes the sovereign authority, and a corresponding belief that no other persons or centre of power is legitimate or duty-worthy?

(3) Is the public proportionately large and well-mobilized into private associations? i.e. do we find cohesive churches, industrial associations and firms, labour unions, and political parties?

Where all these conditions are satisfied the level of political culture may be said to be high; to the extent that they are not, it is correspondingly low.

These conditions are obviously better satisfied in Britain than in Iraq. It is more difficult, however, to say whether they are better satisfied in Britain than in Sweden. Furthermore, this notion of 'political culture' is not unitary. It is a complex of the three conditions, and these can be ranked in different ways. Thus we might find one country in which the public was weak and ill-organized but reasonably united, while in another it was disunited but very strongly organized. For these reasons it would be difficult to arrange societies in a continuous rank-order, and even more difficult to find one that satisfied everybody.

It is not so hard, however, to group societies in a number of broad categories of descending orders of political culture (though borderline cases still offer difficulties). And, for purposes of relating the level of intervention to the order of political culture, it is much clearer.

In the first group, where the order of political culture is highest, all three of the conditions are fulfilled. In such countries, the intervention of the military would be regarded as a wholly unwarrantable intrusion. Public sanction for such action would be unobtainable. Britain, the United States, the Scandinavian countries, Switzerland, Canada, Australia and New Zealand, Eire and Holland are examples. We shall call these countries of a *mature political culture*.

In the second group, civil institutions are highly developed. The public is a proportionately wide one, well organized into powerful associations. Civil procedures and public authorities are well rooted. But, unlike the first group, the legitimacy of the procedures for transferring political power and the question of who or what should constitute the sovereign authority are both in dispute. Germany from the Empire to the accession of Hitler, Japan between the two wars, and France from the Third Republic onwards, fall into this group. So too, as we shall see, does the U.S.S.R. In such countries, the military would have to reckon on a strong public resistance to their interventions. We shall call these countries of a *developed political culture*.

In the third group are those countries where the public is relatively narrow and is weakly organized, and where the institutions and procedures of the régime are in dispute also. Here opinion would not be strongly resistive to military intervention; this opinion, being weak and self-divided, is in a fluid state. At the top of this category we can place countries like Turkey, Argentina and Spain; at the bottom countries like Egypt and Syria, Pakistan, Iraq and the Sudan, or South Korea. We shall call these countries of a *low political culture*.

Fourth come the countries where for practical purposes any government can ignore public opinion – the politically articulate are so few and weakly organized. Mexico and Argentina in the first half century of their existence, Haiti or Paraguay or the Congo today, are of this kind. We shall call these countries of *minimal political culture*.[2]

As long as the listed characteristics persist in such societies, the legitimation of military rule would be *unobtainable* in the first group, *resisted* in the second, *fluid* in the third, *unimportant* in the fourth.

The levels to which intervention is pushed vary according to the group into which a society falls. These four orders of political culture form, as it were, the parameters of the levels of military intervention.

Countries of Developed Political Culture

In societies of this order of political culture legitimation of military rule is resisted. The typical levels of military interference range from *influence* to *blackmail*. The violent overthrow of a government may indeed be attempted, since the military may be rash enough to try anything; but the attempts are rare, brief and unsuccessful. The characteristic methods are those which operate from behind the scenes and the reason is that the civil institutions which are being manipulated are the ones that command effective public support.

Even at the height of their power, i.e. during the Pacific war, the armed forces of Japan spared the constitution and the political institutions it hallowed. True, the parties had been induced to dissolve themselves and perfunctory and unsuccessful efforts were made to constitute a sort of popular 'rally' of the Japanese public. But the Diet continued to sit, and the former party men continued to sit in it and criticize the government throughout the war.

For although the military was powerful in Japan, it was only one element of an old-established and traditional system of which the other elements were also strong. The military had a privileged constitutional

2. There is also a fifth class, with which we shall not be concerned. This might be styled the antediluvian class (the deluge in question being the French Revolution). These are the traditional monarchies where the ideals of nationality, liberty, equality and popular sovereignty have not yet penetrated. Another and better description is perhaps the proto-dynastic societies, societies where allegiance is owed to the dynasty. In these societies the public, as an active and organized force, does not exist. It is a passive body, still in its traditional moulds of kinship and village communities. This traditionally structured opinion exhibits a passive consensus on the mode of transferring power (i.e. through the dynastic line) and on the sovereign authority, the monarch. These proto-dynastic states are fast passing: but the Yemen, Saudi Arabia and Ethiopia still remain. Any military intervention in such states as these would be exercised in the name of the dynasty – as it was in the revolt of the Ethiopian Imperial Guard in 1960.

position; it had strong roots in the peasantry and so a powerful social basis. It controlled an educational system of its own. It enjoyed great prestige, and had centuries of heroic tradition behind it. Despite all this, it had to coexist with other equally well-rooted institutions. There were, first of all, the formal institutions set down in the 1889 Constitution and, because this was an Imperial document, hallowed as sacrosanct – as the Tenno (or Emperor) was sacrosanct. These institutions were the Tenno himself, whose servants they were, and his Imperial Household. There was the *Genro*, the council of the elders of the five clans which had acted till the late 1920s as the effective balance wheel of the whole Imperial constitution. There were the Diet and the Cabinet. Operating through these institutions were rival political 'orders', which had emerged just as the modern army and navy had, at the Meiji restoration of 1868. The great clans of Choshu and Satsuma had laid hold of the machinery of state: having done so, the clansmen gradually split into the military bureaucracy (the *Gumbatsu*) and the civil bureaucracy (the *Kanbatsu*), and thus both had a common clan origin. This civil bureaucracy was a *corps d'élite* recruited by open competitive examination, almost exclusively from Tokyo and Kyoto universities. It had a great professional self-esteem and looked on the other forces, including the military, with arrogant disdain. Thirdly there were the parties. These were first formed from the clans that had been left in the cold when Choshu and Satsuma seized the administration after 1868. Since then they had lost their clan associations and instead were the organs of the newly arrived *Zaibitsu*, particularly the great houses of Mitsubishi and Mitsui. Trade and industry developed with prodigious speed and, with it, urbanization, industrial associations and labour unions. Japan had become a modern industrial state and its public was wide, highly literate and organized. The parties therefore were also a real force. These various forces infiltrated whatever organs of government they could. The military operated through the Supreme Command. The *Zaibitsu* and the *Kanbatsu* rivalled one another by infiltrating the same organs, e.g. the Privy Council, the House of Peers and the Diet. The point is that 'the Parliamentary State had never existed without the concurrent support and coexistence of the bureaucratic and militaristic elements, all of which made up a characteristic Japanese polity.'[3] The history of modern Japan from 1890 to 1945 was a struggle between military, civil bureaucracy, the capitalists and the two political parties.

The characteristic levels of military intervention, therefore, were *influence*, and, from 1930 onwards, *blackmail* – a large-scale offensive against

3. P. A. M. Linebarger (ed.), *Far Eastern Government and Politics*, p. 404.

the civilian elements using political intrigue, constitutional, obstruc-
tion, popular propaganda, and terrorism and murder. But although small
groups of plotters did from time to time plan to destroy the cabinet and
seize power for the army (e.g. the March and October incidents of 1931),
only once did they bring the issue to the test. This was in the February
mutiny of 1936, and its outcome proved decisively that the traditional
civilian institutions of Japan were too pervasive and resistant for overt
military intervention to succeed.

For in the first place, the mutiny was the culminating point in the clash
of two army factions, the Kodo-ha and the Tosei-ha, which, significantly,
stood for outright military rule and covert military manipulation of the
civil authorities respectively. The Kodo-ha envisaged the suppression of the
parties and of the Diet, and the forcible regimentation of the *Zaibitsu*
elements under a military government ruling in the name of the Emperor.
The Tosei-ha envisaged a one-party system, working within the traditional
system, and controlled by the military. Secondly, the mutiny was initially
successful. Two infantry regiments and some of the Guards left their barracks. They split up into murder bands and succeeded in killing a large
number of the senior statesmen. They then occupied a zone in the centre of
Tokyo. At this stage the authorities were completely at a loss, and in no
position to offer any resistance. Thirdly, however, this was precisely as far
as the mutiny went. No senior officers joined the rebels. No popular
movements demonstrated for them. No senior politicians offered their support. And on their side, the rebels did nothing either – except to leave a
mimeographed manifesto at each of the newspaper offices on the next
morning. For four days the rebels and the authorities faced one another in
silence. The decisive action was initiated by the Emperor, usually a passive
spectator of the political scene. Here he made it absolutely clear that this
was a mutiny and that it must be suppressed. With this decision the whole
civil machinery of the state operated once more. Martial law was declared,
troops were brought in from the outside, and the navy prepared to act. The
rebels were summoned to surrender, and finally did so. They were denied
the privilege of a public trial, and, instead, were tried by secret court
martial. Furthermore, unlike previous plotters, the ringleaders were
executed. Fourthly, the ignominious collapse of the rebellion did not
weaken the army's position *vis-à-vis* the civil authorities. It immensely
strengthened it, but not by way of the Kodo-ha. This faction was defeated.
Power in the army passed to the 'control' school, the Tosei-ha. From 1936
it successfully carried out its programme, so that by 1940 the parties had
been dissolved, the *Zaibitsu* harnessed to a siege economy, and ultimate

decisions vested in the military-dominated Liaison Committee. Thus the events of 1936 dramatically exposed the futility of attempting overt military rule, and vindicated the view that, in Japanese conditions, the military must secure their control from within. 'There were limits to its power. It could not rule the country directly and, indeed, preferred the traditional method of indirect rule. It could not dispense with the politicians, the Foreign Office, the bureaucrats and the industrialists. While it had its allies among all these groups it also had its enemies.'[4]

What the February mutiny is to the Japanese experience, the Kapp putsch of 1920 is to the German. During the whole period from 1918 to 1934 the German army had the final word. Yet its role was characterized by two features. In the first place it was always concealed by some constitutional or civilian cloak – even in the Kapp putsch the rebellious army units planned a government under Kapp, a civilian. Secondly, with the exception of the Kapp putsch, it always sought some pretext of legality. Even Schleicher, the inveterate schemer for a military government, sought to achieve this by invoking the State of Emergency under Article 48 of the Constitution. Furthermore, he and his like sought alliances with the Nazis only because they knew that the army could not rule without some powerful mass basis to give it support and colour of legitimacy. One of the reasons which convinced them of this was, precisely, the failure of the Kapp putsch.

The underlying reason lies in the tradition of civil institutions in Germany, and the highly organized nature of the public which supported them. The Empire had inherited from Prussia not only the army but also the bureaucracy and with this the cult of regulations and punctilious legalism. Within the Empire, too, there had grown up – as in Japan – a vast industrialization, so that the public became urbanized, and organized into industrial associations and trade unions. Moreover – unlike Japan – the churches were a powerful civilian force. Thus the Empire was a society in which civilian institutions and legality were important; in which the public, organized by churches, economic associations and political parties, was powerful; and in which civilian organs like the Emperor and the bureaucracy were strongly rooted in tradition. The Weimar period did not destroy the hold of institutions like the bureaucracy or the army upon the public, and strengthened rather than otherwise the organized nature of public opinion. The effect of the 1918 defeat was, rather, to destroy the previous consensus on the characteristics and location of legitimate authority.

4. F. C. Jones, 'The Military Domination of Japanese Policy, 1931–1945', *Soldiers and Governments*, ed. M. Howard, p. 125.

As we have already shown, this brought about a situation of overt crisis lasting from 1918 to the triumph of Hitler, during which the army became the arbiter of German politics. Yet the tradition of civilianism and legality was so strong that, as in Japan, it could exercise power only behind the scenes. The Kapp putsch demonstrated the impossibility of overt action, i.e. the violent overthrow of government for another of a more complaisant complexion.

In February 1920 the German government received the Allied list of war criminals. A nationalist frenzy shook Germany from Left to Right. And the army, from Lüttwitz to von Seeckt, determined to fight rather than comply.

While the Bauer government temporized, General Lüttwitz favoured a march on Berlin. His military colleagues persuaded him to wait until legal means were exhausted. He therefore confined himself to the demand that the government should dissolve the Assembly, and hold new elections for the Reichstag and for the Presidency.

Meanwhile he was in touch with a former civil servant, Kapp, a leading light in an extremely right-wing party whose purpose was to lock up the government and establish an authoritarian régime under a *Reichsverweser*, in which the Prussian virtues of duty and obedience were to be reaffirmed.

Bauer refused Lüttwitz's demands; and Lüttwitz, once he learned that the naval brigade was being taken from him, felt he must act immediately. The President told him to obey orders or resign; that the Reichswehr was not behind Lüttwitz and that if he acted the President would proclaim a general strike. The next day, the government openly dismissed Lüttwitz and issued warrants for the arrest of Kapp. So Lüttwitz marched.

The government fled to Dresden, and Kapp was installed at the Chancellery. Apparently no victory could be more complete. But, again as in Japan, nobody rallied to the new government. No political leaders or parties offered support. Indeed the civil service began to resist and the rest of the Reichswehr were silent. And, at the demand of the government-in-exile, the general strike was indeed proclaimed. The life of Berlin – communications, light, food supply – was instantaneously and totally extinguished. Meantime the wretched Kapp, like the Japanese mutineers, marked time. He did not even have a manifesto ready. It had to be typed by his wife on a borrowed machine and was circulated too late to reach the morning papers. In the face of the strike and the total absence of support, he remained indecisive. Some efforts of Lüttwitz's troops to get the workers back to work led only to some futile casualties. On 17 March, after five days of pointless isolation in the Chancellery, Kapp, accompanied by his hysterical and weeping daughter, fled to Finland. The putsch was over. It left in its wake all the signs of violent civilian resistance – revolts in Saxony and the Ruhr, Workers' Councils everywhere. The General Staff, as Görlitz comments, 'had a new object lesson to demonstrate the absurdity of a military dictatorship without a mass basis'.[5] From then on, the German army, like the Japanese, worked by influence and blackmail. These were the levels imposed by the political culture level of German society.

And the same levels are imposed by the political culture level of France; this is the moral of the Four Generals' revolt of 22 April, analogous in all essentials with the Kapp putsch and the February mutiny. 'France's economic and social structure has gone well beyond the era of *pronunciamentos*,' wrote Maurice Duverger.[6] When, in 1958, Soustelle told a fellow-conspirator that he himself would not initiate a breach of legality but would leave such a decision to the generals, his colleague (a civilian like Soustelle) replied, 'That sentence can only be spoken in Spanish.'[7] The *Treize Mai* (1958) showed that the army could bring down a government and impose a new one. 22 April 1961 just as forcibly showed that it could not stand alone as a rival government to the civil power. For this is the essential difference between the two situations; in the first, the exercise of covert pressures and intimidation to impose de Gaulle; in the second, the open, public and direct seizure of the authority of the state in Algeria in flagrant defiance of the legal order. In 1958, the revolt began with civilians, and the army in Algeria was sucked into it; in 1961, it began with the army and no civilians joined it. In 1958, Massu and Salan put themselves at the head of the civilians reluctantly, first to 'control' them and then to intimidate the National Assembly into rejecting Pflimlin as Prime Minister. When their action only provoked the Assembly into investing Pflimlin they became terrified at their temerity in breaching 'republican legality'. '*Nous sommes foutus*' was Massu's reaction to the news, and the stiffening attitude of the Paris government alarmed the generals still more; but in 1961, the four generals decided deliberately to breach legality and defy the consequences. In 1958 their compromised status led Massu and Salan to clutch eagerly at the suggestion to raise the cry, '*De Gaulle au pouvoir*'; for a change of government was now their best and possibly their only hope of immunity. But in 1958, what transformed their situation was General de Gaulle's public announcement that he was willing to assume the powers of the Republic. To the army – and not merely the generals – de Gaulle

5. W. Görlitz, *The German General Staff*, p. 221.
6. Quoted, A. Werth, *The de Gaulle Revolution*, p. 89.
7. Quoted, P. Williams and M. Harrison, *De Gaulle's Republic*, p. 56.

represented a more congenial régime than the Fourth Republic; to the people and politicians of France he represented an escape from the possibility of civil war. As he himself put it, 'Belonging to nobody I belong to everybody.' If the Fourth Republic began to totter at that point, it was due to de Gaulle, not to Generals Massu and Salan. It was only when civilian sentiment began to swing behind de Gaulle that the army began to plot its breaches of legality and the war of nerves against the Republic. Not until de Gaulle had spoken did the airforce dip its wings in salute over Colombey, and units begin to chalk up their crosses of Lorraine. It was only then that the emboldened General Salan authorized the raid on Corsica and thus for the first time openly broke the laws; and it was only then that operation 'Resurrection' was planned to seize Metropolitan France. The threat of violence was unleashed when – and not until – an alternative civilian government and a supporting public opinion were forthcoming. And by the same token the resistance of the government, powerful and increasing before the name of de Gaulle was canvassed, first faltered, then crumbled, and ultimately collapsed, as de Gaulle's magic name first confused the supporters of the régime and finally captured them.

Treize Mai demonstrated that the army could intimidate a government into resigning – provided the army had powerful civilian support. But it received such support only by adopting as its candidate one who was a masterful public figure in his own right, and a politician to boot. 22 April demonstrated, *per contra*, that by defying this figure it brought against itself the full weight of civilian resistance, and that in face of this it was powerless.

In the early hours of 22 April 1961, the 1st Division of paratroopers entered the city of Algiers and possessed themselves of the public buildings without any struggle. General Challe proclaimed a state of siege and ordered all civil authorities to obey the orders of the army. In this *pronunciamento* he declared that he and his colleagues (Generals Zeller, Jouhaud and Salan) were simply acting to keep their oath, 'the army oath of guarding Algeria'. Within a few hours the garrisons of Oran and Constantine were brought over. As in the Kapp putsch and the February mutiny, the triumph of the army was in all appearances complete. At that moment the situation of the metropolitan government seemed desperate.

Its security services had failed – through complicity, it has since been alleged. The bulk of the army was in Algeria, now in the hands of the rebels. The remainder of the army, situated in Germany, was only doubtfully loyal. At any moment skyborne troops might invade Paris. There seemed nothing to stop them. But the government went to work with the one thing that alone remained to it – its moral authority. And this had been swelled by the overwhelming vote of confidence received by General de Gaulle in the referendum of 8 January only three months before.

It did not compromise, it attacked. It declared the coup 'a grave and premeditated act of indiscipline'. Recalling that the will of the nation had been expressed in the recent referendum, the Prime Minister stated that 'The government is determined to make the will of the nation respected.' The President, General de Gaulle, clamped down upon France the State of Emergency, under the notorious and controversial Article 16 of the Constitution; and then, advancing to the television screen, and speaking directly into the homes of the people of France, he pronounced these grave and defiant words:

> I forbid all soldiers to obey the rebels ... I shall maintain this [my] legitimate power whatever happens, up to the term of my mandate or until such time as I cease to have necessary means to do so or cease to be alive ... In the name of France I command that all means – I repeat *all means* – be used to bar the way to those men ... *Françaises! Français! Aidez-moi!*

Buses, lorries, coaches stood ready to rush upon the airfields and block them against airborne troops. The government asked the people to flock to the airfields if, despite these measures, troops managed to land. Republican and mobile guards in armoured cars and tanks moved to protect the Elysée Palace. The authorities began arming a civilian Home Guard. The security police swept Paris for suspects. The parachutists did not come that night. The next day the government began to form a force of Republican guards and reservists, 10,000 strong. It imposed a financial and shipping blockade on Algeria. As a sign of civilian solidarity, ten million workmen struck for one hour throughout Metropolitan France. Later that day General Crépin, the Commander-in-Chief of the doubtful divisions in West Germany, declared for the government and his formations began to roll towards Paris. The Algerian paratroopers did not come on that night either.

Their delay was fatal. The rebel generals held all Algeria; but nobody (except the inevitable Ortiz and Lagaillarde) joined them. In Metropolitan France nobody demonstrated for them and no politicians came forward to join their cause. They remained in physical control of Algeria; that was all; and that was also all too brief. In the face of their isolation and the growing resistance of the people of France, units which had constrainedly joined the generals began to return to their allegiance. The paratroops marched out of Oran. Rebel paratroops failed to take Mers El Kebir from the fleet. The airforce refused to lift troops to France; some of its planes actually fled to France. Conscript troops, listening to the words of de Gaulle on their transistor sets, became restive or offered passive resistance. Seizing its opportunity the government became still firmer. General de Gaulle ordered all forces in Algeria to use 'all means including the use of arms to stop the insurrection, then smash it and finally liquidate it'. That night, too, the fleet sailed southward from Toulon.

A few hours later, the revolt collapsed. The 1st Division withdrew from Algiers and loyal troops occupied the city. The generals fled save for General Challe who was seized and hurried off to a Paris prison.

In all these three cases – Kapp putsch, February mutiny and the April rebellion – the army, acting alone and in defiance of civilian opinion, was isolated and then defeated by civilian resistances. In all these countries, wherever lawful authority might be thought to lie, there was widespread consensus that it did *not* lie with the military. In all these countries, therefore, the army was powerless to get its way unless and until it had learned that it must work within the current political formula, within the traditions of legitimacy. That meant, from behind some body of civilian leaders who enjoyed a mass backing among the population. After the Kapp putsch failed, the true reign of the Reichswehr began – but from behind the scenes. After the February mutiny, the Tosei-ha faction of the Japanese army had no difficulty in dominating all successive governments until military defeat in 1945. The French army reversed this order of experience; successful in bringing de Gaulle to power in 1958, it failed, like its German and Japanese forebears, in a direct challenge to the civil power. The reason lies in these three countries' order of political culture. Consensus on legitimacy or the modes of transferring political power were not perfect enough for government always to be able to resist intimidation and blackmail: but it was widespread enough, and the organization and mobilization of civilian life were strong enough, to resist the open assumption of power by the military. The characteristic levels of military intervention in such countries were therefore influence (constitutional enough) and pressure and blackmail.

Before leaving countries of the second order, i.e. with a developed political culture, we must, however, consider one other country that falls into this class. This is the U.S.S.R. In this country, the overt displacement or supersession of the ruling group in flagrant defiance of the civil institutions and notably of the Communist Party is as unlikely to occur (and as unlikely to be successful if it did occur) as in Weimar Germany, pre-war Japan and contemporary France. On the other hand, military influence, pressure and even blackmail aimed at ejecting the ruling group of the

Communist Party and replacing it by an alternative party group could occur and, indeed, has done so.

However, to suggest that civil–military relations in the U.S.S.R. may be even mentioned in the same breath as other non-communist countries will strike many as being outrageous. Some will resent the implication that any friction between soldiers and civilians could arise in a workers' socialist republic. At the other extreme, others will object to the U.S.S.R. being regarded as equal in its political-culture level to the other countries we have dealt with here. Another set of objections will come from those who imagine that the relationship of the Communist Party to the armed forces is so peculiar as to be unique, and who think that a category of 'party-controlled' armies must be erected as a special and extraordinary case, not subject to the kind of consideration we have so far been urging. Let us, therefore, take these objections in order; for by doing so we shall in effect be making out our own case for placing the U.S.S.R. at this second level of political culture.

To begin with, civil–military relations in the U.S.S.R. are not frictionless; but a mythology exists which prevents certain folk from perceiving this. The Soviet handbook, *The U.S.S.R. Today and Tomorrow*, tells us that the Soviet army, 'being the army of a socialist state, has certain distinctive features'. Among these it notes particularly that it is 'an army of the people'; that 'contradictions' between the officers and men do not exist because they share the same world outlook; and that it is an 'integral part of the Russian people'.[8] Now in the first place the Soviet army is not an armed militia, not the common people in arms, not a set of partisan detachments or a revolutionary army like Fidel Castro's '3000'. It is an enormous standing force, with a highly professionalized officer corps who, moreover, enjoy a pampered status in society; and it disposes of a discipline which compares with the old Prussian army at its harshest. Second, its classlessness is neither here nor there. 'Bourgeois' officer corps make coups and displace governments that are similarly 'bourgeois' in complexion; and they do so to set up a new government equally bourgeois, but more complaisant to the military. In a similar manner might a 'classless' and indeed a communist army displace a 'classless' and communist government in favour of an equally classless and communist one, but whose policy was more pleasing to the military. And third, this is precisely what successive Soviet governments have feared since the Red Army was established in 1917 – a so-called 'Bonapartist' coup. Furthermore, they did so

8. *The U.S.S.R. Today and Tomorrow*, Moscow, 1959, p. 56.

with good reason. Their relations with their armed forces have been shot through with friction – as witness the Kronstadt mutiny of 1921, the great purge of 1937, and the three military interventions of 1953, 1955 and 1957.

However, the Soviet military is by no means untrammelled in its activities. It has far less scope for intervention than it had in the 1920s and 1930s and much less than the military have in the satellite countries, which are of a much lower order – the third order – of political-culture level. It is tempting to see in the U.S.S.R. a state of 'latent opposition' to the government, as in, say, pre-1958 Iraq. Others who champion the U.S.S.R. see it as a first-order state, 'the most democratic in the world', in which the 'contradictions' of capitalist societies like Britain, Sweden or the United States have long since been transcended and where, therefore, *a fortiori* there can be no doubt as to the mass support enjoyed by the Soviet government. Yet the truth seems to lie between these extreme views. For, firstly, there is a consensus on where legitimacy resides. It is thought to reside in the Communist Party. Its *imprimatur*, its endorsement, is generally accepted as making decisions legitimate and duty-worthy. By the same token, the expression 'anti-party' carries a stigma of usurpation. It may well be that the consensus on this is a fragile one, and a highly artificial one; that it is secured only by continuous unremitting indoctrination and the sanctions of fear; that it rests on acquiescence and above all on long habituation in what is today one of the stuffiest of conforming societies in the world; and that, if cracked by some external or internal blow, a much more mobile and adventurous opinion would rapidly emerge as it did in Hungary and is today emerging in Poland. Nevertheless, at the moment, this consensus exists. Particular acts of the régime are unpopular; but the régime itself is *not* actively unpopular. In this régime, the party, at the moment at any rate, is generally regarded as the legitimate source of authority.

Furthermore, civilian organizations are highly developed. Indeed, the situation today is not unlike that in pre-war Japan. There, as we saw, politics consisted of the interplay of certain massive institutions: the bureaucracy, the capitalist *zaibitsu*, the armed forces, the two parties. The armed forces had to live with and work through these well-established institutions which were, moreover, indispensable to the national life. In like manner, politics in Soviet Russia consists of the interplay of the notables who head and speak for the not always identical interests of massive institutions – in this case the party 'apparatus', the civil bureaucracy (i.e. state apparatus), the managers, the police and the army. Unlike Japan, all these are integrated – as far as integration is possible – by the common element of party membership, and the need to respect the authority of those who, for the moment, lead the party (i.e. its Praesidium). The military must, like the other elements, work with and through these other institutions. It cannot replace them – they are indispensable. Nor can it, any more than they, set up in opposition to the party. This would certainly survive decapitation just as the Democratic Party in Turkey has done, and would be able (as the Turkish Democratic Party was unable to do) to pull into opposition a large part of the mass associations – trade unions, industrial plants and the like – which they have infiltrated. Therefore, all must be done in the name of the party. So long as this is so, the party membership will not only accept, but fervidly execute the decision. The moment this is not so, the rank and file of the party, whose support for a party decision is taken for granted, could and would create massive dislocation.

Thus, two of the features of a high political culture are present: consensus or legitimacy, and well-developed civil institutions, including a party which buttresses this consensus. What it lacks, however, is the third necessary element: fixed and orderly procedures to determine the transference of legitimate authority from one person or group to another. There are no rules for this, and the decision is arrived at by a pure power-struggle inside a group of dedicated oligarchs, who owe their place in the game to the sectors (party apparatus, civil bureaucracy, police, military, etc.) which at the moment they happen to hold.[9] This struggle is unremitting and ruthless: truly, *homo homini lupus*. It is this feature that puts the Soviet Union in the second order of political culture. It possesses tenacious and well-established civil institutions. It enjoys a consensus on what constitutes legitimacy. But the transference of legitimate authority is regulated by no orderly and fixed procedures and is accomplished by a grim and often mortal struggle.

In the third place, Soviet civil–military relationships are not *sui generis* as the catch-phrase, 'party-control', seems to suggest. Certainly, the Soviet Union's monopolistic party, designated both in law and actual operation as 'the leading core' of all Soviet institutions, is a singular feature which has important consequences. But the expression 'party-control of the military' not only explains nothing; it is positively misleading. It explains nothing because it is highly ambiguous. It may refer to the fact that the military are, in the Soviet context, supposed to hold themselves responsible to the party rather than, as in other countries, to the government of the day

9. H. S. Dinerstein, *War and the Soviet Union*, pp. 133–8; R. Conquest, *Power and Policy in the U.S.S.R.*, pp. 46–8; R. L. Carthoff, 'The Military in Soviet Politics', *Problems of Communism*, vol. VI, no. 6, pp. 45–8.

or the Head of State. In short, it may refer to the authority to whom the military owe allegiance. In that case, one would have to establish other categories such as 'Royal' control (as in Persia or the pre-war Balkan countries) where the nature of the army's superior organ has played a significant part in determining the level and the results of military intervention. But in any case, the Soviet army's legal superior might be *either* the Supreme Soviet *or* the Communist Party; Soviet constitutional law simply does not permit of a precise answer.[10] And if it is the Soviet army's *de facto* status we are concerned with, then again, such is the complexity and the reciprocity of the relationship between party and military that no simple answer, in terms of a ruler–ruled relationship, is possible.[11]

On the other hand, 'party control' may refer to a means, a specific means adopted by the Soviet authorities to bring about an identity of view between themselves and the armed forces, i.e. the permeation of the armed forces by partisans of the government. If this is what 'party control' means then it differs only in degree, not *sui generis*, from other armed forces. The effort to make the armed forces conform to one particular political viewpoint is not peculiar to the Soviet Union, or to its satellites or to revolutionary governments. The Greek army was purged of Republicans between 1920–23. Jiménez of Venezuela likewise purged his army of known and suspected opponents. He used secret delators and spies to inform upon suspect members of the armed forces just as the Soviet Union does. The difference between the methods used in the Soviet Union and in these other and capitalist countries is one of degree; no other government in the world demands so high a degree of identity with its programme as does Soviet Russia, and disposes of such a battery of controls to establish it.

Thus the expression 'party control' is highly ambiguous and by itself contributes little to understanding Soviet civil–military relations. This is not all. It can be highly misleading. For if it is intended as an explanation of how or why the military are brought to conform with civilian programmes, it lays stress on the wrong factors. There was indeed a time when 'party control' explained this identity. That was in the days of the civil wars and their aftermath, when the Red Army was fighting for a vaguely expressed revolution against counter-revolution, and when its officer corps was largely composed of ex-Imperial officers. In those conditions, the permeation of the army by communist 'cells', and the flanking of the officers by military commissars, did indeed guarantee loyalty to the revolutionary régime. But, as the army became increasingly bolshevized, quite a different

10. H. J. Berman and M. Kerner, *Soviet Military Law and Administration*, pp. 5–7.
11. ibid., pp.7–9.

problem arose. In 1924, the percentage of officers who were communists was 31 per cent, in 1927 56 per cent, and by 1930 some 90 per cent. The problem was no longer to secure that the army was communist; for it was. The problem was now to secure that its communism – like that of the trades unions, or the party members themselves – was of the right variety. The institution of the Political Command, under the control of the party's Central Committee and with its staff of *zampolits* and *politruks*[12] laced into the army command at all echelons, indeed served to make and keep the army 'communist'. From 1923 onwards, however, and notably after 1930, the problem has been to keep it orthodox. Otherwise the army might have had its own peculiar version of communism, differing from and opposed to the government's or the party leadership's (just as presumably 'bourgeois' armies have their own version of capitalism different from the government's) in which case the civil–military gulf opens once again. Hence the Soviet government's concern has not been confined to indoctrination, which is a necessary condition of civil–military identity but not a sufficient one. The sufficient condition is orthodoxy; and this has been achieved by infiltrating the armed forces with the secret police, the counter-intelligence services of the K.G.B.[13] Above regimental levels there are the special '*OO*'[14] detachments. Below that, the army is permeated by the secret counter-intelligence police. There is simple and convincing proof that party affiliation is no longer the decisive mechanism for securing military loyalty, but that this is accomplished by the K.G.B.'s security network – the proof comes from the great purge of 1937. In it Stalin eliminated 40 per cent of the more senior and between one-half and one-quarter of the junior officers. Yet he did not confine himself to the command officers. On the contrary, the political officers who were supposedly the political tutors, mentors and controllers of the armed personnel, were themselves purged by the O.G.P.U. *in equal degree* with the command staff![15]

12. *Zampolit* is an abbreviation, meaning Assistant Commander for Political Affairs. *Politruk*, another abbreviation, signifies political instructor.

13. The Committee on State Security.

14. *OO* comes from the Russian *Osobyi Otdel*. They are the Special Sections, i.e. counter-intelligence sections. During the Second World War they were renamed SMERSH, an abbreviation for the Russian words meaning 'Death to spies'. These *OO* sections and their work are well described in the latter part of Z. Brzezinski, *Political Controls in the Soviet Army*, pp. 54 *et seq*.

The earlier part of this little but important book contains an account of the party network in the army, and is useful in supplementing Berman and Kerner, op. cit.

15. This general thesis is amply supported throughout J. Erikson's masterly *The Soviet High Command*, which I was privileged to read in galley-proof. For a brief but authoritative description of the party's political and security apparatus inside the armed forces, see Berman and Kerner, op. cit.

How then does civil–military friction arise in the Soviet Union, and what are the characteristic levels of military intervention there?

From its inception, the Soviet government has been obsessed by a fear of 'Bonapartism'. And very properly so. Revolutionary and violent in origin, it justly feared to be overthrown by its own methods. Hence to a degree unparalleled outside the Iron Curtain, it has done all within its power to control its armed forces, of which it nourishes a perennial suspicion. It has sought to do so by three main means. First, it has permeated the armed forces with its own ideology, i.e. by its party members, and has kept these loyal to the leadership by the secret police and the '*OO*' detachments. Second, it has been extremely careful *not* to use the armed forces as an internal police force; instead it has established hand-picked troops, the M.V.D. regiments, for all such repressive work. Finally, it has taken all possible pains to pinch off those motivations which most commonly oppose armies to their civil leaders. It has pinched off a separate class interest in the officer corps; this is as 'classless' as the government itself. It has likewise pinched off regional interest by non-discrimination among its various nationalities. And it has effectively pinched off self-interest. It has pampered the officers, restoring the Imperial epaulettes, titles and salutes, paying them well and giving them social privileges.

Of the usual motivations, as we have listed them above in Chapter Four, only two remain: the motive of the national interest, and the motive of corporate self-interest. These two devils have not only not been cast out by the Soviet leaders' measures; they have been actively provoked by them. First, corporate self-interest. The Soviet armed forces are fully professionalized; but ideological orthodoxy, to which they must pay lip service, hampers their search for military doctrine, just as it hampers biologists or economists in the Soviet Union. The rule of Stalin was particularly frustrating in this respect; for instance, it proved impossible seriously to discuss the issue of 'surprise' in war, since, according to Stalin, this was not important in the long run.[16] In addition, from the very beginning the commanders have chafed at being restricted by the political commissars. They have constantly demanded 'unitary control' as against the party's insistence on 'dual control'. The vicissitudes of the 'dual control' mechanism tell their own story here. The system was introduced in 1918. In 1936, with the increasing threat of war, the command staff began to elbow out the political command on the plea that they lacked technical skills. In 1937, when the purge began, however, 'dual control' was restored in its full intensity, with the commissar coequal with the commander. After the

16. Conquest, op. cit., p. 330 *et seq.*

fiasco of the Finnish war (1940), Marshal Timoshenko, the new Commissar of the Armed Forces, was able to persuade Stalin that the dual command must be abolished and so it was. Then the even greater fiasco of the first month of the German war (1941) brought about its reintroduction. In October 1942, however, it was again abolished and one-man control restored. Marshal Zhukov was ejected from control of the armed forces in 1957 because he ostensibly sought to weaken the already enfeebled political administration still further. In 1960, however, a further change made the command officer himself responsible for ideological training with the political officers responsible to him.

Thus the motive of professional self-interest remains, and is resistive to, ideological requirements. At the same time the régime's very anxiety to indoctrinate and politicize its armed forces in the hope of making them politically reliable may have, and has had, diametrically opposite effects. It may create in them an idea of the national interest different from that of the ruling group; and indeed it has done so. Erikson observes of the period 1923–5, that 'factional work within the armed forces carried with it the threat of splitting the Red Army into two camps' and that 'the control apparatus might not only cease to control but work *against* the interests of the ruling political group in conditions of inner-party conflict'.[17] The logic is obvious. The ruling group of the hour uses the Political Command and the K.G.B. to eliminate the politically unreliable and to promote into authority those who subscribe to their own views. Thus the High Command is committed to a specific political view and is loyal to a particular group of party leaders. Suppose now that these leaders subsequently split into two rival factions: the support of the military may be thrown to either – but it will certainly not stay neutral! And by the same token, when the ruling group splits, both sides will bid for the support of the High Command.

This is precisely what has happened, not once but many times, and the way in which it happens and the consequences for the military illustrate the characteristic levels at which the Soviet military intervenes in politics. In 1923, for instance, the party was divided between Trotsky's minority and the majority who followed the 'Troika' of leaders, viz. Zinoviev, Kamenev and Stalin. Trotsky was still nominally responsible for the Red Army, and the party cells within it tended to support him; indeed the whole Moscow garrison passed to his faction in this way. The Troika therefore sought for a counter-poise and it found this among the 'red' commanders, i.e. those

17. Erikson, op. cit., My italics.

95

who had held only N.C.O. rank or none at all in the Imperial army, as against the ex-Imperial officers whom Trotsky befriended and on whom he much relied. This 'emergent command group' threw its support to the Troika in the vital 1924 Congress and was able to place the control of the Political Command in the hands of one of Trotsky's enemies and to appoint his opponent Frunze as his nominal deputy, but effectively as the controller of the military machine. One of the consequences was that Voroshilov, Budenny, S. Kamenev and the '1st Cavalry clique' generally, were given influential posts and became devoted Stalinists.

Stalin (1930–53) gave the military no opportunity to play an independent political role. Since 1953, however, in conditions of intense competition for the leadership and ever-changing alliances in the top echelons of the party, the military have intervened decisively on three occasions. The first was the elimination of Beria in 1953. It is certain that army units entered Moscow from the outside on the night of his arrest, and it is even said that Marshals Zhukov and Koniev carried out the arrest themselves.[18] The second occasion was the deposition of Malenkov; here the military leaders in the Central Committee cast their votes against Malenkov.[19] The third occasion was in Khrushchev's critical struggle against his opponents on the Praesidium – Molotov, Bulganin, Kaganovich, Malenkov and Shepilov – later significantly dubbed the 'anti-party bloc'. In this, Marshal Zhukov supported Khrushchev, certainly by his voice and authority, possibly by force or the threat of force against the 'bloc', as has been suggested.[20]

In all three cases, the military benefited substantially. Beria, as head of the great rival 'establishment', the M.V.D./K.G.B., was a natural enemy. The armed services could only stand to benefit from the weakening of the security forces. It is significant that immediately after Beria's fall the army received the first high-level promotions since the end of the war. In 1955, the military opposed Malenkov on two important counts: his apparent intention to turn from heavy industry to consumer goods and his pessimism about the effects of nuclear war.[21] As soon as Malenkov had been swept away, the succeeding Bulganin–Khrushchev leadership met the military demands for stockpiling, for military industry and for budget appropriations; six new marshals were created; and Marshal Zhukov was given the Ministry of Defence.

The armed forces reached their high-water mark of influence from 1956 to October 1957 – significantly, the period when Krushchev's battle for the

18. Garthoff, 'The Military in Soviet Politics', *Problems of Communism*, vol. VI, p. 46.
19. Conquest, op. cit., p. 332.   20. ibid., p. 312.
21. Garthoff, op. cit., p. 46. Conquest, op. cit., p. 333. Dinerstein, op. cit., pp. 98 *et seq.*

succession was at its height. Substantially, Krushchev represented and drew his strength from the party apparatus (which he controlled), and his opponents (e.g. Molotov) drew theirs from the state apparatus and the managerial sectors. The struggle came to a climax with Krushchev's plan to decentralize and regionalize the great industrial ministries, a step bound to bring them more strictly under the party *apparatchiks*. During this period the military were Krushchev's indispensable ally. Marshal Zhukov was promoted to candidate-membership of the Praesidium, while the head of the Political Administration of the Armed Forces was correspondingly demoted; and Zhukov was able to wring from the party's Central Committee the decree that 'criticism of the orders and decisions of commanders will not be permitted at [military] party meetings'.[22] In June, Zhukov's support for Krushchev against the concerted opposition of Molotov, Kaganovich, Malenkov and Shepilov seems to have been decisive; it was certainly of massive importance. The reward was Zhukov's promotion to full membership of the Praesidium – unprecedented for a serving soldier.

Yet, as we have suggested, the military's political intervention is effective only when the top leadership is split. With Krushchev's victory over his opponents – not only dubbed an 'anti-party bloc' but also slavishly insulted by a servile party Congress – the rift in the leadership was closed. With it the military suffered a decline in status. Zhukov was stripped both of his Praesidium-membership and his ministry only four months after helping Krushchev to triumph; and he was castigated for precisely those things the leadership had allowed him to do – a sure sign that he had extorted them. He had, in short, advanced military professionalism against the claims of party ideology. The charges against him claimed that he had '(1) violated the Leninist party principles for the guidance of the Armed Forces; (2) pursued a policy of curtailing the Party organizations, political organizations and military councils; and (3) of abolishing the leadership and control of (a) the Party and its Central Committee and (b) the Government, over the Army and Navy.'[23] Under Marshal Malinowski, his successor, the party cells' right and duty to criticize the command was restored.

In the Soviet Union, then, the civil–military relationship is far from frictionless, as is sometimes supposed. The military do have points of view which conflict with those of other components of the party's Praesidium.

22. Conquest, op. cit., p. 338.

23. Conquest, op. cit., p. 339 (quoting the Plenum of 1957). He was also accused of pursuing a 'cult of personality'.

Successive governments have not succeeded in depriving the armed forces of concern for their corporate professional interests, nor in preventing them from having their own variant interpretation of what the national interest requires. These can and have conflicted with the current party line. But the armed forces have not and cannot set themselves up in open contradiction to the party. Such is its legitimacy and such its organized hold on the other civil institutions that the armed forces must work – as do the other great institutions – in its name and upon its leadership. This confines its level of intervention to influence or at the most to pressure or blackmail, by the means described and as in the instances cited.

CHAPTER EIGHT

THE LEVELS OF INTERVENTION
(2) COUNTRIES OF LOW POLITICAL CULTURE

IN societies of low political culture – the third order – the levels of military intervention are much extended. As in states of developed political culture, intervention by pressure and blackmail often occurs; but, in addition, the military are just as likely to come out into the open, overtly overturning governments and installing others (*displacement*) or even *supplanting* the civilian régime for good, installing itself in its place. Among countries of this type are to be reckoned Argentina and Brazil, Turkey, Spain, Egypt, Venezuela, Pakistan, the (pre-war) Balkan countries, Syria, Iraq and the Sudan. There is unquestionably a great gap between countries at the head and the tail of the list. In any other sense than the level of political culture, Argentina and the Sudan are poles apart. Yet politically, there is less of a gap between them than there is between any of them and the states of the second order of political culture dealt with above. The higher up this list of third-order states, the more difficult it proves for the military to retain power without some form at least of civilian trappings, or without organizing civilian support; and the lower down the scale, the easier it is for the military to retain power in their own name and by their own strength. In different ways both Argentina and Turkey differ sharply from most of the other countries in this category. They fall into this category, however, because like the rest – albeit for not quite the same reasons or by the same ways – they too suffer acutely from the absence of consensus, and from the feebleness of the organized attachment to the régime.

We are not the first to bracket Argentina, as far as her political behaviour is concerned, with 'the economically underdeveloped and politically inexperienced peoples just emerging from colonial subjection in Africa and Asia'.[1] It is indeed surprising that this should be so, for at first sight Argentina possesses most of the objective preconditions of political stability. There is no '*patria chica*' here but, on the contrary, a xenophobic and arrogant nationalism. Her institutions have been developed since the Constitution of 1853. Her population is well fed and literate. Hers, however, is a polity gone sour.

1. A. P. Whitaker, 'The Argentine Paradox', *Annals of the American Academy*, March 1961, p. 104.

The procedures for political change have been discredited by flagrant corruption and abuse for a whole century, minus only the fourteen years of Radical rule till 1930. Secondly, notions of legitimacy have been fragmented. The three main sections of society – *estancieros*, middle classes and labour – have all been at cross-purposes, each group opposing the other two. Furthermore, up to 1943 no party had rooted itself among the masses. The traditional Radical and Conservative parties came into being in the localities only at election time. Additionally, the Radicals were split into three factions based on personal loyalties. The only powerful party Argentina has known was that of Perón, and it was an official creation. Thus Argentina, despite its high level of material and literary culture, is afflicted with a kind of *anomie*. Its society is compartmentalized, where each section is at cross-purposes with the remainder. The situation – albeit far less ferocious – resembles the kind of situation in Spain in the twentieth century. And, since the overthrow of Perón there has arisen yet a new cleavage over legitimacy, for his followers still constitute a numerous and hostile force among the electorate. Together with the feebleness of the parties and the hostility of a now powerfully organized labour movement, this has created in Argentina a state of overt crisis.[2]

Turkey[3] approximated more closely to the others, but was still very far removed from say Iraq or the Sudan. The greatest difference lay in her well-organized parties. These, the Republican and the Democratic, were neither transient electoral organizations, nor personalist followings. They had branches throughout the villages and, since the Republic began, had set out to inform, indoctrinate and organize the masses.[4] Yet, for the rest, Turkey's level of political culture was and still is immature. It is, basically, still a country where an intellectual élite (which in this case includes the army officers) is trying to impose western standards on a traditional society. Ever since 1908 it has been passing through a crisis of regeneration:

2. Cf. Whitaker, op. cit., p. 103. The foregoing lines were written without the benefit of Professor Whitaker's admirable essay, and it was with interest and pleasure that I found his own view near to mine. Compare this passage from his Abstract: 'A permanent crisis in Argentina since 1930 has produced extreme fragmentation, as distinguished from pluralism, and has made it necessary for the military actively to protect the stability and integrity of whatever government holds office. Although the behaviour of the Argentines is generally typical of the behaviour of people in underdeveloped countries, Argentina has long enjoyed national independence and has been well developed. The middle class is large and literacy is high.'

3. I have put this in the past tense to refer to the situation as it was before May 1960.

4. Until 1945 (except for two intervals when opposition was briefly tolerated) there was but one party, the Republican People's Party. In 1945, permission was given for a number of dissidents from this party (including Celal Bayar and Adnan Menderes) to form an opposition party and from then till May 1960 these parties competed.

a long time – over half a century of stresses, punctuated by a revolution-from-above in 1923. Localism is still a feature of its society, especially in the Anatolian villages. It is doubtful how far Atatürk's novel conception of a Turkish nationality has superseded the traditional concept of the Turks as being essentially a peculiar part of Islam. Traditionalism still fights a successful battle against the laic, almost Comtist philosophy of the urban élites, and one of the reasons for the 1960 coup was the growing extent to which the Democratic governing party had lent itself to the resistant clericalism of the countryside.

Since the declaration of the Republic, indeed since the Young Turk revolution of 1908, there has been no consensus on the procedures for transferring power. Atatürk's two efforts to create 'loyal opposition' parties both failed; the first, the Progressive Party of Kasim Karabekir, because it was implicated in the Kurdish revolt of 1925; the second, the Liberal Party of Fethi Bey in 1930, because it soon became the vehicle of the clericals and religious fanatics. The formation of the Democratic Party in 1945 and its triumph in the elections of 1950 were widely hailed as evidence that the régime had at last legitimized itself and could henceforth rely on orderly procedures for the transference of power. But the shameless jiggery-pokery by which the Democratic Party manipulated the rules in order to cripple its opponents and to retain its hold on power demonstrates clearly how little agreement existed on the procedures for transferring power.[5]

This disagreement on procedures itself reflects the lack of consensus on Kemal Atatürk's resolute westernization. Since his death in 1938 and the disappearance of his prestigious personality, the history of Turkey has been that of the efforts of the progressive but narrow élite of town-bred western-izers to preserve his reforms against popular reaction. As soon as the

5. The Republican Party's 'Houses of the People' (its local headquarters in the villages) were closed down. In 1953, its assets were confiscated, as were its Ankara headquarters and its newspaper, *Ulus*. Press laws, of ever increasing severity, in 1954, 1956 and finally 1960, crippled the right to criticize the government. In 1957, when there seemed a fair chance that the three opposition parties might beat the Democratic Party by forming an electoral alliance, this right was arbitrarily – and very thoroughly – suppressed by the electoral law of 1957. At the same time demonstrations and processions were forbidden, severe restrictions put upon the right to assemble, and opposition politicians, like Gulek (the Secretary General of the Republican Party), harassed. Without such measures it is unlikely that the Democrats would have won the 1957 election. After that date (though it polled only five or six per cent over the Republican Party) the government tightened its repressive measures, harassing Ismet Inönu, the veteran leader of the Republicans; and finally, in April 1960, suspended all party activities and set up a wholly partisan committee to investigate what were described as the 'subversive and illegal activities' of the Republican Party.

two-party system was introduced in 1945, the reactionary forces among the largely illiterate villagers became a decisive factor. The Menderes government increasingly pandered to this clerical reaction, 'buying votes with religion'. The more it did so the more it drew on itself the attacks of the Republican Party and the press; and therefore the more it felt impelled to suppress them and to alter the rules in its own favour.

Nevertheless, after making due allowance for local peculiarities, as in Turkey and in Argentina or in Spain, the remaining countries at this third level of political culture have common characteristics.

Local particularism is pronounced, and national and local politics operate at separate levels; politics is fought out between urban élites over the heads of the peasants; rooted in one's social influence and power, it is a struggle to secure or expand such influence and power at the national level, and in terms of personal followings. Again, in all these countries, a latent opposition exists between the largely peasant masses on the one hand and the tightly entrenched oligarchy of rulers on the other. Because industrialization is so slight, neither industry nor organized labour are capable of either sustaining or of bringing down the régimes. Urbanization, itself a precondition of dense mass organization, is still rudimentary and the bulk of the population are villagers.[6] The only civil organization of any strength in this type of country is to be found in the Latin American ones, where the Catholic Church exists. In Asia, the native religions – Buddhism, Hinduism, Islam – do not possess such a hierarchical structure. In all these countries, the political parties tended and tend to be as feeble as they were numerous. The only parties of any weight in Latin America have been

6. The following table underlines some of the characteristics mentioned:

| | Industrialization | | Urbanization | Education |
	Per capita energy consumed (in tons) millions	% of population in labour unions	% of population in cities of over 100,000	% of population literate
Argentina	0·97	21·6	37·2	87
Brazil	0·39	4·2	13·2	50
Turkey	0·23	0·8	8·2	35
U.A.R.	0·24	1·1	19·4	25
Iraq	0·48	0·0	16·6	15
Venezuela	2·18	5·5	20·6	69
Pakistan	0·05	0·5	5·9	19
Sudan	0·04	0·5	3·5	10

Source: Almond and Coleman, *The Politics of the Developing Areas* (Appendix).

those few 'labour' parties like A.P.R.A. in Peru or the M.N.R. in Bolivia, or the Accion Democratica in Venezuela, and it is significant that in these countries the military have not had a walk-over. The only other strong Latin American parties have been those with official backing like Vargas's Labour Party in Brazil, Perón's party in Argentina, and the P.R.I. in Mexico. The traditional parties – Radicals, Liberals, Conservatives and the like – are highly personalized parties, led by urban cliques and with few and shallow roots in the villages. The Middle Eastern parties and the South East Asian ones are exclusively of this type. The political institutions of all these countries (until the military revolutions) were recent, tarnished by corrupt manipulation and fraud, often imposed, and hardly comprehended by the popular mass, let alone loved and revered. The Parliament was, to them, a façade for a selfish town-trained oligarchy. The people were not involved in it.

Such then are the characteristics of the third order of political culture. These are countries whose populations have – or had – little attachment to or even comprehension of their political institutions, countries of latent opposition to the ruling group, countries in which there is no clear and well-established political formula; and countries too in which, for the most part, civilian organization is feeble. In such countries, politics does not run in clearly defined channels; there is no widespread consensus on the channels it should run in; and even if there were, opinion is too inchoate to make it do so. Here the legitimacy which attaches to institutions is not paramount as in 'mature' political cultures, nor resistant to overt military rule as in 'developed' political cultures. It is fluid; and, possibly, even ductile. It is easily impugned by the military, and in the least-developed political cultures of this third order, it has been relatively easy for the military to reshape it by a new political formula which legitimizes their own pretensions.

In such societies, military displacement of the government meets a far different reception from that meted out in the societies of the higher orders. In pre-war Germany and Japan as in contemporary France, the overt military coup, as we have seen, has met with such frozen hostility from society's mass organizations as to perish in its tracks. It is rarely attempted, and is doomed to fail. In the societies of a low level of political culture it is often attempted, and is often successful. The public's attachment to its political institutions is so shallow that the military's deposition of the government by force or the threat of force is at least not resisted and more often than not is initially very popular indeed.

The reason for this is threefold. In the first place, the existing institutions are either discredited or incomprehensible. Secondly, these institutions have, usually, abutted in a situation of deadlock where change cannot be brought about constitutionally. Thirdly, in such circumstances the deposition is widely welcomed throughout society because, initially, the military coup means all things to all men. The army is popular not because of what it stands for (which nobody knows, at first), but of what, quite patently, it has fought *against*. This is true of the great bulk of the examples in this class of country (though, admittedly, not of all). In cases where the military has a past record of intervention, their views might be only too well known, as in Spain in 1936 and Venezuela in 1948 and Argentina in 1962. It is true, however, of the history of Argentina between 1930 and 1955, of Turkey in the 1960 coup, of the Spanish coup of 1923, and of the coups in Egypt, Iraq, Pakistan and the Sudan.

In Argentina, for instance, the régime of 1930 was thoroughly discredited. Though the country was reeling from the economic crisis, the octogenarian Irigoyen occupied the Presidential chair, and in his dotage his corrupt subordinates padded the public payroll and helped themselves to favours. Secondly, there was a constitutional deadlock. The Radical Party had come to power in free elections in 1916, and had maintained themselves in power by the same means until 1930. In that year, however, their majority in the Chamber disqualified successfully opposition candidates. This suggested that henceforth the Radical Party itself would 'make' the elections in the manner practised up to 1914. Consequently, when General Uriburu occupied Buenos Aires and deposed the acting President (Martinez),[7] he was wildly applauded; the crowds cheered his troops and showered them with flowers.

In 1943, it was much the same story. The régime established by General Uriburu had proved conservative and unpopular, and was based on flagrant manipulation of the elections. Also, President Castillo, who succeeded the well-liked but incapacitated President Ortiz in 1940, was actively unpopular because of the economic crisis brought on by the war. Once again there was constitutional deadlock: since 1941 Castillo had governed by state of siege and it was clear that he would use this to 'impose' his chosen successor, Patron Costas. Now Costas was the epitome of the hated 'oligarchy'. For all these reasons the military revolt of 1943 which deposed Castillo and installed first General Rawson and then General Ramírez was even more popular – and more misunderstood –

7. President Irigoyen had resigned the previous day, in face of the imminent coup.

than that of 1930. *'Viva la libertad! Viva la democracia!'* shouted the crowds once more.[8]

Similar was the initial reaction to General Gürsel's bloodless coup in Turkey in May 1960 – in the towns at any rate. In Istanbul, cheering crowds hung out flags, danced in the streets and chanted *'Hurriyet, Hurriyet!'* (Freedom, Freedom!). In Ankara, the armed forces were carried shoulder-high. Premier Adnan Menderes's repressive measures had discredited a constitution already tarnished by the tampering with the 1957 election; the university students and professors were outraged at Menderes's interference with the curriculum, the lawyers with the government's arbitrary measures, the press at the suppression of its freedom and businessmen at the maze of import controls. The whole trend of Menderes's legislation since 1953 had been towards the suppression of the Republican Party. With the establishment of the commission of inquiry into the alleged 'subversive methods' of the opposition it was pretty clear that the constitutional channels of change would soon be closed entirely. Once again, if change was to come, who could bring it about except the army?

The military revolts in Egypt (1952) and Iraq and Pakistan (1958) conform to the 'model' even more clearly than the Argentine and Turkish cases. In all of these countries, the purported parliamentary system was mysterious; largely if not entirely alienated from the public; shamelessly manipulated to provide a colour of legality by a narrow, ambitious and

8. Cf. Ray Josephs' *Argentine Diary*, pp. 40 *et seq.* for the first reactions and the subsequent bewilderment. The 1955 revolt, which overthrew Perón, is not so clear a case. In some quarters the Perón dictatorship was popular. The dictator had taken well-chosen steps to win civilian support for his régime and had created a powerful political party for this purpose. In 1955, the régime was certainly hated by the anti-Peronista parties, by the Catholic Church, and by the armed forces. The deadlock situation again persisted, worse than in 1930 or 1943, since Argentina was now a police state, and hence *only* military action could possibly overthrow it. Public reaction to the victory of the anti-Peronista revolt was mixed. While uptown crowds cheered General Lonardi, wrecked the Peronista H.Q. in Buenos Aires, and burned pictures of Perón, pro-Perón riots broke out in the working-class quarters. There was another pro-Perón riot of industrial workers in Rosario.

The altered circumstances of 1955 are due to the nature of the Perón régime which was not a simple military dictatorship at all. It created for its institutions a mass support never previously accorded to an Argentinian government. For the nature of the régime, see below at Chapter Eleven. By contrast, the long-drawn-out sequence of threats and armed demonstrations, culminating in the physical removal and the subsequent imprisonment of President Frondizi in March 1962, went on amid supreme indifference. The armed forces had intervened so often since the overthrow of Perón in 1955 – it is said that President Frondizi had surmounted no less than twenty-three crises in civil–military relations – that the bored and listless public, well knowing that they were politically helpless, simply went about their business.

selfish oligarchy; and therefore tainted with every ill that appeared to affect the nation – corruption, inefficiency, betrayal and 'colonialism'. Each of these countries, furthermore, had come to a constitutional dead-end. The institutions had been manipulated to maintain the rulers in power and would continue to be so. If change were to come, it must be from outside the 'system'. Likewise in Spain in 1923. There the constitutional provisions had been so misused for a century as to appear entirely untrustworthy. The conditions of endemic social disorder only underlined their inefficiency.

In all of these countries the military's deposition of the government was hailed with a delirium of delight – in Iraq, indeed, with an almost cannibalistic orgy. In the Sudan, the discredit of the institutions was of a different order – it was not due to their being tainted with corruption, but to despondency that the one-year-old system had not only not brought the millenium but had brought a quarrel with Egypt and economic relapse. Furthermore, the disintegration of the governing coalition and the impossibility of forging any other seemed to foretoken the ruin of the system. General Abboud's coup was, therefore, greeted with the same round of unthinking applause as in the countries already mentioned.

In all these cases, the public's attachment to their political institutions was so fragile that it not only offered neither protest nor opposition to the military's violent deposition of the rulers, but it danced with delight. Where expediency is suffered to triumph over principle, it is always and only because the principle is not strong enough. So it is in these states, and it is here that they offer their sharpest contrast to the states of the 'mature' or 'developed' political culture.

In these countries, then, the political formula is feeble enough to allow the military to displace the civilian government by violence or the threat of it, i.e. to permit of the military replacing one government by another. But this does not necessarily mean that it is so feeble as to permit of the military supplanting civilian government altogether, and ruling in its own name. In many countries the initial popularity of the displacement is, as we have suggested, because no change is otherwise possible and the situation is such that people have come to believe that any change is for the better. At this first stage the military is an unknown quantity. It is the second stage, when the military have to decide what to do next, which provides the better index of the fragility of the political formula, and the want of civilian organization to support it. To permit the military merely to displace one government for another is one thing; to allow it to rule is quite different.

Now occurs a curious paradox. If civilian organization happens to be strong in countries of 'low' political culture, this condition produces two contradictory effects. It both engenders resistance to military attempts to pass from simple deposition to the complete supplantment of the civil authorities, and yet impels the military to attempt this very thing. The result is a history checkered by short-lived military *interregna* as in Argentina. The reason is this: the previous supporters of the displaced government may be strong enough to stage a return to power and therefore the military must reckon with the possibility of their vengeance. It therefore takes steps to prevent such a return to power and is thus impelled, at some stage, to take full powers to itself. But when it does so it runs into increasing resistance, not merely from the ex-supporters of the government but from all sides. This induces the military either to give way and call for some kind of elections, or alternatively to go into politics itself as a sort of political party, in order to legitimize itself by some plebiscitary or electoral procedure. In either case, it must still fear the results of a fall from power. It therefore continues to play an active political role, if only for self-defence. 'Who rides the tiger can never dismount.' 'Whosoever draws his sword against the prince must throw the scabbard away.' These two proverbs pithily express the logic of the situation.

In countries with a low political culture, where civilian organization is feeble however (and this is true of most), this paradox operates in a kind of reverse sense. The sheer absence of civilian counter-pressures encourages the military to set up a full-blooded military oligarchy; on the other hand, the sheer invulnerability of the military leaves this as a matter of choice, not of necessity.

Examples of the first paradox, i.e. the countries with relatively strong civilian organization, are provided by the Argentine, by Turkey since 1960, by pre-war Greece, and, in some degree, by the course of events in Egypt between 1952 and 1954. Examples of the second paradox, i.e. countries with relatively feeble civilian organization, might be seen in Iraq and the Sudan (for complete supplantment of the civilian régime) and in post-1946 Syria (for successive displacements of the civilian cabinets).

The result is that *all* the countries with a 'low' political culture present to outer appearance similar features, irrespective of how high or low they are in the scale of this category; i.e. they exhibit either displacement or complete supplantment; but the reasons for this differ from country to country as explained.

Let us illustrate this by first examining some cases from the most advanced of the countries in this order of political culture; for instance, Argentina and Turkey. In both, the military deposed the government. In both, once the initial popularity of the coup had passed, the military found themselves drawn further and further towards the total supplantment of the civilian régime, and yet, at the same time, forced more and more strongly to make concessions to the civilian opposition this provoked. In the Argentine coup of 1930, General Uriburu said at first that he would hold new – and honest – elections. But it then appeared from a great Radical victory in the elections for Buenos Aires Province that the very Radicals he had ejected were likely to return. Uriburu promptly declared the Buenos Aires election void, indefinitely postponed the other provincial elections, and declared ineligible the Radical candidates for the Presidential election. He even contemplated cancelling the Presidential election altogether and ruling by force. But his measures, accompanied as they were by a purge of the bureaucracy and the imprisonment and exile of his opponents, now showed up the régime as an undisguised military oligarchy. The civilian resistance appeared too strong to remain suppressed for ever. In this dilemma, Uriburu the soldier gave way to his civilian allies, the Conservative *estanciero* aristocracy, and limited himself to manipulating the elections in such a way as to secure their victory. Thus did he fend off the vengeance which otherwise the Radicals would surely have inflicted. In all, Uriburu's direct military régime lasted little more than one year.

The 1943 coup of General Ramírez ushered in a military oligarchy which lasted some one-and-a-half years. And here again is seen the push–pull towards and away from open supplantment of the civilian régime. On this occasion, unlike 1930, the army plotters – the G.O.U. – had no intention whatever of holding new elections. They unquestionably envisaged some sort of military oligarchy, though their precise plans are still obscure, and indeed it is very likely that they were both disunited and vague on anything but short-term objectives. What is certain, however, is that they had not long been in power before widespread opposition developed, and thrust them into increasing repression. Their opponents – the press, the universities, the trade unions – were struck down in turn; but the more repressive the régime the more unpopular it became. In June 1945, when the industrialists, merchants and cattle breeders signed an open manifesto against Vice-President Juan Perón, the dismayed military began to give way. Elections were promised in July and in August the state of siege was lifted. There now took place a massive all-party demonstration in the capital, the 'March of Constitution and Liberty'. Clearly elections boded ill for the army. The fear of political destruction now prompted the G.O.U. to arrest Perón, in the belief that he was their Jonah. Their effort failed. For one thing, they had no clear alternative to Perón. For another, the *descamisados* counter-demonstrated in favour of Perón. From that point the military took the only possible way out – the one trodden by General Uriburu. They decided that there must be elections, and that their candidate, Perón, must win.[9] He did; and for the moment the political future of the armed forces was secured.

Even the revolt against Perón in 1955, openly committed as it was to the restoration of democratic liberties, manifests much the same preoccupations as in 1930 and 1943. Perón resigned in September 1955, but new presidential elections were not held until February 1958, and in the intervening period of two years and a half the military ruled. For, just as the junta of 1943 had reason to fear the consequences of an electoral triumph of the traditional civilian forces, so the junta of 1955 had to fear the electoral triumph of the Peronistas. The armed forces were themselves split on this issue. General Lonardi, the leader of the junta and the Provisional President, was removed within a few weeks by the anti-Peronista faction in the armed forces; and even as late as November 1956 it proved necessary to remove members of the High Command who wanted to perpetuate military rule, and replace them by officers willing to turn the government over to the politicians and technicians. Again, though elections had been promised for late 1957, at the beginning of that year they were postponed till 1958. All this time the junta busied itself with making Argentina safe for the army. To do so, it had to destroy both the trade unions and the political organizations of Peronism, and to ban the Peronista party from participating in the elections. And, having once intervened in this way, it has been forced to hold up the hands of the government against the Peronistas ever since.[10]

9. For the first year of the military dictatorship, see Ray Josephs, *Argentine Diary*. The motives of the Avalos group in arresting Perón are still obscure, but Blanksten (*Perón's Argentina*) definitely affirms (p. 59) that they regarded him as the reason for the army's unpopularity. For the growing opposition to the régime see Macdonald, *Latin American Politics and Government*, pp. 63–5 and Blanksten, op. cit., pp. 56–60. The elections were marked by pressure and violence from the opening of the campaign till just before election day. Cf. Macdonald, op. cit., pp. 78–80 and Blanksten, op. cit., pp. 64–70. That the elections themselves were orderly and fair is due to the fact that, twelve days earlier, the U.S. State Department had published its Blue Book charging Argentina with collaboration with the Nazis, and this created a xenophobic surge of popularity for Perón at the last minute. Further pressure on the electorate was therefore deemed unnecessary.

10. The armed forces' dilemma was dramatically highlighted by the events of March–April 1962. Much against their wishes President Frondizi had legalized the Peronist party and permitted it to contest the Congressional and Provincial elections. They scored a signal victory, polling over 35 per cent of the popular vote. The armed forces were now torn between their wish to respect constitutionality and their hostility to the Peronists. After ten days of pressure on President Frondizi, who refused to comply with their wishes and resign 'voluntarily' they hustled him off to prison; whereupon their dilemma reopened under his successor Provisional President

The course of affairs in Turkey has run in much the same direction, and for a similar reason – the strength of the political parties.

When General Gürsel overthrew the Menderes government in May 1960, he promised that the army would quit power as soon as a new constitution had been accepted and elections for a new Assembly had been held under it. Those elections were promised for autumn 1961. In the meantime the army ruled. But this rule became more and more repressive as support for the displaced rulers rallied. For the army, in displacing Menderes, was ejecting the free choice of one half of the nation and the leader of a party – the Democrat Party – sufficiently well organized to persist, even when decapitated. Thus from the very beginning the army was forced to pass beyond the simple deposition of a cabinet to the eradication of a mass party. In order to do this, among other things it arrested and put on trial over 400 Democrat deputies and officials, purged the armed forces of 7,000 Menderes officers, attacked the freedom of the press, dismissed 147 university teachers, and arrested opponents and demonstrators all over the country.

The fear of losing power to the Democrat sympathizers worked even more strongly on the armed forces as the time for the elections approached. For instance, to protect themselves from future vengeance, the junta (the National Unity Committee) had a clause inserted in the constitution making the constitutionality of its interim laws unchallengeable. By July 1961, the armed forces had serious cause for alarm. For one thing, new parties were angling for the former Democrat vote – notably the Justice party. Headed by one of the purged officers, General Gumuspala, this party drew its following from former Democrats and from the 7,000 officers who had been dismissed by the junta. Secondly, when the new constitution was submitted to a referendum, over four million voted against it – a sign that the Menderes supporters adhered to their former allegiance. 'The army,' it was reported, 'felt that if this went on the result would even be a reversal of power in which the lives of the revolutionaries would not be safe.'[11]

Their reaction was much as in Argentina. Since they were committed to holding elections, they must make sure of winning them. To ensure this the

Guido. Guido refused to intervent the provinces, cancel the elections, and arrange for an immediate presidential election as the forces demanded. His refusal split the armed forces into two factions: those like Generals Fraga and Rauch who placed constitutionality higher than their dislike of the Peronists, and those like Generals Poggi and Carrera whose preferences were exactly the opposite. The two factions almost came to the point of firing on one another on the Campo de Mayo. Then the navy pronounced itself for the Poggi–Carrera faction, and under the renewed pressure President Guido conceded their demands. See pp. 153–6.

11. *The Times*, 21 September 1961.

armed forces insisted on the execution of the death sentence passed by the Yassiada tribunal on Menderes. In the words of *The Times* correspondent, Menderes's fate was sealed by the very number of his supporters. Two of his colleagues perished with him. Another 460 were sent to prison. Then the political parties were brought together, overawed by the physical presence of General Gürsel, the service chiefs and the Commander-in-Chief of the gendarmerie, were made to vow to 'turn their backs on Menderes and the former Democrat party'.

The armed forces had, however, reckoned without the voters. The election returned the Republicans in a minority. Most of the vote went to the three other parties and particularly to the Justice party which in a sense was the residuary legatee of the old Democrats. In the lower House it had almost as many seats as the Republicans and in the Senate twice as many.

The armed forces were in real peril and could not disengage from politics even if they wanted to. For self-protection alone, they had to bring about a government of their own choosing. They forced the withdrawal of an opposition candidate for the Presidency (a former Democrat), leaving General Gürsel as sole candidate. They vetoed the three smaller parties' attempt to form a coalition to exclude the Republicans. Finally, under 'the scarcely veiled threat of further intervention from the armed forces', the Justice party was forced into a shot-gun coalition with its bitterest rivals, the Republicans, under the Premiership of old General Inönu.[12] The coalition fell to bickering and made no attempt to tackle the domestic problems of the country. Thereupon some of the younger and more radical elements in the army tried to bring pressure upon it. On 23 February 1962, units of the War Academy and the gendarmerie Officers' School and a battalion of the Armoured Warfare School staged a demonstration. They demanded that the National Assembly be dissolved or that at least it be purged of some two hundred of its most reactionary members, and that the constitution be amended. The revolt was put down by the Supreme Command, and the ringleaders arrested, but only after it had felt obliged to take General Inönu and his cabinet into protective arrest. The incident led the Supreme Command to intervene in politics once more: the cabinet and Assembly were presented with a Bill prescribing up to five years' heavy imprisonment for attempts to show or say that the May Revolution was unjustified, illegitimate or illegal, or for those who challenged the sentences passed on the Menderes supporters at the Yassiada tribunal. In addition the Bill proscribed any party which 'praised or defended' the former Democratic party or which claimed to be its 'successor'. Penalties were also laid down

12. *The Times*, 15 November 1961.

for those who maintained that 'democracy cannot be applied in Turkey' (*sic*). *The Times* correspondent noted that there could be 'little doubt that the new measure was a direct result of pressure by the leaders of the armed forces'.[13] It can be confidently predicted that the military will remain in Turkish politics for at least a generation, and that the worst is still to come.

Thus, where civilian organization is at all advanced, as in Argentina or Turkey, a paradoxical result often asserts itself as soon as the initial popularity of the army coup wears off; what began as 'displacement' engenders an urge for 'supplantment'. Having cast off its political neutrality the military fears reprisals from its civilian opponents. The more it represses them, the more nakedly oligarchic does the military régime appear, and the less legitimate. Hence the vicious circle of repression and resistance; and for the army seeking future immunity, the 'perpetual and restless desire for power'. 'And the cause of this,' says Hobbes, 'is not always that [the military] hopes for a more intensive delight than [it] has already attained to; or that [it] cannot be content with a moderate power; but because [it] *cannot assure the power and means to live well, which [it] hath at present, with the acquisition of more.*'[14]

Where civilian opinion is inchoate, and its organization feeble, these considerations do not apply. The armed forces are invulnerable, because the potential civilian opposition is so feeble and confused. In such countries the military may simply topple cabinets, one after another, or alternatively, supplant the civilians and govern overtly in their own name. Syria may serve as an example.

Syria, for instance, is not a nation. The family makes the first claim on personal loyalty, then the tribe or religious group, then the region; and there loyalty stops. The animosity of Aleppo and Damascus, for instance, is one of the motive forces in Syrian politics. 'So far,' comments one observer, 'men have not developed a deep constructive sense of loyalty towards a land, a people, a nation, or a state . . . [Hence] the absence of the concept of the state not only among the common people, but even those whom circumstances bring to power . . .'[15] The Syrian people do indeed share feelings of Arabism, anti-Zionism and anti-westernism with a fanatical and violent intensity; but this is more aptly styled a 'public emotion' rather than a 'public opinion' in the usual sense given to this term.

Political parties, in the sense of organized groupings with programmes and ideologies, hardly exist. This is partly due to the lack of a developed public opinion – and of course this itself is partly the result of the feeble-

13. *The Times*, 5 March 1962.   14. T. Hobbes, *Leviathan*, Book 1, Chap. XI. My italics.
15. Ziadeh, op. cit., pp. 285–6.

ness of the parties. It is also due to the poverty of communications, the low level of literacy, and the dependence of the overwhelming mass of the people upon the large landowners. The result is that most of the Syrian parties are in fact the following of a handful of magnates. The Conference of such parties is not a meeting in which an organized group of members participate but a meeting of a few top people who have been there for a long time and who, from time to time, co-opt to work with them others of similar standing or social interests. The more literate Syrians, however, have tended to move into certain ideological parties: the Syrian Popular Party, a right-wing and activist organization whose policy is the union of Syria with Jordan and Iraq, and the pro-Russian leftist Ba'ath or Arab Renaissance part. But neither of these has had a mass following. The first is proscribed, and the second has been important only when the army used it as its stalking-horse in the days of Colonel Serraj, from 1954–8.

Events in Syria show a characteristic alternation of blackmail, displacement and supplantment. The army is far too strong and opinion too weak for it to have any enemies but those in its own ranks. In March 1949, Colonel Zaim overthrew the civilian government, dissolved Parliament, abolished the political parties, proclaimed a referendum for the Presidency, became sole candidate and was – not surprisingly – elected. Within less than two months a constitutionalist faction of the army led by Colonel Hinnawi arrested him and had him shot. Hinnawi then established a civilian government under army protection. This, the Attasi Pasha government, began to favour the 'Great Syria' notion of union between Syria and Iraq: and thereupon, in December, another faction of the army, led by Colonel Shishakli, arrested Hinnawi, deposed the government and installed one of its own – the el Azam cabinet. This was later (May 1950) replaced by a cabinet led by el Kudsi. Within a year it too was at logger-heads with the army. El Kudsi proposed to transfer the gendarmerie from army control to the Ministry of the Interior, i.e. to civilian control, in order to prevent it interfering in the elections. The army thereupon made him resign and replaced him by el Azam (March 1951). A little later the perform-ance was repeated with a different cast. This time the Premier was Dr Dawalibi. He fell foul of the army partly because he supported the Syria–Iraq union, partly because he too tried to remove the gendarmerie and police from army control. Colonel Shishakli had him arrested in a mid-night coup, and held him until he agreed to resign. Shishakli then ap-pointed his own hack, Colonel Selo, as Chief of State, Prime Minister and Defence Minister 'pending the restoration of Parliamentary life' (December 1951). Next year Shishakli took steps to have himself elected President under a new and imposed constitution and thenceforth ruled personally. His end came in February 1954 when the garrisons revolted all over Syria. Thenceforward Syria returned to the façade of parliamentarianism, with the army controlling events behind the scenes. This was the period in which the dominant faction of the army led by the sinister Colonel Serraj of its *Deuxième Bureau* made common cause with the Ba'ath party and the Independents to terrorize and suppress opposition. This coalition finally ended Syria's independence by bringing it into union with Egypt, in the so-called United Arab Republic, in 1958. The previous parliamentary régime was now swept away. Legislative power nominally resided in a National Assembly nominated by President Nasser and consisting of 400 Egyptians and 200 Syrians – many of them ex-Deputies. The executive power lay in a Regional Executive council of fifteen, also nominated by President Nasser and whose chairman was none other than Colonel Serraj.

This régime lasted less than three years. Not for nothing has it been said that 'even the Prophet himself could not govern Damascus'. On 28 September 1961, a military faction revolted and in a bloodless coup ended the union with Egypt and re-established the parliamentary régime. Having hustled the Egyptian troops and officials from Syrian soil, the junta proclaimed elections, and then retired into the background. Thus it came about that, as in 1951, El Kudsi was President of the Syrian Republic and Dr Dawalibi his Prime Minister.

Exactly six months later the régime was overturned once more, in yet another military coup. Its origin and purpose are still extremely obscure. The original group of conspirators clearly wanted a more radical economic and social policy than the restored landlord régime was providing. There is more than a suspicion too that the government's contacts with Jordan had revived military fears of another move towards the 'Fertile Crescent' notion which had proved fatal to Dr Dawalibi in 1951, and to his predecessors. Even the events are obscure. On 28 March, a group of officers overthrew the Dawalibi government in a bloodless coup and moved to establish a direct military oligarchy. They accepted the resignation of the President, Prime Minister and cabinet, dissolved the National Assembly, and decreed the transfer of all executive and legislative power to the High Command.

Within forty-eight hours, however, the original conspirators found themselves challenged by a second group based on Aleppo. This group demanded the reunion of Syria with Egypt. Planes bombed Aleppo, and then a meeting of the two factions was arranged to take place at Homs. Here – so it appears – the High Command, in the person of General

Zahreddin, the Commander-in-Chief, asserted its authority over both groups. The outcome, at any rate, was an arrangement by which the leaders of both the Damascus and the Aleppo factions were to be exiled, and by which President El Kudsi was to be recalled to office. A few days later General Zahreddin, having nominated a new High Command, proclaimed the restoration of the parliamentary régime. The Assembly was recalled, and a new cabinet, consisting of newcomers with a more leftish tinge than their predecessors, was established. Significantly, General Zahreddin became Minister of Defence in this new government.

Despite the obscurity of the events and the anonymity of the principal actors, four conclusions seem to emerge which substantiate the picture of Syria as a land where the army and only the army decides whether it will rule through civilians or over civilians. First it is clear that between 28 September 1961, and 28 March 1962, at least four separate army factions were involved. The conspirators of 28 September were an anti-Nasser faction. The second, the Damascus conspirators of 28 March, were anti-Nasser but opposed to the views of the first group, both because they favoured more radical economic policies and because they were inimical to an alignment with Iraq and Jordan. The third group, the Aleppo group, were pro-Nasser. The fourth was the personal faction of the Commander-in-Chief, General Zahreddin, who appears to have come forward to prevent civil war between the opposing factions in the army and to have succeeded by reason of his seniority.

Secondly, it is likely that General Zahreddin's decision to return to the parliamentary régime and to reinstate President Kudsi was a *pis aller* – imposed by his desire to stifle the sharp differences of opinion in the army which arose as soon as any one faction seized power. The civilian régime, he might well have thought, was 'the one that divides the army least'. Thirdly, the events clearly show that the abrogation or the restoration of the parliamentary régime owed absolutely nothing to any civilian resistance to military rule. One way or the other way, decisions as to the form of the régime depended entirely on the will or whim or the temporarily dominant faction of the army. Finally, General Zahreddin's action in naming a new High Command (which implies a 'purge' of the previous High Command) and his acceptance of the post of Minister of Defence in the new cabinet, provides the guarantee that the new government has the support of the army and that conversely the army's wishes will be respected by the cabinet.

In the light of all this, General Zahreddin's explanation of why the army decided to reverse its previous decision to establish a military régime and chose instead to reinstate the civilian one, reads like supreme irony – or, perhaps, supreme cynicism? A transitional cabinet such as previously had been contemplated, he said, was rejected because 'it would be responsible to the army and would thereby contradict the principle of constitutional life. The army would not interfere in civilian politics.'[16]

16. *New York Times*, 14 April 1962.

CHAPTER NINE

THE LEVELS OF INTERVENTION:
(3) COUNTRIES OF MINIMAL POLITICAL CULTURE

SARMIENTO's great classic *Don Facundo* describes the turmoils in newly independent Argentina. Mrs Mann, its translator, commented on it: 'The rural districts never made a movement *which revealed a political idea*. It is true that the gauchos followed certain partisans of that epoch, but it was because those partisans were the immediate authority which they recognized: they followed them from personal affection and from the habit of obedience, but *from no political conviction nor from any desire to make any system prevail for their interest as a class.*'[1]

Mrs Mann's distinction is altogether valid; and it points to the existence of a fourth and lowest level of political culture – to societies, usually ones in transition from a static and traditional culture, where the public with views on what is or is not legitimate in politics is utterly negligible and hardly exists at all. In such countries questions as to legitimacy and consensus are irrelevant. One group of these countries are indeed deeply divided – but 'by cultural and ethnic pluralism, by provincialism, regionalism, localism, and casteism',[2] as Carnell says of the new states of South-East Asia, but to which we may with equal justice add many others. Another group, like Thailand, are placid, coherent and still predominantly traditionalist societies which indulge their ruling élites in their struggle for power without feeling at all involved in it. In both cases, what Carnell states of the South-East Asian countries[3] is true of all such states: 'If there is a political "style", it is political crisis. If they must have a name, "fluctuating oligarchy" might possibly be appropriate. The power holders are fluid alternating groups of politicians, bureaucrats, and army officers.'

The characteristic of states at the lowest level of political culture is not that there are 'no people able and willing to hold political ideas' or to act from 'political conviction', but that these are so few and so scattered as to be altogether negligible when political issues are to be decided. These issues

1. D. F. Sarmiento, *Civilization and Barbarism*, trs. Mrs Horace Mann, 1868 (New York, 1960), p. xx. My italics.

2. F. G. Carnell, *Political Ideas and Ideologies in South and South-East Asia* (unpublished paper delivered at the U.K. Political Studies Association, 1960).

3. With the exceptions of India, the Philippines and North Vietnam.

are decided by force or threat of force. In the countries divided by tribalism or race this may involve whole masses in bitter internecine strife, as in the first days of independent Latin America or in the Congo today. In countries not so divided in these ways, as in present-day Paraguay or Haiti and particularly Thailand, these issues are decided by the factions of the professional armed forces with the rest of society as mere onlookers. The power of the military is checked, if at all, only by its technical weakness in the face of savage populations – like Baluba tribesmen in the Congo, or the gauchos in early Argentina, or the barbarous *llaneros* who lanced Bolívar's armies to death in Venezuela. In many cases, however, it is not checked for there is no other organized force in society at all. Government in these societies is (to quote Sarmiento) *'founded upon the unpremeditated consent which a nation gives to a permanent fact'*.[4]

In these states the military's characteristic mode of proceeding is, *par excellence*, by violent displacement or open supplantment of the civilian authorities (the latter mode being far more common and continual than in the countries of the third order of political culture which we have already discussed). Whether in office or out of it, the military rule, often openly contemptuous (like Rosas of Argentina or Diaz of Mexico) of the legal forms.

The military do not require the assistance or even the blessing of civilian institutions or forces to acquire and maintain their power. If they clothe themselves in civilian forms it is but an additional reinsurance, it is not a necessary one. In these countries the military is the sole political force; and as such it is entirely at large.

The Latin American republics in the nineteenth century were in this condition. There, in Garcia-Calderon's words, 'The rude and bloodstained hand of the *caudillo* forces the amorphous masses into durable moulds. South America is ruled by ignorant soldiers. There is therefore no history properly so called for it has no continuity; there is a perpetual *ricorso* brought about by successive revolutions; the same men appear with the same promises and the same methods.'[5]

Some Latin American states are still in this condition. Elsewhere in the world, other states have but recently fallen into it. Among the former, Paraguay or Haiti provide examples; among the latter, Thailand, and Iraq between 1936 and 1941. To illustrate the role of the military in these states and others like them little more is required than a brief chronology.

Paraguay has about one million inhabitants, mostly *mestizo* and, for the

4. Sarmiento, op. cit., p. 130.
5. F. Garcia-Calderon, *Latin America: Its Rise and Progress*, pp. 88 *et seq*.

most part, speaking not Spanish but Guaraní, the native Indian tongue. Asunçión, its capital, with 200,000 population, is not typical. It is the only city of any size in an otherwise completely rural country. Apart from a handful of wealthy proprietors, the population is miserably poor. Cotton is the main export crop; there is little light industry, and no heavy industry at all. About 85 per cent of the people are illiterate. Trade unions are not unknown, but exist on sufferance from the government and under its control. The parties – Colorados and Azules – are personalist cliques. We can omit its nineteenth-century history, dominated by the successive despotisms of the sinister Dr Francia, Lopez I, and the bloodthirsty megalomaniac Lopez II who perished in battle in 1870. From 1870 to 1940 there were fourteen full-scale civil wars and few presidents served out their legal term. Let us begin our more detailed chronology in 1935, the date of the armistice in the Chaco war with Bolivia.

The military were disaffected by the armistice of 1935 and therefore they executed a coup in 1936, installing an ex-serviceman, Colonel Franco, as President. Later in 1936, the army deposed Franco and installed Dr Paiva, the President of the University of Asunçión, who suppressed two army rebellions and governed till 1939. In this, the election year, the army supported Estigaribía, of the Azule faction, who went to the country as sole candidate (*candidato unico*), was 'elected' in 1940 and immediately declared himself dictator. Estigaribía also was an ex-serviceman of the Chaco war. He was shortly afterwards killed in a plane crash. He was succeeded by the Minister of War, Morínigo, another soldier, who instantly converted his provisional Presidency into a thoroughgoing dictatorship, and carried out the most savage repression known since Lopez II's day. He leaned for support on the young army officers of the Colorado faction, and he called his régime 'selective democracy'. In 1943 he was returned as President in an election in which he was the *candidato unico* and in 1944, after some amused contemplation of his opponents, crushed them all: the Francistas (who supported ex-President Franco), the Tiempistas (the university graduates whose organ was *Il Tiempo*) and the nascent trade unions who had been rash enough to strike rather than submit to government control. Morínigo ruled from 1940 to 1948, and up to and including that year had suppressed twenty-six coups. In 1948, another election year, Morínigo selected Gonzalez as Presidential candidate. He was duly elected, as *candidato unico*, by 96 per cent of the votes cast. Six months later, however, yet another army revolt removed Morínigo from his post of Commander-in-Chief, and six months later the military removed his nominee President Gonzalez also. It replaced him by General Rolón, and then, one month later, replaced Rolón by Molas Lopez. In 1949, Molas Lopez submitted to election, again as *candidato unico*. But, not long after his inevitable 'election', he was deposed – not by an army coup this time, but by a congressional manoeuvre. In his place, the Congress chose the popular Dr Chaves, former Foreign Minister, and the leader of the Colorado faction. This civilian interlude was broken in 1954 when, once again, the Asunçión garrison revolted. It overthrew Chaves and installed its Commander-in-Chief, General Stroessner, as President. Stroessner, after jailing his opponents and crushing anew the trade unions (whom Chaves had permitted to reform), was re-elected in 1958 in an election in which as usual he was the sole candidate. Except for a few days in 1959 the country has been governed under a continuous 'state of siege' since 1947.

Haiti, our second example, has a population of three million, for the most part smallholders of negro extraction. At the other extreme is the Haitian mulatto élite, wealthy, cultivated and cosmopolitan. The tiny middle class is made up of immigrants. Trade unionism is embryonic. Parties no longer exist, and even when they did were personalist cliques. The social élite, not more than 3 per cent of the population, plays almost no part in politics while the peasant population is 90 per cent illiterate. Ever since independence the army – now the *Garde Nationale* – has acted as king-maker and king-breaker. From the overthrow of Boyer in 1842 to the United States occupation of the island in 1915, only one President ever completed his term. Admittedly three died in office. But one was torn to pieces by a furious mob, one was poisoned, one blown up and the remaining fourteen were all forced out of power by the army.

The withdrawal of the American forces in 1934 enabled Sténio Vincent, a mulatto member of the élite, to secure election. He benefited by a wave of Haitian nationalism which would have made a hero of anyone who ended the American occupation. Exceptionally, therefore, Vincent served out his full legal term and handed over to his deputy, Elie Lescot, in 1941. In 1946, when a mob of market women stormed the house of Lescot's Minister of the Interior (tearing out the doornails with their teeth), the army never stirred – until Lescot fled. Then it took over and selected Estimé as a Presidential candidate. Estimé began to encourage the formation of trade unions and permitted the formation of political parties. In 1950 he sought to have the constitution amended so that he could succeed himself. Thereupon the officer corps issued a proclamation to the effect that it had unanimously asked the Junta of 1946 to take over again. Its candidate was now the leader of the coup, General Magloire, who as sole candidate was elected President. Like his predecessor, Magloire also sought to alter the constitution so that he could continue in office. He was overthrown by an army coup in 1957 and Daniel Fignolé was nominated President. His widespread popularity and his intention of holding elections as soon as possible immediately aroused the hostility of the army which deposed him within three weeks. The army then nominated Dr Duvalier as sole candidate. Duvalier took office in October 1957 and still rules. He has established an iron dictatorship in which all opposition has been crushed. He has even shattered the power of the army itself – by cross postings and purgings. However, this does not mean that he leans on civilian support, but simply that instead of relying upon the *Garde Nationale*, he has built himself up a 5,000 strong counterforce of palace guards, civilian militia and civilian hoodlums called '*tonton macoute*'.

In Iraq, again, there were no political parties at all until after the war, and even these were mere groupings, with nothing, or almost nothing, in the way of organization. Before the war political ideas hardly existed, and even after 1941 were vague and confused. The façade of parliamentarianism was identified in the popular mind only with its abuses: fraud, speculation, corruption and repression. The régime had no popular roots at all.

Between 1936 and 1941 the army – or rather the rival factions of the army – proceeded by simply deposing one cabinet and imposing another of their own choice. Thus in 1936, General Bakr Sidqui occupied the city of Baghdad, proclaiming that: 'The army . . . has requested His Majesty the King to dismiss the cabinet and form a new one composed of sincere men under the leadership of Hikmat Suleyman . . .'[6] This the King did, and the same pattern was repeated in 1937 when the anti-Bakr faction of the army deposed Hikmat, and so on in 1938, 1940 and 1941. The series ended in the third coup of the year 1941 when, at last, the Regent decided not to lend himself to the technique. He ran away, thus making it constitutionally impossible for Rashid Ali, the army's nominee, to become Prime Minister. Thereupon Rashid Ali turned from displacement to supplantment. He declared the Regent deposed, constituted a military government called the Government of National Defence, and then forced the Parliament to recognize it. This Rashid Ali government was overturned by the British forces in 1941 and the Regent thereupon returned and the constitution was restored.

The military dominate Thailand too; but here the style of national politics is very different from the squalor of Haiti and the carnage of Paraguay. The military coups which have made and unmade constitutions and governments since 1932 have been carried out with moderation and

6. M. Khadduri, *Independent Iraq*, London, 1960, p. 84.

little bloodshed. The public have been onlookers, not participants. Yet the result is military domination as in Haiti, Paraguay and Iraq, and the reason is, once again the total absence of any civilian counterforce to its power. (In this respect alone, and in the political consequences that flow from it, are these societies comparable.)

The essence of the Thai situation is the distinction between the mass of the population and a tiny fraction, possibly 1 per cent of the whole, who form the political public. The bulk of Thailand's population lives up-country, engaged in agriculture. The farmers, who are economically well off and stable and secure in their properties, are both inarticulate and totally indifferent to national politics. Politics is the concern of the drop-sical city of Bangkok, with its million inhabitants, and in this city it is the concern of a very narrow group indeed. Its base consists of those who have had a school education and more rarely a university training. Most of these are employed in the bureaucracy. Above them, and significantly influential, are about one thousand persons – the very highest civil servants, some prominent politicians, a few wealthy merchants and the officers of field rank in the armed forces. At the top, and manipulating these lower levels, are about fifteen persons, mostly military officers but with one or two outstanding civilians. These are the ruling group.

The civil service is both fragmented and docile and plays no independent political role. Members of Parliament may, by unusual talents, succeed in becoming influential but Parliament's importance was derivative only, being a creature of the all-powerful executive (it was abolished altogether in 1958). Trade unions hardly exist, and the 'parties' have little or no extra-parliamentary organization. Each candidate has to get himself elected by his own individual efforts, seconded or thwarted by government interference with the campaign and the counting of votes. These 'parties' have never represented social forces, only cliques.

Government has always come from above and it still does. Up to the coup of 1932, it lay in the hands of absolute monarchs of mildly westernizing tendency and their court circle. This rule was supplanted in 1932 by that of a tiny military–civilian circle, in which the military predominated, and have done ever since. The monarch has been relegated to a decorative role and the military cliques carry out his previous functions in a similarly benevolent autocratic way.

The post-1932 politics of Thailand is the history of three military revolts and their aftermaths: those of 1932, 1947 and 1957. In 1932 a conspiracy was hatched between certain civil servants and officers, disgruntled at bumping up against the royal hierarchy and feeling able to proceed no further. Both groups were western-educated, and both were resentful of the court monopoly of supreme power. This group, having seized Bangkok, ended the absolute monarchy, established a quasi-Parliament, half of which was to be nominated, and proclaimed themselves as 'The People's Party'. Its military wing, led by Colonel (later Field-Marshal) Phibun, soon quarrelled with its civilian wing, led by Nai Pridi, a Paris-educated lawyer, and drove him into exile. Thenceforth Phibun, the soldier, governed the country, first as Minister of Defence and then (in 1938) as Prime Minister. He fell in 1944, and gave way to Nai Pridi: for Phibun had becomes identified with Thailand's pro-Japanese policy during the war, while Pridi had rallied the anti-Japanese resistance. There followed a brief, 'civilian' interlude under Pridi which ended with the second decisive military coup, that of 1947.

This revolt was engineered by the Phibun group. It called for elections, and when these went against it in 1948 it forced out the victorious Nai Kuang (their nominee after the 1947 coup), and established Field-Marshal Phibun as Prime Minister. Then followed a split in the triumphant armed forces. The navy and marines who were hostile to Phibun supported his enemy, Kuang, and in February 1949 staged their own counter-revolt. They were crushed by Phibun's loyalist forces, however. In 1951, the navy and marines kidnapped Phibun and revolted once more only to be crushed again after three days' heavy fighting. Phibun remained Prime Minister until 1957.

But the army was now throwing up younger leaders, and from the fighting of 1951 two emerged as potential rivals to the Field-Marshal. One was Phao Sriyanon, the Director General of Police, the other General Sarit Thanarat, the Commander of the Bangkok garrison. Their chance came after 1955 when after visiting the United States and Britain Field-Marshal Phibun decided to relax the repression, to encourage political parties to register, and to seek an electoral mandate for himself. The elections of 1956, however, were not only conducted with gross irregularity and interference, but (from Phibun's point of view) with gross inefficiency; for the 'official' party barely scraped a majority. General Sarit – who had been a candidate – was able to claim that the elections were fraudulent. To placate him Phibun made him Commander-in-Chief of all the armed forces, and gave him a seat in the patchwork cabinet which he formed in an effort to conciliate the factions he had let loose. Phao, rival to both Phibun and Sarit alike, was also in the cabinet.

Now occurred the third coup, that of 1957. General Sarit and his forces revolted. Phibun fled, Phao went into exile. New elections were called, in which General Sarit's new 'Unionist' party triumphed. General Sarit then appointed his deputy, General Thanom, as Prime Minister while he himself went to the United States for medical treatment. Suddenly reappearing in October 1958, he engineered a bloodless coup, thrust out General Thanom, abrogated the constitution and proclaimed himself absolute ruler. In all, since 1932 Thailand has experienced eight coups, and experimented with seven constitutions. Throughout the whole thirty years, however, the military have been the sole source of political power and the sole instrument of political change.

Changes in the Level of Political Culture

A society's level of political culture is not necessarily static, and indeed it may change very quickly. It is not identical with certain quantifiable objective factors such as the degree of industrialization or literacy, although it is substantially affected by these and to some extent correlated with them. It depends on opinion, and the extent to which this is effectively mobilized. Now this can change very fast in countries with 'low' or 'minimal' political cultures; for very often the reasons for the absence of a political public lie in the prohibition of free association and free discussion, and once these are permitted, organized viewpoints can become a significant political force. This can be seen from the examples of Venezuela or Guatemala. Venezuela had suffered from 1908 until his death in 1935, under the brutal and barbarous tyranny of Gomez. His death set off a train of blind and bloody disturbances which resulted in still further repression under his successor. Nevertheless, parties now formed underground and to such effect that in 1941 the President (General Medina) thought it expedient to sanction them, including even the Accion Democratica. This rapidly built up a real organization, rooted in the villages. It was so effective that by 1943 General Medina found it necessary to establish an official party to combat Accion Democratica in the municipal elections. This in turn led some dissident junior officers in 1945 to seek the alliance of Accion Democratica in their coup of that year and this in turn led to the free elections of 1946 in which Accion Democratica was victorious with a huge majority. The whole of President Jiménez's reign of terror from his counter-revolution of 1948 to his fall in 1958 could not wipe out the latent forces of organized opinion. Thus 1935 was a critical date. Before 1935, one would have been justified in considering Venezuela as a military-dominated state in which the forces of opinion counted for nothing: her whole history was, as Bolívar had prophetically said, 'that of the barracks'. After 1935, certainly after 1941, Venezuela was equally clearly a 'third-order' state in which notions of legitimacy were fluid, but, nevertheless, present and supported by organized opinion. Yet the changes that occurred in 1935 had, obviously, been latent before that time; 1935 simply crystallized them out. President Bétancourt has himself described how:

Now Venezuela had ceased to be exclusively pastoral and agricultural. In the towns and more especially in the oil-fields there had grown up a new social class – the workers. From exile there had returned, alongside the emigrés of fossilized mentality who like the Bourbons had learned nothing and forgotten nothing, groups of young men nourished on modern social disquietude. The people began to encounter their future organizers and leaders: men who like the Argentine generation of the 1850s had filled the interminable hours of exile and prison with the study of new social doctrines and experiences. The masses' ardour for a truly democratic life and the realization of their eminently just slogan 'Get rid of Gomez-ism' found channels in the democratic political parties, in the trade unions, in the militant students' organizations and among the organized leaders, all of which began straight away to fill with life.[7]

The same is true of Guatemala. Today, even under the reactionary rule of President Ydígoras, the parties and the trade unions, feeble though they be, are of some political significance. Before 1944 they did not exist at all. The country had been ruled by a succession of long-lived dictators, the last of whom, Ubíco, had ruthlessly suppressed all opposition, and dismissed all protests with the words, 'My justice is God's'. He fell in 1944 not as a result of any organized movement at all, but simply by the tacit withdrawal of support by all the elements that had hitherto acquiesced in his dictatorship. From then onwards an unbridled frenzy of discussion and organization took hold of the urban population. It was this that was canalized into supporting the returned exile, the schoolmaster Arévalo, and it was under him that the way was prepared for Major Arbenz to become his successor. Then followed the mass organization of the peasants by the legalized Communist Party, drawing the Indians for the first time into politics. After Arbenz was deserted by his army in the face of the counter-revolutionary invasion of Castillo Armas, much of this was undone; but enough has remained to make the unions and the parties of some political significance.

Thus our classification of régimes according to their levels of political culture is always provisional. Latent forces lurk in society and may crystallize out after some cataclysm or accident. Factors such as the self-consciousness of opinion or the strength and durability of public associations are more volatile and more subject to rapid alteration than the

7. Bétancourt, op. cit., pp. 80–81.

economic and social factors with which Marxists deal. Yet even these material factors are much less immediately apparent than the 'vulgar' Marxists tend to credit, and therefore what Engels said of the difficulties of Marx's historical materialism is equally true of our own approach. Engels wrote:

Even today, when the specialized press concerned provides such rich material, it still remains impossible even in England to follow day by day the movement of industry and trade in the world market and the changes which take place in the methods of production in such a way as to be able to draw a general conclusion, for any point of time, from these manifold complicated and ever changing factors *the most important of which, into the bargain, generally operate for a long time in secret before they suddenly make themselves violently felt on the surface* . . . It is self-evident that this unavoidable neglect of contemporary changes in the economic situation, the very basis of all the processes to be examined, must be a source of error. But all the conditions of a comprehensive presentation of current history unavoidably include sources of error, which, however, keeps nobody from writing current history.[8]

Summary

We may summarize the relationship between the levels of intervention on the one hand and the levels of political culture on the other by means of a diagram, thus:

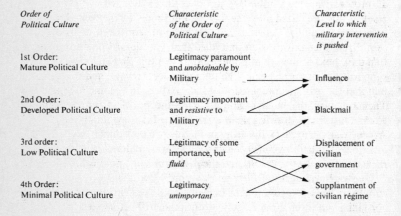

Order of Political Culture	Characteristic of the Order of Political Culture	Characteristic Level to which military intervention is pushed
1st Order: Mature Political Culture	Legitimacy paramount and *unobtainable* by Military	Influence
2nd Order: Developed Political Culture	Legitimacy important and *resistive* to Military	Blackmail
3rd order: Low Political Culture	Legitimacy of some importance, but *fluid*	Displacement of civilian government
4th Order: Minimal Political Culture	Legitimacy *unimportant*	Supplantment of civilian régime

8. F. Engels, *Introduction to Marx's Class Struggles in France* (Marx–Engels' Selected Works, Lawrence & Wishart, 1958, vol. 1, p. 119).

CHAPTER TEN

THE MODES OF INTERVENTION

WE have seen that intervention may be pressed to four levels: influence, blackmail, displacement and supplantment. These levels of intervention are attained by certain characteristic methods, alone or in conjunction with one another. They may be listed as:

(1) The normal constitutional channels.
(2) Collusion and/or competition with the civilian authorities.
(3) The intimidation of the civilian authorities.
(4) Threats of non-cooperation with, or violence towards, the civilian authorities.
(5) Failure to defend the civilian authorities from violence.
(6) The exercise of violence against the civilian authorities.

These six methods are specifically related to the level of intervention in question and the relationship may be expressed thus:

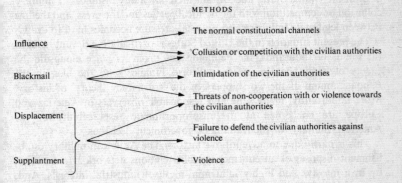

From 'influence' to 'blackmail'

In all countries ruled by civilians, the armed forces may try to convert the rulers to their own point of view. They have both the right and the duty to attempt this. They are in no better, but certainly no worse a moral position than any departments of the civil administration which also have the right and duty to persuade the government to their point of view. Such discussion or persuasion cannot be regarded as 'intervention'. This by definition is the military's *imposed* substitution of its policies, or of its person, for that of the civilian government.

'Influence', however, can become something not far removed from blackmail, as soon as the military advisers threaten to apply some sanction should their advice not be followed. The question is: what kind of sanction constitutes 'pressure' or 'blackmail'? We can readily agree that the threats of physical coercion or of disobedience are unconstitutional in any circumstances and that views accompanied by such threats are, clearly, blackmail. What are we to say, however, of a threat merely to create political difficulties for the government – to rouse legislative or public opinion against it to the extent, possibly, of causing its overthrow? In some circumstances, this might be deemed the maximum extension of military influence; in others, an example of unwarranted pressure and, as such, a case of blackmail. The line between the two is a tenuous one. This can be seen by comparing the cases of, say, the United States and Britain with certain other cases. The issue is: what in each case are the 'normal channels' of military participation in framing national policy and how far have the military moved outside these? Do the 'normal channels' include the military's mobilization of public or legislative support against the government of the day? In the history of both the United States and Britain there are many instances of military collusion or competition with the political parties and the press; and the line between legitimate influence and political pressure becomes hard to draw.

The present situation in the United States is particularly relevant here. In the minds of thousands, the Pentagon has taken its place alongside the Elders of Zion, the Freemasons, 'World Finance' and the like, in the Pandaemonium of the worshippers of the 'conspiracy theory' of history. More importantly, many sane and responsible observers in America and Europe are concerned at the disproportionate responsibility of the American military for the framing of government decisions.

This is partly due to adventitious factors. The American military establishment disposes of an enormous public-relations network.[1] It is caught up in a massive and highly influential mesh of industrial interests. And, since 1945, events have made it less and less possible to divorce questions of defence from those of foreign policy.[2] All this has added to the disquiet about its role in policy formation, the more so since the developments are of recent growth and contrast sharply with the subordinate role of the military up to 1941.

More fundamental to this enhanced role is, however, the effect of the

1. See particularly, M. Janowitz, *The Professional Soldier*, Ch. 19, 'The New Public Relations'.   2. ibid., Chs. 13 to 16.

American system of government itself. This forces the military to collude with or combat other political forces under a spotlight of constant publicity. In this it is neither better nor worse off than any other government agency in the United States. The generals and admirals are accused of 'speaking out of turn', and of uttering sentiments which are bigoted, or contrary to official policy, or which deal with matters – like foreign policy – which are no concern of theirs. They certainly do do these things. Often, the publicity given to their views is not intended by them and reflects administrative errors in clearance.[3] Often it results from the casualness of American officialdom or leakages to reporters. In many cases it stems from a characteristic American loquacity and lack of administrative self-discipline. Yet in all these cases it is not only not censured by the American public but is positively defended on the grounds that 'the public have a right to know'. It must never be forgotten that the American panacea for any policy problem is publicity. In this respect the military are no more open-mouthed or undisciplined than the civil administrators.[4]

Even more important, though, is the effect of the separation of powers. This creates rivalry and tension between the President and the Congress. The three services, albeit brought together in the Joint Chiefs of Staff Committee, think as three separate services. They have different notions of strategy and are in constant competition for limited funds. Thus each disgruntled service – or even part of a service – can play off the Secretary of Defence's decision against the Congressional committees, which, under the constitution, have the right to conduct hearings. This right of appeal has made the private discords public and has also multiplied such discords: for no service will consider compromise until it has essayed the appeal to Congress. Hence two results. In the first place, the public come to know of the 'non-official' views of each section of the armed forces. This may not be due to an officer's disloyalty to the President, but to the moral conflict he is forced into when a Committee questions him as to his own personal views.[5] Secondly, bureaux or services may prompt their supporters in the

3. Cf. Lt-Gen. J. M. Gavin, *War and Peace in the Space Age*, pp. 169–72, for a leakage due to poor clearance arrangements in the Department of Defence.

4. On the other hand, officers *have* abused the opportunity (given them by a National Security Council directive of 1958) to carry out open propaganda, of most reactionary tendency, against leading Americans and the United States Government itself. They have 'indoctrinated' their troops with such views. They have also sought to dominate civilian thinking by organizing anti-communism courses, Freedom Forums, lectures, etc. (See, for instance, 'U.S. Officers abuse their power', *The Times*, 13 September 1961.)

5. Cf. Lt-Gen. J. M. Gavin, op. cit., pp. 166, 168–9; Gen. Maxwell Taylor, *The Uncertain Trumpet*, pp. 112–14.

Committees to ask leading questions.[6] The result is open propaganda by each branch of the service, which is fully reported and often exaggerated in the press; and bitter mutual recriminations on strategy and tactics between the proponents of the different views. In 1948, Secretary Forrestal had to deal with the 'air force revolt': in 1948, Secretary Johnson had to cope with the 'admirals' revolt'; and in 1956, Secretary Wilson had to cope with the army's calculated leakages of information. The American system leads indeed to what has been called 'legalized insubordination'. In all this, both those Congressional groups who are disinterestedly concerned with a Presidential decision, as well as those who have been influenced by a military interest, are empowered to engage in lobbying. Professor Huntington cites three types of such lobbying. First come attempts to make the Administration construct certain types of weapons; e.g. the Joint Committee on Atomic Energy has played an important part in prompting the decision to build the H-bomb, Polaris and I.R.B.M.s. Secondly, there are attempts to prevent cuts in favourite forces (e.g. the marines) or supply more money to others (e.g. the air force). Finally, Congress investigates matters of strategy, e.g. the 1951 MacArthur hearings, the 1956 Symington Airpower hearings or the 1957–8 Johnson Missile investigation.[7]

In a word, the American governmental system and its tradition of publicity *forces* the military not only to speak out but to establish relationships with political forces. It does the same to all interested groups in the United States – both to administrative groups and to private ones.[8] The very pressure of the system forces the military to shout just as loudly – indeed, more loudly than – the rest; and each service must, simultaneously, try to shout more loudly than its fellows. This gives an impression of a vast military influence in government, whereas it is evidence only of a vast amount of necessitated noise. It has some arbitrary and unpredictable effect on readjusting the relative budgets of the three services: but it is questionable whether it enhances the influence of the military as a whole *vis-à-vis* the civil authorities. One observer, at any rate, thinks that the boot is on the other foot and that 'so far from the military element expanding at the expense of the civilian government, it is arguable that the civilian has

16. Lt-Gen. Gavin, op. cit., p. 167.

7. Professor S. R. Huntington, 'Strategic Decision Making in the U.S.A.', unpublished paper, delivered to the 7th Round Table of I.P.S.A., 1959. Cf. also, his more recent 'Interservice Competition and the Political Roles of the Armed Services', *American Political Science Review*, March 1961, pp. 40–52. Janowitz, op. cit., Chs. 17, 18, 19.

8. Cf. S. E. Finer, *Anonymous Empire*, London, 1958, pp. 92–3.

constantly and inevitably encroached on the military.'[9] He argues that in both the United States and Britain the budget has been the decisive factor in determining military policy and that this has been firmly controlled by the civilians; and it must be owned that this thesis finds very considerable support from the account given by General Maxwell Taylor, in his *Uncertain Trumpet*.

Given then the preconditions of American constitutional law and usage, it is more judicious to consider the American military's efforts to exercise political pressure as an extension of their legitimate means of influence, rather than as blackmail.[10]

In Britain, the cabinet system lessens the military's opportunities to mount Parliamentary pressure against the government; and, furthermore, the lobbying of M.P.s by service chiefs is a breach of constitutional usage, if not of a fixed convention. Yet Britain has had her experiences with service lobbies not dissimilar to those of the United States. We have already had occasion to mention the struggle between Lloyd George, the Prime Minister, and his service chiefs, notably Sir William Robertson, in the 1917 period. That the outcome was so long delayed was due to Robertson's political support, in Parliament, in the press and among the public. And, in the period before the outbreak of the First World War, two rival factions at the Admiralty each sought to bring political pressure to bear on the government. On the one side was the First Lord, Lord Fisher, and on the other Admiral Beresford. Fisher captured the Navy League (a powerful pressure group), and recked nothing of lobbying M.P.s or sending his 'journalistic Janissaries' to secure a favourable press. Neither did his opponents, the so-called 'Syndicate of Discontent'. Their supporters split off from the Navy League to form the Imperial Maritime League;[11] they too had their 'Big Navy' press, and they sought and found support in Parliament especially among the Conservative opposition.

Though such efforts are unusual and unconventional, they are not necessarily unconstitutional. Whether one is to regard them as the legitimate

9. M. Howard, 'Some Reflections on Defence Organization in Great Britain and the U.S.A. 1945–1958', unpublished paper delivered to the 7th Round Table of I.P.S.A. on Civil–Military Relations, 1959.

10. I expect from this, of course, the propaganda exercises mentioned in the footnote on p. 142 above. There is no excuse whatsoever for this flagrant abuse of public position and public funds.

11. Cf., for instance, *The Passing of the Great Fleet* by H. F. Whatt and L. G. H. Graham Horton, the joint founders of the Imperial Maritime League (1909). The whole of this episode is described in detail in A. J. Marder, *From the Dreadnought to Scapa Flow*, Oxford, 1961, vol. I. See especially Chapters V and VIII.

extension of influence or as the beginnings of political blackmail depends on how one regards serving officers' unauthorized disclosure of information to the press and to politicians. If one stresses the right of the legislature to be informed and to redress grievances, then these were techniques of influence: if one stresses the duty of serving officers to obey their superiors, then they must be regarded as efforts at blackmail.

However, in both Britain and the United States the policies advocated bore strictly on professional matters. Sections of the military were vying with other sections to have their professional claims met.[12] This is very different from other cases where the military have *corporately* opposed the civilian authorities, and advocated a policy which was less about professional matters than it was a general political programme.

The most striking of such cases is that of the Japanese armed forces in the 1930s. The Japanese military, particularly the army, acted like a political party in all senses but one – it did not put up candidates. From 1935 it openly assumed responsibility for the training of youth, and thereafter its 'thought supervisors' and inspection commissions began to operate in the schools. Students were encouraged to spy on their fellows. Officers came in to instruct the school-teachers on 'morals'. In addition, jointly with the Department of Education, it published millions of propaganda pamphlets which put the army case for expansion and war abroad and for a controlled economy at home, and were distributed to the schools and colleges, and to every village. Officers toured the country lecturing in factories, schools and village halls, and in all this the extensive ex-servicemen's associations and the Japanese Women's Society for National Defence gave vociferous assistance.

In addition, however, the law and convention of the Japanese state assigned to the military an autonomous political rôle. The cabinet had to include the Ministers of War and of the Navy and by convention also these had to be officers on the active list and so under orders. (In 1913 the rule was abrogated and the ministers could be drawn from the retired list but in

12. Cf. Janowitz, op. cit. 'The [American] military profession is not a monolithic power group. A deep split pervades its ranks in respect to its doctrine and viewpoints on foreign affairs, a split which mirrors civilian disagreements. Instead, the military profession and the military establishment conform more to the pattern of an administrative pressure group, but one with a strong internal conflict of interest. It is a very special pressure group because of its immense resources, and because of its grave problems of national security. The military have accumulated considerable power and that power protrudes into the political fabric of contemporary society. It could not be otherwise. However, while they have no reluctance to press for larger budgets, they exercise their opinion on political matters with considerable restraint and unease. Civilian control of military affairs remains intact and fundamentally acceptable to the military; and imbalance in military contributions to politico-military affairs – domestic or international – is therefore often the result of default by civilian political leadership' (p. viii).

practice the concession had little effect. The rule was restored in 1936.) Hence the military could break a cabinet by withdrawing their representatives and refusing to appoint others until and unless they were satisfied with the choice of the other ministers. The military made frequent use of this power to bring pressure on the civilians. It would be otiose to catalogue all the occasions;[13] a selection from the 1936–7 period will suffice to illustrate the technique. In 1936, the Emperor called on the ex-Foreign Minister Hirota to form a cabinet. The army was by now determined to block party government. It, therefore, nominated General Terauchi as Minister of War, and Hirota was able to form his cabinet only after securing Terauchi's (i.e. army) approval for each and every one of the cabinet members. For instance, Hirota's first choice for Foreign Minister was Yoshida – a liberal. 'But naturally,' commented the American Ambassador, Joseph Grew, 'the army wouldn't have him for a moment and it was soon announced that Hirota had run into hot water and was having difficulty in forming his cabinet and that General Terauchi, his choice for Minister of War, would not serve unless radical alterations were made in Hirota's slate ... It took Hirota four days to smooth out his differences of opinion with the army ...'[14]

The Hirota cabinet was indeed a 'puppet of the army';[15] it diverted 46 per cent of the budget to the armed forces. In January 1937, the civilian–army differences again came to a head. When Hamada of the Seiyukai Party launched a parliamentary attack on the army's political activities, General Terauchi claimed it had been insulted and the War Office issued a midnight press statement criticizing the régime of political parties and parliamentarism. Hirota resigned. All the negotiations for a new cabinet were now set afoot once more. This time the Emperor called on General Ugaki. In vain. 'It was the army and solely the army which was responsible for the failure. All other important groups in the country favoured Ugaki.'[16] Furthermore, in the army it was the Kwantung army faction (i.e. the army in Manchuria, led by General Itagaki, its Chief of Staff) who refused to have Ugaki. Ugaki was regarded as too moderate, as he had once concurred with his civilian colleagues in a cabinet which had cut down the size of the army.

---

13. Cf. C. Yinaga, 'The Military and the Government in Japan', *American Political Science Review*, vol. 35, pp. 529–39.

14. J. Grew, *Ten Years in Japan*, pp. 160–61; cf. also Shigemitsu, op. cit., p. 108.

15. Shigemitsu, op. cit.

16. *Foreign Relations of the United States*, Department of State, Washington, 1937, vol. IV, pp. 703–14.

The next choice for Prime Minister was General Hayashi. He tried to bring in the extremist General Itagaki either as War Minister or Vice-Premier, but was blocked by the other army factions and by the navy. His cabinet was 'vetted' by these groups and, as a consequence of their pressure, once again no party politicians were appointed to the cabinet.[17]

Other armies, e.g. the Spanish army in the decades before the First World War, also tended to act like a party, and bring pressure upon their civilian colleagues; but this Japanese example must suffice to illustrate the technique of bringing pressure to bear upon the civilian government by collusion or competition with civilian politicians.

Blackmail: intimidation and threats

The Japanese example of collusion and competition with civilians may be regarded as influence or blackmail according to taste. When we consider military intimidation of politicians by violence and by threats we are quite certainly at the level of blackmail.

In Japan, the army's competition with the parties was accompanied by the murder of prominent politicians. This was not of deliberate set purpose; many of the assassins were not soldiers but civilians, and even the soldier-assassins were not acting under orders. Nevertheless, the murders were carried out in the army's interest; the murderers (save in 1936) got off lightly for that reason; and the army benefited. In 1930, the anti-militarist 'Lion' Hamagauchi was shot by a right-wing patriot and died of his wounds. In 1931, a plot was uncovered to blow the whole cabinet to pieces and install a military junta. In February 1932, a former Finance Minister, Inoye, was murdered by the right-wing 'League of Blood' and Baron Dan, of the house of Mitsui, was killed a month later by a young naval officer. In May 1932, Prime Minister Inukai, who believed in a peaceful policy towards China, was murdered by a group of cadets and officers. They had a field day in court where they basked in public sympathy and not one received a capital sentence. 'The military are still supreme and still form a dictatorship of terrorism,' wrote the American Ambassador Grew in early 1933. 'There seems little doubt that Saito [the Prime Minister] was told to fall in line or else there would be an internal crack-up in the country commencing with the assassination of himself and others who had opposed withdrawal from the League of Nations . . .'[18] The climax of the murder campaign occurred in the February mutiny of 1936. The rebels' plan was to kill every important member of the cabinet, and several were indeed sur-

17. For other examples cf. K. Colegrove, 'The Japanese Cabinet', *American Political Science Review*, vol. 30, pp. 916–19. 18. Grew, op. cit., pp. 73–4.

prised in their homes and shot down. This time the Emperor had a say in the repression; as far as he was concerned, the rebellion was an act of mutiny. The rebel officers were denied the public trial they coveted and the ringleaders were executed. From then on the campaign of assassinations ceased.

A very different but evidently most effective variant of the technique of frightening the army's political enemies, practised in Syria between 1955 and 1956, was the judicial 'frame-up'. Here the army colluded with certain favoured political groups, while terrorizing their political opponents. The leader of the military faction was the young head of the Syrian army's *Deuxième Bureau*, Lt-Col. Serraj, and the political faction he favoured was the Ba'ath party.

The Ba'ath party came into prominence in 1954, when elections were held after the deposition of the dictator Shishakli. The majority of the Chamber were Independents. Also about twenty-eight members of the People's party and thirteen of the National party were returned (these were the older nationalist parties and represented the socially powerful classes). But there were also returned sixteen members of the Ba'ath party. It was a radical party of the urban intelligentsia which proclaimed Arab unity with a strong pro-Egyptian slant, denounced imperialism and hence the West, and stood for 'positive neutralism', and favoured social reforms.[19] Its view had made much headway among the junior army officers. Serraj co-operated with the Ba'ath, whose success in the 1954 elections (it had only two members in the previous Parliament) has been ascribed[20] partly to army funds and army support.[21]

As head of counter-intelligence, Serraj had a secret budget and controlled a network of agents and spies. He now used his position to destroy the Ba'ath's enemies. The first to be crushed was the small, activist, right-wing Popular party, which hated and fought the Ba'ath and stood for the union of Syria with Iraq. The occasion was the assassination of Colonel Malki, the Deputy Chief of Staff, and brother to one of the Ba'ath leaders. The assassin (a sergeant) committed suicide, but the government stated that the assassination was part of a plot by the Popular party. Seventy-five civilians and thirty army officers were charged with complicity and tried by

19. For two different assessments of the Ba'ath, see W. Z. Laqueur, *Nationalism and Communism in the Middle East*, and G. Majdalany, 'The Arab Socialist Movement', *The Middle East in Transition*, ed. W. Z. Laqueur, pp. 324–50.

20. Cf. W. Z. Laqueur, 'Syria: Nationalism and Communism', *The Middle East in Transition*, p. 328.

21. It will be remembered that the army controlled the *gendarmerie*, and that this was influential at election time (see p. 113).

the office of the military investigator. The death sentence for twenty-six executive members of the Popular party was demanded,[22] and the party itself was dissolved. It was as a result of this trial that Colonel Serraj first emerged into prominence. This was in 1955. One year later, *The Times* was describing Syria as being 'in the grip of a military dictatorship' headed by Serraj.[23]

Serraj struck his second blow on 8 January 1957, when forty-seven Syrians including some of the leading politicians were tried by court martial for conspiring to overthrow the government by armed revolt, with backing from Britain, France, Turkey and Iraq. Among the accused was the ex-dictator Shishakli. Only three of the defendants were acquitted. Nearly all the accused were right-wing or moderate politicians and the effect of the trial was to purge the opposition in the parties and the armed forces.

The third blow was the expulsion of three United States officials in August 1957, on the grounds that they had been preparing a plot to overthrow the régime. Four days later Serraj purged the senior appointments in the Syrian army, and replaced the Commander-in-Chief by Brigadier Bizri, believed (by *The Times* correspondent) to be a Communist party member.

Concurrently, the Syrian Parliament took on a more and more anti-western, pro-Soviet and pro-Egyptian cast. The independents teamed up with the Ba'ath to form a majority group. Many of the old People's party and other oppositionists began to feel the pressure of the government and some of the most prominent of them fled. The President of the Chamber was replaced by Akram Hourani, the leader of the Ba'ath. In this way was the stage set for the union of Syria with Egypt – with Colonel Serraj as the Syrian Minister of the Interior.[24]

A more usual form of political blackmail than the one described is the military threat to refuse to defend the government or to attack it unless its demands are met. This is what the French forces in Algeria threatened to do unless de Gaulle came to power.[25] Likewise in Greece in 1936, where the army officers threatened to revolt if a government were formed which depended on communist support. Some of the most vivid illustrations of

22. Three were sentenced to death, but the sentences were not carried out.

23. *The Times*, 28 November 1956.

24. Later, he became President of the Executive Council of the 'Northern region' of the United Arab Republic (September 1959). He resigned in 1961, after quarrelling with the Egyptian Commander-in-Chief, Hakim Amer, and his resignation was immediately seized on by the Syrian officers to launch their revolt against Egypt on 28 September 1961. Serraj was imprisoned until he contrived to escape to Egypt after the coup of 28 March 1962.

25. See p. 86 – the threat to launch 'Operation Resurrection'.

this technique come from the earliest days of the Weimar Republic. In early 1918, Field-Marshal von Hindenburg threatened President Ebert that unless he took action against the Spartakists, the Field-Marshal would 'act on his own responsibility and would employ all the means at his disposal against them'. Ebert perforce gave way and allowed troops to enter Berlin.[26] A few days later, the Soldiers' Congress put forward its 7-point demands: officers were to be elected, power was to reside in the Soldiers' Councils, the regular army was to be supplanted by a civil guard, and so forth. These the Field-Marshal positively refused to obey. 'I decline to recognize the ruling of the Congress,' he said. 'I shall oppose it by every means in my power. I shall not permit my epaulettes or my sword to be taken from me. Now as before, the Army supports the Government and expects it to carry out the promise to preserve the Army.' Ebert replied that this must therefore end in civil war. 'It is not we who began the quarrel,' was Hindenburg's reply, 'and it is not our business to end it. We have taken our decision and it is irrevocable.' Once again the government gave way to this bullying.[27]

Displacement and supplantment

The displacement of a government or the supplantment of the civilian régime are brought about in three ways.

(1) The first is the same as we have already described, viz. by a threat to revolt, or, alternatively, to refuse to defend the government against its foes. So far we have described this as a technique of blackmail, but it can also be a technique for displacement or supplantment.

The Iraqi coups, 1936–41, illustrate this. Not all of them were carried through by physical violence. In some the mere threat was sufficient. Bakr Sidqi's coup of 1936 was indeed a physical one, but the counter-coup of 1937 which displaced his puppet cabinet was executed by threats. It happened thus. When Bakr Sidqi was assassinated in 1937, Prime Minister Hikmat decided to arrest the ringleaders. The Mosul garrison supported them, however, and accordingly declared that it had 'severed relations with Baghdad'. It was soon joined by three other garrisons, but the Baghdad garrison stayed loyal. Just as it looked as if civil war must break out, an outlying portion of the Baghdad garrison also defected. Thus nearly all the Iraqi garrisons had declared they would not obey the government. In these circumstances Hikmat simply resigned.

The fall of Hikmat's successor, Midfai, was brought about even more

26. Wheeler-Bennett, op. cit., p. 31.   27. ibid., p. 33.

simply. He owed his elevation to the army coup just described. By 1938 the coup faction had broken into two, one of which was known as 'The Seven'. At the end of 1938 it decided to overthrow Midfai. Having concentrated their forces and put them on the alert, the conspirators had the Premier told at a private party that unless he resigned the forces would march. Midfai immediately agreed to yield, and next day he and his colleagues formally tendered their resignation to the King, in the presence of the Chief of the General Staff and other leading army officers.

Likewise in Spain, during the period of the *Juntas de defensa*, 1917–23. When these sprang up in 1917 the Minister of War promptly ordered the arrest of the leaders. The Juntas retorted with an ultimatum, and the cabinet, not even assured of the support of the monarch, had no other course than to resign. The general strike and the disorders in Barcelona which broke out immediately afterwards then made civil government entirely dependent on military support and thenceforward cabinet after cabinet fell as a result of the Juntas' threats of disobedience. When, in 1917, they insisted on La Cierva being Minister of War, the Prime Minister (Dato) had to resign and the whole of the succeeding cabinet had to be built around La Cierva.

In 1919 the Sanchez Toca government fell owing to army opposition also. In this case the Juntas had imposed certain conditions on officers studying at the *Escuela de Guerra*. Some captains who declined to accept the conditions were brought before a Court of Honour and told to resign. Civilian opinion was shocked, and the Sanchez Toca government decided to allow an appeal to the Supreme Council of War, but the Juntas brought pressure on the War Minister and he, in turn, refused to allow the captains to appeal to the Supreme Council. The cabinet thereupon resigned. Later, in 1922, the scene repeated itself. By this time the disaster at Anuel had occurred and was casting its shadow over Spanish politics. The Prime Minister was Maura; but, in deference to the Juntas, he had had to appoint to the Ministry of War that same La Cierva whom the Juntas regarded as their spokesman. Civilian opinion demanded an inquiry into the Anuel disaster. Maura complied, only to meet the enraged protests of La Cierva and the Juntas. It was now that Maura, resigning, issued the famous words: 'Let those who prevent government govern instead.'

(2) A second way in which the military can bring down a government or supplant the civilian régime is by refusing to defend the government from civil disorder. It was in this way, for instance, that General Song Yo Chan, the Chief of the General Staff of the South Korean army, brought about

the downfall of President Syngman Rhee. On 15 March 1960, President Syngman Rhee won his fourth term in a flagrantly rigged election. A nation-wide revolt followed. Student demonstrations started in Seoul and spread. In April, the police fired on crowds marching on Syngman Rhee's residence, with dreadful consequences – 115 dead and 777 wounded. General Song called on the President to say that the army would probably refuse to shoot if the students rioted again, but Syngman Rhee took no action. A few days later the issue came to a head. Three hundred Seoul University teachers were gathered at the National Assembly building to protest; yet the army tanks rumbled past them, apparently unheeding. By curfew time (7 p.m.) the crowd had become enormous, and once the army loudspeakers proclaimed their sympathy with the demands for new elections, almost the whole population turned out. Under army protection a student delegation waited upon Syngman Rhee and secured his resignation. The next day the successor government of Chung Huh was formally installed.

Another example is the fall of the Arbenz government in Guatemala, in 1954. By that year the bulk of the army's officers had become disinclined to fight for President Arbenz. On 5 June the General Staff sent him a memorandum recommending the curbing of the communists, only to have the President reject it and state that he would maintain his policies. A fortnight later Castillo Armas and his column invaded the country with about 1,500 poorly equipped men and was checked after an advance of twenty miles. The only engagement was the Battle of Chiquimula in which only a few hundred men were involved, and where the casualties totalled a mere seventeen. There the army remained passive until, a few days later (27 June), representatives of its officer corps met the President and secured his resignation. A temporary military junta took over and on 2 July made terms with Castillo Armas.

(3) We now come to the final method of displacing a government or supplanting a régime – the use of violence. And here we must distinguish.

The expression commonly used is 'coup'. When we come to examine this closely, it is clear that it is a general term. In Europe, with its more limited experience of such matters, the expression *coup d'état* is not specifically distinguished from say, a *coup de force*, and we use the expressions 'military revolt', 'mutiny', 'rebellion', 'coup', 'revolution' interchangeably without asking what precisely has happened. Latin Americans, with their closer acquaintance with the phenomenon, distinguish. For them 'revolution' is a portentous word, signifying some massive alteration in a country's social structure. Mexico talks, accordingly, of its Revolution of

1910 and wears this as a badge of pride. Military despots also lay claim to the term for their own successful conspiracies, just as it is common experience that the more authoritarian a régime, the more anxious it is to label itself a democracy.[28] They will claim that theirs is 'no mere barracks-revolt' (cuartelazo) but a true 'revolution'. The people know otherwise and employ other terms.

The first is the *golpe de estado*, literally the *coup d'état*, but which to them signifies the seizure and elimination of the person of the head of state. The second is what Europeans usually think of when they use the term *coup d'état*, as in the '*coup d'état* of Louis Napoleon': and this, in Latin America, is the *cuartelazo*, the 'barracks coup'. Most of the exercises of violence discussed in these pages – the Egyptian coup of 1952, the Iraqi coup of 1958, the Japanese, German and French coups of 1936, 1920 and 1961 respectively, were specifically cuartelazos. Sometimes the golpe is carried out at the same time as the cuartelazo.

Sometimes the cuartelazo, failing, is repressed by loyalist troops and sometimes it leads to civil war. If either happens it is surely the result of a miscalculation for the whole point of both golpe and cuartelazo is to carry out the displacement or the supplantment with the minimum of bloodshed.

(*a*) *Golpe de estado*. From cases already cited, we can select two clear instances of a successful golpe, unaccompanied by further violence. The first is the removal of President Ramírez and his replacement by General Farrell in Argentina in 1944. The officers' clique (the G.O.U.) were enraged when Ramírez broke with the Axis powers and decided to overthrow him. A group of officers, with Perón prominent among them, burst into the Casa Rosada and, with pistols levelled at his head, forced him to resign. 'Fatigued by the intense tasks of Government which have obliged me to take a rest,' ran his letter, 'I delegate on this date the position which I occupy to the person of H.E. the Vice-President of the Nation, Brigadier-General don Edelmiro J. Farrell.'

We have mentioned the coup (cuartelazo, really) led by Colonel Zaim of Syria by which he made himself dictator in 1948, and how he himself was soon overthrown by a counter-coup.[29] This counter-coup was a classic golpe de estado. In the small hours of the morning, President Zaim and his Prime Minister were arrested in their homes by a group of army officers, summarily tried by a tribunal of officers sitting as the Supreme War Council, sentenced – and shot. The conspirators then issued proclamations announcing the trial and execution of the 'tyrant' and 'traitor'; denounced his wickedness and misdeeds; and promised democratic government.

28. See pp. 220–21.   29. See p. 113.

It may seem that this method of displacing a government is too simple to be valid. It is certainly speedy and immediate, but to be successful it has to be anything but simple. To succeed it requires the most shrewd assessment of political forces in the country and the most careful planning. It demands the organization of a cadre of leaders and sub-leaders, the appointment of the take-over men in advance, and, if necessary (as with Zaim), arrangements for propaganda against the victim. It also requires 'reinsurances' such as a plane or a car to make a get-away if the plot is unsuccessful.

(b) *Golpe and cuartelazo combined.* More usually, the golpe is the culminating act of a cuartelazo. Two examples are by now familiar to us. The February mutiny of 1936 in Japan was a cuartelazo in which the rebels seized control of central Tokyo, and simultaneously, as we saw, sent out murder-bands to hunt down and kill members of the cabinet. Technically speaking, it failed because its leaders had made none of the 'follow through' arrangements listed above. In Iraq, on the other hand, Brigadier Kassim had prepared his ground; and then, having seized Baghdad, he proceeded to murder the Regent and the King and then, later, to hunt down and kill Nuri-es-Said, the Prime Minister.

One other example, not previously referred to, will help to complete the picture. It comes from Colombia, where, by 1953, President Gomez had created a terrible sense of national disaster. The country was plunged into a barbarous civil war. Gomez then quarrelled with the army. He refused to sanction the arrest of a certain industrialist who was suspected of plotting to kill the Commander-in-Chief, General Rojas Pinilla. The cabinet resigned in protest, whereas Gomez decided to arrest Rojas Pinilla. Rojas got to hear of this. He sent tanks to surround the Presidential Palace, forced the President's resignation and next morning assumed power as Provisional President.[30]

(c) *The cuartelazo.* Like the golpe, the cuartelazo demands very careful preparation. To succeed it needs a masterly computation of the balance of not only the civilian political forces, but of the reactions of the different branches of the service and of the different garrisons or units. With the differentiation of the various arms the calculations have become formidably complex and where cuartelazos fail, it is usually because such calculations have gone awry. For the premise on which the cuartelazo is based is the unity of the armed forces: that, in the words of von Seeckt when asked to suppress the Kapp putsch, 'Reichswehr does not fire upon

30. But without any intention to become so. He had acted in self-defence and after the golpe offered the Presidency to two politicians – who refused – before proclaiming himself. Cf. Tad Szulc, *Twilight of the Tyrants*, p. 224.

Reichswehr'. The assumption is that the uncommitted garrisons and units will stand aside at first, and then jump on the bandwagon if the movement looks like succeeding. The result often justifies the assumption and accounts for the fact that a whole régime can often be subverted by a handful of troops, and that so many of the cuartelazos – like the Turkish one for instance – are bloodless. On the other hand the calculation may be quite false from the outset. The French generals' cuartelazo of 1961 failed to estimate correctly the reactions of the navy, of the air force and of the conscripts.

The cuartelazo follows a classic pattern, not simply in Spain where it has been described as a 'highly formalized play', but in all countries. If the terms used here are mostly Spanish, the procedures described occur everywhere – in Thailand, Iraq, Egypt, Europe, as well as Spain and Latin America. In chronological order they are:

   (i) The *trabajos*, or tentative testing of opinion.
   (ii) The *compromisos*, i.e. the 'deals', and the commitments to take part.
   (iii) *Action!* The treason of a single garrison or barracks.
   (iv) The *pronunciamento*, manifesto, proclamation or *grito* (cry).
   (v) The march on the centres of communication towards the capital *or* the seizure of communication centres, and government buildings in the capital.
   (vi) The announcement that the government has changed hands.
   (vii) The appointment of a military junta to assume government, the promise that the change is merely provisional, together with the rounding-up of opposition.

To show the universality of the pattern, let us look at three diverse examples: the Bakr Sidqi cuartelazo in Iraq (1936), the Neguib–Nasser cuartelazo in Egypt in 1952 and the Pak cuartelazo in South Korea in 1961.

General Bakr Sidqi had won a great reputation in Iraq in 1936 as the effective suppressor of the tribal revolts. A number of politicians looked to him as the strong man who could renovate Iraq. He himself took Kemal Atatürk as his model of the soldier-reformer.

At the autumn manoeuvres, Bakr Sidqi was appointed acting-Chief of the General Staff, since the Chief of the General Staff was himself on leave. These manoeuvres were to take place in the Khana-quin-Baghdad area. Bakr Sidqi therefore decided to march on the capital before they took place. He took into his confidence the Minister of War, Abd-el-Latif Nuri. Then, back at his headquarters, north of Baghdad, he revealed his plan to some of his officers: the 2nd Division was to stay behind to defend the frontier while he would send the 1st Division up to stage the attack. Having explained these plans, he and the Minister of War jointly drew up a petition to the King, demanding the resignation of the cabinet. The two men also drew up their Proclamation to the people of Baghdad, and decided that the 1st Division should be called 'The National Reform Force'.

They had their successor-government ready in the person of Hikmat, one of the Ahali group of reformers. On the eve of the march, Hikmat received his copy of the petition, while copies of the Proclamation were issued to reliable army officers for distribution next day. Meanwhile the air force had been sounded and agreed to support the plot by sending a few planes to Bakr's headquarters.

That night the 1st Division moved and pitched camp in the northern outskirts of Baghdad. The next morning, as the march into the city began at 7.30 a.m., Bakr Sidqi declared it under military occupation. One hour later the planes flew over, dropping copies of the Proclamation, while army officers and some policemen also helped to distribute it.

The Prime Minister called the cabinet. Not very enthusiastically, he suggested resistance. The King simply remained silent. Thereupon the Prime Minister tendered his resignation. The cuartelazo was over.

In Egypt, the plotters were that band of ardent and rebellious spirits who came to call themselves the 'Free Officers' and who, after being scattered in cross-postings during the war, came together again after 1945. They then dreamed of overturning the government and the defeat in Palestine in 1948 made them more urgent; but the earliest date by which they were likely to succeed was, to their mind, in 1954 or 1955. But after the sack of Cairo in 1952 and the fall of the Wafd, police activity increased and the Free Officers had to think of an immediate blow. Hence their search for a 'front man' and Neguib was approached. He had been in almost constant contact with the Free Officers for the last year, when Hakim Amer (Nasser's friend) became his A.D.C.

The police were now so active that the group felt they must act at once, if at all. Their difficulty was that they were all staff officers and had no fighting troops. The circle of conspirators therefore had to be widened. Al Shafi of the cavalry agreed and so did Shawki of the infantry: but Mehanna of the artillery not only refused but gave reason to believe that he was actively hostile.

The date chosen was 5 August when the Court and the cabinet would be at Alexandria, the summer capital. However, on 20 July news arrived that King Farouk was about to dismiss his ministry, and appoint the redoubtable

Sirri Amer as Minister of War. It was also rumoured that all fourteen of the conspirators were to be arrested. They thereupon decided to strike in the next forty-eight hours and met on the appointed day to lay their final plans. It now appeared that the Chief of the General Staff had wind of some plot, so they decided to march one hour earlier than arranged. Shawki and his 13th Infantry Regiment, together with Sadiq's tanks, occupied G.H.Q. and arrested the Chief of the General Staff. Muhieddin's armoured cars threw a cordon round the military areas of Abbassia and Heliopolis. Al Shafi's tanks, meanwhile, occupied the strategic points in the centre of Cairo and seized the telephone exchange, the broadcasting station, the railway and the airports. By 3 a.m. the conquest was complete and the Free Officers in G.H.Q. proclaimed General Neguib as Commander-in-Chief of the army, and informed the British and American embassies. At 4 a.m. the Prime Minister telephoned from Alexandria to General Neguib to find out what had happened, but was inclined to make light of the affair. The decisive moment occurred when the conspirators learned that the powerful El Arish garrison had come over. Only now did the conspirators make their appeal to the public. General Neguib explained to the reporters that the officers' aims were legality, continuity and democracy; and at 6 a.m. the *pronunciamento* of the movement was broadcast. Meanwhile an emissary, the firebrand El Sadhat, offered the Premiership to the officers' choice, the politician Ali Maher who, temporizing a little till he saw the army was in full control, finally agreed. Next day (24 July), Ali Maher waited on the King in Alexandria and emerged as Prime Minister with a list of ministers in his pocket. Two days later the army presented its ultimatum to the King, who had no choice but to agree and abdicate. The initial aims of the cuartelazo were all secured.

To turn to South Korea: there Major-General Pak, aged 44, had apparently been plotting to seize power for some time; but the student riots, the fall of Syngman Rhee and the subsequent elections in 1960 had overtaken him. The new Prime Minister's plan to reduce the size of the army, and his early retirement of some prominent officers presented Pak with his opportunity. His difficulties lay in the reaction of the United States forces in Korea, in the attitude of the frontier troops, and in the need for a senior commander, since he himself was merely the chief of operations. It is reported that he and his fellows called on General Chang, the Chief of the General Staff, and threatened to kill him unless he led the enterprise. Accordingly, at 3.30 a.m. in the morning of 16 May 1961, infantry, marines, tanks and paratroopers occupied Seoul, and by dawn were in complete possession. However, the cuartelazo was not yet fully successful. The

Prime Minister had escaped and was in hiding. The commander of the United States forces refused recognition. The attitude of the frontier troops was still in doubt. And a group of senior officers had barricaded themselves in and seemed about to offer resistance. But the officers surrendered, the American troops did not move, the frontier troops defected to the insurgents and within two days the ex-Premier had given himself up. The almost bloodless coup had been effected by a mere 3,600 men out of an army numbering 600,000.

These examples illustrate various aspects of that basic pattern we have described; but, since all were very neat, and all were successful, they give the impression that a cuartelazo is an easy short cut to power. It should be remembered therefore that far more cuartelazos fail than succeed. Furthermore, some meet so much resistance as to turn into civil war.

Since the fall of Jiménez in 1958, there have been several unsuccessful cuartelazos in Venezuela. As an example, we may consider the attempt of April 1960. At 3 a.m., a former War Minister, General Castro Leon, crossed from neighbouring Colombia to San Cristobal (about 400 miles from the capital) and assumed command of its 500-man garrison from his fellow conspirator, the colonel commanding. By radio he broadcast a recorded appeal to other generals to join him.

In Caracas, the President convened the heads of the armed forces, and together they and the President telephoned all garrisons and state governors. The air force was ordered to strafe the rebel headquarters and to fly in local troops, but the weather made this impossible for some time.

Matters went worse for Castro Leon however. The state national guard refused to join him. He sent 150 men to capture the local airfield. They deserted to the government forces. He sent another 180 troops to capture a second airfield. They were held off by 200 hastily armed peasants. By the time the loyal planes were about to attack, Castro Leon had fled and the cuartelazo was crushed.

The abortive cuartelazo of June 1955 in Argentina was a more complicated and far more serious affair. It began with a totally unexpected attack on the Casa Rosada by navy aircraft. As they dropped bombs, machine guns from the Navy Ministry began to fire into the Casa Rosada, and a few minutes later a line of rebel marines advanced.

Perón had received ten minutes' warning. It was enough. Truckloads of soldiers roared off towards the rebel marines and, supported by tanks, drove them back. Tanks and light artillery besieged the Navy Ministry and forced it to surrender. The battle seemed over by the early afternoon when suddenly a new wave of planes soared over, strafing and bombing. The loyal tanks now advanced again and captured the rebel airbase. The pilots gave up and flew off towards Uruguay and the cuartelazo was over. It had cost 360 dead and about 1,000 wounded. Why had it failed? First of all, fog had hindered the plan. It prevented both planes and ships from moving freely and prevented the seaborne landing on the Buenos Aires waterfront. Secondly, the *compromisos* had not kept their word; they had not joined in.

Between the clean-cut successes which we have described, and the complete failures, some cuartelazos develop into a brief but bloody civil war. The second and successful Argentine cuartelazo of September 1955 was of this kind.

It differed from the June rising in two ways. First, all three services joined in. Second, the rising began in the provinces and converged on the capital.

It began in the night, when rebel troops occupied Cordoba, Arroyo-Seco and Curuzu-Cuatía, while rebel sailors took over the naval base of Santiago (near Buenos Aires) and that of Puerto Belgrano (near Bahía Blanca). Perón's troops counter-attacked fiercely. At the end of the first day's fighting they recaptured Santiago, and at the beginning of the second day had entered Arroyo-Seco and Curuzu-Cuatía, while troops were marching on Puerto Belgrano and Cordoba. Now the rebel leader, General Lonardi, issued his *grito*, denouncing the dictator; and while the battle for Cordoba raged, the news came that the Second Army (in Western Argentina) had defected to the rebels and held San Luis and Mendoza. As the day turned against Perón, the navy threw its weight into the battle. It had silently concentrated on the Uruguay shore and now Admiral Rojas announced that the fleet was heading up river for the capital and would bombard it unless Perón resigned. Next morning observers could count no less than twenty-one rebel warships in the river. The movement was decisive. The navy gave Perón until 10 a.m. on 19 September to resign unconditionally. After some prevarication he did so, and took refuge on a Paraguayan gunboat. Truce talks were held at sea between the loyalist and rebel commanders and on 21 December both sides proclaimed General Lonardi as Provisional President.

One feature that must strike any observer of cuartelazos is the extent to which they discount civilian reactions. One of the considerations in their planning is, to be sure, the steps to be taken to *paralyse* civilian reactions: hence the securing of the centres of communication, the telephone offices and the radio station, and hence also the immediate imposition of a curfew and the ban on demonstrations. All this assumes that civilian reaction will be weak enough to be paralysed, and it also assumes that the loyalist elements will not be prepared to arm the populace.

The explanation lies in what has been said in Chapter Seven; on the whole, the military are sensible enough not to attempt cuartelazos in countries where civilian resistance is likely to be considerable. Cuartelazos take place in countries with a relatively low level of political culture, precisely because it is in such countries that the military realize they can discount civilian hostility or even count on civilian support. Mad-dog acts like the Kapp putsch, the Japanese February mutiny and the generals' revolt in France are exceptions to the usual military techniques in such countries, i.e. threats, intimidation, or collusion with civilian politicians.

Nevertheless, so unpredictable is the human temperament that somewhere, sometime, under severe provocation, any soldier may be tempted to chance his arm. In countries with powerful civilian forces, this leads, as we have seen, to the withering away of the revolt. But where the military are arrogant enough to strike and the civilian forces opposed to them strong enough to resist but too weak to triumph, the cuartelazo can lead to the most appalling tragedy. This is what happened in 1936 in Spain. The Spanish army had been nurtured on bloodless victories like those of 1923 and 1930 – or equally on bloodless failures like Sanjurjo's in 1932. It had been blooded on strikers and Catalans too long to have anything but a contempt for civilian resistance. It was politically too ignorant and too contemptuous of politicians, especially liberal ones, ever to dream that they might resist – and resist by arming the population. Above all it did not realize that by 1936 the forces of the left were themselves spoiling for a fight – that they were anxious to have a revolution, but, since 'their' government was in power, unwilling to start it. For the first time the Spanish army had, in its arrogant ignorance of political tendencies, unwittingly 'picked someone its own size'. The anarchists, the trade unionists, the Basques and the Catalans were just as eager to fight as the army was.

General Mola's conspiracy followed the usual Spanish course, save for the fact that this time the generals thought it wiser to have some civilian supporters, notably the Carlist levies. Hitherto they had preferred to act as '*nosotros solos*' (ourselves alone). But, otherwise, the rising was planned as cuartelazos are. By the time they had completed their plans, the only forces that seemed unpledged to them were the newly formed Republican Assault Guards and the small air force. In addition they had the Carlist levies, and the promise, if necessary, of planes and tanks from Germany and Italy. The plans were extensively and meticulously worked out. On this hypothesis, the plot appeared certain to succeed. There can be little doubt today that the generals regarded the whole affair as a typical cuartelazo which could be expected to occupy all Spain, except possibly Barcelona and

Madrid, in a day or so, after which the government as usual would lose its nerve and capitulate. The cuartelazo was, however, only half successful, for Barcelona and Madrid and Valencia passed to the government forces, and the navy remained loyal. Furthermore after its overtures for compromise were rejected by the rebels, the government's reaction stiffened and it took the course which alone could make civilian resistance effective: it armed the population, a population only too eager to fight. The cuartelazo, neither successful nor aborted, turned into the carnage of the frightful three years' war.[31]

31. Cf. Brenan, op. cit., esp. Chap. XIV; also H. Thomas, *The Spanish Civil War*, London, 1961, pp. 95–170.

CHAPTER ELEVEN

THE RESULTS OF INTERVENTION – THE MILITARY RÉGIMES

LITTLE effort has been made to distinguish between various classes of military régime. The problem is certainly a difficult one. To begin with not all régimes of military *provenance* are military régimes, although in practice most of them, in fact, are. A régime of military *provenance* is any régime that has owed its establishment to some military intervention. The Vth French Republic is certainly a régime of military *provenance*, but it is not a military régime. The Second Empire of Napoleon III was a régime of military *provenance*, but not a military régime, and likewise the Turkish Republic until 1960, and the Mexican Republic today. For a régime to be a 'military régime', there must be evidence that the government is in the hands of the armed forces or that it acts entirely or predominantly at their command.

Again, even among the military régimes themselves, there are clearly quite different types. For instance, *The Times* correspondent felt able (28 November 1956) to describe Syria under Colonel Serraj as a concealed 'military dictatorship'. Now if this were indeed so, it was obviously not the same kind of dictatorship as Colonel Nasser's, or General Franco's, or Field-Marshal Sarit's.

However, there are certain obstacles to classification. Perhaps we ought to regard military régimes simply as a set of techniques used by the military to carry out their policies rather than as political or constitutional structures. For many of the forms thrown up are created in conditions of illegality. Even more about them is fluid and personal. The formal constitutional structures give no guidance as to how the régime works and where all that is clear is that authority is being exercised only after personal struggles behind the scenes, it is often impossible to find out who or what is the dominant force.

We propose therefore to distinguish three broad types of military régimes. The *first* is indirect rule, where nominally a civilian government rules and takes constitutional responsibility. This type of military régime comes about when intervention is carried only to the level of blackmail (which presupposes a civilian government being blackmailed by the military) or of displacement (which presupposes one civilian government being changed for another).

The *third* is direct rule. Here (as in Turkey, 1960–61) the army itself assumes responsibility, although it may well appoint a civilian cabinet (as in the Turkish or Sudanese cases) to carry out its policies. Elsewhere (as in Argentina, 1943–5) it may rule through a junta of its own members. This form or technique obviously only occurs when the military have supplanted the civilian régime.

In between (and therefore the *second* type) comes a kind of régime which, for want of a better name, may be styled 'dual'. Such a régime rests on two pillars: the army is one and the civilian party or some organized civilian opinion is the other, and the ruling oligarchy or despot is at the head of both. More military dictatorships take this form than is at first realized. For the individual who has been hoisted to power *qua* leader of the armed forces often tends to immerse himself in the functions of government, and as he does so he begins to dissociate himself from active command of the armed forces and to build up other and civilian forces on which to rely. Sometimes this dual régime is constitutionalized. The royal dictatorships, that peculiar phenomenon of the inter-war Balkans, may serve to illustrate this constitutional pattern; for instance that of King Carol of Rumania, resting on the National Renaissance Front on the one hand, and the police and army on the other. More common, as we shall see, are the *de facto* dual régimes. The clearest case of all is the Perón dictatorship; for Perón's powers rested just as much on his Justicialist Party and the *descamisados* as it did on the army, and it was precisely this fact that enabled him to play off one force against the other. Now whereas the indirect-rule régimes stem from the levels of blackmail and displacement, and the direct-rule régimes from the level of supplantment, dual régimes may stem from any one of these three levels. Where the military overtly take on certain official responsibilities for government alongside and among the civilian forces, this represents the borderline between the blackmail or displacement of these authorities on the one hand, and their supplantment of them on the other. If the military went further than this, they would be supplanting the civilian authorities. If the military did not go as far as this, they would be blackmailing or displacing the civilian authorities, not supplanting them. This overt assumption of certain official responsibilities alongside the civilian forces is the maximum manifestation of what we have called blackmail and displacement or the minimum manifestation of what we have called supplantment.

Thus we recognize three main types of military rule: indirect, dual and direct. This classification can be elaborated to distinguish between two kinds of indirect rule and two kinds of direct rule. The first kind of indirect military rule may be styled 'limited', or perhaps 'intermittent'. Here the military intervene only from time to time to secure various limited objectives. In contrast, stands 'complete' or continuous indirect rule, i.e. when the military control all the activities of the nominal government.

Likewise there are two kinds of direct rule. The first, like that of Brigadier Kassim in Iraq or General Gürsel in Turkey,[1] is direct military rule – unqualified. (Though this does not rule out the use of civilian cabinets established by the junta and taking its orders and acting in its name.) But, as we shall see, such juntas feel naked in a world swayed by moral beliefs; and they frequently begin to establish ancillary civilian organizations, like the National Union in Egypt, or put themselves through the forms of a plebiscite, in order to acquire an aura of legitimacy. The essence of such electoral manoeuvres and civilian ancillaries, however, is their dependence on, or rather their emanation from, the military junta. The régime is a direct military régime decked out with some civilian trappings. We shall style it, therefore, 'direct rule, quasi-civilianized'.

We can thus recognize the following forms of the military régime:

> Indirect: limited
> Indirect: complete
> Dual
> Direct
> Direct, quasi-civilianized

Furthermore, these forms of military régime express the levels to which the military have pushed their intervention. We showed at some length how those levels were related to, indeed conditioned by, a country's level of political culture. By the same reasoning then, the form of military régime is related to and conditioned by the country's order of political culture. We can, as before, express this graphically in the form of the table on page 152.

Indirect-limited military rule

The classic examples of this type of régime are inter-war Germany and Japan, to which we have already devoted much attention. We can fairly style the Japanese experience, 1931–45, as indirect and limited military rule. As we have seen, the range of matters the military controlled was very limited at the beginning of this period but grew more and more extensive after 1936, reaching its maximum with the progress of the Pacific War.

The objectives of the German army – with one exception, the Schleicher

---

1. Before the return to constitutionalism in October 1961.

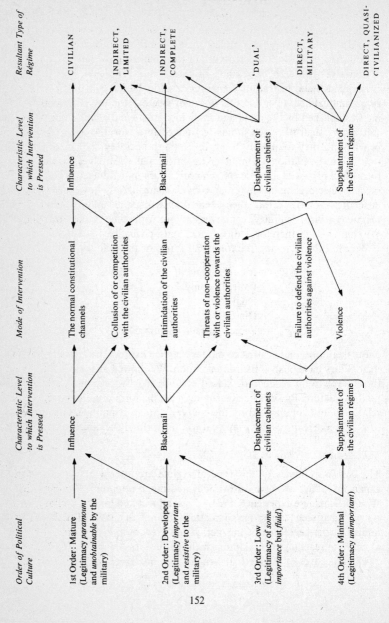

period 1930–32[2] – were always limited. It was and intended to remain, a *Stand*, i.e. an Order. The hard core of its purpose was the limited objective of establishing itself as an autonomous corporation in a powerful state. Furthermore, after the Kapp putsch which thenceforward served as its classic warning, the army worked within, not against, the legal framework. This had been its method under the Empire, and it reverted to it after 1920.[3]

These Japanese and the German examples illustrate indirect rule in 'second order' states, i.e. those of developed political cultures. There, respect for forms and attachment to institutions was strong enough to prevent the military attempting to establish anything but an indirect form of rule. The nature of this kind of rule is therefore possibly expressed more vividly by current practices in Argentina. Here is a country of the third order of political culture, in which the armed forces have, from time to time, exercised rule directly, or in dual harness, or indirectly. At the moment (1959–62), Argentina affords a perfect illustration of military indirect-limited rule. Basically, its political dilemma is this: the military, having overthrown Perón in 1955 in the name of parliamentarism, are committed to excluding the Peronistas from power; while the politicians, for their part, realize that they can secure their electoral and political triumph only by wooing the ex-Peronista officials and the ex-Peronista vote. This led to repeated military pressure on the President, Arturo Frondizi. In July 1959, after Perón had published what he claimed was a pre-election pact between himself and Frondizi,[4] a number of the military men demanded changes in the government. The whole cabinet was therefore sacked except for the Minister of the Interior and the three service ministers. In September 1959, the anti-Peronista Commander-in-Chief, General Toranzo, again threatened military action and thereby forced President Frondizi to dismiss his Minister of War (General Carlos Anaya) and replace him by General Larcher who had spent four years in Perón's prisons. In October 1960, there was another head-on clash. This time the military disagreed with the government's policy for the oil-fields. As the dispute sharpened they demanded a purge of Peronistas from the administration and an accompanying battery of anti-communist measures. This time the President held out and the only notable to resign was the unfortunate War Minister, the anti-Peronist General Larcher, since the army

2. For this episode and the dual rule it introduced, see pp. 159–60.

3. For the legalism of the army see p. 83.

4. Frondizi only won the Presidency because ex-President Perón instructed his followers to vote for him.

regarded him as having been too tepid in urging its case.[5] But the battle was not over. General Larcher was succeeded by General Fraga, whom the military placed in the cabinet to see that their demands were met. In April 1961, the army tried to submit an ultimatum *via* General Fraga, demanding 'fundamental changes' in the government's attitude to the ex-Peronistas, an end to corruption, and a new 'order' in politics, education and the national economy. This time, however, the army was divided. A good proportion supported General Fraga who refused to press these demands on the President, and in consequence it was the Commander-in-Chief (General Toranzo Montero) who resigned and the civil power that triumphed.[6] That this did not mean the permanent defeat of the military was soon shown, in February 1962, when the armed forces compelled President Frondizi to give way on an important matter of foreign policy. At the Punte del Este Conference of the Organization of American States, Argentina was one of the countries which refused to vote for Cuba's immediate exclusion from the Organization. But President Frondizi thereupon found himself compelled by military pressure to break off diplomatic relations with Cuba.

This incident was but the prologue to the immense drama in civil-military relations which took place in March and April 1962. It began with the Provincial and Congressional elections of 18 March. For the first time since the fall of Perón, the Peronistas were being allowed to contest the elections. Hitherto they had been able to show their discontent only by abstention from the polls. The innovation was a manoeuvre of President Frondizi, who supposed that Peronism was on the wane. The elections proved a rude shock. The Peronistas polled 35 per cent of the popular vote and won five of the Provinces, including Buenos Aires. The President immediately 'intervented' the five Provinces, while the armed forces met in angry conclave to decide what to do next. Some favoured ousting the President, others not. At first there was talk of a military pact with Frondizi: he would be expected to invite all the democratic parties into a coalition government, to try to combine the fractured Radical party, to revise the trade union regulations and to ban the Peronists again. However most of the navy officers and a group of influential colonels refused to agree to this arrangement. While they exerted pressure on their colleagues to demand the resignation of the President, whom they held responsible for the resurgence of Peronism, others called in ex-President Aramburu to mediate. But Aramburu was unsuccessful: every grouping in Argentina's public life seemed to have its own exclusive policy. Frondizi's

5. *The Times*, 13, 14 and 18 October 1960.   6. *The Times*, 4 April 1961.

Congressional opponents condemned the 'intervention' of the five Provinces and demanded that the results of the elections be respected, while at the other extreme the navy made an official demand for the President's resignation. While Frondizi himself positively refused to resign both the President of the Senate and the President of the Chamber of Deputies (who were respectively the second and the third in line to the Presidency) positively refused to accept the Presidency if it was vacated.

The extremist factions in the military became more prominent. The navy, adamant for Frondizi's resignation, was reportedly moving ships to Buenos Aires. General Rawson commanding the Third Cavalry division, demanded that Frondizi be ousted by force. On the other hand, Frondizi's intransigent Radical Party, which was the largest in the Chamber and altogether controlled the Senate, declared that it would quit the Congress if the President were forced from office. The military extremists retorted to this by moving troops into Buenos Aires and seizing the Casa Rosada itself. Nevertheless, he still refused to resign, and his Secretary for War, General Fraga, supported him. But General Fraga was promptly isolated by General Poggi, the Commander-in-Chief, the President was prevented from calling an extraordinary session of Congress, and the Minister of the Interior forbidden to broadcast to the nation; and on 29 March the President was arrested and imprisoned on Martin Garcia Island, while Vice President Guido was sworn in as Provisional President.

This did not however end the crisis. It simply renewed it. On 19 April the three service Secretaries demanded that the President should take immediate action against the Peronist parties. Specifically they demanded that the elections should be cancelled, the Peronist parties banned and the remaining Provinces taken over by military interventors. The President refused and his entire cabinet resigned except for the three service Secretaries. Thereupon army units began to move into the capital, at the order of the Commander-in-Chief, General Poggi. At this point, however, the renewed military pressure met an unexpected check. General Poggi's troops were opposed by the Buenos Aires garrison, led by General Rauch. While the two bodies of troops faced each other across the Campo de Mayo, General Rauch accused both General Poggi and the Secretary for War (General Carrera) of issuing ultimata to force the President into unconstitutionality. Both Carrera and Rauch were induced to resign their commands. The peace was kept in this way but the deadlock was unresolved. Once again, the navy proved the deciding factor. It insisted that President Guido fulfil the military's demands. On 24 April, therefore, the Provisional President issued decrees interventing all the remaining

Provinces, cancelling the results of the Provincial elections and calling a new Presidential election for the month of July.

These vicissitudes, with the army intermittently exerting control over the civil power on certain particular matters, illustrate the military régime of the indirect-limited type.

Indirect-complete military rule

One of the clearest examples of this type of régime is provided by Cuba from the Revolution of 1933 to Batista's election to the Presidency in 1940. All through that time ex-Sergeant Batista, as Commander-in-Chief of the army, was the effective government, but he exercised its rule through a series of puppet-Presidents who were made and broken as occasion served. Batista first seized power in September 1933 and established the usual military junta. It was headed by Dr Grau San Martin, one of the students' leaders, and with student support he became the first of Batista's Presidents. After the army had suppressed a counter-revolution (November 1933) it replaced the students as the dominant power in the government. Batista decided that Grau must resign in favour of Colonel Mendieta, the leader of the Nacionalista Party, but Grau refused and was supported by the left. Batista thereupon chose a compromise candidate, Hevia, the Secretary of State for Agriculture and leader of the 1931 rising against ex-President Machado. As the military took over all the municipal and provincial governments, Hevia took the oath of office on 16 January 1934. Thirty-two hours later he resigned and, significantly, addressed his resignation not to the Revolutionary junta but to where it mattered – to Colonel Batista. Hevia was Batista's second President, and his successor, Colonel Mendieta, became the third. Labour and the students were displeased. Violence erupted. The army broke the strikes, suspended constitutional guarantees, and put the island under military control. Half the cabinet protested and demanded the return of constitutional guarantees, but Batista refused their demand and continued with his repressive policy well into 1935. By this time the four main parties had agreed that an election should be held in December 1935. They even nominated their candidates. Unfortunately, at the very last minute, they quarrelled over the electoral law. Provisional President Mendieta thereupon resigned in despair and was succeeded by the Secretary of State, Barnet, who thus became Batista's fourth President. Under Barnet, a few days later, the elections were finally held and Gomez was elected in an orderly election – the first constitutional President since 1933 and, as the event was to prove, Batista's fifth President. Gomez straightway alienated Batista and the army by ejecting

3,000 civil servants to make way for party men. It so happened that most of them were military reservists and as Commander-in-Chief Batista expressed the army's displeasure. He had at this time evolved a plan for the army to establish and operate special schools for workers' children, and to finance these by a levy on the sugar crop. Gomez disapproved of the army meddling in such things. The Congress however was subservient to Batista. It passed his Bill, and when President Gomez vetoed it, it impeached him – ironically enough – for 'violation of the constitution' and 'coercion of representatives', among other things. Thus ended the fifth Batista President, to be succeeded by the Vice-President, Laredo Bru. As to who really governed there was no doubt. The Laredo Bru cabinet was largely Batistized; the Secretary of State and the Secretary of Defence were both soldiers, the Secretary of Health was a major of the reserve, the Secretary of Agriculture, Lopez, was a familiar of the Commander-in-Chief. And two days after the inauguration, it was Colonel Batista, the Commander-in-Chief, and not the President, who announced the programme of the new government.

Shortly after this, Colonel Batista stood for the Presidency himself, and was successfully elected (1940). He thus brought to an end this episode, in which he had been *de facto* ruler while the nominal rule was in the hands of six successive Presidents – a period, in our terminology, of indirect-complete military rule.

Dual rule

We have already pointed out that this kind of régime takes variant forms. The decision as to what is and what is not a 'dual régime' turns on one's estimate of how real and how powerful are the civilian forces on which the government relies. There can be no doubt, however, that the Perón dictatorship was a régime of this type. By every account, it reposed upon a 'soldier–worker alliance', on a 'curious and uneasy partnership'[7] between the armed forces and the trade-union movement and Peronista Party which Perón built up. The army was, as Blanksten puts it, a 'fundamentally indispensable bulwark of the Perón régime';[8] but so was the organized working-class support which Perón commanded. He 'intervented'[9] the C.G.T. in 1943, and soon captured it by arresting and imprisoning any leaders who showed rebelliousness, and, finally, imposed on it a secretariat of five men, all Peronistas. From about 300,000 in 1942, Perón built it up, by 1953, to some 800,000; and it was *his*. The other civilian organization on

---

7. Blanksten, *Perón's Argentina*, p. 306.   8. ibid.
9. i.e. he installed government '*Interventors*' to run the unions.

which he relied – and indeed of which he was the head – was the Peronista or 'Justicialist' Party. Formed in 1949 it was a compound of certain nationalist groups, of some 'collaborationist' Radical leaders (promptly expelled by their party) and, for the most part, of the Argentine Labour Party once its independent leaders (like Cipriano Reyes) had been removed. This party was a real one, in the sense that it was a doctrinaire party of a quarter-of-a-million card-carrying members, and had a national organization rooted in the constituencies.

The régime was 'dual' because both elements were essential to the régime, and because Perón stood at the apex of both; it was a sort of 'personal union', not of two territories (like Austria–Hungary) but of two organizations, one the army, the other civilian. Perón was, *de facto* and *de jure*, the head of the armed forces; he was, at the same time, 'Chief of the [Peronista] movement', and might countermand any of its decisions, supervise elections of candidates, and determine its agenda.

Perón survived by playing one organization against the other. It was the yelling *descamisados*, not his military colleagues, who, on the famous 17 October 1945, made sure that he would run as the Presidential candidate. The Peronista militia helped to scotch the cuartelázo of June 1955. After that revolt, Perón played for time by promising relaxations until, on 31 August, he addressed a crowd of 100,000 supporters outside his Palace and urged them (with glances, it is said, at the officers by his side) to kill all those who tried to 'get in our way'.

His courtship of the armed forces also rose and fell according to the political requirements of the moment. In Perón's first term, his civilian support was powerful enough to permit him to reduce military appropriations. He halved the army budget between 1945 and 1949; he brought the building of barracks and the like to a halt; half of his cabinet were civilians. In his second term, however, the emphasis was the other way. Economically the régime was failing; and Evita Perón, an inestimable ally to her husband, died in 1952. Perón began to moderate his pro-labour policies, and therefore sought to strengthen his support among the military, particularly the navy which had always been hostile.

The Franco régime of Spain may also be regarded as a 'dual' régime, but the case is not as clear-cut as Perón's. It turns on whether we regard the civilian forces in Spain – the Monarchists and the Falange – as in any sense a counterpoise to the views and the influence of the army. If we regard the Falange and the Monarchists as quite uninfluential, we should best classify the régime as a direct but quasi-civilianized régime, i.e. we should be saying that the army is still the sole effective source of power and authority, and that the syndicates and the pseudo-Cortés and the Falangist Party itself are simply civilian trappings, emanating from and dependent on the army. To complicate classification still further, it appears that the influence of the Falange has considerably fluctuated – being very powerful in 1943, for instance, and thereafter suffering a sharp check. The plain facts, however, are simply that the Head of State and Prime Minister (General Franco) is also 'Head of the F.E.T.' (the Falange) and 'Head of the Armed Forces'. Furthermore, the F.E.T., albeit gravely weakened since its prime, *is* a mass movement, and, more importantly still, controls the workers' syndical organizations in which elections began to be held from 1944. In addition, monarchist sentiment (no monarchist *party* is allowed) is a powerful force which the Caudillo can bring into play if necessary. Most observers describe Franco's position as playing off the Falange, the Church and the army. If this is really so, this régime also would appear to be of a dual nature, albeit not as clear-cut as that of Perón.

Both these régimes arose in countries of 'low' (third order) political culture, where notions of legitimacy were fluid: the Argentinian régime was a military retreat from their bare-faced oligarchy of 1943–5, the Spanish was a retreat from the brutal armed rape and military occupation of Spain between 1936 and 1939. Such régimes may also arise, however, in countries of the second order, i.e. of developed political culture, where legitimacy is resistive to the military's supplantment of civilianism, and where the military typically operate on the government by non-violent means. In these countries the dual régime represents an advance from the typical indirect covert form of military régime, into the open. The Schleicher cabinet of 1932, in Germany, provides an example of what we mean. Up to that point the army had been represented in the government by the Minister of War (whether he was a civilian or, like Gröner, a general). Schleicher was Minister of Defence in von Papen's government; so far this is a simple case of indirect and covert army rule. The Schleicher Chancellorship of December 1932 represented a very different state of affairs – a jump into the open. Schleicher was the acknowledged leader of the officer corps. He now became, simultaneously, Chancellor and Minister of Defence. By this move, the army, whose leader he (doubly) was, assumed a direct and overt constitutional responsibility. As for Schleicher, like Perón, his power also reposed on two pillars: the Reichswehr, and the parliamentary forces, together with their backing in the country, as well as the whole mystique of civilian legitimacy which surrounded the office of Chancellor. The fact that his civilian supports were feeble compared to Perón's and collapsed under him in short order must not obscure the basic pattern: Schleicher was at the apex of two organizations, civilian and military.

Direct military rule

This is, at least, an unsophisticated form of régime, easily recognizable; and examples abound.

In its purest form it may be found in the Primo de Rivera 'Directorate', 1923–5. As already explained, de Rivera was the Captain-General of Barcelona, and his *pronunciamento* was supported by the leaders of a number of other garrisons and finally accepted by King Alfonso XIII. A temporary junta took power in Madrid, in preparation for his arrival. On entering the city, the general dismissed this junta and organized what he called a directorate, which was to govern Spain for the next two years. It consisted entirely of military men. Furthermore, for each of Spain's military regions a Brigadier-General was appointed. This directorate was a collegiate body, collectively responsible to the dictator who was the Sole Minister. Once it was established, the Sole Minister dismissed the Cortés, so that he also became the sole legislative organ; and then he proceeded to dissolve all the municipal councils and replace them by associates and representatives of the military policy, while government representation in state-subsidized concerns was also taken over by military men.

The Rawson–Ramírez–Farrell régime in Argentina, 1943–5, is a similar example of direct rule by the military. With one exception (the Finance Minister) everyone in General Ramírez's cabinet was a military man. In all the Provinces, the civilian administrators were removed and replaced by military men also, and most of the mayors of cities were replaced by young colonels. Another direct military régime was that established in Venezuela in 1948, after the military overthrow of the constitutional government. Government was taken into the hands of a three-man junta, all army officers. In 1950 one of these (Chalbaud) was murdered in mysterious circumstances and the two remaining triumvirs thought it expedient to replace him by a tame civilian; but the junta continued to rule in the name of the armed forces until the decision, in 1953 (which we shall discuss later), to 'legitimize' the régime by holding elections.

Many of the contemporary military régimes are of this nature. The Sudanese régime is simply a military oligarchy led by General Abboud, in which trade unions and parties were tolerated only so long as and in so far as they served the oligarchy's purposes (in July 1960 the parties were suppressed and their leaders arrested). The Iraqi régime is the personal rule of Brigadier-General Kassim, though nominally he is but the chairman of a three-man supreme council of state, and rules through a cabinet composed partly of civilians and partly of soldiers. In South Korea (since the cuartelazo of May 1961) the supreme power has been assumed by the junta of the successful officers, styling itself the Supreme Council for National Reconstruction. After seizing power it lost no time in suspending the constitution and ruling by decree.

In Turkey (1960–61) the pattern was different. Indeed it was quite complex, and in this respect vividly illustrates the point we made at the beginning of this chapter – the fluidity of institutions, the mingling of *de jure* and *de facto* elements which make the description of the military régimes so contingent, if not subjective, a process. The coup leaders established themselves as a 'Committee of National Union', consisting of 38 officers (later reduced to 22). This Committee forthwith set up a cabinet consisting of 15 civilians and 3 army officers, nominating its leader, General Gürsel, as Head of State, Prime Minister and Minister of Defence. Press reports make it quite clear that all major decisions were taken by the Committee of National Union. For instance it was the Committee that drafted the provisional constitution; and this, it should be noted, gave it power to control and if necessary dismiss the cabinet.[10] The Committee was the organ that gave the government the directive on which it was to base its plans for the country's future;[11] which dismissed the 157 professors; which enforced residence on the 55 feudal landowners; and which, above all, insisted on the Yassiada trials of the Democratic ministers and deputies.

But another complexity emerged later, when the time came to consider the new constitution which the Committe had always promised. This was considered by a Constituent Assembly (nominated, but containing a high proportion of party politicians), but *jointly* with the Committee which appears to have exercised not only a right to initiate proposals but also a right of veto. A further complication only appeared in June 1961, a year after the initial seizure of power. Members of the Committee were not permitted to hold direct army commands. In June the Committee tried to get rid of the air force chief, General Tansel, by sending him on a mission to Washington, whereupon there was a 'sort of rebellion, in the air force' (including the 'buzzing' of Ankara with low-flying jet aircraft) which forced the Committee to reverse its decision. Evidently the active military command was, by now, an autonomous power in the *ad hoc* régime established by the coup of 1960. *The Times* correspondent significantly reported that there had been a growing breach in recent months between the High

10. *The Times*, 14 June 1960.   11. *The Times*, 12 September 1960.

Command of the armed forces and the National Unity Committee. The former resented the Committee's interference with military appointments, and, more generally, was dissatisfied with its conduct of the nation's affairs since the *coup d'état*.[12] In September *The Times* reported: 'The Army has lately moved more into political focus and has to a large extent taken over the running of the country during the critical period of the [Yassiada] trial, verdicts and elections. The power of the 22-man Junta, not to mention the purely nominal 18-man civilian Government, has relatively declined. For example, the whole Government and a large part of the Junta were known to have opposed the executions of the former leaders, but when the judgments came to be confirmed, the Army and the Air Force insisted on a minimum of three death sentences being carried out . . .'[13]

Later in October, another report explained: 'For some months it has been clear that the real rulers in Turkey have not been in the Junta, who are powerless and partly discredited, but a secret cabal of some two hundred officers in the armed forces known as the *Ordu surasi* (the council of the army). This powerful body is said to include the chiefs of the air and naval staffs, and to have the patronage, though not the actual membership, of the elderly chief of the General Staff, General Cevdet Sunay. Four or five extremist members of the Junta are also in it, and it is said to have highly-placed civilian members in the ministries. It was primarily *Ordu surasi* which insisted on the execution of Mr Menderes, Mr Zorlu and Mr Polatkin. . . .'[14]

Before concluding, it is worth while to draw attention to one institutional distinction that does occur among this type of régime. It will have been noticed that in some cases the nominal as well as the effective government lies with a military individual or junta of individuals. Thus in South Korea, or in the Primo de Rivera case or that of the Venezuelan military régime between 1948 and 1952, both nominal and effective power rests in the hands of a military individual or group. In other cases, however, while effective power resides with a revolutionary junta of officers, the nominal power (or possibly administrative power) lies with some other especially constituted body. Thus after the Egyptian coup of 1952 (which we shall discuss in some detail below), effective policy-making power resided in the Officers' Revolutionary Council, which instructed the cabinet (and even, for some time, the nominal Revolutionary military leader, General Neguib). The Turkish case already described provides another example. In the Sudan, effective government resides in the Supreme

12. *The Times*, loc. cit.   13. *The Times*, 21 September 1961.
14. 'A Vote against Kemalism', *Economist*, 21 October 1961, p. 233.

Council of the armed forces, composed of 12 officers; and this has nominated a Council of Ministers, 7 of whom are on the Supreme Council while 5 are civilians.

Direct military rule in its brute form, unjustified by any other principles than its own success and its vague promises to do well by the people, is a short-lived form of rule. It often pretends that it is transitional – a provisional form about to lead to something else. And, in a sense, this claim is true – willy-nilly. Such régimes *are* transitional. In some cases, as in Argentina after 1945, they recede to a dual type of régime, or (as after 1955) to a form of indirect rule. In others, however, where circumstances or the ambition of the victorious soldiery dictate that the power they have won shall not be laid aside, the military junta seeks some endorsement of popular approval; and the régime thereby moves *forward* to a quasi-civilianized type of régime. The military still rule; but they clothe themselves with the evidences of civilian support.

The reasons they do so have already been recognized. They are implicit in all that has gone before; legitimacy breeds power. Even a mock legitimacy is more compulsive to citizens than that flagrant absence of any right to rule that inheres in the sword. Other reasons creep in, to be sure, particularly in those countries of the fourth and lowest order of political legitimacy like Haiti, the Congo and Paraguay where it little helps or hinders a government's hold on the populace whether it be regarded by them as legitimate or not. The need of such régimes for diplomatic recognition may be a compelling factor; likewise the ruling junta's desire to be on all fours with the constitutionally based governments with whom it has contacts and whom it fears and envies. There is, in the comity of established governments, something second class, parvenu, about an *ad hoc* or provisional régime. Hence such governments seek, as they put it, to 'regularize' the situation. But the chief motive is the internal importance of establishing a claim to govern. In the first place, they slam the door of illegality in the face of rivals seeking power by the same means as the government has acquired it. In the second place, they do, or at least may, win over a section of civilian sentiment to that feeling of habitual obedience owed to a legal and lawful superior which is the bedrock of any governmental stability.

Sometimes the process of quasi-civilization is a simple endorsement by the electorate. Then the military can claim to be the elected choice of the people. Often it goes further with the creation of all manner of what purport to be organs of democratic self-expression. Whether one or the other or both, they all have the same object: to hoodwink the native population and bamboozle the world. Their success in the latter object is remarkable.

The Latin Americans, whose experience of such endeavours is longer than that of the Arabs and the Asians, and whose political sophistication (or cynicism) is considerably more developed, have, in their usual way, developed a special vocabulary for the processes of simulating popular support. They talk of *continuismo* – the tacit setting aside of the expiry of the constitutional term of office; of *imposicion* – the government, like Nasser's, 'imposing' its candidate or its party and then arranging for these to be elected. And there is *candidato unico* – seeing to it that, one way or the other, the official candidate shall have nobody to contend with. We have already seen the operation of the *candidato unico* in Paraguay for the last dozen elections. But Paraguay ought not to be singled out by the finger of scorn. In the Egyptian presidential election Colonel Nasser was the *candidato unico* also.

The various modes by which direct military rule is tricked out in the regalia of legitimacy and civil affection are best explained, however, by looking at a number of direct military régimes and observing the steps they took. Peru (1948–56) provides a fine clear case of *candidato unico*. In 1948, General Odría overthrew the lawful elected government and made himself autocrat with an all-military cabinet. The press was censored, constitutional guarantees of freedom suspended, and the death penalty imposed for 'political crimes'. Congress was prorogued. But at the same time the régime was passed off as provisional – for General Odría promised elections 'at an early date'. After two years of this, the General resigned in favour of his Vice-President in order to stand as Presidential candidate. (Such nicety, in view of what was to happen!) Since the only really powerful opposition party, the A.P.R.A., was proscribed, General Odría found himself with only one electoral opponent – the General Ernesto Montagne. But Montagne's nomination papers were declared fraudulent and his candidature rendered void, and General Odría was returned unopposed by an 80 per cent poll. Thenceforth he governed Peru as its constitutional President, with a docile Congress and a cabinet half of whose members were military.

The régime of General Rojas Pinilla, in Colombia, was much less orthodox. Rojas had seized power[15] amid the enthusiasm of the populace who were sick of the *machetismo* in the hinterlands and looked to Rojas to pacify the two sides. Rojas quickly developed his own creative ambitions, however, and became increasingly radical, grandiose and oppressive. From

15. See p. 141.

beginning to end his rule was based on the army and he fell when, appalled at the popular insurrection which raged against him in May 1957, the army withdrew its support and told him he must resign. Rojas tolerated a legislature but this was a Constituent Assembly selected for a special purpose, so in 1957 he created another and subservient one. His cabinet certainly contained civilians but he, as President and head of the cabinet, maintained that he was responsible only to the armed forces, and he dubbed his régime 'the Government of the People and the Armed Forces'. Rojas made no serious attempt to create his own civilian backing (as Perón did) and he tolerated the existence of the traditional and the powerful Liberal and Conservative parties. In this he really had no alternative, for these parties, exceptionally for Latin America, were thoroughly rooted in popular life. Rojas did realize, however, that the régime looked increasingly naked, and in 1956 he began to talk about something he styled a 'Third Force'. However, nobody knew or knows to this day whether this meant 'Army and People', or whether it presaged the foundation of an official party. This was a very odd régime, and only Rojas's concession to such legitimizing devices as his legislature, and his notions of 'Third Force' and so forth would place it in this quasi-civilian category. If one decides that such trappings were too insignificant to be rated, it might be better to regard this as a direct, unqualified military régime.

The way by which the Primo de Rivera régime of Spain 'civilianized' itself was a mysterious plebiscite. In 1925 de Rivera replaced the all-military directorate with which he had governed since 1923 by one made up of civilians. Next year he held a four-day plebiscite which gathered 6,700,000 votes – recorded by whom, and how many by each voter has never been made clear.[16] In 1927 he created a Supreme National Assembly, purportedly to 'represent all classes and interests'. Not surprisingly, it was nominated by the dictator. It met for twenty-four hours in each month and was advisory only. Primo de Rivera also created the Patriotic Union of 'good citizens', who carried out monster demonstrations in favour of the régime. The whole of this was so much flim-flam and disappeared like a bubble in 1930 when the army expressed its non-confidence in the dictator, and power silently slipped from him to General Berenguer.

The whole of this farce resembles what has happened in Egypt since 1952, but as Egypt is particularly relevant to another aspect of the military régimes, it will be described below. As a concluding example of the quasi-civilianization of a direct military régime, we shall therefore take the Jiménez dictatorship in Venezuela. After seizing power in 1948 the military

16. Madariaga, op. cit.

junta suppressed the Accion Democratica Party but permitted the C.O.P.E.I. (Christian Democrat) and U.R.D. parties to continue. As already explained, the régime was an unqalified military oligarchy. Three years later, however, the junta decided to 'constitutionalize' it. Why? Opinions differ. Some say that Jiménez wanted Caracas to be the site of the Pan-American conference, others that certain oil contracts were being held up until a constitutional government came into existence. In any event, Jiménez decided that his army government would seek endorsement from the people. To this end the Accion Democratica remained under proscription, civil liberties were 'regulated'; and, above all, any political parties seeking to contest the election had to be licensed by the authorities – a process which involved police surveillance over the whole of their overt activities.

The government now created its own party, the F.E.I. (Frente Electoral Independente), a new body designed to bring about 'a massive adhesion to the national army and Colonel Jiménez'.[17]

The elections took place in freedom and secrecy and with no disorders on 30 November 1952. They were to establish a Constituent Assembly to revise the constitution: but as this Constituent Assembly was also to designate the provisional President the elections took on the aspect of a Presidential race. By the end of the first scrutiny it became clear that the proscribed Accion Democratica vote was being cast for the other and constitutional parties but against the government-sponsored F.E.I. The first broadcast returns showed U.R.D. with 54 per cent, C.O.P.E.I. with 15 per cent and the F.E.I. with only 25 per cent. At this point the broadcasts stopped abruptly. Perez Jiménez dissolved the military junta and with the endorsements of the chiefs of the six distinct sections of the armed forces, proclaimed himself provisional President. His *apologia* is worthy of record. 'Although it is true,' he broadcast, 'that the basic factor of the Republic is the normal evolution of constitutional life – yet what is also certain is that the accomplishment of the national well-being which will give Venezuela the grandeur she deserves stands higher than this.'[18] After a brief but very effective repression, only 71 deputies of the Constituent Assembly remained free to convene. Indeed the true number is really 50, since 21 of those who attended were 'candidate' members. Both the U.R.D. and the C.O.P.E.I. members were absent. The Constituent was a mere rump. It was this body that endorsed Perez Jiménez as Provisional President.

But now, according to the Constitution, the government should proceed

17. Bétancourt, op. cit., p. 554; cf. L. B. Lott, 'The 1952 Venezuelan Elections' (*Western Political Quaterly*, vol. X, no. 3, pp. 541–59).

18. Bétancourt, op. cit., p. 558.

with the municipal, the Congressional and the (true) Presidential elections. Instead, in the words of Romulo 'Bétancourt, 'the usurpation pretended to constitutionalize itself, for itself, and by itself, in April 1953, through one of the most cynical displays of contempt for the norms of representative government recorded in American history.'[19] *This rump and servile Constituent Assembly itself* nominated the members of the national Congress; the Deputies of the State Assemblies; the councillors for some hundreds of local government areas; the judges of the Supreme Court; the Procurador General; and, finally, of course, Perez Jiménez as the constitutional (no longer provisional) President of the Republic!

Dynamics of the military régimes

Commonly, the form taken by the military régime in a given country does not stand still. It is usual for one type of régime to change into another. Now these changes do not tend to take place among the types we have classified in any arbitrary fashion, but almost as though these types represented a kind of scale or spectrum and the changes took place up or down it. This is not altogether surprising because, roughly speaking, the scale runs parallel with the depth of military intervention.

The table

> Indirect: limited
> Indirect: complete
> Dual
> Direct
> Direct, quasi-civilianized

corresponds broadly to covert intervention, then overt intervention, then the supplantment of the civilian régime, and – in its final manifestation – the intent to perpetuate and institutionalize this supplantment. With quasi-civilianization the régime moves out of the realm of the provisional, and purports to be a régime in its own right.

It is, therefore, very common to find 'runs' or 'sequences' of régimes, up and down the 'scale' represented by this table of régimes. These runs or sequences occur as the military decide to seek increasing control of the situation (e.g. Syria, Egypt) or, alternatively, appalled at their embroilment and fearful of the wrath to come (Argentina, Turkey), to disengage from politics. Consider Argentina, for instance. Here the indirect-limited rule of the pre-1943 period was succeeded by the Rawson–Ramirez–Farrell régime of direct rule (1943–45); this (marking the beginning of the military retreat)

19. ibid. Cf. *Time*, 16 April 1953.

by the dual régime of Perón (1945–55); and this, finally, by the present period of indirect limited rule under the provisional Presidents Lonardi and Aramburu, then President Frondizi and now provisional President Guido. Or consider Venezuela: first the period of direct military rule up to 1945, shattered by the cuartelazo of 1945 and the establishment of the indirect-limited rule of the soldiers under the Accion Democratica government, 1945–8: this, in turn, was followed by a reversion to direct military rule by Perez Jiménez (1948–52), and this, again, by a quasi-civilianized régime (1952–8). Then came a sharp break when the military decided to disentangle themselves from the régime. Their feelings were partly occasioned by the quite formidable underground civilian opposition to the constitutional President, which broke out into open disturbances after the grotesque 'plebiscite' which purportedly re-elected Jiménez in 1957; partly due to their dislike of the unpopularity accruing to them for having to repress such disturbances; but also, and very significantly, because the 'quasi-civilianized' régime had tended to erode its connection with the armed forces and to rely increasingly upon a secret police. Romulo Bétancourt, when in exile, quite prophetically pointed out this feature as early as 1956. The first reaction of the armed forces to the public disturbances was (successfully) to demand the exile of the Chief of the *Seguridad* and of the Minister of the Interior. When the disturbances continued, however, the leaders of the armed forces decided to disengage. They withdrew their support from Perez Jiménez and returned to the régime of indirect-limited rule (1958 to the present).

Syria provides an enlightening sequence, in so far as it illustrates how the armed forces, having taken the first overt step to interfere with civilian processes may be compelled to go further and further until at the end they must themselves become the government. The elections of December 1949 returned a Chamber favourable to the much-canvassed union with Iraq. That very night Colonel Shishakli carried out a *coup d'état*, and imposed a cabinet of his own choosing. This heralded the first phase of army rule, that of *indirect-complete* rule. Cabinets were formed by a number of politicians but, as Dr Ziadeh puts it, 'Cabinets governed the country but all knew the army ruled'.[20] In November 1951, however, a new cabinet, formed under Dr Dawalibi, refused to be a puppet and looked suddenly dangerous to army interest.[21] Colonel Shishakli struck again, thus ushering

20. A. Ziadeh, *Syria and the Lebanon*, p. 112.

21. It was deemed to be favourable to the union with Iraq and, more immediately, it was said it was about to transfer the *gendarmerie* from the army to the civil authorities. The *gendarmerie* controlled the elections.

in the second régime, that of *direct* military rule. As Chief of the General Staff he headed a military junta styled the Supreme Military Council – of a type familiar enough by now. In this capacity he forced the President of the Republic and the Prime Minister to resign and appointed his familiar, one Colonel Selo (Minister of Defence and spokesman for the army in the preceding cabinets), as Head of State, Prime Minister and Minister of Defence. Colonel Selo in his turn appointed an all-civilian cabinet, but this took orders openly from the Chief of the General Staff, Colonel Shishakli.[22] This period of direct military rule is drearily familiar, resembling those already described. The Chamber was dissolved, the courts and civil service purged, the political parties suppressed.

This régime now gave way to the third type, the *quasi-civilianized* régime. The manner in which this was brought about shows, parenthetically, how little the civilian cabinet and how much the armed forces counted for. For General Shishakli,[23] *qua* 'President of the Supreme Military Council', sent the draft of the new constitution to Colonel Selo as Head of State and Prime Minister, and asked his cabinet to hold a referendum on the draft; which they did.

This ushered in the quasi-civilianized military régime. Shishakli had now formed his own party, the Arab Liberation Party. This was the sole party fighting the election and Shishakli was the sole candidate for President. Needless to say the constitution was approved and Shishakli was elected President. His 'constitutional' régime lasted only till February 1954. In the course of 'civilianizing' his régime he had lost contact with the conspiracies in the army. His military enemies now overthrew him and the system reverted back to the *indirect-limited* régimes (1954–8) in which Colonel Serraj was to distinguish himself as already described, then to Egyptian domination (1958–61) until it returned again to indirect-limited government (1961–2).

However, no example equals that of the Egyptian régime either for the completeness of the stages it has passed through, or the ordered logic of their sequence and the light it throws on the compulsions of the military. For the Egyptian officers did not conspire to supplant the civilian régime at all. They were much too unselfconfident for that. They set out to *displace* the government, and replace it by a nobler one; but appetite grew by what it fed on, and they were led, month in and month out, down our table of régimes until they ended up as the new governing class, ruling behind a screen of civilian forms. In the course of this, too, they made a true revolution,

22. A pattern similar to that of the Sudan under General Abboud today.
23. Shishakli had by this date promoted himself to the rank of Brigadier-General.

both in the sense of altering the balance of social classes and of nationalizing or controlling the economy, but also in that they completely set aside and indeed destroyed the former ruling class, and set themselves in its place. This example is a model. The Argentine, Venezuelan and Syrian cases have shown a limited number of transitions, in each case followed by a decisive retraction from overt power. The Egyptian case illustrates the military moving down the whole spectrum of forms of régime, and, for the moment, stabilizing itself in the quasi-civilianized type.

Initially, the Free Officers' conspiracy had neither intended nor expected to govern. Neguib declared that 'our movement has nothing to do with politics',[24] and Nasser himself thought of the officers as a 'commando vanguard'; that once he and his associates had purged the bad elements, 'good politicians' would run the country. Therefore the first thing the victorious plotters did was to engineer the downfall of the cabinet and ensure the installation of Ali Maher as Prime Minister; and the second thing, to secure the abdication of King Farouk. Thus began, on 23 July 1952, phase one – the régime of *indirect-limited rule*. Ali Maher chose his own cabinet. For their part, the Free Officers established an Executive Committee. It intervened to secure certain conditions; for instance, it secured rises in military pay and it established a special military court to try the leaders of the Kafr el Dawar cotton-mill riots. But it was unable to get Ali Maher to enact its cherished land-reform law, and it came up against increasing resistance from the old style politicians, e.g. Nahas Pasha and the Wafd, and from the Moslem Brotherhood.

From between some time in August and September, the control exerted by the Executive Committee of the Free Officers became increasingly complete, exemplified in such incidents as their arrest (7 September) of forty-three of the older politicians. This transitional period may be regarded as the second phase – that of *indirect-complete rule* by the soldiers and it led on 7 September to a formal change in the institutional arrangements which ushered in dual rule. Ali Maher was dismissed. In his stead, General Neguib, the Chairman of the Free Officers' Committee, also became the Prime Minister of an all-civilian cabinet. In his Pooh-Bah capacities as Prime Minister, Minister of War and Marine, Commander-in-Chief and Military Governor of Egypt, Neguib's power now rested on two pillars, the military and the civilian. The reality of the military component may be attested by the decision of 30 September whereby each government department was afforced by thirty officers, 'to supply these with progressive administrative elements and to ensure close co-ordination of army policy

24. Wheelock, op. cit., p. 12.

and administrative action'.[25] The reality of the civilian component was no less. The deputy Premier and Minister of the Interior was Soliman Hafez, an opponent of the Wafd, and the cabinet was supported also by an anti-Nahas faction of the Wafd, led by Fahmi Gomaa. Four cabinet ministers, besides, formed a new political 'party'.

This *dual régime* found itself – indeed thrust itself – into a struggle with the two most powerfully organized segments of public opinion – the Moslem Brotherhood and the Wafd. On 10 December 1952 the strain proved too much. The army, determined now to be master, jettisoned their civilian allies and moved into the fourth phase of *direct military rule*. On 9 December practically all the politicians were dismissed from the cabinet and replaced by civil servants, and on 10 December General Neguib announced that the 1923 Constitution to which lip service had hitherto been paid was abrogated. Authority, he proclaimed, had now passed to a 'transitional government'.

The succeeding moves conform to the same dismal pattern of overt military rule which we have described for other countries such as Argentina. All political parties were abolished and their funds seized. Politically insecure officers (e.g. Mohanna) were arrested. Former ministers were indicted before special courts. There was no need to make special provision for the suspension of individual guarantees as the country had been under martial law since before the revolution. Institutionally, important changes were made. The whole authority for government was transferred to a newly created Revolutionary Command Council (the R.C.C.) which was composed entirely of members of the Executive Committee of the Free officers. A three-year transition period was announced before 'constitutional government' would be resumed. In the meantime, 'the Leader of the Revolution will exercise the power of supreme sovereignty. . . . [His] powers will apply to the right of appointing and dismissing ministers who will have executive authority in their respective spheres of work: and the R.C.C. and the Council of Ministers will form a Congress which will discuss the general policy of the State'.[26] In practice the final authority rested with the R.C.C. which had a weekly session with the civilian ministers.

This period of rule lasted as had been decreed until January 1956, i.e. for three years. During that time, however, the Officers' movement was forced to its critical decision: was it going to rule the country, or was it going to disengage? As we have seen, the Argentine army, twice faced with this decision – in 1930 and 1945 – was not prepared to wear down civilian

25. *Keesing's Contemporary Archives*, 1952, 12537B.
26. 10 February 1952, *Keesing's Contemporary Archives*, 1952, 12846A.

resistance and remain in power. Instead it disengaged and returned to indirect rule. The Turkish army was faced with the same decision in 1961 and made a similar judgement. In the R.C.C., the desire to disengage came from General Neguib, and the determination to hold on, to become a new ruling class, was held by Nasser. A first attempt to oust Neguib, on 28 February 1954, failed and for the succeeding month preparations went ahead for elections and a return to legitimacy. On 28 March all this was reversed. A classic golpe de estado was effected; Neguib was seized and later demoted, and the decision to maintain power reaffirmed. Nasser became Prime Minister in a cabinet of a different type. Henceforth *all* members of the R.C.C. were cabinet ministers.

The '*Gleichschaltung*' of civilian life continued. Nasser emerged undisputed master, with the army purged, the civilian organizations destroyed, the universities stifled, the Wafd and Moslem Brotherhood both shattered and all political parties banned.

The direct military régime of Nasser passed into its final phase, that of *quasi-civilianization*, in 1956. This was the end of the 'transitional' period, as had been promised. A set of bogus institutions was offered – bogus because they were mere emanations, ancillaries of the army. On 16 January 1956 a new constitution was offered the country, a constitution with a powerful President and a comparatively feeble but elected Assembly. This was submitted to a plebiscite in June. No other parties than the official 'National Union' were permitted. The plebiscite showed that Colonel Nasser (nominated for President by the R.C.C.) was 0·1 per cent more popular than the constitution. He received 99·9 per cent of the votes and the constitution only 99·8 per cent.

Thereafter the R.C.C. was dissolved, and all cabinet ministers who had been officers had to drop their titles (except of course the Commander-in-Chief). The régime had to show itself civilianized. How genuine that civilianization was may be gleaned from the following: there are no independent parties, only an official organization, the National Union, the creature of the government. The National Assembly was an appointive body, handpicked by President Nasser.[27] The press is nationalized, and entirely government-controlled. The government, then, is Colonel Nasser and his handpicked circle of assistants, almost entirely military. The basis of the government is the army which has done well, socially and financially,

27. It has since been dissolved, pending a new constitution. The Assembly did show some independence and boldness. It also did useful work in revising Bills that came before it. But it had no standing in high policy matters, of course, and no means of bringing pressure on the President who created it.

as well as politically, out of the régime. The institutions are so much flim-flam to conceal the elemental truth: that this is still military rule, albeit with fancy trappings.[28]

The return to the barracks: (1) abdication

Overt rule by the military, whether direct or quasi-civilianized, raises two further questions. The first of these is: what induces the military to terminate their rule? The second is whether and how far it is possible for a military régime, starting with quasi-civilian institutions, to proceed to give real life to these and ultimately to re-civilianize itself.

In either case two facts must always be borne in mind. In all countries of the fourth (minimal) order of political culture, as in a great majority of those of the third order, the military is so strong *vis-à-vis* the civilians that it tends to lose little of its significance by substituting indirect for direct rule. Secondly, in such countries – particularly those with weak civilian bases such as Syria, Thailand, Paraguay – the usual consequence of the fall of one military régime is the immediate installation of another.

The cases we have to consider, therefore, are those of such third-order states as Argentina, Colombia, Venezuela in South America; Egypt, Pakistan, Syria and Iraq in Asia. Immediately a difficulty appears. The direct or quasi-civilianized military régimes which have collapsed in the near past and so afford a basis for generalization are all Latin American: to be precise those of Perón (1955), Odría (1956), Rojas Pinilla (1957) and Perez Jiménez (1958). The Asian régimes are still in being[29] and one of them, Nasser's, will shortly be ten years old. Thus the basis of our experience is very narrow. It has also to be said that, however tenuous the information about the conspiratorial cells and organizations that planned the military supplantment of civilian rule, such as the G.O.U. in Argentina or the Free Officers in Egypt,[30] there is far far less known about the conspiracies, the methods, or the motives of the military men who decide the *return* to civilian rule, and so bring the overt rule of the military to an end. In fact we know next to nothing of this. Nobody prominent in such enterprises has vouchsafed to write his memoirs.

28. This is not to say that Colonel Nasser or even the régime is not popular. I think it is. The point is it does not, or dare not, *depend* on its popularity for its continuance. It depends on the armed forces, and accepts public popularity as a kind of bonus.

29. Ayub Khan's direct-military rule has given way to the new constitution since these lines were written. It is too early to say whether this marks genuine abdication by the military, or whether it is not a mere quasi-civilianization of military rule. If Professor Newman's strictures on the Constitution ('Democracy under Control', *The Times*, 16 March 1962) are correct, it is the latter. I am, at present, strongly inclined to take this view.

30. See pp. 32; 57–8.

On the basis of the limited evidence which is all that is available, it appears as though the 'return to the barracks' – what we have called the military's 'disengagement' from overt rule – occurs through the cumulation of three conditions: the disintegration of the original conspiratorial group, the growing divergence of interests between the junta of rulers and those military who remain as active heads of the fighting services, and the political difficulties of the régime.

When a cuartelazo has been successful and the civilians have been thrust off-stage as in South Korea or the Sudan, it still remains true that the 'military' as such cannot rule, but only a handful of them. An individual, or a junta, installs himself in power in the name of the armed forces, and is immediately faced with the problem of guaranteeing their loyalty, a loyalty weakened by the example of subversion which they have just learned. The bulk of the armed forces, i.e. those not called on to govern, are treated to a vigorous regiment of rewards and punishments. Some part of the reward is corporate: better pay for all ranks, perhaps certain tax-free privileges, new equipment and the like. For instance, in Paraguay, after the coup of 1954, the military budget rose to 50 per cent of the total; in Argentina, during the 1943–5 period (when the G.O.U. were in full command), the military appropriations for 1944 were double those for the preceding years, and in 1945 were larger than the entire rest of the government budget for that year. Or again, as in Egypt, one of the first actions of the victorious junta was to raise army pay. The arms trade with Russia which the Arab military régimes, e.g. Egypt, Syria, Iraq, have pursued, is one of the consequences of the military régime which requires the ruling junta to give the military new and expensive material to play with, material which the West has been too slow to deliver. Certain aspects of industrialization are also part of the huge mass bribe which is necessary to hold the loyalty of the military: e.g. the exploitation of the oil-fields in Argentina, which, as far as the military are concerned, must be developed even without benefit of foreign capital; or the armament factories which President Nasser has established in Egypt and which he now proposes to develop until they are capable of turning out heavy equipment.

At the same time the military junta hands out governorships, senior administrative posts, comptrollerships of various kinds, ambassadorships, not to speak of the top policy-making posts. For those of reliable political opinions, promotions are rapid. Political intervention, once it has occurred, breaches the former political neutrality of the armed services. The ruling junta, therefore, must, of dire necessity, ensure that the key commanders are well-affected.

Simultaneously with the rewards go the punishments. The numbers of officers purged by the ruling junta is often very high. The numbers purged by General Gürsel appear to have risen to 7,000. The numbers purged in Egypt between 1952 and 1954 alone are, to public knowledge, some 500 – the full figure is probably higher.[31] At the same time, a secret-police system has to be organized throughout the armed forces. In the Venezuela of Perez Jiménez, for instance, it was not long before the armed forces had become insignificant compared with the *Seguridad Nacional* under Estrada. This controlled all the mainsprings of the state, and, in Bétancourt's words, the army became 'a virtual prisoner of the vast apparatus of espionage, delation, tortures and assassinations created by the political police. What began as an instrument to terrorize the civil population has finished by investing the very cadres of the officer corps, in the army, the navy and the air force and the National Guard.' 'Venezuela,' he said, 'suffers the rigours of a régime which continues to talk in the name of the armed forces but which in reality governs and despotizes over the country with the almost solitary support of a hypertrophied Himmler-like police.'[32]

Such, then, are the positive policies the ruling junta tend to pursue to secure their rule, and, thereby, the overt rule of the military. The first of the three weaknesses that tends to develop in this situation is the disintegration of the ruling group – not necessarily the junta, though this often does disintegrate, but the wider circle of officers which have borne it to power. Parenthetically we may remark that nothing is more natural, nothing more to be expected. It is difficult enough for civilian cabinets not to disintegrate, and the Praesidium of the Communist Party of the Soviet Union is from time to time cleft into ferocious factions. The military conspirators seize power with considerably less in the way of common policy or ideology than these civilians. Furthermore, the way in which they have come to power is by treason and violence; for one faction to oppose its opponents by these means is just as valid as the way in which both in alliance originally seized power. The military junta, quasi-civilianize itself how it will, has the lie in the soul. It suffers from the vice of origin. So it is that practically every successful act of military supplantment has been succeeded by a struggle among the victorious conspirators. In Egypt, after 1952, Mohanna, one of the Free Officers, had to be cast out because he supported the Moslem Brotherhood, then Neguib and his supporters such

---

31. 25 September 1952: 450 dismissed; 16 January 1953: 16 tried and dismissed; 6–22 June 1954: 15 tried and imprisoned.

32. Bétancourt, op. cit., p. 572. The first reaction of the army to the popular outbreaks which shook the régime in late 1957 and early 1958 was, significantly, to demand and secure the dismissal and exile of Estrada, head of the Seguridad. See p. 168.

as Mohieddin were defeated and purged in their turn. In the Argentine (1943), the G.O.U. first put up the War Minister Ramírez, as provisional President, then withdrew him for General Rawson and finally reinstalled Ramírez. When Ramírez, bowing to necessities, decided it was necessary to sever relations with the Axis, the G.O.U. decided to depose him and did, substituting General Farrell. Then, anxious at Perón's rapid rise – though he had been in the forefront of the deposition of Ramírez – they imprisoned him and only released him from fear of the *descamisados*, and because by then (15 October 1945) they had run out of ideas and leaders. Likewise, after the overthrow of Perón in 1955, it was only a matter of weeks before General Lonardi, who wanted to conciliate the ex-Peronistas, was made to resign in favour of General Aramburu who favoured a tough line. In Venezuela, after the cuartelazo of 1948, there was the rivalry between Colonel Chalbaud and Colonel Jiménez, ended by the murder, in mysterious circumstances, of the former: in Guatemala, the rivalry between Colonel Arana and Major Arbenz – likewise terminated by the mysterious murder of the former. Turkey, since May 1960, saw first the collision between General Gürsel, the Head of State, and the right-wing radical group led by Alparslan Türkes, and then, in 1961, a further collision between General Gürsel and the anti-Türkes group, led by General Madanoglu.

Policy differences are not the whole story. Although this is more difficult to prove, for obvious reasons, there is no doubt at all that purely personal rivalries often play a profound part in disintegrating the ruling military group. And this again is very natural. These officers have all been at the Military Academy together, have worked in the same offices, taken part in the same exercises; they have in fact formed part of a closed society all their working lives. The temptation for any number of them to say that General X, who is now the provisional president, is a blockhead is overwhelming; the temptation to say it of *Major* this or *Colonel* that, no more exalted in rank than oneself and yet now the Head of State, is far more compelling and embittering.

In summary: the 'ruling group' of the military, i.e. those who take over the government of the country after the cuartelazo, tends to disintegrate. In addition, however, a gulf tends to open between this governing group of the officers and those who remain behind in active command of the armed forces. We have already parenthetically cited a most recent and dramatic case of this: the refusal of the Turkish air force to obey the orders of the National Unity Committee in the matter of General Tansel's posting overseas, the general grievance of the active service commanders at the 'interference' of the National Unity Committee: i.e. at the twenty-two officers who participated in the cuartelazo and were then running the country, and, finally, their clash with the National Unity Committee on the issue of executing Menderes.[33]

Past experience shows that it is very rare for the leader of the military conspiracy to retain for long the loyalty both of the country at large and of the armed forces. Men like Kemal Atatürk have been able to do it, but the majority of the leaders thrown up by military revolts are very inferior in calibre compared to him; and indeed, to be truthful, by any world standard of statesmanship.

The new, ex-military rulers, it seems, find it increasingly hard to govern the country and yet, at the same time, to retain their former grip on the armed forces. In the first place, they may be tempted to lean on civilian support, and this is apt to rouse the jealousy of the armed forces. The military's opposition to Perón sprang partly from their resentment at this alliance with the labour movement; the same thing is true of the Guatemalan army's opposition to Major Arbenz. Secondly, the ex-military ruler often takes decisions which appear politically compelling to him in his position of ruler, but which offend the soldiers who continue to react with a blind impatience. General Ramírez of Argentina, for instance, finally recognized that he must break off diplomatic relations with the Axis; but the G.O.U. would not forgive him and removed him for General Farrell. Thirdly, it would appear – the direct evidence is limited – that as the ex-military ruler becomes immersed in politics and administration, he loses touch with military politics; his rivals edge themselves into key positions, then form private understandings with one another for self-protection or self-advancement; and all this takes place clandestinely. The arts the ex-military dictator used to attain his pre-eminence are available to those left behind in active command positions. It is rare to find an ex-military ruler like Batista, who was able to maintain the affection of the armed forces eight clear years after he had voluntarily stepped down from power in 1944. Finally, the political purges and the activities of the security police annoy the armed forces and may well be more effective in arousing resentment against the ex-military ruler who relies on these methods than in maintaining loyalty. As we have seen, the activities of the security police were one of the armed forces' grievances against Jiménez in Venezuela; and in Turkey General Gürsel and his Committee of National Union were very exercised indeed by the activities of the 7,000 or so officers whom they had dismissed.

33. See p. 162.

Weakened by the disintegration of the original faction, and with the civil–military tension beginning to accumulate once more, these new and ex-military rulers are in no position to meet any serious political opposition. Their régimes are suppressive, not totalitarian. They do not, as the people's democracies do, inculcate a positive philosophy of the régime throughout every walk of life. They do not, as the people's democracies do, absorb to themselves every interest, association and institution of social life. Even in Perón's Argentina, which among such régimes had gone furthest towards totalitarianism, society was highly pluralistic by Soviet standards. In none of these régimes has private industry been abolished;[34] in many of them the political parties, or the less innocuous of them, were permitted to operate; and even in Peru and Venezuela where the mass parties (A.P.R.A. and A.D.) were illegalized, they maintained a successful moral hold over the masses. The military governments have been, as it were, simply superimposed on the top of these elements. Thus the conditions have been present for demonstrations and for dislocations of civil life which, though easily suppressible by a united and resolute soldiery, might well serve to make an impression upon a régime where the original conspirators are at loggerheads and where the rulers and the military have once more begun to drift apart. Add to this the fact that few of the military dictators or military juntas seem to have much political capacity. It is like the occasion when somebody complained to Victor Hugo that his cook, who was also his mistress, had served a very poor meal and Hugo retorted that, after all, one could hardly expect her to be good at everything. There is no good reason why generals, colonels or majors should make good politicians and a fair number of *prima facie* reasons why they should make very bad ones. In any event, few of the now fallen dictators seem to have been very capable as politicians. Most of them, for instance Perón and Jiménez and Rojas Pinilla, were thoroughly bad economists. Most of them – Perón and Rojas Pinilla, for instance – quarrelled with the Catholic Church. In all these régimes there came a point of mass civilian protest, with the industrialists, students and the church, and sometimes the manual workers, united in joint protest. At moments like these, everything turned on the attitude of the armed forces; and the fact is that these in many cases decided suddenly to jettison their ex-leader and to relinquish open rule. In these Latin American cases, one reason is that, as far as experience shows, the armed forces are morbidly concerned with their popularity. Unlike the Spanish army, withdrawn into itself and utterly untouched by the intellectual and emotional movements of surrounding society, the military in

34. This abolition is now (1961–2) taking place in Egypt.

Argentina, Colombia, Peru and Venezuela seem to have been sensitive to such currents and these appear to have affected their resolution.

The fall of Rojas Pinilla of Colombia in 1957 illustrates the way in which an overt military régime is apt to crumble. By 1957 Pinilla had quarrelled with the businessmen. He had run up a considerable adverse balance of payments. He had quarrelled with the church; partly because he had tried to centralize all social welfare activities in the government's hand and partly because he had tried to capture the church-supported Union de Trabajadores. In May, Rojas decided to arrest Leon Valencia, the joint candidate of the united Liberal and Conservative parties. This news sparked off a student riot, and for a whole day the students demonstrated through Bogotá while police and troops looked tensely on. That night the General-President moved 35,000 troops into the city.

But resistance spread. Ex-President Camargo stepped in to organize the city's leading businessmen and bankers in a commercial strike. Next, the Primate issued a pastoral letter, not his first but certainly his bitterest attack on Rojas. This proved to be the conclusive argument for the heads of the armed forces. After a four-hour conference, they deputed the Commander-in-Chief, General Navas, to tell the President he must go. At first Rojas refused to believe it. Three hours later he was persuaded. As he broadcast his resignation to the nation, power passed to a junta established with the object of liquidating the military régime and returning the country to civilian rule.

The return to the barracks: (2) re-civilianization

A second fashion of withdrawing from the political arena is also conceivable. Could it not happen, we may ask, that these quasi-civilian organizations and institutions – these official 'parties', these official congresses or assemblies – might some day take on a life of their own? Could the régime not pass thereby from a quasi-civilianized military régime, like Egypt's, to a re-civilianized one?

What would be the criteria of such re-civilianization? Briefly, that policy decisions should be taken through these civilian organizations and by the methods peculiar to them; and that they should be taken autonomously, *proprio motu*, and not under the covert or overt dictation of the military leaders. One must not necessarily expect that the military should lack influence, perhaps a very wide influence. Nor must one necessarily demand that the régime should be an effectively representative system. It would suffice if its chief personnel, its principal policy makers, and its characteristic modes of making policy were all civilian.

179

Only two régimes of military provenance seem to fit this description: Mexico and pre-1960 Turkey. Both cases are somewhat peculiar. In the first place, the military movement that endowed them with their civilian institution was very unlike most of the movements we have been considering. All those originated as conspiracies in which the regular armed forces displaced or supplanted the civil authorities. The Mexican and Turkish cases approximate much more nearly to wars of liberation such as have been waged in Indonesia or in Algeria and the armies more nearly resembled revolutionary armies, like those of the two countries mentioned, than a normal regular standing army. This distinction is very important. Such armies tend to incorporate every active element of a nation including many which are usually regarded as the antithesis of the regular soldier, such as the intellectual, the author and the politician, just as the 'new army' that the British regulars fought hard to prevent in the 1914–18 period contained all these elements. For this reason such armies do not tend to feel the sentiments of military pride and corporate self-identity as much as the regular armies. Furthermore, as liberation armies, their ideology tends, initially at any rate, to favour popular participation in government.

In the second place, in both these cases it has taken a long time for the 're-civilization' to strike root. It is now forty-two years since Obregón became President of Mexico and the same period has elapsed since Kemal Atatürk entered the scene.

In Mexico, cuartelazos of the usual type continued down to 1938 when General Cedillo's was crushed, and it was not until 1946 that Mexico had its first civilian President (Alemán) since the Revolution. As late as 1937, the army was still recognized as dominating the situation. The occasion was President Cárdenas's experiment in giving the military official representation as one of the parts of the P.R.M.,[35] the official party. When critics protested he said: 'We have not put the army in politics. It was already there. In fact, it had been dominating the situation and we did well to reduce its influence to one vote out of four.'[36] It is in the last twenty years that re-civilization has become marked and the apparent autonomy of the military lessened.

The Mexican military are still important – indeed, vitally important – to the continuance of the régime; but in the sense that they assist the civil power, not dictate to it. Since 1929 there has been built up beside the military a vast organized bloc of civilian interests – the bureaucracy, the

35. The Party of the Mexican Revolution now the P.R.I. (Party of the Institutionalized Revolution, or of Revolutionary Institutions).

36. Lieuwen, op. cit., p. 114.

white collar and professional workers, manual labour and the peasantry: all the mass organizations in the country except two − the private capitalists and the Roman Catholic Church. This great bloc is the official party, the P.R.I. Its candidates always win; its workers always get favours; and so it has become a vast national bandwagon, on which practically everybody seeks to climb. The struggles between its bureaucratic, agrarian and labour sectors are adjusted inside the high councils. The local pork-barrels are delivered to its field workers and organizers. So vast and pervasive is this great political machine that even those who do not belong to it find their path smoothed if they do business with it; and this is true of the Mexican army today, which still represents one of the great interests which no President would fail to consult, which is closely tied in to the apparatus of Provincial government, and which still generates an enormous influence on politics. *But* it does this today inside the framework of the party, not as an external force hammering at the party. In this great civilian hive, the President is Queen Bee, even down to his prerogative of selecting his successor. This he does with an eye to all the pressures and counter-pressures in the party and with a view to selecting the candidate most likely to be able to conciliate all of these. Characteristically the Presidents are nowadays being drawn from the party apparatus or the civil administration. Cárdenas himself, albeit a general, had been President of the party's executive committee. President Alemán (1946) had, among other things, managed the election campaign of his predecessor (and selector), Avilo Camacho; President Cortines had managed the election for his predecessor (and selector), President Alemán; and President Lopèz Matéos had likewise managed the election for his predecessor (and selector) President Cortines. What could be more uncharacteristic of military institutions, what could reek more heavily of the civilian and the politician?

This system is not so much an endorsement by the military as an outgrowth of what, as late as 1929, was still a military domination of the country. The post-revolutionary period (1917–29) was characterized by a sort of half-military *caciquism*, with the former revolutionary generals each in charge of a zone or district. The formation of the P.N.R.[37] in 1929 gave a civilian colouring to this still military tenure. The key figure was the regional or State *caudillo*, who still had his revolutionary following, which, in turn, had a following among the 'popular classes'. The president (whether Obregón or Calles) was a soldier and all the regional bosses were soldiers too. The end of the '*tormento*', the period of civil war, had meant

37. The Party of the National Revolution. The name was changed in 1937 to P.R.M. (Party of the Mexican Revolution); then, in 1945, as explained above, to P.R.I.

merely that these regional and state generals were now styled Governors or Zone Commanders: from generals they became *caciques*. In 1929, General Calles convened these ex-generals and got them to fuse into a party, known then as the P.N.R. Each local machine became institutionally linked with the whole. The President, as *jefe maximo*, dealt only with his *caciques*; they in turn with their subordinates; and these, with the people. But since the *cacique* could only hold his following by granting them favours, so the demands of the population were forwarded upwards and in return services – the 'pork-barrel' – were provided downwards.

From this beginning grew today's great P.R.I. machine. Successive Presidents mobilized sectors of the civil population and brought them into the party, which soon became organized on a three-sector basis of labour, peasantry and bureaucracy. To enhance their own office they strove to perfect this machine since it held all nominations and indeed elections in its hands. It was and is a perfect mine of patronage and hence of civilian political power. In perfecting its mechanism they magnified their own power. At the same time these successive Presidents strove to de-politicize the army. The unsuccessful revolts in 1923, 1927 and 1928 helped, for they enabled the President to purge the officer corps. The vacancies were filled by younger men, professionally trained in Mexico's own military schools, or sent abroad for training.[38] By the end of the Second World War, the old 'politicals' had been largely pensioned off and the new army – much smaller than its revolutionary original of 1920 – was professionally trained.

It has taken Mexico over forty years to reach this stability. The power of civilianism has been phenomenally increased as compared with the beginning of the period, i.e. the last days of Porfirio Diaz, when indeed it would be difficult to say civilianism had any strength at all. In the first place, the last forty years have provided the public with a political formula, a legitimizing myth. This is the myth of *The Revolution*, an epic-movement which means most things to most Mexicans; and since '*c'est par le malentendu universel que tout l'univers s'entend*', this has provided a consensus unbelievable in the riven Mexico of the nineteenth century. Secondly, the official party has successfully claimed to embody this Revolution. Thirdly, and therefore, it is through the party and with the party's sanction that political decisions have become publicly acceptable. And, finally, this party is, as we have said, a huge civilian bloc. Thus at one and the same time the area of disputes over political legitimacy has been narrowed and a very powerful and extensive civilian organization to back up the institutions of governments has been created; and although nobody could claim that the

38. See Lieuwen, op. cit., Chapter 4, for the steps taken.

representative system was democratic, it is nevertheless true that government and governed are linked by material self-interest, and this is satisfied on both sides through the procedures of the party. The rank and file of the P.R.I. have little say in nominating candidates, and parties other than the P.R.I. have no chance of defeating the candidates it puts up. The higher echelons of the party make the nominations and these are tantamount to election. In all this the President has the final say.

Thus the public is not autonomous; and it may be precisely this that has most served to subordinate the military to the civil hierarchy. For an autonomous public might select a Presidential candidate (like General Mugica[39]) whom the military would not tolerate. Or it might advocate some new Santa Anna who would be opposed by powerful civilian forces, such as organized labour. Or the competition for votes between the parties might drive these to adopt policies which, once again, could open the old rift between military and civilian. Precisely because the President has to cope with the pressures within his party, and not with those of the public, he is dealing with forces under his control. All decisions are taken in the light of the balance of forces, of which the military is one of the most powerful. In Mexico, the President is able to take a considered view of alternatives instead of being committed by the mandate of the electorate, and able to conciliate rival factions in private instead of having to choose one or the other in public; it may well be that this is one of the most important of the reasons for the renascence of civilianism in Mexico.[40]

The Turkish case bears many resemblances to the Mexican. Its collapse into military interventionism in 1960 by no means signifies that the institutions planted by the military had not struck roots. Rather the reverse: they had become autonomous.

These institutions were, certainly, the endowment of the army. 'The incantatory flourish of constitution, parliament, party and election does not hide the basic fact that the Republic was established by a professional soldier leading a victorious army and maintaining himself, in the early stages at least, by a combination of personal and military power.'[41] But here, even more than in Mexico, the military took on the nature of a revolutionary army of liberation rather than the corporate viewpoint of a professional officer corps, as in the Latin American and Middle Eastern

39. A very left-wing candidate.
40. For the Mexican political system, see particularly: R. E. Scott, *Mexican Government in Transition*; I. B. Simpson, *Many Mexicos*; H. F. Cline, *The United States and Mexico*, and *Mexico, Revolution to Evolution*.
41. B. Lewis, *The Emergence of Modern Turkey*, p. 364.

examples of quasi-civilianized régimes. The army was as much the agent of the Turkish nationalist movement as its inspiration. The movement that threw out the foreigner and established the Republic was, indeed, a co-alescence of the army with the popular movements known as the 'Associations for the Rights of Anatolia and Rumelia'.[42] And the way this movement developed – in its Grand Assembly at Ankara, in contrast to the manoeuvres of the discredited puppet government of Istanbul – enhanced this representative quality. Secondly, both the army and the Assembly were in violent reaction against the intervention of the officer corps (as such) in politics and its supplantment of the civil régime.[43] For the government which had brought the country to prostration had been, since 1908, precisely that indirect-complete military régime of the Committee of Union and Progress, and Mustafa Kemal and the Assembly were strongly op-posed to the Committee's aims and methods. Thirdly, neither Assembly nor army could, even if they wanted to, stand against the towering figure of Mustafa Kemal, and Kemal quite deliberately wanted his country to become a westernized parliamentary state. He backed it with his army; and he overtopped the army itself;[44] but his ideal was not a military-dominated régime, but a parliamentary one. The great statue to him at Ankara shows him not in military uniform – he, the Ghazi! – but in western evening dress. Both he and Ismet Inönu renounced military titles; and the constitution subordinated the military to the civil power. From as early as 1909, Mustafa Kemal had opposed the mingling of military and political respon-sibilities as fatal to the strength of the army and equally fatal to the effec-tiveness of government.[45] 'To be victorious in the internal affairs of a country is due less to any army than to the successful offices of govern-ment.'[46] The Constitution of 1923, among other things, forbade Deputies to hold military office. The military were separated from the internal police and security forces: in the countryside the gendarmerie was responsible for law and order, and this was controlled by the civilian Ministry of the Interior and only came under the General Staff for routine administrative purposes. In the towns, the civilian police force likewise came under the Ministry of the Interior and had no direct relationship with the armed forces.

42. D. A. Rustow, 'The Army and the Founding of the Turkish Republic', *World Politics*, 1949, pp. 513–52; esp. p. 544.   43. ibid., pp. 545 and 549.

44. Lewis, op. cit., p. 364. See Rustow, op. cit., p. 549, for Atatürk's quarrel with, and triumph over, his fellow generals.   45. See the quotation above, p. 31.

46. Quoted, D. Lerner and R. R. Richardson, 'Swords and Ploughshares: The Turkish Army as a Modernizing Force' (*World Politics*, vol. 13, no. 1, p. 20). The article is a valuable contribu-tion to the theme discussed in the text.

Kemal's instrument of government was the party – the People's Party, and, until 1945, the sole party. This was to be the transmission belt between government and people. It was closely tied in with the state organs; for most of its life the Minister of the Interior and the party's Secretary General were the same man, and the Vali was the chairman of each Vilayet party organization. The People's Party was a true and deep-rooted organization, too, not a simple 'front' organization to give the régime the mere trappings of civilianism. It was the direct successor of the revolutionary Association for the Rights of Anatolia and Rumelia and took over its assets. It was not a party for the seizure of power but one for maintaining it. It created a nation-wide constituency organization and its local officials were, everywhere, the agents of the régime. It established People's Houses for propaganda and educational work all over Turkey and later, in 1940, set up 'People's Rooms' in the smaller towns and the villages.

This party had no rival (with two short-lived exceptions) until 1945 when some of its dissidents were permitted to form the opposition Democratic Party. Until then, and indeed until 1950 when it fell from power, the People's Party was the institution through which policy decisions were taken. As long as Atatürk was alive, he took those decisions; but he had them executed through the Assembly and the party. He did not call in the army. Ismet Inönu, his successor, was far less absolute, but he followed the same civilianized course.

As long as the People's Party was the sole party, the identity of régime and military was not difficult to maintain. The over-riding personality of Atatürk guaranteed the quiescence of the army till his death in 1938. Ismet Inönu, his lieutenant and successor, also had a great hold on the army's loyalty. Indeed a persistent rumour has it that the selection of Ismet Inönu as President in 1938, instead of Celal Bayar (a civilian) was determined by the army. Neither with Atatürk nor Ismet Inönu in command was an estrangement between party and army likely to take place. Furthermore, the fact that the party was an instrument of government, not a register of public opinion, made it relatively simple – as in Mexico – for any possible collisions to be averted by backstage diplomacy.

The formation of the Democratic party in 1945 and its victory in 1950 radically altered the situation. For the first time the electorate became independent; and as the two parties bid for its votes it became clear that a divergence opened, for the first time, between the views of the army and the views of a civilian administration carrying out a popular mandate. The coup of May 1960 was the consequence.

That coup and what has followed under the direct military régime of

General Gürsel does not prove that the civilian institutions of Turkey were a sham. Paradoxically, it proves the reverse: that the two parties had become genuine parties, and that the Assembly was the authoritative arena of policy making. The subsequent difficulties of the military junta in repressing the supporters of the Democratic Party, the resistive 'No' vote in the referendum on the new (1961) constitution and the results of the 1961 election all point to the same conclusion. As long as Kemal lived, his civil institutions were quasi-civilian only, for his will always prevailed. As long as the People's Party held sole power, i.e. till 1945, the institutions were still quasi-institutions; they were given no chance to function. Since then they have been given this chance; and they have turned out to be real institutions, and not shams.

Thus the Mexican and the Turkish cases both demonstrate the possibility of the military endowing the country with civilian institutions and retreating away from politics into professionalism. But for the reasons given the military movements that initiated these institutions partook of a popular nature; the armies were not the typical regular standing armies but popular in character; and in any case, the institutions thus set up have broken down under the test of political stress in Turkey and have not yet been subjected to such a test in Mexico. Mexico and Turkey do not demonstrate that a quasi-civilianized military régime, such as that in Egypt today or in Venezuela or Colombia up to 1958, may denature itself, and turn into a civilian régime. The circumstances of the Mexican and Turkish revolutions are themselves too dissimilar from those of the Middle Eastern and South American cuartelazos to make the argument admissible.

CHAPTER TWELVE

THE PAST AND THE FUTURE OF MILITARY INTERVENTION

1

THE experiences of Rome, of the medieval Italian city-states, of England under the Commonwealth and the Protectorate; the activities of such corps as the Mamelukes, the Janissaries, the Streltsi; all these seem to attest the antiquity as well as the perennialism of military intervention in politics. Nevertheless these differ in essential aspects from the military interventions of today for which they provide analogies rather than antecedents. The military intervention that we have been describing is a modern phenomenon, not yet two centuries old.

Rome has bequeathed the terms 'dictatorship', 'Caesarism' and 'Praetorianism', the last two of which are sometimes used as synonymous with 'military intervention'. Certainly, the situation in the later Empire where the Praetorians and later the legions literally made and undid the Imperial succession amid a welter of carnage seems to represent the *ne plus ultra* of military intervention. Objective conditions in the Empire largely corresponded to those we have styled states of low or minimal political culture. Any rule of succession had long disappeared. Civilian political forces, even a recognized aristocracy and governing class, had long since atrophied and the Roman Senate had been reduced to a cipher. At the same time the Empire, on the defensive against the Barbarians, was totally dependent on the armies and on the generals. The armies represented the only coherent formations capable of making or at least of enforcing any political initiative. Yet for all this it is hard to find any political motivation behind the armies' activities, from the wars of Marius and Sulla onwards, other than individual self-interest – the desire to put their own man in office, to receive better pay and conditions, and donatives. They had no social and political programme, and did not conceive themselves as a separate identity set against the rest of society. Indeed they acted as separate units struggling against one another. 'In the strict sense, the Roman soldiers were not partisans. They did not fight for a certain thing but for a certain person. They recognized nothing but their leader, who attached them to himself by raising immense hopes; but since their leader, defeated, was not able to fulfil his promises, they went over to the other side.'[1]

1. Baron de Montesquieu, *Grandeur et décadence des Romains*, Ch. 13.

The despotisms of the Italian *condottiere* are not true antecedents either. Here again, the forces acted for pelf and out of loyalty to their chief. Their rule was illegitimate and recognized to be so by the citizens they had subjected. Macchiavelli's *Prince* is simply a primer for such usurpers. It purports to tell them how to acquire legitimacy, and, if this proves impossible, how to corrupt or to break the resistance of the citizens. The Streltsi and Janissaries were king-makers and king-breakers, like the Praetorians, for reasons of personal loyalty and to ensure respect for their special privileges.

Only the political role of the English New Model Army may be deemed a genuine precursor of what the last century has brought forth. Its social composition; its political organization; its ideological basis; its corporate political view, whereby the Army Council treated as an independent power with the civilian authorities – all these prefigure the 'revolutionary' armies of the twentieth century. Like the standing armies of the modern era, too, it sought to validate the claim to rule by claiming to be representative of the people, and if not the people, of the Godly: and like them it was drawn irresistibly into rejecting one after another the legislatures that purported to represent the people – whether the Long Parliament, or its Rump, or the army-nominated 'Barebones' Parliament – until in the end it was dragged into ruling overtly through the Major-Generals. But though we may reckon it a true antecedent, it was a unique one. Its history and significance were buried in insular obscurity and misunderstanding for two centuries. It generated no forces either of attraction or repulsion throughout the world which could stimulate further adventures on the same pattern. It is in this respect that it essentially differs from the event which is the true seed plot of military intervention as we know it today – the French Revolution and Empire. Herein were engendered or nourished five factors, processes, movements – which separately and conjointly form the necessary conditions of military intervention.

2

The first of these factors is the professionalization of the officer corps. A professionalized corps of this kind contrasts sharply with the aristocratic officers or the soldiers of fortune which it replaced. To some extent military professionalism works against intervention in politics. Confining the armed forces to their specialized role, it implies leaving the politicians to theirs. By the same token, however, such professionalism also impels the military into politics. To begin with it opens a gap between the armed forces and the politicians: for under the old régimes, policy-making and the task of fighting lay in the same hands – those of the aristocracy. Secondly, the anxieties of the professional officer impel him, as we have already seen, to intrude into the politician's control over foreign affairs and even over domestic matters where this frustrates and impinges on the military task.

The second factor is the rise of nationalism and of the nation-state. The nation replaces the dynasty as the object of military loyalty. Nationalism provides the military with a civic religion and an overriding set of values. Because they have a unique role as guardian of the national territory, they regard themselves and are much regarded as the ultimate repositories and custodians of the nation's values. Three highly significant consequences flow from this. First, where nationalism has gripped the masses, the armed forces tend to become the visible symbol and the pledge of nationhood and independence and to attract an esteem for that reason. Secondly, nationalism provides the military with an ideology and possibly even a programme; in this it contrasts sharply with the sentiment, among the forces of the old régimes, of loyalty and enthusiasm for a dynasty or a personage. Thirdly, whereas in the old régime loyalty to state and to ruler were synonymous, in the nation-state this is no longer necessarily so. There, it must first be demonstrated to the military that the government they serve is synonymous with and representative of the nation. There is no logical reason why they should not regard an alternative government, and even themselves, as more representative and more worthy of the nation than the government in office; and since their transcendent duty is loyalty to the nation this may entail a duty to be disloyal to the government.

The third factor, closely associated with the second both historically and logically, is the substitution for the divine authority of kings of the dogma of popular sovereignty. Sovereignty is believed to reside in the people; and the people are identified (as in Siéyès' '*Qu'est-ce que le Tiers État?*') with the nation. From Rousseau sprang the doctrine, in Sir Henry Maine's words, of 'The People (with a capital P), the Sovereign People, the People the sole source of all legitimate power. From this came the subordinate of Governments, not merely to electorates, but to a vaguely defined multitude outside them, and to the still vaguer mastership of floating opinion. Thence began the limitation of legitimacy in government to governments which approach democracy.'[2]

Since that time, he remarked (i.e. 'since rulers became delegates of the community'), 'there has been no such insecurity of government since the century during which the Roman emperors were at the mercy of the Praetorian soldiers'. This is truer today than when he wrote it some eighty

2. Sir H. Maine, *Popular Government*, p. 158.

years ago. In the dynastic state, the most the military could do was to replace the monarchy. All they could do was to exercise indirect rule and influence, through the person of that monarch. Only the monarch conferred legitimacy, and he was corporeal, visible, tangible. The dogma of *vox populi vox dei* is more amenable since there is no hard and fast definition of what is *vox* and what is *populus*. Any person and group, including the army, which succeeds in mustering a mere semblance of popular support can claim to be the lawful government; and indeed, it is not even necessary to go so far. It is possible to argue that the claimant represents, if not the actual observed will of the people, then its 'real' will – what is in its true interest, or what represents its higher morality, and so forth. By this token any faction can seize power and legitimize itself in the name of the sovereign people. Thus the path is laid wide open for the military to intervene and to supersede the civil power altogether, on the plea that they embody the sovereignty of the people.

The fourth factor is closely connected with both the rise of nationalism and of the dogma of popular sovereignty. It is the emergence of what, for lack of any better term, we may call 'the insurrectionary army', i.e. an army working for the liberation of the national territory or for the overthrow of the social order. Insurrectionary armies therefore have a rudimentary ideology. Furthermore, they draw their strength from the public at large and tend to be representative of the whole population. In them intellectuals, scholars and natural leaders transform themselves into fighting men and may show unexpected and unsuspected gifts of military skill, administrative ability, and diplomacy. Insurrectionary armies intervene in politics *ex hypothesi*; this is why they have come into existence. Their significance lies in their legacy to the state once victory has been won and they disband. In the nature of things their leaders tend to become the rulers of the new state, for in the first place these armies have acted as a forcing ground for talent, and secondly they are clothed with all the prestige of liberation. Thus the successful army of insurrection tends to provide the leadership in the new order; and this may perpetuate a tradition of military intervention in politics. Where nationhood and revolution have come as the bequest of the army, the army regards itself – and is often regarded – as having a privileged position as custodian and guarantor. We have noticed, for instance, how the Turkish army has regarded itself as the guarantor of Kemalism which was its gift. In like manner began the military *caudillismo* of South America. 'As the generals of Alexander disputed, after his death, for the provinces of Europe, Asia, Africa, the remains of the imperial feast, and founded new dynasties in the flood of Oriental decadence, so the lieutenants of Bolívar dominated American life for a period of fifty years. Flores in Ecuador, Paéz in Venezuela, Santa-Cruz in Bolivia and Santander in Colombia governed as heirs of the Liberator.'[3]

Finally, intimately connected with nationalism, with popular sovereignty, and with the armies of insurrection, is a fifth factor: the emergence of new states from colonial subjection and their attainment of sovereign independence. Few of these, historically, have been as the U.S.A., and possessed a genuine and significant historical 'formation' in civilian politics and self-government. Most of these countries were rent by economic, ethnic and religious cleavages. Concealed and repressed by the authoritarian colonial régime these divisions burst into the open as soon as it was withdrawn. They were often exacerbated by the dogmas of nationalism and popular sovereignty through which independence had been won and which sapped the traditional basis of society without supplying a moral equivalent. Thus many of the new states faced independence with a passionate nationalism on the one hand and a need for strong central government on the other: a sure invitation to military intervention.

3

These five factors – or movements – all arose within a decade of one another. All sprang, by action and reaction, from the French Revolution and Empire. In some respects the American War of Independence was a precursor; therein are to be found a doctrine of popular sovereignty, an insurrectionary army, a secession from colonial rule. But its doctrine of popular sovereignty was a qualified one, trammelled by representative institutions, limited government, and an elaborate system of checks and balances – not to speak of the dominance of a ruling group who were successfully determined to resist the rule of majorities. The insurrectionary army, drawn from the citizens as it was – the Continental Army – was modelled on the English regular forces; and its leaders had no intentions of launching a 'people's war'. Furthermore its avowed purpose was to combat, among other things, standing armies, the quartering of armed troops on civilians, and the military enforcement of 'works of death, desolation and tyranny';[4] so that, only six months after the war had come to an end, the great Continental Army had been reduced to a mere 700 men. As for the secession from the British Empire, unlike the majority of new states,

3. F. Garcia-Calderon, *Latin America: Its Rise and Progress*, p. 87; also J. Beneyto, 'Los puntos de partida de la organizaçion politica hispano-americana', *Estudios Politicos*, Madrid, no. 91, p. 148.   4. The Declaration of Independence, p. 1776.

the newly independent colonies had received a long historical formation in statecraft and had thrown up to govern and administer themselves one of the most talented generations of leaders that civilization has seen. Furthermore, nothing that occurred in the world of that day could have an impact comparable to one that occurred in the country which dominated the cultural life of all Europe – France; certainly not an event occurring in a far-off and empty continent on the periphery of a Europe which was already on the march to its century of world domination. And, finally, in so far as the features of the American Revolution were exercising an influence abroad, they were swallowed up, overwhelmed, by the paroxismal violence, the colour and the drama of the events in Paris from 1789.

(1) *Popular sovereignty*

The notion that 'sovereignty resides essentially in the nation' was explicitly stated in the 1789 *Declaration of Rights of Man and the Citizen* but it was qualified by the retention of Louis XVI as King of the French. The crucial step towards the position that sovereignty resided *absolutely* in the nation occurred when the Paris mob stormed the Tuileries and massacred the Swiss Guards. This was the famous *journée* of 10 August 1792. The balanced constitution came to an end; the insurrectionary Commune of Paris seized control and terrorized the National Assembly; and on 22 September 1792 the Monarchy was abolished and the Republic proclaimed. From this point, the Revolution assumed the unqualified authority of popular sovereignty. Two months later it proclaimed it as a universal to be backed by the force of French arms. 'The French nation declares,' ran its proclamation, 'that it will treat as enemies every people who, refusing liberty and equality or renouncing them, may wish to maintain, recall or treat with the prince and the privileged classes: on the other hand it engages not to subscribe to any treaty and not to lay down its arms until the sovereignty and independence of the peoples whose territory the troops of the Republic shall have entered shall be established and until the people shall have adopted the principles of equality and founded a free and democratic government.'

From this moment all the old notions of 'legitimacy' were on the defensive: whether a dynastic right or prescriptive right or simple acceptance of long usage and tradition. By 1885, Sir Henry Maine was able to observe that 'Russia and Turkey are the only European states which completely reject the theory that governments hold their powers by delegation from the community.'[5] From this moment, too, the voice of the people began to speak, as it has never ceased doing, 'in tongues'. Popular sovereignty was

5. See H. Maine, op. cit., p. 9.

assumed to justify the despotism of the Jacobins, and did, in fact, justify the despotism of Napoleon. It was held to be immanent in the Jacobin seizure of the Paris Commune; in the storming of the Tuileries on 10 August 1792; and in the subsequent domination of the National Assembly by the Jacobin-dominated mobs of Paris. It was held to be immanent, likewise, in the *journée* of 2 June 1793, when the Jacobin Paris Commune invaded the Convention and brought about the fall of the Gironde. It was held to be immanent in the Jacobin usurpation and the Terror. But it was equally held to be immanent in the *journée* of the 9 Thermidor 1794 and the fall of the Jacobins, and in their persecution after the 1st Prairial. It was likewise held to justify the suppression of the royalist-dominated sections of Paris in the *journée* of Vendémiaire 1795. Not once in all these *journées* were the people of France consulted; but not once in all of them was the action taken not carried out in their name. When the people were genuinely consulted, it was to make Napoleon First Consul, then Life Consul and finally Emperor. The infinite malleability of the new political formula was fully grasped by the Corsican. 'The appeal to the people,' he wrote to Thibaudeau in August 1802, 'has the double advantage of legalizing the prolongment of my power and of purifying its origins. In any other way, it must always have appeared equivocal.'[6] And again: 'I did in no way usurp the crown; I picked it up from the gutter. The people set it on my head.'[7] With the French Revolution the Pandora's box had been opened. Popular sovereignty might mean government by popular consent; equally well it might not. Rulership now lay open to anyone who could sufficiently colour his claim to represent the sovereign people.

Furthermore, the history of this time simply foretokened what have since become political commonplaces; the tendency of one usurpation to breed another and the tendency in such circumstances for the military to become the decisive factor. The first is vividly illustrated by a speech which Robespierre with his characteristic humourlessness sincerely believed to be a self-justification. 'After a coup,' he said, 'it is not possible to mark the precise point at which the waves of the popular insurrection should break.' ... 'Why,' he asked, 'do you not put on trial simultaneously the municipality, the electoral assemblies, the Paris section and all those who followed our example? *For all these things have been illegal – illegal as the Revolution, as unlawful as the destruction of the throne and of the Bastille, as illegal as liberty itself.*'[8] What Robespierre unwittingly implied, Napoleon

6. Quoted, *Napoléon: Vues Politiques*, Paris, 1939, p. 65.

7. ibid., pp. 66–7. To Montholon, at St Helena.

8. Quoted J. L. Talmon, *The Origins of Totalitarian Democracy*, p. 102. (My italics.)

boldly proclaimed. 'Do you think,' he asked the Conseil d'État in 1800, 'that the 18 Fructidor, the 18 Brumaire, even the 10 August were regular and obtained general consent, that you should wish unremittingly to place the institutions which those *journées* brought forth above those consecrated by time and tradition?'[9]

When all the *journées*, and all the governments they established, were either equally irregular or equally the will of the people, the sword crept in as the arbiter. That the Revolution as such began, was due to the revolt of the *Gardes Françaises* on 12 July 1789. Thenceforward the dissolution of discipline in the army proceeded apace, and in its default power passed to the National Guard with its units in the Paris sections. It was during this period until 1795 that the usurpation of power was carried out at the hands of the population of Paris, in *journées* of a popular and insurrectionary character. By 1795 the army was reconstituted and became a political force once again, and from that year became ever more obviously decisive.

It first re-entered politics in Vendémiaire 1795. Determined to perpetuate themselves, the members of the outgoing Convention passed the 'law of the two-thirds'. By this, two-thirds of its successor legislature under the new constitution (the Council of Five Hundred) was in the first instance to be made up of members of the Convention. A clamour immediately arose in the sections of Paris, now under Royalist influence. On 13 Vendémiaire they marched on the Tuileries. Facing them, under Barras, were the regular forces, with Napoleon in command of the cannon. The 'whiff of grapeshot' established the regular army once again as the ultimate bulwark of the civil power.

In this action of Vendémiaire 1795 the army perpetuated the rule of the Thermidoreans. In Fructidor 1797 it was called by one faction of these Thermidoreans to proscribe and suppress the other. This is the first *coup d'état* which, being carried on by a civil faction with military support and using electoral malpractices which have since become a commonplace, has an authentically modern tang. The troops under General Augereau advanced on the Tuileries and arrested the opposition representatives. When one of them asked Augereau by what right he did so, the General replied: 'By the right of the sword.' The rump of the Council of Five Hundred was then surrounded by troops and forced to pass the law by which the elections in 49 Departments were annulled, and the triumphant faction charged with filling the vacancies. All newspapers were placed for one year under the inspection of the police, and the Directors received the right to proclaim any commune in a state of siege.

In Napoleon's 18 Brumaire 1799, the process reached its term. Both the

9. *Napoléon: Vues Politiques*, p. 46. To the Conseil d'État.

objective conditions and the state of mind of the soldiery were ripe for further intervention. France was passing through an overt crisis. The Directory could not rely on any middle opinion, but was caught and tossed between the two great forces of Royalism and Jacobinism, equally hostile to one another and to the Directory itself. Incapable of relying on either, the Directors were forced to rely on the army, first to repress one faction and then the other – the celebrated policy of the *Bascule*. While the feebleness and corruption of the Directory brought its prestige to a nadir, by the same token the prestige of the army which alone kept the Republic from invasion was at its height. The war policy of the Directory played into its hands, for the Directory's incapacity to feed, clothe and equip the army, its connection with speculators and *fournisseurs*, and its very civilianism, brought the army to hate and despise it and to blame it for all their misfortunes. Not all the generals were on Bonaparte's side in the 18 Brumaire (Augereau and Bernadotte stood by the Jacobins), but no serving officer of any description had any use for the Directory as it stood. When Siéyès and his colleagues 'looked for a sword' to overthrow the Directory they found first Joubert, and on Joubert's death, Napoleon. Had Napoleon not been available there can be little doubt that sooner or later they would have found a third candidate.

(2) *Nationalism and national sovereignty*

Nationalism and national sovereignty were proclaimed at the same time and by the same formula as the doctrine of popular sovereignty. It was Siéyès who first, in his *Qu'est-ce que le Tiers État?*, boldly identified People and Nation and claimed for the Nation what Rousseau had claimed for his 'general will'. What the Revolution did was to dramatize the idea of the Nation, to make Frenchmen self-conscious of their common bonds, and above all to furnish a symbolism and imagery which gripped the imagination of the masses and provided them with a heady and fanatical religion. If we must put a date to the first manifestation of this spirit it would surely be 17 June 1789. That was the day when the *Tiers État*, rejecting the role of part of an Estates-General, proclaimed itself the *National* Assembly. Then followed the 'federation' demonstrations, through 1789 and 1790: meetings of citizens all over France which greeted the suppression of the ancient Provinces by 'abjuring every distinction of our provinces, offering our arms and our wealth to *la patrie* for support of the laws which come from the National Assembly'. These demonstrations culminated in the vast nationalistic fête of 14 July 1790, in the Champ de Mars where 50,000 delegates from all over France took the federation oath and swore '*fraternité*'.

The war of 1792 and the fear of invasion brought the new-born patriotism to a delirium. Nowadays *La Marseillaise* is no longer the marching song of the patriotic levies of the Rhine army, but merely another national anthem, albeit with a more stirring tune than most. At all events few people seriously ponder its (many) verses. Yet these, and more particularly the first, vividly illustrate the fervour of pristine and frenetic French nationalism. The verse calls for resistance to barbarous invaders, invaders who will murder one's sons and comrades: invaders who, however, are also political enemies – the tools of tyranny. Defence of the people and defence of the new-won political order are merged in one. The verse is not addressed to the regular army. It does not (like *God Save the Queen*) refer to the dynasty. On the contrary it is addressed to *citizens* (not subjects); and to the '*enfants de la* patrie' – that is to the common and equal bonds uniting all Frenchmen in their capacity as nationals. For their use of '*la patrie*' is a neologism. Till then, France had been described as *un royaume*, and *patrie* was defined by the Academy (as late as 1776) as the *pays*, the part of the country in which a man happened to be born.

Meanwhile in the interior the Revolution established, or rather sought to establish, patriotism as a new religion on the ruins of the Roman Church. To this end was instituted the *décadi*, and the cult associated with it. 'The *décadi*,' writes Vandal, 'the final and culminating day of the *décade*, was chosen for the celebration of the cult which had become the religion of the State and was commonly styled the decadal cult. For let us not forget that the Revolution, frighteningly anti-Christian as it had become, remained religious. It still retained a passion for liturgies, a frenzy for rites, and spent part of its time inventing religions. The decadal religion was nothing else than the organized cult of the Nation. On the appointed day, in a solemn or a pastoral setting, the administrators of each canton assembled the population around the altar of the Nation, read out and passed comments on the laws, delivered lay sermons, catechized children, recited the characteristics of civic value – all to the accompaniment of singing and the organ.'[10]

It was the armies of the Revolution that carried the nationalistic contagion to France's neighbours. The armies came as liberators and stayed as tax-gatherers, plunderers and rulers. In reaction to their arrogant nationalism, the nationalism of the invaded and oppressed peoples awoke. If we are to put a firm date to this it might well be the famous *Dos de Mayo*, 2 May 1808, when the people of Madrid arose against the French and initiated the savage war of the Spanish priests and people against the infidel

10. A. Vandal, *L'avènement de Bonaparte*, Paris, 1905–7, vol. I, pp. 30–31.

foreigner. Yet simultaneously with this rising a furious hatred of the French had awoken in Prussia.

Humiliated by Jena and the disastrous peace, 'all', wrote Stein, 'thirsted for revenge; plans of insurrection which aimed at exterminating the French scattered about the country were arranged ... the incubus of the French garrisons, of marchings through the country, indescribable provocations, kept alive the hatred of [the] French.'[11] This was the year in which Fichte published his *Addresses to the German Nation*, the first major pronouncement of German nationalism – an unconscious commentary, as Seeley called it, on the Spanish conflict.

(3) *Popular armies*

The armies with which the Republic fought its wars were not truly insurrectionary or revolutionary armies. Their nucleus consisted of the old regular troops, while the engineer and artillery corps had retained most of their former officers. The admixture of volunteer and the '*levée en masse*' did not make them insurrectionary or fully 'popular'. But the army of 1795 (by which date the amalgam of the old and new elements was complete) was a new military phenomenon nevertheless. First of all, its officers were no longer the old aristocratic class but freely drawn from the ranks of professional talent: it was therefore imbued with a zeal for the Republican social principles of equality which had permitted them to rise. Secondly, the volunteers, brigaded with the old regiments, leavened the mass with their fervour for the nation and for the Revolution and so gave the whole force a dynamic and self-conscious ideology.

The success of this army in carrying the war into the enemies' countries not only provoked the enemy peoples into a counter-nationalism of their own, as we have already seen; it also produced a similar military reaction. In Spain the anti-French reaction produced an entirely new kind of army and of warfare, viz. genuinely insurrectionary forces made up of the people at large, and irregular warfare – the *guerrilla*, i.e. the 'little war'. Popular risings had occurred before; the revolt of the Netherlands is a classic case. The Revolution did not produce a new phenomenon, but vastly stimulated an old one.

This Spanish experience was a true example of an army of popular insurrection. It was not immediately copied in Europe. Its first imitations were to be found in the Spanish colonies themselves, where for the next ten or fifteen years civil wars began to rage, of frightful ferocity; and then, after these, in the Balkans where the Greek people rose against the Turks.

11. Quoted, J. R. Seeley, *Life and Times of Stein*, vol. II, pp. 26–7.

(4) *Professionalism*

While nations and causes which had no army were creating armies of their own and adding the terms *guerrilla* and partisan warfare to the dictionary, those which did have armies were developing them in the opposite direction, i.e. by purging their political and their amateur characteristics, and creating instead a professional organization. Here Prussia was the pioneer. The army reforms of Stein and Scharnhorst mark the first self-conscious effort in Europe to professionalize the officer corps. Humiliated by Jena and Auerstadt, King Frederic William III appointed a Military Reorganization Commission in which Stein and Scharnhorst were dominant. Their object was twofold: first to regenerate Prussian nationalism and at the same time 'bring the army and the nation into a more intimate union'; and next to raise the competence of the officer corps from the morass of abysmal ignorance and inefficiency to which the aristocratic monopoly of entrance had brought it. The first was achieved by Stein's social reforms, and by the system of national military conscription and training. The second was begun with the famous decree of 6 August 1808. 'A claim to the position of officer,' it ran, 'should from now on be warranted in peacetime by knowledge and education, in time of war by exceptional bravery and quickness of perception . . . All social preference which has hitherto existed is herewith terminated in the military establishment and everyone, without regard for his background, has the same duties and the same rights.'[12] To this end any young man of seventeen years who had served three months in the ranks could take regimental examinations for admission to the rank of cornet; and before the cornets were admitted to the rank of lieutenant they had to sit a further examination in Berlin. At the same time the military schools were thoroughly reorganized; the old schools were dissolved and three new schools of war established, and a Superior Military Academy was founded in Berlin wherein selected officers were given three years' advanced training. The competing military agencies whose rivalry had helped bring about the *débâcle* of Jena were subordinated to a new and centralized Ministry.[13]

The professionalization of the Prussian officer corps took place in two movements. In the first part of the century, the stress fell on opening up the career to talent, and on the need for educational qualifications. The second movement took place midway through the century. Here the stress was on the development of a General Staff and the provision of advanced military education. By 1875 the Prussian officer corps was fully professionalized.

12. Quoted, Craig, op. cit., p. 43.   13. ibid., pp. 37–65.

The qualification for entrance was educational, an examination system was in full swing, and the provision of centres of military education was complete. Advancement proceeded by merit. A General Staff had been formed. All these features formed part of one interlocking system: and the officer corps which was the product enjoyed to the highest degree a sense of corporate identity.

France followed Germany, but at one remove. Britain was still slower. Nevertheless it would be true to say that at the beginning of the nineteenth century none of the three countries possessed a professional officer corps. By 1914 all did.

(5) *The emergence of new states*

The American War of Independence was the first in which colonies declared their secession from a European empire, and established their independent statehood. Nevertheless the new United States which arose was not typical of the majority of the emergent states of today. Ethnically it was homogeneous. Social tensions were not marked. It suffered from no sectarian cleavages. It was endowed with great natural wealth and a busy and inventive population. It possessed vigorous institutions of self-government, and a superabundance of persons with the will and skill to operate them. Within a few years of independence it was able to do something unique in the annals of colonial independence movements – to establish an administrative system more pure and more efficient than the metropolitan country's.[14]

Therefore if we are to seek for the antecedents of what is typical (though by no means universal) in the emergent states of today, we shall have to look elsewhere than the birth of the United States, and it is in the revolt of the Spanish American colonies that we find it.

These emergent societies stood in complete contrast to the thirteen colonies. Their peoples, even the narrow class of the wealthy, had no experience of self-government. The populations were bitterly self-divided. The Creoles hated the Spanish, and both feared the bulk of the population, composed of illiterate and brutalized Indians in a state of serfdom and slavery. Locality stood aloof from locality, native tribe from native tribe, the countryside from the towns and the rich from the poor. The church had its fanatical partisans; equally, its fanatical opponents.

Few new states have ever arisen with a less promising start. Independence was a protracted business which plunged these societies into

14. S. E. Finer, 'Patronage and the Public Service', *Public Administration*, Winter 1952, pp. 329–59.

unremitting and unbelievably hideous civil strife and anarchy for some fifteen years. Here the servile war of the slaves of Haiti against their French owners served as the prologue. That war began in 1790 and ended in 1804 with Haiti as an independent state. On the mainland, however, events marched on the heels of the affairs of Spain. The deposition of Ferdinand VII by Napoleon (1808) created a legal hiatus of which the aspiring Creole elements soon took advantage. In Rio de Janeiro, the Provisional Junta assumed power in 1810, but independence was not proclaimed till 1816. In Venezuela, the extraordinary *cabildo* established itself in 1810 and in 1811 a Congress proclaimed independence. This was followed by Cartagena. Meanwhile in Mexico, Hidalgo took up arms against the Spanish authorities in 1810, and on his death Morélos continued the struggle. Independence was proclaimed in 1813. But all these movements, with the exception of those in the Plate provinces, had foundered by 1816. It was not till after 1820 that, one by one, the insurrectionary armies triumphed and independence became a fact.

4

Contemporary military intervention is the fruit of the five factors which emerged from the paroxysm of the French Revolution, between 1789 and 1810: the doctrine of nationality, the doctrine of popular sovereignty, the insurgence of popular armies, the professionalization of the armed forces and, finally, the emancipation of Imperial dependencies.

Of these five factors two are primary, the others derivative. The primary factors are the dynamic novel doctrines and emotions of nationalism and popular sovereignty. The military effects are derivative: on the one side the formation of popular armies to advance these doctrines – what Burke called 'an armed doctrine' – and, on the other, the professionalization of armies the better to withstand them. The movement for colonial independence is doubly derivative: from the new doctrines, which merge into the doctrine of national self-determination, and from the popular movements and if need be popular armies to achieve this.

So it was in Latin America. This represents the first triumphant emanation from the cockpit of Europe.

From the close of the Napoleonic period, the 'armed doctrine' has spread wider and penetrated deeply. Today few countries have not felt in some measure the appeals of nationalism and popular sovereignty. The two notions tend to work in double harness. Sometimes the demand for popular sovereignty has preceded nationalism, sometimes it has been the other way about; but the leads and lags were never very lengthy, and in most cases the two notions marched together.

The first half of the nineteenth century saw them more or less take possession of the west, north and south-east of Europe. In the next quarter century, Central Europe – Germany and Austria – began to succumb. By 1878, only in Turkey and Imperial Russia was there no concession, even implicit, to these principles; and both significantly were 'prison houses of nationalities'. Yet by 1910 both had caught the contagion. Russia had experienced the 1905 Revolution and established the Duma; Turkey had experienced the Young Turk Revolution and the Committee of Union and Progress (1908). Meanwhile Asia was beginning to stir. In India the Congress was established in 1886; in China the Boxer Rebellion (1900) was the forewarning of resurgent nationalism. These portents were followed by significant action: the Persian revolution of 1905–6, the Indian Congress's demand for representative institutions and even (its minority's view) independence, and the 1911 Revolution in China. The First World War acted as a reagent. With 1919, the principle of self-determination became one of the dogmas of the post-war European settlement, nationalism had awakened in the Arab lands, was rampant in China and India, and was just beginning its career in South-East Asia and sub-Saharan Africa.

The world had hitherto been parcelled out into vast multi-national states, commonly called empires. Now these began to disintegrate. We have already seen how the Spanish and Portuguese colonies in Latin America won their independence. Their example had been followed by the nationalities (Serbs, Greeks, Rumanians) of Turkey-in-Europe. By 1878 these were almost, and by 1914 entirely, independent of the Turk, along with the Montenegrins, the Albanians and the Bulgarians. With the First World War a third great wave of secession arrived. The German, Austrian and Russian empires collapsed leaving behind a string of new states. The Ottoman empire also disintegrated leaving its Arab successors as temporary and conditional spoils in the hands of the British and French: Egypt itself, Syria, Transjordan and Iraq. Thus a band of young and brand-new successor-states to the four empires stretched in an arc from the Polar Sea to the Persian Gulf.

We are still witnessing the effects of the fourth great wave – the aftermath of the Second World War. One empire has indeed advanced: Russia reabsorbed the Baltic states and reduced all South-Eastern and Eastern Europe (including half Germany) to dependency. But overseas, in Asia and then Africa, the British, the Dutch, the French and the Belgian empires have disintegrated. In Asia there came into existence Indonesia, the four successor-states to French Indochina, Malaya, Burma, Pakistan, India and Ceylon. In Africa, first Tunisia, Libya and Morocco became independent, and then, with the creation of Ghana, began the liquidation of all the European possessions south of the Sahara with the (present) exceptions of those of Spain and Portugal.

In this way did nationalism, popular sovereignty and the emergence of new states – three interlocking factors – sweep through the world. The remaining two factors of our five spread with them, viz. insurrectionary armies, and professionalized armies. Latin America and the Balkans had liberated themselves by their own popular levies. After 1917 so did the succesion states to Russia and to Austria. The Red armies of Russia, the Kuomintang (and later the communist) forces of China re-enacted an ideological warfare last seen in the era of the French Revolution. This kind of warfare flared up again in the aftermath of the Second World War. When the movement was dominated by the nationalist ideology it led, as in Indonesia and in South Vietnam, to the national independence of the country under nationalist leadership. When it was dominated by the communists its fate was various: successful in China, Yugoslavia and North Vietnam, unsuccessful in Burma, Malaya and Greece, it brought the first three into the totalitarian camp, but in the last three enhanced the status of the triumphant nationalist forces.

In all such countries, as soon as the fighting was over, the authorities made haste to convert the levies into a regular army and to professionalize the officer corps. In those countries like India and Pakistan and Ghana and Morocco where independence was conceded peacefully, a professional force was part of the Imperial legacy. In either case, professionalization was the rule. This professionalization – our fifth decisive factor in the evolution of military intervention – had been developing at the same time as nationalism and popular sovereignty were extending. By 1914 every major world power, including the United States and Japan, had professionalized its forces. Thereafter the newly independent states adopted the same methods, mostly by sending their officers abroad or by inviting military missions of the great powers to train their forces at home. The more advanced established their own indigenous systems, based on the overseas model.

In this way, the factors of special significance for military intervention have become all but ubiquitous.

5

The dynastic state and the colonial dependency have now all but disappeared. In their place stand over one hundred sovereign states, equipped with professional forces, and founded on the twin formulae of national self-determination and popular sovereignty. The conditions that permitted of military blackmail in Germany and France, and of the displacement or even supplantment of civilian governments in Portugal and Spain have thus penetrated all these countries. The results are most marked in the ex-imperial territories, and these bands of successor-states form so many seismic zones of preternatural military eruption.

In terms of chronology there are, first (1810–24), the Latin American successor-states to Portugal and Spain. Secondly (1829–1914), the Balkan successor states to the Ottoman empire, and Turkey itself: Serbia, Greece, Bulgaria, Rumania and Albania. Next (1918–46) come two sets of states: the successors to the Russian, German and Austrian empires in Eastern Europe (the Baltic States and Poland), and the Arab successor-states to the Ottoman empire; these states, Iraq, Syria, Lebanon, Jordan and Egypt, became sovereign at various dates after 1918, but all were fully independent by 1946. So far, every one of the states named or mentioned has suffered from continual military intervention in its politics. Finally (post 1946), there are the successor-states to the Dutch, Belgian, French and British empires. Many of these are less than ten years old, but already Indonesia, Laos, South Vietnam, Burma, Pakistan, Sudan and the Congo have experienced military intervention.

In terms of geography there are really two zones. The first is Central and South America. The second is a huge arc. It begins in the Baltic with the three former Baltic states and sweeps down through Poland into Rumania, Greece and Turkey. It turns south to the Nile Valley into the Congo and also east through the fertile Crescent, through Persia and Pakistan to Burma, Siam, and ex-French Indochina, until it ends in Indonesia. Practically the whole of the military eruptions of today, when they are not occurring in Latin America, take place in those areas of this great arc which are still outside the Soviet and Chinese systems.

Some ancient states like Persia have suffered military intervention, and others also, like France and Germany and (notably) Spain and Portugal. Likewise some new states like India (notably) and Ceylon have so far proved immune. But, in general, military intervention, especially in the more open and extreme forms, is outstandingly a characteristic of the new, not the older states. There are two principal reasons for this. It is in these states pre-eminently that legitimacy has been shaken and is still in dispute. Secondly, these states are the ones in which, for the most part, the material conditions for fostering and sustaining powerful civilian organizations are still lacking. There is a third, supplementary, reason which applies to a minority of these states: the pre-existence of a tradition of military intervention.

(1) *In search of legitimacy*

The constitutive principles of the new state are indeed nationalism and popular sovereignty. It is in the name of these that the state has emerged into independence. This does not mean, however, that the new state is either a nation or a democracy. These principles are norms and slogans, not facts. They are carried and proclaimed by the westernizing ruling élite. They have in varying degree penetrated a class of 'transitionals'. But they are not yet accepted by the masses who are still traditionalistic. For these, the older loyalties to dynasty, religion, tribe and locality still make the principal appeal. The proportions of the population which make up these three groups vary from society to society. In all of them, however, the westernized group is a tiny fraction, and the transitional and traditional classes the bulk of the population.[15] What Carnell says of the new states of South and South-East Asia applies, broadly speaking, to *all* the successor-states except the three Baltic states. They are, he writes, 'transitional societies deeply divided by cultural and ethnic pluralism, by provincialism, regionalism, localism and caste-ism. Tiny westernized élites of politicians, bureaucrats and army officers are groping tentatively and experimentally for appropriate ways of substituting national consensus and economic growth for a fragmentary traditional social structure and a backward rural economy.'[16]

For once independence has been won, it becomes clear that the principles of nationality and popular sovereignty are insufficient to promote national consensus. The parties that have come to power on the slogan of national independence either give way to more extreme and more socially conscious parties, or seek to project the fervour of nationalism into an indefinite future. Of the former, the traditional nationalist parties of Syria are an example.[17] Of the latter, the nationalisms of Presidents Nasser and Nkrumah are characteristic. For Egyptian and Ghanaian nationalism, these leaders substitute an indefinite and less tangible 'anti-colonialism'. Nasser proclaims that the Egyptian people have a mission to lead, simul-

15. Cf. D. Lerner, *The Passing of Traditional Society*, Free Press, Illinois, 1958. This work is a statistical appraisal of the situation in the Middle East. At the time of their research (1950–58), Professor Lerner and his associates established that Turkey and Lebanon showed the greatest penetration by Western ideas, Persia and Jordan the least. Egypt and Syria came midway.

16. F. G. Carnell, *Political Ideas and Ideologies in South and South-East Asia*, U.K. Political Science Association, 1960.

17. W. Z. Laqueur (ed.), *The Middle East in Transition*, p. 122.

taneously, the Arab zone, Islam and Africa.[18] Nkrumah, in his turn, dedicates Ghana to irredentism: the mission to liberate and even to federate Africa. In this vein the struggle for independence is declared permanent. It is projected forward, ever forward, so that the pristine enthusiasms of independence should be prolonged indefinitely.

Nor does the dogma of popular sovereignty assist consensus. It does just the reverse. These new states are rarely nations. Hatred of the imperial power is not the same as national self-consciousness, and beyond this political consciousness is usually very low. In these circumstances popular sovereignty accentuates provincial particularism, communalism, tribalism and lays the westernizing élites by the heels. Nationalism and popular sovereignty succeed in discrediting the traditional belief systems, or at least in displacing them, but not in supplanting them. The result is a confusion and tension over legitimacy – over what form of rule, which political values, are duty-worthy. Hence the new leaders' quest for some national ideology that will synthesize nationalism and popular sovereignty with the traditional values and so provide the population with a new faith to live by and the governments with a new political formula to govern by. Arab nationalism roots itself in a deep strain of pan-Islamism. Nehru takes refuge in eclecticism, U Nu of Burma in a kind of Buddhist Marxism, Ngo Diem of South Vietnam in a so-called *personnalisme*, and Sukarno in a Marxist-tinctured '*gotong-rōjong*'.[19]

Indeed, in many new states their constitutive principles of nationalism and popular sovereignty may be not merely inadequate to produce consensus, but positively inimical to it. Such is the experience, indeed, of some European states with more complete historical formations than many of the new states. After the making of Italy it was necessary to 'make the Italians'. Spanish nationalism, which turned Napoleon out of the peninsula, subsequently proved incapable of absorbing and transcending Catalonian separatism. A great number of the successor-states to the empires are *polyethnic* societies and here the dogma of nationality, successful in uniting the various communities against the imperial power, soon acts as a dissolvent. For these communities begin to become conscious of *themselves* as nations, and to demand self-determination. Why not? Where is the principle of self-determination to end? Why should it not end just in the constitution of as many states as there are nationally self-conscious minorities? Imperial India was willy-nilly rent into two at the time of independence; but, faced with Sikh demands for a separate Sikh state, Mr Nehru

18. Laqueur, op. cit., pp. 22, 129–44, 145–65. Lerner, op. cit., pp. 403–9.
19. Carnell, op. cit.

declares that 'we will tolerate no further division whatever happens. Even if it is civil war, it will be civil war.' Partition was enough, indeed too much – India was still suffering from the effects of the creation of Pakistan; any further divisions would break her beyond redemption.[20] In Kenya the mere prospect of independence has sparked off an alarming tribal self-consciousness. The two main parties are themselves tribally based, K.A.N.U. on the Kikuyu-Luo combination, K.A.D.U. on the Masai and other tribes. The former demand a unitary state. The latter, fearing Kikuyu dominance, demand a federal system based on tribal divisions.[21] In Ghana, Nkrumah insists that 'in the higher reaches of our national life, there shall be no reference to Fantis, Ashantis, Ewes, Gas, Dagombas, "strangers" and so forth but that we should call ourselves Ghanaians – all brothers and sisters, members of the same community – the state of Ghana'.[22]

And, by the same token, in such societies popular sovereignty also acts as a dissolvent. As in Indonesia – a prize exhibit – it has brought about faction and conflict which serves to advantage in homogeneous societies, but which in self-divided ones simply accentuates the local, tribal, ethnic, religious and class differences.

Thus in such societies the political formula is elusive, legitimacy still at large. Of the three elements constituting a high level of political culture these lack the first two: consensus on the legitimate locus of sovereignty and consensus on the procedures for establishing morally valid public decisions.

The third constituent of a high level of political culture is a sufficiency of civilian organization, willing and capable of sustaining and defending the society's political institutions. In most of these societies this too is lacking. And this is directly related to their backward state of economic development. The material preconditions for adequate civilian organization do not yet exist.

(2) *The material preconditions for civilian consensus*

Such civilian 'organizations' as the new states do inherit are inimical to its constitutive principles of nationality and popular sovereignty. Tribal and religious and ethnic 'organizations', which are the lot of most of them, are, as the previous section shows, more likely to pulverize the new state than to

20. *The Times*, 7 October 1961.   21. *The Times*, 6 October 1961.

22. Quoted by D. Austin, *Parties in Ghana, 1949–60*, U.K. Political Studies Association, 1960. See for an extended discussion, H. L. Brettan, *Political Problems of Polyethnic Societies in West Africa*, I.P.S.A., World Congress, 1961.

integrate it. They threaten a relapse into 'overt crisis', a situation where the government – any government – can rely on no section of civilian opinion without simultaneously bringing on itself the hostility of all the rest: a situation where there is no natural majority, only mutually exclusive and hostile minorities.

The civilian organizations needed to sustain and nourish the civil institutions are the integrating ones like trade unions, businesses, voluntary organizations and political parties which are not mutually exclusive and which cross the tribal, ethnic and religious boundaries to produce functional organizations with a good deal of overlapping membership. Now these are essentially modern institutions. That the basis of political organization underwent an historical development from kinship to territory has often been remarked; neighbourhood units supplanted the family, gens or tribe as the unit of political activity. Since then the process has moved on, and an essential characteristic of the modern state is that the territorial unit has given way to the functional one as the basis of politics.

Functional associations can only develop, however, when certain material preconditions are met. Trade unions, business corporations, voluntary societies and the like reflect a high degree of social specialization. This in turn requires a high level of commercial intercourse and industrial activity, and a fairly high level of national income to provide the necessary 'social surplus'. Also such associations cannot emerge without an adequate level of communications and of literacy. The absence of these precludes all but the most rickety and ephemeral of functional associations;[23] their abundance not only makes them larger and more durable, but enables them to become politically aware, self-conscious and articulate.

In most of the new states, the material conditions are not sufficiently advanced to homogenize society; are too developed to leave it in its traditional state; but are just developed enough (so far) to exacerbate divisions. The industrial proletariat is too weak to be accepted as a legitimate constituent in the political process, too strong and too wretched not to be an extreme and disruptive force. Literacy, education and mass-communication have not gone far enough to permeate the masses but they have developed sufficiently to create, over and against these rural masses, an urban élite of modernizers. It is a mistake to attribute political instability to a low standard of living. This is common in traditional societies and compatible with very stable politics. The instability arises in the movement away from traditionalism. It is the introduction of sharp and as yet localized social discontinuities that makes for instability. It is accentuated,

23. D. Lerner, op. cit., *passim*; also S. M. Lipset, *Political Man*, London, 1961, pp. 61–71.

as modernization takes its hold and literacy and communications increase, by the people's exposure to the possibilities of receiving a more attractive kind of life.

These conclusions are borne out by empirical investigations. It has been shown for instance that urbanization, communications, literacy and political participation are interdependent and that the higher a society stands in one respect the higher it tends to stand in all the others.[24] Another survey, of forty-eight states in Europe and Latin America, showed that the less wealthy, the less industrialized, the less educated and less urbanized a society, the less politically stable it was likely to be.[25] C. Issawi reached similar conclusions, though by different methods, for the Middle East. 'Democracy does not thrive in the present-day Middle East,' he found, because 'the economic and social basis which it requires is as yet non-existent. That basis presents the following aspects: size of territory and population, level of economic development, distribution of wealth, industrialization, homogeneity of language and religion, degree of education and habit of cooperative association.'[26] These conclusions, found to be true for Latin America and the Middle East, are just as applicable to the new states of South-East Asia and to Africa.

(3) *The relevance of the military tradition*

The difficulties of such new states are affected by a third factor – their mode of origin. Some, an increasing number in the lengthening catalogue, have got off to a good start. These are the countries where severance from the imperial power has occurred by agreement and indeed, with an imperial endowment to set the new state on its path. The new state is left with a working administration, and even with administrators and advisers. In many cases, such as Ghana, Nigeria, Malaya, it starts off with a favourable balance of trade and its reserves and balances stand high. More rarely, but notably in India, the imperial connection has gradually brought about the westernization of an extensive middle class, and equipped it with modern professional and administrative skill.

Such states start off with a tradition of civilian control. Furthermore, their armies have been trained in this tradition: that their function is to come to the aid of the civil power, and for the rest, to preserve the strictest political neutrality. A number of the successor-states did not begin life so peacefully. The Latin American states almost without exception secured

24. Lerner, op. cit., pp. 55–65.   25. Lipset, op. cit., pp. 45–76.

26. C. Issawi, 'Economic Foundations of Democracy in the Middle East', W. Z. Laqueur (ed.), *The Middle East in Transition*, pp. 33–51.

independence only after the raising of insurrection and the creation of their own popular levies among scenes of hideous cruelty and carnage. Here independence was a gift of the military and the military have never suffered the population to forget it. 'One heritage of the war was a militarism of monstrous appetite. So ... in all Hispano-America the Presidency of the Republic was considered, *de facto*, as "the highest rank in the army".'[27]

Of the recent successor-states, Burma, Indonesia and South Vietnam had to rely extensively on their armies, either to achieve independence or to reduce the chaos which attended such independence. As a result of Japanese occupation policy all three possessed national armies. When the Japanese left, these forces served as the military instrument of the nationalist movements, prepared, if the need arose, to contest the return of the Europeans. In Burma, independence was granted without fighting, but the new state was immediately faced with civil war: the communists, the Karens and finally the Shan areas all revolted. The army, not unnaturally, acquired much prestige as the guarantor of the national identity; and as a result it stepped in (or was called in?) when civil government under U Nu reached an impasse in 1958, and ruled the country for two years under its General, Ne Win. It stepped in again in 1962 to prevent Karens, Shans and the like from attaining federal status. South Vietnam, as part of French Indochina, was involved in the nationalist struggle against the French. When the movement split and North Vietnam became communist-dominated, the area of South Vietnam remained the stronghold of forces which, though anti-French, were also strongly anti-communist. After partition in 1954, the new government of South Vietnam found itself contending with domestic dissidents each with a private army – viz. the 'sects' – the Bao Dai and the Hoa Hao, and the force of river pirates known as the Binh Xuyen. In these circumstances the Prime Minister, Ngo Diem, gave battle and won. Here again, then, nationhood has been a gift of the military. The current struggle against the communist Viet Cong has still further elevated its importance. In these circumstances it is not surprising that the régime is a façade-régime in which supreme power lies with the President, Ngo Diem, relying on army support. Finally, in Indonesia, the Japanese-created auxiliary army of Indonesians fought the Dutch from 1945 to 1949 when independence was finally granted. In this country, pulverized by party strife, the military are involved in political decisions at all levels. At the centre they have been accorded a quota of seats in President Sukarno's nominated legislature (1960); at the extremities, they

27. J. Beneyto, 'Los puntos de partida de la organizaçion politica hispanoamericana' (*Revista de Estudios Politicos*, No. 91, p. 148).

revolted in 1956, established regional councils and embarked on civil war. In order to crush this revolt the central government was forced to fall back on martial law and for two years, 1957–8, most policy decisions were taken by military decree. The revolt has now faded out but at local and regional levels the army officers still continue to act as policy makers, coordinators, leaders and channellers of political activities;[28] and General Nasution, army Chief of Staff, has become a man to watch.

In these new states, then, legitimacy is contestable; the material preconditions for the development of powerful civilian associations are still lacking; and some suffer from the grand handicap of having received independence at the hands of the armed forces. They would, therefore, seem to be peculiarly vulnerable to military intervention in politics. The historical record so far would seem to attest this, too. The oldest of the successor-states – the Latin American republics – have suffered from endemic military eruptions, and even after a century-and-a-half only Argentina, Mexico, Chile, and possibly Uruguay and Costa Rica can be deemed effectively 'national' states. The remainder are either melting-pots in full bubble like Brazil, or societies still just as riven by ethnic and class divisions as those of Asia and Africa. The next oldest of the successor-states, those of the Balkans and Eastern Europe, used to suffer likewise from endemic military intervention. And of the post-war successor-states, Syria, Iraq, Egypt and the Sudan, Pakistan, Burma, Vietnam and Indonesia have all succumbed: as have their neighbours, Turkey and Persia and Thailand, which, though ancient independent states, have likewise felt the impact of westernization.

6

The Prospect

In nearly all the new states, the modernizing movement has tended and tends to move through two phases – nationalistic euphoria, followed by social discontents. Independence (or, in the case of ancient states like Turkey and Persia, 'national revival') raises the party or coalition that has secured it to power. Examples, such as the Indian Congress, the Ghanaian Convention People's Party, the Tunisian Neo-Destour and the Nigerian National Council could be multiplied. These dominant parties are usually associated with and draw support from an heroic leader – a Nehru, Sukarno, Nkrumah, Bourguiba, Nyerere, Kaunda or Banda. This pre-

28. G. M. Kahin (ed.), *Government and Politics of South-East Asia*, pp. 204–5. J. Mossman, *Rebels in Paradise*, for the civil war.

eminence of the charismatic leader is one of the most striking features of the first stage of national resurgence, and where a new state loses such leaders, as Pakistan lost Jinnah and then Liaquat Ali Khan, its political future is immediately jeopardized.

The nationalist dynamism springs from fierce and even immeasured denunciation of one single theme – the iniquities of foreign rule. Once independence is achieved, however, the question is, what is to be done with it? This problem dissolves the pristine unity of the nationalist movement. To begin with, dissidence need no longer be considered a betrayal of the nation in the face of the imperial power. Also, the members of the nationalist movement have been reared in an oppositionist mentality; therefore disagreements tend to spread over domestic methods and policy, and over nationalism itself.

Again, much that was reprehended as the cynicism of the colonial power turns out now to be inseparable from the exercise of government itself – or so the nationalist government will claim. And as the nationalist leaders become office holders so their mentality and motivation alters. 'Party H.Q.,' reports a reliable observer of the Ghanaian C.P.P., 'is today a shadow of what it used to be. It is no longer the centre of operations for a vibrant and effective nationalist movement. The life of the party is now government and government handouts, and the party followers are on the political dole or trying to get on it.'[29]

Also, the social problem rears its head. It is particularly embittered in societies where (as in the majority of new states) there are wide discrepancies in wealth. It becomes much more acute as the result of certain new characteristic economic policies of the new states. For life under independence has to be shown to be visibly either richer or at least more purposive than under colonialism. In the first case, government is tempted into conspicuous expenditure, e.g. 'Ghanaian Airlines', or the grossly uneconomic minimum wage laws in Egypt. In the second case, it is tempted into capital development projects which absorb more than the country's domestic surplus permits. Whichever the case the state's initial endowment of gold and foreign exchange reserves runs out. This accentuates the clash between left and right wings.

Where there are ethnic and other minorities, these assert their own individualities, the more so when the dominant party or leadership is controlled by some culturally dominant group. The outlying Indonesian island revolt against Java; the Karens and Shans against the Burmese; the Tamil speakers of Ceylon against the Sinhalese – and so forth.

29. David Apter (1957), quoted Almond and Coleman, op. cit., p. 297.

Thus it happens that just when the inherent forces of disintegration manifest themselves and strong purposive government becomes necessary, the government's prestige and moral authority is tarnished. In some such cases only the charismatic personality of an heroic leader – a Sukarno, a Liaquat Ali Khan – stands in the way of dissolution.

What then are the prospects for the new states? There seem to be four possibilities.

(a) *Civilian quasi-democracy.* We have already seen that Mexico and Turkey evolved, over a period of some forty years, a dominant 'official' party arrangement, which was nevertheless not totalitarian. Such a party was sensitive enough to outside criticism and inside pressures to reflect public opinion: it was dominant and independent enough not to bow to it; and it was well organized enough to harness civilian associations and loyalties behind the institutions it utilized. Thus it was able to close the gap between the westernizing and urban élites and the traditionalist and rural masses. Issues were compromised inside the framework of the party instead of being blown up, by electoral competition, into major crises over legitimacy and procedures. At the same time the more important civilian organizations were tied into the party which, with its firm mass basis, served to underpin the civil power.

Now in some of the newer states, the nationalist party or coalition that has become the ruling party at independence is clearly moving in a similar direction. One might cite Ghana, Tunisia, Guinea, the Ivory Coast, Senegal, Somalia, Tanganyika and Nyasaland. All have thrown up dominant or single-party systems. Even more significantly, some of these parties have deliberately decided to perpetuate and to institutionalize this situation. In India, the Congress Party is dominant because of its prestige, its leadership, its patronage and its 'machine'. It has not (or not yet) needed to grant itself a legally privileged position. In Ghana, in Guinea and in Tunisia it has. In Ghana, for instance, the C.P.P. government has voted itself special powers to arrest and detain its opponents, and has, in a series of purges, virtually expelled the opposition from Parliament and intimidated, proscribed or exiled its leaders. At the same time it has absorbed all the significant civilian organizations of the country: the United Ghana Farmers' Council, the Trades Union Congress, the Co-operative Movement, the ex-servicemen's and women's organizations and so forth. And Nkrumah pronounces its identity with the state, saying: 'The Convention People's Party is Ghana. Our Party not only provides the Government but is also the custodian which stands guardian over the welfare of the State.'

This is a pattern which is likely to spread. Handled efficiently the official or dominant party system might conceivably provide a civilian alternative to military rule.

(b) *Civilian 'open' democracy: India.* The most hopeful evidence for the possibility of democratic civilian government is the successful experiment in India, for her handicaps are such as to make one wonder how the subcontinent is governed at all, let alone in a liberal spirit. It is true that India possesses certain advantages. She has a dominant personality in Nehru; a widespread and educated middle class which supplies her officers, administrators and professionals; a well-trained civil service; a social policy which, even if it does little to bridge the gap between rich and poor, at least visibly tries to do so; and, finally, a dominant party rooted in the villages. Yet this has to be set against apparently crushing handicaps far greater than that of almost any other successor-state. Her size: a population of some 380 millions; one of the lowest average *per capita* incomes in the world; widespread illiteracy; a multitude of linguistic and communal divisions. As long as the Indian experiment prospers, the possibility of a stable democratic order for the new states is possible too. Other states may not possess all India's advantages (though many of them began life with a fair number of them), but none start off with a tithe of her handicaps.

(c) *Civilian totalitarianism* (*communism*). In practice, militant communism has been far less successful than might have been expected. It has arrived either with the Russian armies (Eastern Europe and the Balkans) or with Chinese military support (North Vietnam). Nevertheless the possibility of further advance is very real. In many of the new states the Communist Party, even underground, is the only cohesive and disciplined organization in the country outside the army. It is possessed of a coherent doctrine, held with tenacity and pressed with fanaticism. It is equally prepared to lead insurgent masses or, as in Guatemala and Cuba, to infiltrate a popular movement, and emerge in control of the key organizations of the state.

It makes a special appeal to new states in difficulties once the first fervour of nationalism has worn off. Its class-war doctrine finds supporters where the disparities in wealth are great, where the nascent proletariat is at its most frustrated and extreme, and where the contours of pigmentation, wealth and political power are visibly seen to coincide. And these conditions obtain in a very large number of the new states.

Secondly, the Soviet example makes a special appeal to anti-Westernism, a feeling which is understandably widespread in the former Asian and

African possessions of the European powers and which, in the form of anti-Americanism, is very much alive in Latin America. The Soviet system is seen as a way of westernizing without having to humiliate oneself by copying the West; indeed, by turning one's back on it. Furthermore, it seems a 'get rich quick' system as opposed to the laboriously slow pace which the Western model appears to demand. And both the Soviet Union and China have tried to portray themselves as former colonies which have become rich and powerful after shaking off the imperial yoke.

Finally, it is demagogic, in that its appeal is both popular and also authoritarian. It therefore attracts the young and idealistic, but also the disappointed or 'failed' professional or technician or army officer. Government is to be *for* the masses: but *by* an élite. The intellectual, the white-collar worker, the officer are quite prepared to be that élite.

(d) *Military intervention.* Yet none of the preceding alternatives seem likely to spread or to take a firm hold. The open democracy of India is the most unlikely of all. The new states lack, as we have seen, the ideology and the social basis on which alone this open system, with its orderly representative system and tolerated opposition can thrive. The majority doctrine gives full reign to all the particularisms – ethnic, communal, class – by which these imperfect societies are riven. It may be that the Indian experiment proves successful and that other countries can follow suit. But it seems unlikely that they will be many; and they will be inherently unstable. Even in Latin America, with 150 years of experiment behind it, the only open systems that appear to be working smoothly are those of Uruguay and Costa Rica. Well-developed nations with a long historic formation like France and Germany and Japan have relapsed from open democracy into military intervention. It is hard to see why states with much less united communities should do any better.

Nor does the single – or dominant – party pattern enjoy a fairer prospect. First, even if such parties establish themselves successfully, they have a tendency to go stale. The Egyptian Wafd Party went stale in this way, and finally the initiative passed to the activists – the Moslem Brotherhood and the army. The Indian Congress runs the same risk. Its great advantages are its leader, Mr Nehru, and its triumphant history; but the first is not immortal, and as Taya Zinkin says, 'History knows no gratitude ... The Congress has lost an enormous amount of prestige, despite its immense achievements and this ... has translated itself into a widespread series of open quarrels ... In nearly every state there are dissident and rebel groups and the party discipline has crumbled. But these are not the causes of decay, they are the symptoms. The cause is the alienation of

Congress from the modern educated.'[30] A similar staleness is reported from the very much younger C.P.P. of Ghana. 'Comrades,' Nkrumah said in 1959, 'it seems to me that maybe from complacency and exhaustion some of our older party members seem to have lost in some degree the early spirit of zeal.'[31]

Secondly, it is no easy thing to prevent such parties from breaking up. They try to be all things to all men; they seek to incorporate all important organized sections of opinion: they seek to dominate and politicize all politically important voluntary bodies outside their ranks. In trying to accommodate all these interest-groups, the Mexican P.R.I. has lurched from left to right, but has held together. The Turkish People's Party did not, and was finally constrained to allow its dissidents to hive off and form the Democratic Party – with disastrous results fifteen years later. The Burmese A.F.P.F.L. split into two factions in 1958 and so prompted the military interventions of General Ne Win. The Pakistan Muslim League splintered into knots of politicians carrying on a purposeless game of general post. And at the moment of writing the Ghanaian C.P.P. is passing through an acute crisis, which must either lead to a split or a purge. (The arrest without trial of fifty of Nkrumah's opponents which accompanied this crisis was significant in that half of those arrested had, till recently, been keen supporters of the government.)

In any case, by no means all new states start off with such dominant party systems. This was unknown in Latin America and the Balkans, uncommon in the Near East. Among the more recent states, the Sudan, Nigeria, the Congo and some half-dozen of the ex-French territories have multi-party systems and will soon be joined by Uganda and Kenya. In Asia, Ceylon and Indonesia have multi-party systems. These lists are illustrative, not exhaustive. In these countries the multi-party systems tend to institutionalize and deepen the pre-existing social, ethnic, religious and tribal divisions in society. They enfeeble authority and render it unintelligible. In Indonesia, where the sole unifying force in government is the personality of Sukarno, his recent activities provide a grotesque commentary on multi-partyism in a new and divided state. The 1955 elections provided a legislature composed of Sukarno's own P.N.I., the Muslim Masjumi Party, then the Muslim Ulama Party, and in addition the communists, the socialists, the Christian Party and the Catholic Party. Between 1957 and 1959, the islands revolted against Java, and effective political

30. Taya Zinkin, 'India and Military Dictatorship', *Pacific Affairs*, vol. XXXII, no. 1, March 1959, pp. 90–91; cf. K. M. Pannikar, *Common Sense about India*, Chap. III.

31. Austin, op. cit.

control had to be handed over to the central government's military forces. By 1959 the President was telling his four-year-old Constituent Assembly (still working out the new constitution) that he wanted a Presidential cabinet to rule 'without interference or opposition as conceived by the system of liberal democracy'[32] – a very understandable desire. Since the Constituent Assembly demurred, he dissolved it. He then proceeded to form a new cabinet in which the Chiefs of Staff were significantly included, and personally nominated a new legislature from which his opponents, the Masjumi and Socialist parties, were excluded. Finally he banned these parties altogether and subjected all political activities to tight government control. His new system is itself underpinned only by a tacit accord between Sukarno's own party (P.N.I.), the Communist Party and the army, and the tension between the last two is increasing. This unstable situation will almost certainly be punctuated, if not terminated, by alternate communist and military bids for supreme power.

Under either alternative, then – whether of open or 'guided' democracy – the likelihood of social disintegration is very great. The legitimacy of the governing body is in dispute, the procedures unintelligible, and the society is riven by mutually incompatible factions. These are societies living on the edge of overt crisis, liable to erupt as soon as the initial euphoria of liberation dies down and its symbols tarnish. In such circumstances either the government becomes a mere spectator while opposing groups tear each other to pieces, or else, conscious of its responsibilities, it summons the army to its support and crushes these factions down. Now we have run into these situations before. The first is a typical Primo de Rivera or Ayub Khan situation ('a perfectly good country has been turned into a laughing stock'). In situations like this, sooner or later even an army trained in the British tradition of political neutrality will act like one trained in the Spanish traditions of supercilious inter-meddling, and will supplant the civil power. The second is a typical von Seeckt situation. Its life entirely dependent on the army, the government becomes a mere pawn and the army exercises indirect rule, by blackmail or pressure.

The third alternative, attempted communization, is *at present* only likely

32. 'President Soekarno said today that political and economic liberalism were mother and child to growing capitalism which ultimately would resort to Fascism. This was capitalism's last effort to preserve itself. "We do not want Fascism," he said when opening his newly-nominated Parliament. "This is why we brought liberalization to an end and replaced it with Gotang-Rojōng (mutual help) democracy".' (*Daily Telegraph*, 17 August 1960). This reminds me of 'Kingfish' Huey Long, the Governor (and dictator) of Louisiana. 'Senator,' asked a newspaper correspondent, during the 1930s, 'Senator, do you think we're going to get Fascism?' 'Sure,' replied the Senator, 'but we'll call it anti-Fascism.'

to bring about an identical result, but more quickly. For most governments, most populations and – not unexpectedly, therefore – most armies
today, communism is still unattractive: so unattractive that they are
prepared to fight it. Examples to the contrary exist but so far there are not
many. Communist success in Laos, for instance, is due to the Royal
Laotian Army's lack of offensive (and even defensive) spirit against the
Pathet Lao. In time, still more governments and populations and armies
may become indifferent. At the moment, however, the communist challenge appears to government and army as merely one more divisive or
rebellious factor among all the others. On past form, the communist challenge takes the shape of either a formidable party challenge (as in
Indonesia); or a powerful grip over workers' and peasants' organizations
(China, North Indochina, Greece, Guatemala); or armed insurrection; or
all together – as in Burma, Vietnam and Greece. Most governments in the
new states therefore see communists as another of the divisive forces in
society, along with tribalism and communalism and so forth. As long as
they do so, the communist challenge will simply push the government into
the hands of the military, and even give the military both the reason and
the opportunity to supplant civilian institutions altogether. Communist victory is likely to take place, for the moment, only in the areas where Soviet
Russia and China enjoy a favourable geographical position. All this may
change, *and would certainly do so if the world balance tipped in favour of the
East*.

Of all the alternatives therefore the most probable is some form or other
of military intervention – possibly indirect or 'dual', but more often than
not overt and direct. We do not mean this will become a universal pattern.
It would be surprising if one or two of the new states did not make a
success of some kind of open democracy, and still more of some variant of
one-party rule, while some fringe territories are likely to be overrun by
communism. We mean no more – but certainly no less – than that military
intervention, of which we are even now seeing a good deal, will not only
continue but become very much more common. The arrival in these countries of nationalism and the principle of popular sovereignty, together with
the presence of a standing army, has rendered them just as liable to military
intervention of the modern type as the European lands from which these
principles originated; while the inherent fragmentation of their societies,
their lack of consensus, and the shallow popular basis of their new institutions, make them much *more* vulnerable to the consequences of nationalism,
popular sovereignty and standing armies than the European originals –
certainly not less vulnerable than Spain and Portugal and Germany.

This will seem more than harsh to the many generous-minded westerners who see in the new states of Asia and particularly Africa a new birth of freedom, a pristine political innocence now that the mire of colonialism has at last been sloughed off. 'The world's great age begins anew, the golden years return.' To them it may smack, not of a melancholy scepticism but some ironic *Schadenfreude*, or what is worse, racialism.

But to say that a society is ready and able to govern itself is not the same as saying that its people are ready to govern themselves. It may mean simply that a few of its people are just as capable of governing the mass as were the administrators and agents of the imperial power. And in most cases this is just what it does mean. What is the military dictatorship of Pakistan[33] and the Sudan but Governor-General's rule with a native instead of a British Governor-General and army? What is the pattern of rule in the Middle East but a reversion to the Ottoman and Mameluke pattern – a combination of a military oligarchy, the permanent officials, and the 'learned' class.[34] What is the pattern of rule in Thailand but the rule of absolute monarchy *redivivus*, with a soldier instead of the monarch exercising absolute power over a traditional society? What is and has been the pattern in most Latin American republics but vice-regal authority writ large in the hands of all-powerful Presidents? Forms of government (no less than theories, as Sir Henry Maine would have it) possess that faculty of the hero in the Border ballad – 'when his legs were smitten off, he fought upon his stumps'.

The Latin American states have been 150 years in the making: most of them are still half made, still unstable. The Balkan states with about half that lifespan until absorbed by the Soviet Union were still, at the end of the process, imperfect nations rocked by instability and military intervention. With the exception of Lebanon all the Arab states of the Middle East have succumbed to military rule. Except for India and the Philippines (Malaya is too recent an example) no new state in South and South-East Asia is stable, Pakistan and Siam and Burma have experienced military rule, and one, Indonesia, is in dissolution. The African states, in being and to be, are unlikely to enjoy a different fate. Their societies are no more coherent and their economies no more advanced than those of their predecessors in independence. And there is absolutely no reason to suppose that they possess a greater political capacity than other cultures and nations. The past history of Haiti, Liberia and Ethiopia hardly encourages that belief.

33. Now expired, in favour of the new constitution.

34. A. Hourani, 'The Decline of the West in the Middle East', *International Affairs*, April 1953, p. 180.

And this is to reckon without *mimesis*. Among unstable states, particularly those with a rage for innovation, military intervention has proved to be highly contagious. To take but a few examples of recent date, there is good evidence that it was the success of Perón in 1945 that inspired the wave of military revolts in Paraguay (1947), Peru (1948) and Venezuela (1948). The 1936 revolt of Bakr Sidqi in Iraq was inspired by Atatürk's example and led to the succession of coup and counter-coup between 1936 and 1941. The Egyptian military revolution of 1952 provided the inspiration for the abortive coup in Jordan in 1957 and the successful ones in Sudan and Iraq in 1958. Likewise, the Iraqi coup, the dictatorship of Ne Win in Burma, and the circumstances of General de Gaulle's accession to power in 1958 afforded welcome precedents for General Ayub Khan's dictatorship in Pakistan.

In all likelihood, then, those of the new states which are not overtaken by totalitarianism and attracted into the Russian and Chinese orbits will oscillate for a long time to come between military régimes and civilian restorations. The past patterns of Latin America and the Middle East are likely to occur in the newest states in Asia and in Africa.

*

At this point we ought to conclude. But, precisely at this point the question of values is sure to be raised. 'Are these dictatorships and revolts and pressures desirable?' it will be asked. 'Are they good or bad?' Now, first of all, it is no part of this study to answer such questions; we have tried to explain why and how this world pattern of military intervention has arisen and why it thrives. However, even if we were disposed to try to answer such questions, there is no scientific canon by which to do so. Our answer would depend on a prior disposition, entirely subjective, as to what goals we regard as most important. There are some today who are willing to overlook the despotic nature of any régime providing that it acts or claims to act in the name of the masses; or that it purportedly 'raises the standard of living'; or that it serves the cause of anti-colonialism, etc. There are others who, on the contrary, will refuse to extenuate any despotism whatever on the high ground that it is the antithesis of liberty and justice.

Four things may however be fairly said. The first is that in a large number of cases the frequency of military intervention is a proof that the society is as yet politically immature and unfit for representative institutions. John Stuart Mill, for whom representative government was 'the ideally best form of polity', was himself almost over-eager to assert this. If the people are not ready to fight for these institutions, if they are too little valued for this, he wrote, they seldom acquire a footing; and even if they do they 'are sure to be overthrown as soon as the head of the government or any party leader who can muster force for a *coup de main* is willing to run some small risk for absolute power'. Unless the people are able to take sufficient interest in public matters to permit a public opinion to form, the 'selfish and sordid factions' which arise by the flattering and bribery of their politically unselfconscious fellow-electors can, as in Spanish America, 'keep the country in a state of chronic violence and civil war'. 'A despotism, not even legal but of illegal violence, will be alternately exercised by a succession of political adventurers and the names and form of representation will have no effect but to prevent despotism from attaining the stability and security by which alone the evils can be mitigated and its few advantages realized.'[35] Mill recognized the 'necessity' of some despotic régimes; but he saw them for what they were, as a *pis aller*. He did not, like today's pimps of tyranny, pretend that the despotism was superior to the system of representative government; and nor do we.

However, secondly, in a large number of the cases we have cited, the corporate self-interest of the military has itself signally contributed to this political immaturity. If in some cases, like that of Atatürk, military intervention has been tutelary and constitutive, in the vast majority of cases it has not. Earlier in this book we analysed the mixed motives of the military. It is for the reader to make his own judgement; but in ours, in a vast number of cases this intervention has been little or nothing more than an attempt upon feeble but nevertheless operative civilian institutions by a small group of wilful men armed with lethal weapons, nurtured in arrogance, and pricked on by pride, ambition, self-interest and revenge.

Thirdly, whatever the motive, the result is some form – direct or indirect – of corporate despotism. Whatever our views on the ends which such régimes may serve, and however desirable these may seem to be, we have the duty, first and last, at least to recognize them for what they are: as despotisms. Yet here is a list of official 'styles' with which some of our despots have decorated their régimes:

Nasser:	Presidential Democracy
Ayub Khan:	Basic Democracy
Sukarno:	Guided Democracy

---

35. J. S. Mill, *Representative Government*, Everyman ed., p. 220. I have changed the tense.

Franco:	Organic Democracy
Stroessner:	Selective Democracy
Trujillo:	Neo-Democracy

The one style missing here is 'democracy', without qualification.

Lastly one ought to contemplate the more common of the excuses for military intervention in a highly critical spirit: some of them are more than usually specious. A common justification, for instance, is that the intervention was desirable in order to preserve order in a highly disturbed political situation. So it well might be, but one must first inquire whether this result could not have been achieved by the military coming to the aid of the civil power instead of attacking and supplanting it, as in Spain or Pakistan or Burma. Another common excuse is that the military régime has created greater social equality and material prosperity than its civilian predecessor. Again, this may be true in particular cases; but one ought to bear in mind that there are few military régimes of which this can be unequivocally asserted, while there are numerous examples – the régimes of Arbenz, or Rojas Pinilla, or Jiménez or Perón or Kassim, for instance – where the effect was the disorder if not the ruin of the economy. By any world standards military régimes have shown less than average capacity for statesmanship or economics. And yet, even if it could be shown without doubt that the military intervention had indeed brought material well-being and political stability to a country, it is necessary to ask one final, because transcendently important, question: whether the short-term political and economic gain is not likely to be overbalanced by a longer-term catastrophe? For, in most cases, military intervention has put a stop to constitutional evolution. We have seen that the military engage in politics with relative haste but disengage, if at all, with the greatest reluctance. Armed forces or the leaders whom they have raised to power have indeed been known to withdraw from active politics and retire into a scrupulous neutrality; but, in the historical record, these are very rare. More usual is the situation described earlier in this book: those armed forces that have tried to disengage from politics have had to hasten back as soon as their quondam political enemies came within sight of regaining power, while those that have elected to remain and rule have been ejected only by popular revolt, or by further military revolts of their own malcontents. In most cases the military that have intervened in politics are in a dilemma: whether their rule be indirect or whether it be direct, they cannot withdraw from rulership nor can they fully legitimize it. They can neither stay nor go. If ever we are asked to endorse a military régime, therefore, we must surely ask ourselves whether any immediate gain in stability and prosperity it brings is not overweighed by the very great likelihood that, for an indefinite time to come, public life and all the personal expectations that hang upon it will continue to be upset, wilfully and unpredictably, by further military threats, blackmail or revolt.

There still remain those very numerous cases where, as we have seen, the military are so powerful and the civilian forces so inchoate and feeble that, come what may, the military are bound to dominate politics. Here, we are not called on to endorse anything. We are merely called on to attest to a fact. Whatever our private opinions of these régimes, we have to recognize that the state of society makes them inevitable. Our attitude to them can only be, in Dante's words,

. . . come colui che piange e dice.

CHAPTER THIRTEEN

THE MAN ON HORSEBACK – 1975

1

TWELVE years have passed since the last chapter was written; the course of events has strikingly confirmed the predictions made there. The number of stable liberal-democracies has not significantly expanded, the number of totalitarian communist states has not contracted and the single- or dominant-party systems in new states have proved as fragile as suggested. In contrast, these twelve years ending 31 December 1974, have witnessed 101 more *coups*, thirty-five more states have been affected, and the countries governed by men who came to power as a result of military intervention now number thirty-eight. They represent 25 per cent of the world's 150 independent states and comprise some 55 per cent of the population of Latin America, nearly two-thirds of the population of the Arab states of North Africa and the Middle East, and a like proportion of the population of sub-Saharan Africa. And this is to count only 'hard core' cases: it excludes régimes which exist only by courtesy of their military forces such as Jordan, Morocco and Iran, and those where the military, though temporarily disengaged from active politics, continue to dominate political life, like Guatemala, Nicaragua, El Salvador and the Dominican Republic.

The flood of facts has swept away some of the fashionable theories of the sixties: for example, that Latin America, having purged itself by 1960 of all military régimes, had finally entered its civilian phase,[1] that Africa was 'different' and incapable of being 'Latin-Americanized',[2] that the one-party system was an effective barrier to military take-overs.[3] Equally, it has cast doubt on others which hailed the military as the great modernizing force in otherwise backward societies.[4]

Yet, by the same token, this long train of military interventions has called into being an increasingly voluminous literature. Work on civil–military

1. E. Lieuwen, *Arms and Politics in Latin America*, New York, 1960, p. 171.

2. W. F. Gutteridge, *Military Institutions and Power in the New States*, London, 1964, p. 144.

3. e.g. T. L. Hodgkin, *African Political Parties*, London, 1961, p. 169; F. R. von der Mehden, *Politics of the Developing Nations*, New Jersey, 1964, pp. 65–6; and cf. the discussion in S. E. Finer, *Comparative Government*, London, 1970, pp. 524–31.

4. Cf. below, at pp. 260–66.

223

relations has, in fact, become a great growth-industry in sociology and political science. Some of this literature criticizes my approach and my arguments (or some of them); some of it, on the other hand, confirms or even elaborates upon them, and some of it uses approaches or raises issues to which I devoted little attention or none at all. The use of aggregate data and statistical analysis, for instance, has been abundant, if not in most cases fruitful. As for new issues, two are outstandingly important: the relationship between military intervention and 'development' (political and/or economic); and the problem of military disengagement from politics – how, in other words, a military force that has intervened can withdraw so as to bequeath to its society a durable civilian régime.

In short: there have been more events – more theorizing on these events – and more and continuing reflection by myself on both. What ensues is the outcome of those reflections.

2

MILITARY INTERVENTION

Military intervention is, clearly, a product of two sets of forces – the capacity and propensity of the military to intervene, and conditions in the society in which it operates. The events of the last twelve years and the current state of theory prompt a reconsideration of what I said on each of these two counts when I first wrote this book.[5]

1. *The Military*

A. *The capacity to intervene*

In very brief compass, the argument I advanced was that since the armed forces tend to be the most highly organized association in the state, since they are a continuing corporation with high sentiments of solidarity, often of great prestige and symbolic status, and since too they are more lethally armed than any other organization, they possess an all but irresistible capacity to intervene. Consequently, the rest of my discussion was largely devoted to inquiring as to why they might (or might not) wish to do so (i.e. to 'motivation' or 'mood'). Today I would wish to add two important modifications to this rather simplistic model.

5. Cf. S. E. Finer, 'Armed Forces and the Political Process' in J. Gould (ed.), *Penguin Social Sciences Survey*, London, 1968, pp. 16–33; and S. E. Finer, *Comparative Government*, London 1970, Chapter 2, 'The Military Régime'.

(i) Size and firepower

Statistically minded researchers have devoted much labour to trying to relate the size or cost of armed forces to the incidence of military intervention.[6] They might as well have scrutinized the entrails of a dead fowl. The size of the armed forces is of major importance in deciding whether it can police a country and how it can govern, *after* it has taken over;[7] but bears no relationship to the failure or success of a *coup*, or the number of *coups* attempted. It has been shown that it need take only a handful of troops to overthrow an entire régime. Less than 150 paratroopers were necessary to overthrow President M'ba in Gabon, and a like number to overthrow President Olympio in Togo in 1963. Six hundred troops out of an army of some 10,000 sufficed to destroy the Nkrumah régime in Ghana in 1966. The entire Northern Region of Nigeria was subverted in the January 1966 *coup* by no more than some 500 men and thirty officers.

The reasons for this have already been explained at pp. 141–8, they lie in the very nature of the *coup d'état* as a device for seizing power: the *coup* is the more successful, the more bloodless it is. It is not mounted to be a civil war, and if a civil war results that is the measure of its failure. The conspirators do not dare seek the complicity of the entire forces, since this would breach security. For this same reason the strike-force must be as small as appears consistent with success. Hence the essential components are secrecy, surprise and the neutralization in various ways of the bulk of the armed forces, in order to permit the sudden seizure of all communication and power centres while the government is being taken by force. It is then assumed that the remainder of the armed forces, out of corporate solidarity, will not fire on their brothers and will rally to the new, military, government.[8]

(ii) Self-division

But a second qualification does have major implications in respect to the number of *coups* attempted, as well as to the stability or otherwise of the post-*coup* régime. This qualification may be put in the form of a query: to what extent is it permissible to talk of '*the* military' as though this were a single monolithic unit? Self-divisions in the armed forces have already been discussed above, at pp. 139–48 (in connection with the *coup*) and pp. 173–9 (in respect of the disintegration of the military régimes); but it is

6. C. E. Welch jr (ed.), *Soldier and State in Africa*, Evanston, 1970, pp. 268–9; R. D. Putnam, 'Towards Explaining Military Intervention in Latin American Politics', *World Politics*, vol. XX, October 1967, pp. 100–101.

7. For the Nigerian case, cf. R. Luckham, *The Nigerian Military*, Cambridge, 1971, pp. 90–93.

8. E. Luttwak, *Coup d'État*, London, 1968.

desirable to make more explicit what in those pages is largely implicit and parenthetical. For experience has shown that for a number of quite different reasons, 'the military' may be much less solidary and united in peace-time conditions than on the field of battle, and more disunited still when society has become politically or socially convulsed. To begin with, military *centralization* is sometimes defective. The larger military establishments are divided into services – sea, air and land – and each service is split into different arms, e.g. artillery, infantry, armour: all personnel are parcelled into different commands, garrisons, barracks. The military *coup* originates in some or other of these only. Other services, arms or garrisons may have different views: a *fait accompli* may make them acquiesce – but is, equally, a green light for them to bide their time and conspire in their own turn. Again, military *hierarchy* is sometimes defective. Usually, one can assume that 'the military' is the officer-corps: but this is not always so. The Cuban *coup* of 1933 was led by one Sergeant Batista and his N.C.O.s against the officers. The Sierra Leone *coup* of April 1968 was an N.C.O. revolt. The breakdown of the Congolese Force Publique in 1960 was an N.C.O. revolt against the Belgian officers, and there is ample evidence that the second Nigerian *coup* (July 1966) was fuelled by rank-and-file pressure on the commissioned officers. But, on the whole, these are unusual cases and in most cases the equation of 'the military = the officer corps' still holds. However, this officer corps is itself not necessarily a corporate unity, and many are the examples where military intervention is the work of junior officers, as opposed to the brigadiers and generals. This often reflects a generational gap, the generals being steeped in a pre-technological training and a socially conservative set of values, the younger men having been trained abroad in technological warfare, and exposed to the flood-tides of nationalism and radicalism.

Other divisive factors may also appear. The ethnic composition of the force may fragment it under stress, as in Zaire 1960–65, in Nigeria 1966–70, or, in modified form, in the Syrian army in the late sixties, as officers of the Alawite minority extended their grip on the command positions. Similarly, forces may be divided by political allegiance: this has been a pronounced feature of the Syrian and Iraqi armies since the sixties and largely accounts for the frequency of *coups* in those two countries. To take another example, the Argentinian military split into at least three factions after overthrowing Perón in 1955, some prepared to 'manage' the ex-Peronistas, others determined to suppress them, and others again – the 'Naseristas' – who wanted to suppress parliamentarianism altogether and rule directly, in the army's name.

226

The Portuguese experiences since the successful *coup* of 25 April 1974 vividly illustrate the self-division of a military establishment and go far to explain the erratic course that the revolution has pursued. At the time of the *coup* the navy was highly radical, the airforce was conservative, while the army contained a wide range of opinions. It was divided in many different ways, each somewhat overlapping the others. To begin with, there was and still remains a division between the regular career officers and the 'conscript' officers, and indeed the discontent in the army began (as early as 1973) when the junior career officers began to complain about their pay and conditions; and became acute in March 1974, after the government had decreed that the officer-training course was to be reduced from four years to one year. In the eyes of the career officers, this gave the 'conscript' officers an advantage over them and degraded their own professional self-esteem. It should be noticed that the Armed Forces' Movement is a movement of the regular career officers – not of *all* the officers; and the Movement's institutions, e.g. its Assembly, consists only of the career officers. Secondly, the generation gap is very marked indeed. The movement began, in 1973, as 'The Captains' Movement'. When the *coup* of 1974 was planned, senior officers were certainly brought in, and the first military Junta, of 25 April 1974, was composed exclusively of high-ranking generals and admirals. Subsequently, at every lurch to the left, these senior officers have been disposed of, and the process culminated in a decree of late 1974 which considerably lowered the retiring age for the more senior ranks and enabled the Supreme Revolutionary Council to retire them prematurely. This generation gap partly, perhaps largely, overlaps with the class composition of the officer corps: on the whole the senior officers came from the well-to-do latifundist and mercantile oligarchy that virtually controlled the life of Portugal, while these junior officers came mainly from lower-middle-class families. This, in turn, partly explains the political self-division in the army's ranks – but by no means wholly, since there is clear evidence, even at the time of writing, that many of the junior officers, perhaps a majority, still follow a line which is highly conservative by the standards of the Supreme Revolutionary Council. The army, from the inception of the *coup* down to the present moment, has been very divided as to policy. It had soon split into an extremely radical leftist faction, and a rather conservative one, this being led by the new régime's provisional President, General Spinola. The left-wingers have consistently seized the initiative and shown considerable cunning; they were able to oust Spinola, and carry on a continual series of purges among all three of the Services. The army is also split, however, on the issue of whether to return power to the civilians, which means to the political party leaders, or whether to retain it; and here again the radical faction, the Portuguese equivalent of the 'Naseristas', have been able to get their way, and have imposed on the parties a draft constitution which guarantees the military a position of supreme power for a period which is fixed, at the moment, at 'three to five' years. A further split then developed: after the elections of 25 April 1975 to a Constituent Assembly – elections which showed how slender was the Communist and ultra-left hold on the Portuguese electorate – one faction of the army proposed to abolish all the parties and create a new official party, drawn from the left, to act as the Armed Forces' Movement's political ancillary (and that it would be a mere ancillary was made quite clear); while another faction insisted on retaining the competitive party system. These were the so-called 'pluralists'. At the moment of writing, the latter have just carried the day, and the parties continue their operations. But the majority for the pluralists was very very slender.

It may therefore be an act of oversimplification to talk of '*the* military', and in so far as that term is used, it should be regarded as an expression of convenience rather than an affirmation that the various services, arms, corps and units of the armed forces, the officer corps and the other ranks, are all solidly and unanimously together – though in certain instances this may be so. The distinction ought to be made for each particular case.

Two conclusions follow from this. In the first place, it is usual to assume that the more united and centralized the military establishment, the greater its capacity, and *therefore*, the higher the number of *coups* it attempts. Events have shown the truth is the very reverse. The more inchoate the military establishment, the *greater* the number of *coups*, as one element or faction after another seeks to counter or to emulate the success of those of the military establishment who have seized power. The numerous *coups* in self-divided armies like the Syrian, Iraqi, Ecuadoran, or Bolivian or Argentinian armies demonstrates this vividly. Secondly, by parity of reasoning, the *weaker* will tend to be any régime established by the intervention of such self-divided forces: for the temporarily victorious elements find themselves under threat from other, rebellious, units, and this goes far to explain why *coup* is so often followed by counter-*coup*, and why in so many instances what was erected by one military *coup* is pulled down by another.

B. *The disposition to intervene*

'To intervene,' I wrote (p. 20) 'the military must have both occasion and disposition. By a "disposition" we mean a combination of conscious motive, and of a will or desire to act.' I was surprised to find Professor

228

Dudley complaining that 'this leaves unexplained that which it seeks to explain. It is like saying "X cries because X is disposed to cry", which is to explain nothing about why X is crying.'[9] It is like nothing of the sort. The disposition to intervene was analysed (in some 20,000 words) into the mood that triggers and the motives that, alone or in combination, may impel. Those motivations, it will be remembered, are five – the national interest, the class interest, the corporate interest, the regional or particularistic interest, and the personal interest. Of course, if Professor Dudley is really concerned for an explanation of why certain men in certain situations feel humiliation, fear, shame or rage, or why they should care for country, class, creed or corporation, he is unquestionably right; but then that task did not seem to be imposed on me. Given the wide extent of the field to be covered, I felt it proper to start with the Deluge and pretermit the Creation of the World.

A more intriguing complaint has been that the *coups* seem to exhibit radically different motivations, leaving some critics to conclude that each *coup* is a unique event. This conclusion is illusory, and is most probably due to the limited number of *coups* they have compared together: for five basic motivations which operate singly or in combination mathematically permit of no less than thirty-one different 'combinations', each containing any five or four or three, or two or simply one, of these motivations. So, if we take say, five of the military interventions of 1972–3, we are likely to find that no two precisely resemble each other: the 1972 Ghana *coup* seems to have been motivated primarily by corporate considerations and those of the national interest, the Afghanistan *coup* of 1973 by personal motives and consideration of national interest, the Ruanda *coup* of 1973 by personal and ethnic considerations, the Chilean *coup* of 1973 by a mixture of national interest, class interest and corporate interest.

My five 'motivations' are, methodologically speaking, a checklist derived from considering (in 1962) about one hundred military interventions. The general consensus appears to consider it as neither too economical (in which event analytically distinct motivations would have appeared under the same heading) nor too elaborate (in which case, similar motivations would have appeared under different headings). However that may be, it is at best a tool of convenience, empirically derived from case studies, and has no higher scientific status than that. Nobody appears to have suggested any substantial addition or subtraction, with one highly topical exception. This relates to the motivation which, at p. 38, is described as 'regional'

9. W. J. Dudley, 'The Military and Politics in Nigeria', in J. Van Doorn (ed.), *Military Profession and Military Régimes*, The Hague, 1969, pp. 210–11.

interest. The Nigerian *coups* of January and July 1966 and the subsequent civil war drew vivid attention to ethnic interest (Ibos versus Hausa-Fulani) and indeed, *coups* in many other African states, such as the Dahomey *coups* of 1966 and the first Ghana *coup* (also in 1966) had strong ethnic overtones. But, at the time I wrote the original chapters, the sub-Saharan *coups* still lay in the future and the Burmese *coup* of 1962 (which also had strong ethnic overtones) occurred just as the book went to press. The nearest to the ethnic motivation which was then at hand lay in Pakistan (p. 38), and this was regionally distributed. Had I been more prophetic, I would have re-named the 'regional' motivation as 'particularistic', so as to embrace not only regional but ethnic and confessional particularisms, and this is why I have now substituted this expression in this chapter.

But while this quintuple checklist has not come under criticism as such (with the exceptions just noted), and while little that is conceptually novel has been added to the 'national interest' motive (though materials illustrating its many-faceted nature have been abundantly forthcoming), a number of new considerations have been urged in respect to the motivation of class interest and corporate interest, and to the relationship between them. These views have such far-reaching implications that they must be examined closely.

I have made clear that in certain instances 'the class interest of the military is of great – and sometimes decisive importance' (p. 35), and shown, for instance, how the lower-middle-class make-up of Latin American armies made them revolutionaries in respect to the 'old oligarchy', but counter-revolutionary in respect to industrial labour (pp. 37–8). Nevertheless, by listing as many as five possible motivations for intervention I implicitly rejected the view that class interest was the sole motive. Yet this is the view currently taken by a number of highly qualified scholars. For Manfred Halpern, the Arab armies have become 'the principal political actor or instrument of a new middle class'.[10] José Nun, in a major article entitled 'The Middle Class Coup', has propounded the view that the Latin American armies are nowadays middle-class armies, and as such 'assume responsibility for protecting the middle class'.[11] The armies of sub-Saharan Africa are likewise characterized as of a middle- or lower-

10. M. Halpern, 'Middle East Armies and the New Middle Class', in J. J. Johnson (ed.), *The Rule of the Military in Underdeveloped Countries*, New Jersey, 1962, pp. 278–9. Cf. M. Halpern, *The Politics of Social Change in the Middle East*, New Jersey, 1963, Chapters 4, 13.

11. J. Nun, 'The Middle Class Coup', in C. Veliz (ed.), *The Politics of Conformity in Latin America*, Oxford, 1970, pp. 66–118.

middle-class origin similar to that of the civilian politicians and bureau-crats.[12]

Each of these 'area' arguments could be taken on their own merits – or demerits, which are several.[13] The general drift of these arguments has, however, been brought together in a synthesis of great power and intel-ligence by Sam Huntington, in a chapter of his book *Political Order in Changing Societies*.[14] This chapter, entitled 'The Praetorian State', is a most impressive and original addition to the study of military intervention.

The details of Huntington's argument are complicated and, in many cases, controversial – time-scales vary arbitrarily, special allowances have to be made for different areas, different states, in some cases for different events. But the main thrust is this. First, he is talking only of what he calls 'praetorian societies' (of which more below). These are societies where the political institutions are not strong enough to channel and contain sectional and group interests, which for their part express themselves in direct, often violent action against each other and the public authorities. (Roughly speaking, these praetorian societies correspond with my own 'states of low or minimal political culture' in phases of 'overt crisis'.) Even advanced societies can lapse into this praetorian state. Secondly, in these societies as in other well-institutionalized (hence non-praetorian) societies, the armies are drawn from the middle classes. Thirdly, these praetorian societies have passed or are passing through three stages of development: oligarchical, radical middle-class, and mass-participant. Huntington says that at some point in the oligarchical stage the army becomes predominantly middle class in origin and moves against the oligarchies and so initiates a phase of radical reforms which admit middle-class civilian groups to power. This phase is often marked by a hurly-burly in which one faction of the army deposes governments established by another faction, or in which the army alternately establishes and deposes middle-class civilian governments. Thus, in this, the oligarchical stage, the military is progressive and its *coups* are 'breakthrough' *coups*, while in the radical middle-class stage,

12. P. L. Van den Berghe, 'The Military and Political Change in Africa', in Welch, op. cit., pp. 262–6. Cf. Luckham, op. cit., p. 109.

13. e.g. Perlmutter's criticism of Halpern – Amos Perlmutter, 'Egypt and the Myth of the New Middle Class', *Comparative Studies in Society and History*, vol. X, no. 1, October 1967, or the critiques of Nun, viz. D. Canton, *Military Interventions in Argentina 1900–1966*, Instituto Torcuato di Tella, 1967, and M. Kossok, *Potentialities and Limitations of the Change of the Political and Social Function of the Armed Forces in the Developing Countries: Latin America*, Mimeo, Paper presented to the 7th World Congress of Sociology, Varna, Bulgaria, 14–19 September 1970.

14. S. P. Huntington, *Political Order in Changing Societies*, Yale Univ. Press, 1968.

THE MAN ON HORSEBACK

the military is a participant. But, as the suffrage is extended and the proletarian and other popular sectors organize and seek power, the military stop them by assuming a 'guardian' role and overthrowing governments (like Perón's or Goulart's, in Argentina and Brazil respectively) that ally themselves to these populist movements. The middle-class military thus turn into conservatives, and their *coups* become *veto-coups*. In his words: 'As society changes, so does the role of the military. In the world of oligarchy, the soldier is a radical: in the middle-class world he is a participant and arbiter: as the mass society looms on the horizon he becomes the conservative guardian of the existing order.'[15]

Now there are two separate issues here – whether the *effects* of military intervention are as stated, and this has a bearing on a later topic, viz. the relationship of the military to 'modernization'; and whether the *motivations* of the military merely include or consist uniquely of a perceived class interest; and this is the present issue. In the historical record, the military have indeed, as Huntington affirms, overturned the oligarchies and in due course repressed popular mass movements (with this important qualification, that these movements are ones outside the direction and control of the military). Some statistical evidence supports it also. In Latin America, 1935–64, the proportion of 'reformist' *coups* fell from 50 per cent to 17 per cent, while the proportion of violent *coups* rose from 13 per cent to 33 per cent.[16] However, the scholar who collected this evidence has since reported (1975) that the data for the last decade do not support this trend line. Another study shows that in states where the middle class has become an appreciably large element of the working population (over 10 per cent), military rulers either did not sponsor economic changes or even discourage them.[17]

Turning from effects to motivation, however, not only does there appear to be no evidence to contradict my view (p. 35) that perceived class interest has frequently been a military motivation, but the actions and the statements of the military in the Greek *coup* of 1967, or the Uruguay and Chile *coups* of 1973, provide further corroboration. The question is whether this is the *sole* motivation of military interventionists. And there are good negative grounds for supposing that this is *not* so, which are derivable on logical grounds from Huntington's text itself, and good

15. Huntington, op. cit., p. 221.

16. M. Needler, 'Political Development and Military Intervention in Latin America', *American Political Science Review*, September 1966, pp. 616–26.

17. E. A. Nordlinger, 'Soldiers in Mufti', *American Political Science Review*, December 1970, pp. 1131–48.

positive grounds for re-asserting 'national' and 'corporate' interest as additional motivations which, however mixed up they may be in practice, are analytically distinct.

These negative reasons stem from the notion of the 'middle class' that the various proponents of the thesis entertain. In Huntington's book, for instance, it is clear that this is not a united homogeneous class; if it were, it would be possible to suppose a unitary view, and further, to suppose that any segment of the class – and this could be the military – would 'represent' that view. But the middle class turns out to be an aggregate of (*inter alia*) 'professions and literary intelligentsia, merchants and industrialists, lawyers and engineers'[18] – in short, a residual category of all those who are not latifundists, peasants or proletarians. (And not even 'all' of those. Are clergymen and priests not 'middle class'? If not, why not?) Far from displaying a common attitude, this purely categorical group can and does throw up civilian governments whose attitudes and policies are so repugnant to the military as to invite collisions and overthrow.[19] It even appears that sections of this categorical group are revolutionary, and may seek allies among the *Lumpenproletariat* or peasants to overturn the – presumably – middle-class order.[20] It must follow, therefore, that in between the limiting cases of confrontation with the old oligarchy at one end, and the proletariat and peasants at the other, there must be a whole range of cases where the military's motive for intervention is something *other* than 'middle-class' interest as such.

Positive evidence points to this conclusion also. First, the notion of a one-to-one relationship between social class and attitudes ignores the results of later 'socialization', notably that of schools, and – in this context – military academies. An élite group can subdivide into two with diametrically opposed political views, though all shared similar background characteristics.[21] More specifically, a study of Swedish officers, made in 1962, showed that although not more than 24 per cent came from the 'upper class', 85 per cent of the total showed preferences for the Conservative Party (which was supported by only 16 per cent of the electorate).[22] Again, a study in West Germany shows that the proportion of Bundeswehr officers supporting the right-wing F.D.P. and C.D.U. was about *double* that

18. Huntington, op. cit., p. 210.

19. Cf. Huntington, op. cit., p. 200 (for Africa) and pp. 224–5 (for Peru).

20. Huntington, op. cit., pp. 300–304.

21. I. J. Edinger and D. D. Searing, 'Social Backgrounds in Élite Analysis', *American Political Science Review*, 1967, pp. 428–45.

22. B. Abrahamsson, *Military Professionalization and Political Power*, London, 1972, pp. 42, 102–3.

among the population at large and nearly double that among self-employed and professional people.[23] An important investigation into Dutch officers' attitudes showed that on six items measuring 'hawkishness' and 'militarism' military personnel scored higher than civilians: and more specifically, that military cadets scored higher than conscripts and conscripts higher than 'pure' civilians.[24] The reasons for this specific and differential outlook of the military and particularly the officers is the result of a number of processes, not of social origin. For one thing, officer cadets are a self-selected group who choose the military profession because in some measure its 'image' or values are congruent with their own. For another, the military itself exercises a measure of selection, by rejecting candidates who do not come up to the selection board's image of the military and the military outlook. Thirdly, professional education provides a substantive content and rationale.[25] Finally, the profession itself, and the largely self-sufficient and sealed-off nature of the institution, consolidate the effect of all these processes.

All these, rather than social origins, provide the source for the military's concepts of 'the national interest'. It is striking how frequently the *coup* leaders' vision of the ideal turns out to be the values and organization of the army at large. 'The military,' it has been said of the Nigerian army in 1966, was held to be the

exemplar of values that should be copied by civilian institutions; and ideas of honour were generalized from the collectivity of the army to that of the nation. When the military took part in politics, it did so on a vaguely articulated premise that it was desirable for it to reconstruct government and society in its own image, in accordance with the values of which it was believed to be the unique standard-bearer . . .[26]

The same could be demonstrated of the 'Colonels' régime' in Greece after 1967, or General Ongania's in Argentina after 1966, and indeed, of a wide variety of others.

This skein of selective induction, professional training and social code, along with the organization and often the social self-sufficiency of the military establishment, give rise to the narrower corporate interest of the military: a continuing corporation which has acquired or aspires to a certain social status, political significance and material standard. Interestingly, it has been suggested that this, and not so-called 'middle-class values', is what results from the increasingly middle-class composition of the officer corps.

23. ibid., pp. 102–3.

24. H. Tromp, 'The Assessment of the Military Mind', as reported in Abrahamsson, op. cit., p. 100.   25. Cf. Abrahamsson, op. cit., Chapters 3–9.   26. Luckham, op. cit., p. 279.

Probably the most salient result of the fact that so many military officers originate outside the traditional upper class ... is rather that they cease to identify themselves in terms of their social origins but instead transfer their primary group identification to the military service itself, which has created a new style of life for them, and has made it possible for them to advance socially ... This is likely to heighten, more than most observers have seemed to appreciate, the extent to which the political decisions of military officers are dominated by concern for the corporate self-interest of 'the institution' itself.[27]

This statement was prompted by a Latin American example: but a fascinating corroboration comes from the Nigeria situation, where the army officers, *c.* 1966, were of relatively lowly origin – clerks, school teachers, minor civil servants, of distinctly lower educational attainment than their civilian peers, and consequently enjoying lower prestige. In compensation these officers, therefore, espoused the 'officers are gentlemen' code to the degree of caricature. 'Low prestige led them to search for their own differentiated sphere of military honour with which to protect and validate their position in society.'[28]

In concrete terms this corporate self-interest reflects itself in demands for bigger budgets and better pay, etc.; in intense and lethal opposition to the constitution of any rival armed forces like workers' militias or presidential guards; and in a determination to have a say in public policy-making. The last is particularly marked among armies which, like the Argentinian, have never fought a war for over a century and are unlikely to have to in any immediate future: such military establishments actively search for a new role – and find it in a claim to participate in or even superintend the development of the nation.[29]

The last twelve years' crop of *coups* has produced numerous examples of the corporate-interest motive. Despite the claim by many Africanists that the African armies are less corporate-minded than Latin American ones, very many African *coups* have been prompted by this concern. President Olympio of Togo was murdered by the soldiers in 1963 because he had cut the military budget; so, in the words of a *coup* leader, showing his 'profound contempt for the military'. When Prime Minister Dacko of the Central African Republic deposed President Backasso in 1966, one reason was to make good cuts in the military budget and another was the claim that

27. M. Needler, *Anatomy of a Coup d'État: Ecuador, 1963*, Institute for the Comparative Study of Political Systems, Washington, 1964, p. 45.

28. Luckham, op. cit., p. 109.

29. Cf. A. Craig, 'The Argentine Armed Forces and Their Role in the Nation, 1955–1970', unpublished Ph.D. Thesis, University of Manchester, 1973, especially Chapter IV, 'The Changing Role', pp. 155–209.

the President had secretly established a 'pro-Chinese Popular Army' to eliminate his opponents. (It might be noted that the total strength of that country's regular forces at that time amounted to no more than 600 infantry!) A significant reason for Col. Boumédienne's overthrow of President Ben Bella in Algeria in 1965 was concern for the future of the Liberation Army which he commanded: in 1964 Ben Bella had founded a popular militia, to act as a counterbalance. On assuming power one of Boumédienne's first measures was to dissolve this force. In both the Ghana *coups* corporate interest played an important part. In 1966 the army resented the run-down state of their equipment and expressed fear and jealousy of Nkrumah's well-equipped and Russian-trained Presidential Guard; in 1972, when Lt-Col. Acheampong overthrew Dr Busia's government, the military spokesmen, apart from charging the latter with 'malpractice, mismanagement and arbitrary dismissals', also accused him of 'victimization of military and police personnel' by stripping them of the 'few amenities' they had enjoyed since Nkrumah's time. (Apparently, for the first time they were being asked to pay their own electricity and gas bills.)

We can find equally numerous examples elsewhere. The incident that touched off the Brazilian 1964 *coup* was the President's support for naval mutineers; likewise, in Chile, 1967, certain leaders of the armed forces had become alarmed and angry over an attempted mutiny in the navy in the August preceding the *coup*. One of the most detailed and well-informed studies of a Latin American *coup* is Martin Needler's account of the 1963 *coup* in Ecuador. This was officially justified by the charge that the government (headed by the reformist President Arosemena) was in complicity with 'communist subversion', which 'had placed the existence of the Fatherland in mortal danger'. Needler explains how he had taken this justification at face value at first and concluded that the fierce anti-communism expressed by the military was due either to class interest, or religious sentiment, or even to their belief that their primary duty was to conserve public order. Only later, after investigation, did he find the basic reason: 'the military were strongly anti-communist because they feared that in the event of a communist assumption of power the army would be disbanded and replaced by a militia as had happened in the case of Fidel Castro's coming to power in Cuba'.[30] I have already noted an identical fear in the case of the Guatemala *coup* of 1954 (p. 49). It so happens that the rash of military régimes throughout Latin America had subsided throughout the fifties until in 1959 only two régimes, perhaps, could be said

30. Needler, op. cit., pp. 40–41.

to be of this kind. Then the military *coups* began again in the sixties so that at least fourteen of the present régimes are military or military-supportive ones.[31] There is a strong case, corroborated by the Ecuador example, that this recent wave of military intervention is, at least in part, 'prompted by the armed forces' fear for their own survival in the face of the Castro insurgency in Cuba, the liquidation of the Cuban military establishment and Castro's alliance with the Soviet Union'.[32] Surprising it may seem, but corporate self-interest played a major part in the Chilean coup of 1973. Arturo Valenzuela, in a forthcoming book (*Breakdowns and Crises of Democratic Regimes*, edited by J. Linz and A. Stepan) makes this case very strongly. According to his account the Chilean military felt their monopoly of coercive power threatened by the creation of socialist *cordones industriales* (a militia); resented Allende's interference with the seniority system after he had appointed a new Commandant of the Carabineros over the heads of seven ranking generals; and took offence at the extreme left-wingers' incitement of the rank-and-file to disobey government orders by their officers. In the Portuguese *coup*, also, corporate self-interest has played a major part. It has already been shown that the seeds of disaffection in the army were sown when the 'conscript' officers received concessions which, in the eyes of the regular career officers, were disparaging to their professionalism. Most significant, however, is surely the fact that less than a year after a *coup* designed and proclaimed to restore democratic freedoms, including free elections and an assembly that would then permit the people to decide their own future, the Supreme Revolutionary Council has decided to stay in office for the next three to five years at least, and to reduce the political parties and the newly elected Constituent Assembly to mere vestigial appendices.

Corporate interest, therefore, is clearly a powerful and frequent motivation for military intervention; so much can be deduced with certainty from the case-study approach followed above and earlier (pp. 41–9). But it has recently received a most striking corroboration from a scholar using a statistical approach. In those Latin American states (1950–67) whose military were not politically involved, the average proportion of defence expenditure to the central government's expenditure was 9·3 per cent; for those with intermittent military involvement, it was 14·1 per cent; for those ruled by the military *circa* 1960, it was 18·5 per cent. In between 1960–65,

31. To wit: Bolivia, Brazil, Ecuador, El Salvador, Guatemala, Haiti, Honduras, Nicaragua, Panama, Paraguay, Peru, the Dominican Republic, Chile and Uruguay.

32. E. H. Hyman, 'Military Power and Political Change in Latin America', in *Survival*, I.S.S. London, vol. XV, no. 2, March–April 1973, pp. 68 and 71.

the first group of states increased their military expenditure by 2·8 per cent annually, the second group by 3·3 per cent – but the third group increased it by 14 per cent. What applied to Latin America, applied, in a broad sense, to a sample of seventy-four states (including Latin American ones). The proportion of G.N.P. devoted to defence was almost twice as large in countries ruled by the military 1957–62, as in countries whose military were not politically involved.[33]

2. *Society*

When *The Man on Horseback* was published, one reviewer commented that it was 'a most un-military book' – because, presumably, it dwelt so heavily on the nature of society as a determinant of whether and in what form military intervention occurs. This emphasis has been re-affirmed, however, as an organic part of a general theory of military intervention, in one of the most striking and original works to have appeared on the subject. This is Sam Huntington's *Political Order in Changing Societies*. 'The most important causes of military intervention in politics,' he writes, 'are not military, but political and reflect not the social and organizational characteristics of the military establishment, but the political and institutional structure of the society.'[34]

The causes which produce military intervention in politics . . . lie not in the nature of the group but in the structure of society. In particular, they lie in the absence or weakness of effective political institutions in the society.[35]

There is an:

absence of effective political institutions capable of mediating, refining, and moderating group action . . . social forces confront each other nakedly; no political institu-

33. Nordlinger, op. cit., p. 1135.   34. Huntington, op. cit., p. 194.

35. ibid., p. 198. It might seem that in making so bold an assertion, Huntington is claiming that the structure or motivations of the military in a given country at a particular time have no bearing on whether it intervenes or not. I do not believe that Huntington would ever make such a claim. After all, any military intervention, anywhere, is an act of volition. I believe that the unqualified nature of the statement springs from his thesis that a 'Praetorian society' is one in which all main groupings in society are both politicized and given to direct action: wherefrom, by definition, it follows that the military also is politicized and given to direct action. Huntington does not pursue this matter further in this particular book because (so it seems to me) its subject is political development and the intervention of the military is only incidental to this subject. In a similar but opposite sense Janowitz has been construed as insisting that military format and motivations etc. are the unique determinants of military intervention; yet it is perfectly clear (Janowitz, op. cit., pp. 24–30, and pp. 75–100) that Janowitz is acutely aware of the importance of the societal factors.

tion, no corps of professional political leaders are recognized or accepted as the legitimate intermediary to moderate group conflict. Equally important, no agreement exists among the groups as to the legitimate and authoritative methods for resolving conflicts.[36]

Given a society of this type, the participation of new classes or sectors in the polity 'exacerbates rather than reduces tensions. It multiplies the resources and methods employed in political action and thus contributes to the disintegration of the polity.'[37]

By a remarkable (and historically speaking) quite misleading synecdoche Huntington has styled this anomic, pulverized and agitated society *Praetorian*. As he says,

praetorianism in a limited sense refers to the intervention of the military in politics and clericalism to the participation of religious leaders. As yet, no good word describes extensive student participation in politics. All these terms refer, however, to different aspects of the same phenomenon, the politicization of social forces. Here, for the sake of brevity the phrase 'praetorian society' is used to refer to such a politicized society with the understanding that this refers to the participation not only of the military, but of the other social forces as well.[38]

The features of this 'praetorian society' are, clearly, the same as those in my own 'lower levels of political culture' – and indeed, have been seen as such by other scholars;[39] the absence of agreed procedures, the dissensus on these as well as on substantive issues, the fragility of institutions, i.e. in their ability to channel and contain the collisions that these issues evoke – in short, the shallowness of the roots the institutions have put down, as reflected in the lack of a widespread sentiment of their legitimacy or widespread organized support.

There are, of course, important differences between 'praetorian society' and 'levels of political culture'. (It must be remembered at the outset that Huntington's book is only parenthetically concerned with military intervention, and that his major interest is the relationship between the 'strength' of political institutions and increasing mass participation in politics – and all this seen in a developmental, hence a time-dimension.) To begin with, though both abstractions are concerned with the strength or fragility of political institutions, our criteria for assessing these are not the same: Huntington has four 'criteria', while my own list puts three

36. ibid., p. 198   37. ibid.   38. ibid.
39. M. Lissak, *The Deceptive Agent of Modernization: A Comparative Analysis of Civil–Military Relations in Thailand and Burma*, 2 vols. Mimeo, The Hebrew University of Jerusalem, Israel, 1975, Chapter I, p. 71.

'questions', and these are different from his. (This is not of fundamental importance: all it means is that different indicators are being selected – a pragmatic issue of the relative fruitfulness or utility or practicability of one set or the other.)

Secondly, Huntington divides societies into two major groups, not into 'four levels'. He distinguishes those[40] with 'effective' government, and those with 'debile' ones. These roughly overlap my categories of 'Mature' and 'Developed' political cultures on the one hand, and 'Low' and 'Minimal' on the other.[41]

The third difference is that the tension in the Praetorian Society is generated in the dialectic between institutional strength and the extent of popular participation, so that Huntington's 'ladder' is a developmental one, one registered over time. There is oligarchical praetorianism, radical middle-class praetorianism and mass praetorianism, corresponding to the extent of popular participation. In my 'levels of political culture', on the other hand, there is no time-dimension as such – the analysis is static and the 'levels' are determined (basically), in respect of the tension between dissensus/consensus on the one side and the strength and range of the organization of the various publics on the other. The result is that whereas Huntington's praetorian state is an identical condition, undifferentiated except in its temporal phases, I envisage a continuum of four conditions but undifferentiated (unless implicitly) in respect to time. This distinction reflects the different objectives of our two studies, Huntington's being that of political development, my own the causes, methods and results of military intervention.

My notion of the 'political-culture levels' has by now achieved a certain currency. However, the form in which it appears in the original book has proved capable of some elaboration, and this can clear up some ambiguities and explain what at least one critic sees as a certain paradox in the conclusions it may entail. I published these modifications to the concept as long ago as 1968.[42] However, the nature of this chapter makes it appropriate, indeed essential, to incorporate them here.

Before doing so, though, it seems proper to notice a certain methodological objection which has been raised *in limine*. The 'four levels' are measured, it will be recalled, by (*inter alia*) the strength and the widespread acceptability of civilian institutions. But, it has been objected, 'we can only know *for sure* [our italics] what the cultural level is if we never have a military intervention or if there is a resisted intervention (the Kapp

40. Huntington, op. cit., p. 1.   41. ibid.   42. Cf. footnote 5, p. 224.

putsch, for example). At all other levels we must be unsure.'[43] Certainly we cannot know *for sure* – but there are very few things, if any, that we know 'for sure' in the field of social science. In any other sense, the statement is not only not true – it is very puzzling as well. It is puzzling because, if the implication is that the historic absence of military intervention *proves* the cultural level (presumably 'Mature'), then by parity of reasoning the 170-odd *coups* of Bolivia's independent history also 'prove' its cultural level (low or minimal). But, of course, both implications are unwarranted. The fact that a state has not hitherto suffered a military intervention is not in itself evidence that it will suffer a *coup* tomorrow. Britain has been *coup*-free since 1688 but we do not infer its level of political culture from this fact; we do the reverse and explain the absence of *coups* by the tenacity, deep-rootedness, adaptability and durability of its civilian institutions. A 'failed putsch' is not in itself evidence of 'developed' political culture. It would have been absurd for an observer in July 1973 to have concluded that since Chile had at that moment experienced a 'failed putsch' it was a country of 'developed political culture': for a successful *coup* occurred a few months later. Obviously, if a state has not suffered military intervention for nearly three hundred years this is strong confirmatory evidence of an otherwise independent assessment of the strength and durability of its civilian institutions. Obviously, too, when a state like Bolivia has experienced over 170 interventions in a century and a half – and four of these in the last eleven years – this is strong confirmatory evidence of what we can learn from other sources, viz. that its civil institutions are relatively feeble.

A similar misunderstanding seems to underlie another critic's objection, that in stipulating, as one indicator of political culture, the existence or otherwise of 'a wide public approval of the procedures for transferring power', etc., I have come close to assuming what I have to explain – for (he says), '*coups*, revolutions, violence', etc., 'would enter into any assessment' as to whether such wide public approval existed.[44] This would only be so if I had anywhere stated that the *only* evidence for the absence of 'wide public approval', etc., was *coups*, revolutions, violence, etc.: but this is *not* what was said. Plainly, no intelligent man would ignore the Bolivian record in writing a prognosis, any more than a doctor would ignore repeated cases of cardiac failure as a *prima facie* case for prognosing further failures: but only as a *prima facie* case and never as an explanation. He would proceed

43. R. E. Dowse, 'The Military and Political Development', in C. Leys (ed.) *Politics and Change in Developing Countries*, Cambridge, 1969, p. 224, fn. 1.

44. R. Luckham, 'A Comparative Typology of Civil–Military Relations' (*Government and Opposition*, vol. 6, no. 1, 1971), p. 11.

to examine his patient and establish a diagnosis: and this might show that the condition that gave rise to the previous medical history had ceased to exist.

To turn to the substance of the matter – the four levels of political culture themselves. The criteria invoked were basically two. The first was the extent to which wide public approval existed for the procedures for transferring power and a corresponding belief that no exercise of power in breach of these procedures was legitimate; and this was coupled with the existence or otherwise of a wide public recognition of what or who is the sovereign authority and a corresponding belief that no other persons or bodies are legitimate. The second criterion is the width of the political public and how well organized it is in associations like trade unions, churches, political parties, etc. (pp. 78–9). In brief, the first two questions refer to the existence of legitimacy accorded to procedural consensus, the second to the width and depth of organized public opinion. For simplicity's sake I shall use this two-fold and not the three-fold criterion, and call it, for brevity, 'consensus' and 'organization'. Where both are high, the level of political culture is 'mature', where both are very low, the level is said to be 'minimal'.

Now I clearly noted (p. 79) that 'this notion of political culture is a complex of three conditions, and these can be ranked in different ways', so that a continuous rank-order of societies was difficult to arrange. I also noted as one possible consequence that while one society might have a public that was weakly organized but reasonably united, in another it might be strongly organized but disunited (p. 79). And, indeed, in listing the states of a 'low' level of political culture, I pointed out that although this comprised states like Argentina, Turkey, Brazil, and Syria, Iraq and the Sudan, 'there was a wide gap between the two sets since the first, unlike the second, had relatively strong civilian organizations . . .' (p. 79).

But if the three-fold criterion is reduced to the dual one, it does become possible to produce a consistent rank ordering, as shown in the table on page 243, first published in 1966 and, in its present form, in 1970.[45] Minimal opinion and minimal organization (minimal political culture) rise to (possible) high dissensus with feeble organization (low political culture), which rises to (possible) high dissensus with high organization (developed political culture) which culminates in high consensus with high organization. Of the two variables the state of public opinion is a some- what discontinuous one: for specific reasons, it may, at any level, dissolve into acute dissensus or resolve into consensus (though, in practice and for

45. S. E. Finer, *Comparative Government*, p. 549.

Level of political culture	Characteristics of public opinion	Typical methods of intervention	Levels to which intervention is pressed	Resultant régime
1. Mature	High organization, High consensus	(a) Constitutional methods, to (b) Collusion and/or competition with civilian elements	(a) Constitutional, to (b) Dubiously legitimate pressure on civilian authorities	Constitutional
2. Developed	High organization, High dissensus (= overt acute crisis)	(a) Collusion and/or competition with civilian elements, to (b) Blackmail*	(a) Constitutional, to (b) Dubiously legitimate pressure on civilian authorities, to (c) Blackmail	Constitutional, to Indirect military
3. Low	Feeble organization and possibly also High dissensus (= latent chronic crisis)	(a) Blackmail (b) Threats of violence (c) Violence	(a) Blackmail (b) Displacement of civilian cabinets (c) Self-substitution for civilians	Indirect or Direct military
4. Minimal	Insignificant organization, Insignificant political opinion (= power vacuum)	Any method	Any level	Indirect or Direct military

* Threats to withhold support, etc.

reasons explained in the text, very many Third World countries tend to have either little public opinion or a highly dissensual one). So in 'developed' political cultures the table does not state that they live in a *permanent* state of high dissensus, only that they are more likely to lapse into dissensus than the societies of 'mature' political culture. The second variable, however, *is* continuous: it is the width and depth of organized public opinion – so that states like Turkey or Greece or Chile or Argentina, at the 'top' of the 'low-culture' category, nudge states at the bottom of the 'developed' culture levels.

In these states, according to the extent of 'organization', dissensus produces polarization, and hence a state of overt crisis (p. 66). Where civil institutions are well developed, this tends to deter the military from staging a *coup* – it will prefer blackmail and pressure; or, if some elements do stage a *coup*, it will be smothered. In the more highly organized states of the low-level political cultures, like Greece or Turkey, or Brazil or Chile, civil institutions and organizations are not nearly so powerful, nor so respectfully regarded, as at the 'developed' level. For all that, they are not negligible, and this is why, 'the higher up the list of third-order states, the more difficult it proves for the military to retain power without some form at least of civilian trappings, or without organizing civilian support...' (p. 99), as has been amply demonstrated in Chile, Greece, Turkey and Argentina, for instance.

By the same token, however, the higher up this list the greater, by definition, the amount of civilian opposition the military must count on meeting should it decide, not to threaten or blackmail the government, but to overturn it. (It may prefer blackmail and threats, as in Turkey, 1971, or Uruguay, 1973.) It is likely that the military seizure of power and particularly its consolidation will prove bloody and protracted, the repression of opponents vicious and thorough, and the military 'colonization' of civilian institutions far more thoroughgoing than in countries which, however self-divided, have narrow and feebly organized political publics. This is borne out by what has occurred in Brazil (since 1966), Greece (1967/1974) and Chile (since 1973).

This may serve to explain what one scholar puts as an objection: that the 'greater strength of civil institutions in [say Argentina and Greece] has itself been a factor which tends to widen the extent of military intervention'.[46] This is because he has inferred that I thought that as one moved up the scale from the 'minimal' level of political culture to the 'mature' level there would correspond a smooth and continuous gradation from high

46. R. Luckham, *The Nigerian Military*, op. cit., p. 5.

degrees of intervention at the bottom to zero at the top. On the contrary, where the culture level is minimal, the military may or may not intervene – they are 'at large'. From thereon, the degree of intervention increases up the scale; but as we should expect from the analogy of warfare, it reaches its maximum of violence and scope precisely at the threshold beyond which the perceived power of civil institutions to oppose acts as a deterrent to confrontation and overthrow by open violence.[47]

3

THE MILITARY REGIMES

1. *Types of Military Régime*

Many things have been or could be said about classifications; here I will mention only three. First, a classification or typology is for *use*; a classification which helps in explaining one set of phenomena may be useless for explaining others. 'Animal, mineral, vegetable' is useful in the study of pigments, but totally useless for the study of warfare. Secondly, there is need for economy – the categories must be neither so many as to make comparison impossible nor so few as to make contrasts impossible. Thirdly, the criteria of comparison and contrast should be explicit.

I based my own classification (pp. 149–51) on two criteria: the extent to which the military (or its 'representatives') control the major policies of the society, and the degree of overtness with which they do so. So, in broad terms, the military may fully control, or partially and discriminatingly control policy: and do either thing openly, half-openly or covertly. The effect is to generate five major categories of military régime: direct rule, either open or 'quasi-civilianized', dual rule, and indirect rule, either continuous or intermittent.

This is what might be called a 'structural' classification, since its object is

47. R. Luckham, 'A Comparative Typology of Civil–Military Relations', pp. 10–11, and *The Nigerian Military*, pp. 4–5. In these places Dr Luckham has stated as objection what I thought was clearly explicit in my text at the pages cited, viz. that the three criteria of 'level' can vary independently, and that the span of countries in the '*low*' level is very wide. Furthermore, Dr Luckham does not seem to have seen my reformulations of the 'culture-level' concept, as put in *Penguin Social Sciences Survey*, 1968, or *Comparative Government*, 1970. I note that Huntington (op. cit., pp. 229–30) makes the same point as I when he notes that 'As society becomes more complex, it becomes more difficult for military officers, first, to exercise power effectively, and then, to seize power successfully ... By its very nature, the utility of the *coup* as a technique of political action declines as the scope of political participation broadens ... As participation broadens ... and society becomes more complex, *coups* become more difficult and more bloody ...'

to define the relationship of the armed forces to the exercise of authority at a given point of time. It will not serve to illuminate other aspects of the nature of a military régime. To do this, we should have to adopt other criteria, and erect on them a different classification.

One such is based on the allegedly political and social tendency of the régime – commonly expressed in terms like 'left/right', 'progressive/reactionary', 'reformist/conservative': these are all loaded terms, but for all that, some fairly neutral answers are possible. It seems wise however to defer this discussion to the section on 'development', at the end of this chapter.

Another aspect in which observers have become interested over the past years is what, for want of a better term, might be called the constitutional role of the military. One difficulty here is that this role has to be defined in the light of the military rulers' proclaimed intentions, and this is a somewhat illusory premise: they may be intentionally misleading, or become so through force of circumstances, or by conscious change. The issue has arisen because a (limited) number of military governments have, since 1962, not only proclaimed their intention to retire to the barracks once they have purified public life, but actually done so: in Turkey in 1962, in Ghana in 1966, in Sierra Leone in 1968. These, therefore, have to be distinguished from (most of) the others.

A provisional way of distinguishing régimes by the military's (professed) constitutional role, is to begin by distinguishing those where the military are clearly intent on remaining in power or at least on controlling those in power, for an indeterminate or, at the lowest, very long time to come. These régimes are of two major kinds. The first is comparatively rare. It is the product of a premeditated programme for military or military-dominated rule. Such (it is alleged, at any rate) was the character of the G.O.U. régime in the Argentine in 1943 (though it collapsed after two years); also of the Nasserist faction of the Egyptian Free Officers after Neguib had been eclipsed in 1954. Since the second military *coup* in Greece of 1973 it can be said with the benefit of hindsight that it must have been the view of an important section of the Greek military establishment ever since the first *coup* of 1967. In my own private view, it will be established in some years' time that such was also the view of an extremist element in the Chilean armed forces who seized the opportunity provided by the economic and political crises of late 1973 (which must have brought the military in, in any case) to stage the *coup* and seize power for themselves. This kind of régime may be styled the '*programmatic*' kind.[48]

48. This correlates with what Janowitz, op. cit., p. 16, calls '*designed* militarism'.

Much more numerous are the cases where the military seize power with no clear profession of intending to abandon it, or else place this in a fairly remote future. General Onganía, representing all the armed forces of Argentina, made it clear in 1966 when he overthrew President Illia and became President that he envisaged military rule for at least another ten years. We can class together with régimes of this kind others where the Junta promises a return to 'democratic rule', but incorporates or states its intention to incorporate clauses in a future constitution that will give the armed forces a permanent and legal share in future governments: as for example, in the Greek Constitution of 1968, and the proclamation of the Chilean military spokesman (General Leigh) on 21 September 1973. As I have already stressed in a different context, this is precisely what the Portuguese Armed Forces Movement has done. This movement, its statement of 23 December 1974 proclaimed, would remain above politics but as 'an interpreter of the will and desires of the Portuguese people'; and in April 1975, three weeks before the elections to the Constituent Assembly were due, it compelled the main political parties to agree in advance to a constitution which *inter alia* established the A.F.M. in power for the next three to five years, during which time it would have the power to approve and veto all legislation. Unlike the previous category rulers, those in this category have no very explicit programmes: they claim a sort of 'doctor's mandate'. Régimes of this sort may be styled *permanent* (*pragmatic*) régimes.

The second major category comprises régimes which are explicitly designed to be temporary. The first sub-group contains the Juntas that come to power claiming a similar 'doctor's mandate' for setting all things right like the previous group, but specifically promising that they do not envisage permanent political rule. Lt-Col. Acheampong's *coup* in Ghana, 13 January 1972, was of this kind: all that was promised was that the military would govern by decree until a new Constitution was drawn up. Régimes of this kind tend to be suppressive, veto-devices, checking what are to be alleged to be destructive policies and processes. We may style it a '*holding*' type of régime.

The second sub-group in this category is more clearly distinguishable: it is avowedly transitional to a competitive civilian type of politics, and the aim of the Junta is stated to be the necessary preparations for this end. Egypt, 1952–4; Turkey, 1960–62; Nigeria, 1966; Ghana, 1966–9, are examples of this type. This, of course, was how the Portuguese experiences commenced. 'As soon as possible,' ran the Junta's Declaration of 25 April 1974, 'a general election for a Constituent National Assembly whose powers, by its representation and free election, will permit the nation to choose freely its own form of social and political life.'

This is not a very satisfactory classification, simply because the professed objectives of the Juntas are rarely what occurs in practice. In 1966, General Onganía envisaged at least ten years' military rule, but he himself was ejected by his fellows in 1970 and in 1973 the armed forces as a whole abdicated power altogether. In contrast, each successive *coup* in Iraq since 1958 has generated promises of elections in the near future, but these have never occurred and the military are still in control.

Similarly in Portugal. After the generous Declaration cited above, the Jacobins took over. The evolution of the Portuguese military revolution has so far resembled the course of Egyptian events, 1952–4, with General Spinola doubling for Neguib. Once Spinola was forced out of the country as a consequence of what I solemnly affirm history will demonstrate was a deliberately contrived fake 'counter-coup' (11 March 1975), the Supreme Revolutionary Council was formed, and forthwith stated the intention that the military should stay and direct government for the next three to five years.

Before leaving this topic, however, it seems appropriate to comment on two terms which have come into the literature and to consider their relationship to what has just been said. The first is the so-called '*guardian*' role of the military. As used by Huntington[49] it seems to be the equivalent of the early Roman dictatorship, i.e. *temporary* rule to 'return the purified polity to the hands of the civilian authorities'.[50] As such, it is clearly confined to the second, 'temporary' category as defined above, and more specifically to the 'transitional' sub-type. But Huntington goes on to elaborate on the 'ideology' of guardianship – the 'tutelary principle' or 'principle of supermission'. This is identical with what I described in chapter 4 as 'custodianship' (pp. 30–34), and as 'the providential mission of the soldiers as in this sense, saviours of their countries' (p. 28). Now, 'guardianship' is a motive – the motive of the national interest; and in this sense, then it motivates military in *every single one* of the four types of constitutional roles listed above.

Furthermore, it even transcends this list which comprises only those régimes where the military is ruling directly and in its own name. For the military may play 'the guardian', both before a *coup* and after it, and both within the limits of direct rule or well outside any such thing. For as I showed (pp. 30–34), while some military establishments conceive of guardianship as necessitating overt rule, others see it only as the *poder moderador*,

49. Huntington, op. cit., p. 226.   50. ibid.

the arbitral or veto function, from above or outside the functioning political system. This latter role has sometimes been called 'referee' action, and it characteristically expresses itself in either what our main typology calls intermittent rule, either direct or indirect (overt or covert).[51]

Returning then to the structural classification used in the text – has anything occurred to suggest modification? As far as it goes, it seems capable enough of discrimination between military régimes. For instance, the régime of Lt-Col. Acheampong in Ghana (1972) is an unqualified direct régime, as was that of General Gowon in Nigeria (1966, deposed 1975); that of the Greek Colonels 1968–73, direct quasi-civilianized; that of General Park of Korea, where he drew his support from the army and from his official party (the Democratic Republican Party) in relatively free elections, a dual régime; the régime of General Suharto which reposes on his control of the army but also upon the support of powerful civilian sectors is also a dual régime. In both of these countries however the balance is shifting away from a balanced 'dual' character to the direct, if quasi-institutionalized, type. The process started in Korea in 1972 when President Park forcibly abrogated the Constitution so as to permit himself to become life-President – and moreover, a President who was no longer responsible to the Assembly but to a newfangled National Conference, a non-partisan elected body comprising over two thousand representatives. Fearing that this presaged the end of elections in Korea, the constitutional opposition redoubled its criticisms of the President and his ruling party. In the face of this the President's popular support waned and his régime has become increasingly repressive and autocratic – and by the same token, more army-based. In Indonesia the developments towards an easier relationship with the civilian *aliras* ('currents') ended when the student *alira* – which includes the intellectuals, journalists and the like – opposed the visit of the Japanese Prime Minister, Mr Tanaka, in January 1974. Their protests led to widespread rioting, and since that date the régime has relied increasingly on coercion. 'Indirect-continuous' characterizes the Brazilian régime from December 1968 to November 1969 – during which period the military, far from respecting the Congress it had half handpicked, or the new Constitution it had had drafted, reacted in the person of its hand-picked President (General Costa e Silva) to dissolve Congress and restrict civil liberties, and then, in late 1969, when the President suffered a stroke, set aside the constitutional provisions for replacing him, promulgated a new procedure by decree, nominated its own candidates, and,

51. Cf. A. R. Zolberg, 'Military Rule and Political Development', in J. Van Doorn (ed.), *Military Profession and Military Régimes* (Mouton, The Hague, 1969), pp. 176–99.

having reconvened Congress, got it to invest them as President and Vice-President (1 November 1969). As for 'indirect-intermittent', this characterizes the régime in Turkey since 1962, with governments based on a competitive party system, but where the military have made frequent incursions into politics to warn and threaten party leaders, to force the pace on party coalitions and, in 1971, to deliver a 'memorandum' to the Prime Minister which was in effect an ultimatum calling for immediate political and economic changes, and securing the imposition of martial law.

At least two alternative classifications have since been put forward. In *The Military in the Political Development of New Nations*, Morris Janowitz drew up a five-fold typology. Like mine, it is structural; its chief difference is that it extends to civil–military relations generally, not simply to 'military' régimes. These themselves are divided into two basic types: the 'civil–military coalition' and the 'military oligarchy'.[52] The 'fine print' does indeed contain further distinctions, but in the 'civil–military coalition' type they do not refer to structural relationships, (e.g. 'intermittency' or 'dual' régimes) but to the *constitutional role* of the military as defined above (p. 246), viz., its 'referee' role or 'transitional' role. The 'military oligarchies', however, are, rather like my own 'direct régimes', divided into the narrowly repressive, and the quasi-civilianized (though not under these names).[53]

A more ambitious classification has been attempted by Robin Luckham. This too encompasses the entire range of civil–military relations, not just 'military' régimes. Its major innovation is to introduce, as a criterion, not just whether civil power and military power are respectively 'high, medium, or low' but the kind of *boundaries* of the military establishment in any individual country. This term 'boundary', borrowed from sociology, is shorthand for the exclusiveness with which a social sub-system (like the military) conducts transactions – it can do so exclusively with other members of the sub-system, at one end of the scale; or as much or more with persons outside the sub-system as with those in it; or both or either for certain particular kinds of transactions. In the first event (total exclusiveness) he calls the military's boundaries 'integral'; in the second event 'permeable'; in the third event 'fragmented'.

Though it helps us to distinguish more clearly between military régimes and revolutionary ones, the classification does not add a great deal to classifying the former. Only three types of régime in his typology would qualify as military ones by my own definition. The first two are what (borrowing from Huntington) Luckham calls the Guardian State and the Praetorian State. The difference between these relates to the 'boundaries'

52. Janowitz, op. cit., p. 5.   53. ibid., pp. 7–8.

of the army in each case. 'Guardian States' have armies with 'integral' boundaries, 'Praetorian' ones, with fragmented boundaries, hence splits and factions in the armed forces, and a good deal of civil–military coalition. In addition, he stipulates a situation called 'political vacuum' – which seems to overlap my 'minimal political culture'. The 'fine print' does not elaborate any structural relationships that have not yet been dealt with. On the contrary, Luckham's major forms of 'Guardian State' are direct rule (either unqualified or quasi-civilianized); alternating rule (which is not a structural feature at all – it is not the same as 'intermittent rule', but relates to the transit of régimes); 'catalytic' action – which is not a type of rule at all, but simply one of action to replace civilian authorities, instead of supplanting them (cf. p. 78): and 'covert rule', which, of course, uses an entirely different criterion again, relating to *level*. Although the classification scheme as a whole is very comprehensive and highly ingenious, it does not significantly help in the study of military régimes as such. This is because it is designed for a different purpose; like Janowitz's it relates to the entire range of civil–military combinations together, and not just the military régimes.[54]

For all this it must be recognized that the two classification schemes I have offered – the one distinguishing constitutional roles, and the other distinguishing political structures – cannot discriminate certain highly important and relevant characteristics of military régimes. Take, for instance, two '*direct*' régimes: Thailand (till the fall of the military government in 1973) and Burma (till the quackery of supposed 're-civilianization' in 1971). The *way* the military chose to rule in these two countries was entirely different, and so the working constitution and texture of political life was entirely different also. The Thai military married into, negotiated with and entrusted wide discretion to the bureaucratic and business communities. The Burmese military hated the bureaucracy and took private enterprises into their control. There is a great need for a classification that can handle distinctions of this kind. It might prove fruitful, for instance, to establish 'levels' of governance, and parameters of its power as a framework for comparison. Levels would range from (1) *Control*, i.e. general steering of otherwise largely autonomous and self-sufficient sectors and organizations, to (2) *Direction* of these, to (3) *Administration* of these, e.g., *via* the 'colonization' of the government departments, business corporations, trade unions and the like by military officers. In the cases mentioned, the Thai régime goes little beyond (1); the Burmese takes in all three.

This classification could then be wedded to the (well-known) four-fold parameters of 'power': its scope, or range (how *much* do the military

54. R. Luckham, 'A Comparative Typology of Civil–Military Relations', *passim*.

control, direct or administer), its resources-base (legitimacy, coercive and material resources, etc.), its means (force, patronage, economic concessions), and its efficacy (the probability it will be obeyed).

This suggestion points to one simple fact: the greatest gap in the literature at this moment is the absence of detailed case studies of more than a handful of military régimes.

2. *The Transit of Régimes*

We now have many more examples of the rise, transformation and fall of military régimes than in 1962, when the only direct-régimes that had collapsed and formed a basis for generalization numbered a mere four (p. 173). What has been borne out beyond question is the final generalization (at p. 221). 'In most cases the military that have intervened are in a dilemma ... they cannot withdraw from rulership nor can they fully legitimize it. They can neither stay nor go.' So arises that 'transit régimes' described on pp. 167–73. The military run up the scale of intervention from indirect-limited intervention to direct rule and (except in the rare cases of reconstitutionalization) back again. To take a few supplementary examples to bring the record up to date. First Argentina: up to 1962, as already described in the text, this country had passed through direct rule (1930), indirect-limited rule 1930–43, direct rule 1943–5, dual rule 1945–55, indirect-limited rule 1955–66, and direct rule 1966–73. In 1973, the military abdicated to the aged President Perón, victor in free elections voluntarily arranged by the military – in sheer desperation at finding any other alternative. Perón died in 1974 and was succeeded by his widow, who had been his Vice-President. It seems unlikely that this civilian interlude will last much longer. Next, Brazil: Brazil is a singularly interesting case: it was never clear to me why, if my general argument was correct, the Brazilian armed forces had not taken over the government. Instead, up to 1962, they had played a balancing role, first left, then right, as the *poder moderador*. In 1964, however, they finally took over power and since that date have tried – as so many intervening armies do – to wield power and yet not seem to. Thus Brazil has gone through indirect-intermittent rule, 1955–64; direct rule, 1964–7; indirect-intermittent, 1967–8; indirect-continuous, 1969–75. In Ghana, the single-party régime of Nkrumah was overthrown in 1966. There followed direct rule, 1966–9; civilian rule, 1969–72; direct rule, 1972. Turkey has followed a sequence of direct rule, 1960–62, followed by indirect-intermittent rule since that date, sometimes within a hair's breadth of a return to direct rule.

The reasons for the relatively short life-span of most direct régimes and the troubled and contingent existence of 'civilian' régimes that succeed them can be seen more easily than twelve years ago, and summarized more clearly.

First, the military are not necessarily competent to govern even moderately complex societies. Their usual practice is to team up with the civil bureaucracy; but for it to succeed, the bureaucracy must be competent – not always the case – and even if competent, its advice must be heeded; and this does not necessarily happen either. However, the military are now in command and are seen to be. Their previous assets of neutrality and political innocence have been spent. To whom can the population turn if the military prove no better than the 'politicians'?

At this point, earlier remarks concerning the splits and differences within the armed forces attain their critical importance. Policy differences open – few military leaders, we have already noted, come to power with a clear-cut programme. Also, personal rivalries come to the surface. Thirdly, a ruling Junta comprises only a few officers: the rest (and this 'remainder' is being continually refreshed by recruitment) have no direct say in the government, and their distance from it may turn into active alienation in so far as the younger officers come from a different generation and have received a different and more advanced training than the Junta.

One consequence of disillusion is a succession of new *coups*, or counter-*coups*. In Iraq, for instance, the 1958 *coup* was followed by an unsuccessful one in 1959, a successful one in 1963, an unsuccessful one in 1966, a successful one in 1968, an unsuccessful plot in 1973.

Another consequence is that the Junta, uneasy at being in the 'hot seat', uncomfortable at its exposed position, seeks to withdraw from direct rule. In certain cases – Venezuela and Colombia are interesting examples – the military completely *disengage*: since the overthrow of the military régimes in 1958 these two countries have both reverted to civilian rule. So also, it will be remembered, did the Ghanaian army in 1969, and the Turkish military in 1961.

Now this is a hazardous venture, for the prospect that haunts all military Juntas who contemplate withdrawing from politics is that their political opponents, the very men they chased from power, will return after all. In that event, the Juntas' careers – even their lives – will be at risk. Furthermore, some *coups* at any rate are made for a principle – anti-Peronism in Argentina, competitive party politics in Ghana, Kemalism in Turkey, anti-leftism in Greece and in Chile. If the military's enemies return, all the past intervention will have been for nought. How limpidly, how innocently has the Portuguese Admiral Coutinho expressed this, almost as though it was a self-evident truth: that the reason for the militarily imposed draft constitution which guarantees that the military shall continue to govern the country for the next three to five years was that – in his own words – 'otherwise the Armed Forces' Movement could lose – through accidental results from an uncertain electorate – its position as the driving force of the revolutionary pact'.

Consequently, an almost perennial element in a withdrawal is an attempt to provide against the return of political opponents and a retreat from political principles. When the Ghanaian armed forces returned power to the civilians in 1969, for instance, they made sure that the old C.P.P. of Nkrumah was not reconstituted, that certain ex-Nkrumah politicians should not be able to participate, and – beyond that – that the 'Presidency' should be a triumvirate, one of whom was a military man. In Turkey, after 1961 an act of indemnity was passed preventing legal proceedings against the military for the trial and execution of Menderes and his supporters; also the armed forces were given representation in the Upper House, while the Presidency was occupied by a General.

In short, the military take steps to control the successor régime. Sometimes this is by legal and constitutional provision. Sometimes it is by re-casting the constitutional structure that will control the future. For instance, the Brazilian military, in direct control after 1964, and anxious to disengage, did not so do before completely re-shaping the constitution. The political parties were reduced to two, one of them 'official', multitudes of political opponents were deprived of political rights, and the electoral laws were altered. In this way Congress was made compliant, while later laws gave the President vast new executive scope, gagged the press, and endowed the authorities with sweeping powers to act against communism and other 'subversives'.

This done, the military may feel secure enough to withdraw. But for how long? This depends on how well the post-withdrawal civilian régime lives up to the expectation of the military. To the extent that it does not, the military will re-intervene at the level of exercising pressures, extending ultimatums and so on. This is what the Turkish military have been doing ever since 1961; it was what the Argentine military did from 1958 to 1966. The direct régime gives way, not (save exceptionally) to a civilian régime, but to the indirect military régime, usually of indirect-intermittent type.

But the military find this dangerous also. To control the government tightly (as in Brazil today) involves rigging elections, favouring one party over another, etc.; and so the military's freedom of action is limited, and its claim to political neutrality tarnished. On the other hand, to control too loosely may lead to what they always fear – the return of their political enemies or the dismantling of their handiwork. Elements in the armed services will begin to press for a return to direct rule. The wheel will then come full circle. The military will mount yet another *coup* and resume direct rule once more.

The classification of régimes, from direct to indirect, possesses therefore a useful characteristic in drawing attention to the dynamics of military régimes, and providing the framework for analysing them. Two things remain to do. The first is to supplement the foregoing analysis by an important observation of Sam Huntington.

As Huntington puts it, an army that intervenes has two basic options – to retain power or return it to the civilians. But its strategy in either case may be to restrict political participation, or expand it: this generates four paradigm cases:[55]

(1) *Return and Restrict*

This is characteristic of what the Argentine military did after overthrowing Perón in 1955: the return to civilian rule and election was qualified by limitation or the banning of Peronist organizations. It was characteristic too of the Ghanaian military in restricting ex-Nkrumah organizations.

(2) *Return and Expand*

This is notably what the military have done in Venezuela, where the 1958 overthrow of Jiménez (in which the military were accomplices) permitted freedom of action to their former *bête noire*, the Accion Democratica party: likewise, in Colombia since the fall of Rojas in 1958, where the military have welcomed back and cooperated with the banned traditional parties (the Conservatives and the Liberals).

(3) *Retain and Restrict*

As we have shown, this is what the Brazilian military have done since 1964 (p. 254 above). The Greek military followed the same course.

(4) *Retain and Expand*

The idea is an old one: to widen the political arena, and give the military a power base outside its immediate social and political enemies, in short, to 'call new social forces into existence to redress the balance of the old'.

55. Huntington, op. cit., pp. 233–7.

Perón did this, but the military did not follow him. Arbenz met a similar fate (p. 125). At the moment the Peruvian military appear to be attempting this in their efforts to mobilize the peasantry behind them.[56] In Portugal, junior officers have been sent as missionaries into the deep countryside to politicize and activate the conservative peasantry.

3. *Military Disengagement*

There are two levels of military aloofness from active politics: what might be termed short-term and long-term, or contingent and necessary, or, better than these, disengaged and neutral. Let me put it this way. I have maintained that military intervention is the product of two sets of forces, the capacity and volition of the armed forces to intervene on the one hand and the condition of the society on the other. The cases I have been dealing with are those of the Third World where, as I have argued, the social conditions are favourable to military intervention and, on the whole, the will to intervene exists also. The states of mature political culture, on the other hand, are those where the will to intervene is lacking and also the conditions of society are unfavourable to intervention.

Now it is possible to conceive of states where the conditions are favourable to intervention: a latent chronic crisis of legitimacy exists, and all governments are abnormally dependent upon the support of the military – *but* the military lack volition. This is quite a different situation from one where, whether the military lack volition or not, a consensus exists, civilian counterforces are strongly organized, and the conditions for the success of a military takeover are highly unfavourable.

In the first case cited, the military will be *disengaged* from active politics; in the second they will be *neutral*. In the first, the reason for the absence of military intervention is to be found in the mentality of the military leaders. In the second, irrespective of this mentality, it is to be found in the nature of the society itself. In the first, the situation may change with a change of military mentality. Not so in the second, where a profound cleavage of society would be necessary before any intervention could succeed. In the latter, the attitude of the military is a neutral one: to serve alternating sets of leaders with impartiality. In the first it is not neutral: it is temporarily uninterested.

In the Third World military disengagement is not only possible, it is quite common. But military neutrality – that is another matter.

56. Cf. G. W. Grayson, 'Peru's Revolutionary Government', in *Survival*, I.S.S., London, May–June 1973, pp. 130–36.

First, a number of states exist where the military have not hitherto intervened and where they show no current signs of wishing to do so. Such states include the Hashemite Kingdom of Jordan and the Kingdom of Saudi Arabia. But this is not to say that the armed forces of these countries are not liable to intervene in an immediate future. For, in the last resort, the rulers of all these and similar countries depend upon the support of their army. This has been put to the test several times in Jordan: in 1957, for instance, or in 1966 after the Samu raid. The reason the military have not intervened (apart from the abortive 1957 plot which was confined to a small element) is that on the whole it is well affected towards the person of the monarch and the kind of régime that he runs. If, on the other hand, King Hussein wished to make peace with Israel (for instance), it is not inconceivable that his army might depose him. In all these countries the military are the first reserve of the civil power, and it is in this sense that civil power exists by their complaisance. Libya provided a supreme example. The monarch reposed on nothing save the now hollow support of his tribe, the Senussi – who lived in the wrong part of the country anyway. Political parties had not been permitted to form. The monarchy fell the moment a handful of officers took command of the armed forces and declared the Republic with themselves as the new government.

Additionally there are a number of states where the military have intervened in the immediate past, but have since disengaged. They still form the first reserve of the civil power; they could, if they wished, overthrow this power as on past occasions; but they no longer have the disposition to do so. They permit the civilian authorities to govern, and they refrain from active interference. Spain is a European example. Colombia, Paraguay and South Korea provide further examples. Reasons why the military do not seek to intervene are various. In Colombia they are fairly clear: the military were used by the military President, Rojas Pinilla, in a particularly bloody and murderous campaign to put down the private warfare known as *la violencia*, and the Rojas régime was terminated by the army's withdrawal of its support, followed by a pact between the two rival parties (the Conservatives and Liberals) whose antagonism had – nominally – provided an excuse for *la violencia*. The military still find it in their interest to support this arrangement. In Spain the situation is not the same. The military support the régime, in the first place because they have confidence in the *Caudillo*, General Franco, and secondly because it is the sort of régime in which the traditionally privileged status of the military and its traditional hatreds (e.g., of Catalan separatism) have been fully recognized. Spain is not a military régime: the army does not as such play an important role in policy making. Nor is the army the main institution by which social discontent is subdued; this is done by the Civil Guard. But the military do constitute the great reserve of support to the régime. Much the same reasons – general contentment with their privileged position and confidence in the head of state – explain why the military support the régimes in Paraguay and South Korea, both of which issued from military coups.

All states of this kind – both those which have witnessed a military coup in the immediate past and those that have not done so – are what are sometimes described as *military supportive* states. In the Third World this is not only the commonest form of 'disengagement' from active intervention, but the only form possible. And the reason for this is that for an indefinite time to come the structure of society in the states of the Third World will continue to make their governments unduly dependent upon military support for their survival. As long as this condition obtains, so long the disengagement of the military will be of a temporary, contingent nature. This is likely to be as true of the recently disengaged armies of Sierra Leone, Pakistan, Thailand and Argentina as it was of the Sudanese army, which, disengaged 1964–9, returned to active intervention in 1969; or the Ghanaian which, disengaged in 1969, intervened again in 1972.

But of long-term disengagement, disengagement of a 'necessary' character, there are few examples. Historically the best examples are those supplied by the régimes of Napoleon I and Napoleon III in France; of Kemal Atatürk in Turkey; of the P.R.I. party in Mexico; and of de Gaulle in France.

In order to arrive at this disengagement, four conditions must obtain:
(1) Firstly, that the leader imposed by the military on the state (usually a military man but not necessarily so) shall positively *want* his troops to quit politics. This was true of both the Napoleons, of Atatürk, of the post-Cárdenas presidents of Mexico, and of de Gaulle. It was, however, true of many other ex-military heads of state: for instance, of Jiménez of Venezuela, or Kassem of Iraq. It is in the interest of the head of state that the soldiers go back to their barracks; it gives him a free hand in running the country and at the same time seems to free him from military plots. But the second set of ex-military leaders cited did not meet the further conditions, which include:
(2) That the ex-military leader, now the head of state, shall be able to establish a régime which is capable of functioning without further military support. This the Napoleons, Kemal Atatürk, the Mexicans and the former president de Gaulle succeeded in doing; and it may be that General Park of

Korea will succeed in this, too. But it is precisely on this point that nearly all other post-intervention régimes have failed. As has been pointed out, they still have to rely on military support as their reserve power, so that they are *military-supportive* and not genuinely re-constitutionalized states; (3) That this viable régime shall be favourable to the armed forces – as it was in all the cases cited;

(4) And finally, that these armed forces shall have sufficient confidence in their leader, the head of state, to be prepared to return to the barracks when he tells them. This again was true in all the cases cited.

But these four conditions are to be found nowhere outside those cases. Castelo Branco of Brazil sent his soldiers back to their barracks and they obeyed him; can the present régime survive without them? Events subsequent to December 1968 suggest not.

Each of these conditions, with the exception of the first, poses difficulties for a post-intervention régime in the Third World. For, as I have argued, these states are for the most part those of low or of minimal political culture – states of latent chronic crisis, where opinion is feeble and often self-divided. And because of this, all these states require a strong executive – a requirement the 'single party' was devised to meet, although it has failed to do so. To this extent all these states are ones whose governments are abnormally dependent on their armed forces. And indeed this is just why they *have* experienced military intervention: for in any such case of dependency the armed forces can simply blackmail a government out of existence by refusing to support it – let alone go to the trouble of overthrowing it.

The second of the four conditions will be just as hard to fulfil in the post-intervention phase as it was in the pre-intervention phase. These societies do not change overnight just because a general or a colonel or a captain has taken over the direction of the government.

Nor will the third and fourth conditions necessarily be complied with, though they are much more feasible than the one just cited, which seems incapable of being met in any near future. For, as we have had occasion to see, it is not often that a post-intervention régime proves acceptable to the military: on the contrary, the military are wracked with anxiety lest their former opponents return. And finally, it is mistaken to suppose that the serving officers necessarily trust the military man who is now the head of state just because he has climbed there with their support. On the contrary, the annals of military intervention show more often than not that the ex-military head of state is, after a time, envied or even despised by his former supporters. Military leaders like Kassim (Iraq) or Rojas (Colombia) or

Jiménez (Venezuela) soon become hated and feared by their former colleagues; and in the wake of defeat it was clear that Nasser also incurred the wrath and contempt of his former associates. And quite apart from these personal considerations, the cleavage of attitude between junior and senior officers, between the radicals and the reformers, will continue to create military unrest focused against the head of state.

The best that the Third World states can look to, then, for the immediate present, is disengagement of a contingent and temporary nature. A genuine neutrality of the armed forces because they are satisfied with the régime, and because the régime for its part does not have to court their satisfaction, is only likely in the industrial societies of mature or at least developed political culture. The preconditions for neutrality are, in short, that the successor régime must be one that *neither needs the military nor is needed by it*. The latter precondition may be fulfilled, in the sense that the military may feel assured that its political future and the future of its leaders is secure. But the former is not likely to be realized. The most likely outcome of one military coup and one military régime in the Third World is a second coup and a second military régime, separated by bouts of indirect military rule, monopartism and feebly functioning competitive party politics – an alternation of these three types for a considerable age to come.

4

THE MILITARY AND MODERNIZATION

It must have become clear, as this chapter has proceeded, that we are in a far better position to discuss the causes, course and consequences of military intervention than in 1962, because the range of countries affected and the number of *coups* mounted are so much greater; and because we have had another decade in which to assess the performance of the military régimes. Indeed, the early sixties were almost the worst imaginable time to write on these matters because all but two of the Latin American military régimes had just been swept away, and the African military régimes had, with one or two exceptions, not come into existence. Of the new states of the post-World War period, it was the Arab ones – Egypt, Syria, Iraq and Sudan – which made nearly all the running.

This did not deter observers from predicting great things for the then incipient military régimes. God may not be on the side of poor and developing countries but the academics are: and it really did seem as though whatever newfangled experiment in despotism was adopted in these states, it was the appropriate answer to their backwardness and poverty. When the one-party system spread like a rash through the Third World, the one-party system was all the rage (even though most of such régimes were only two or three years old).[57] As military *coups* exploded over the Third World, a host of apologists rushed forward likewise. Since the régimes were for the most part only two or three years old at the most, these apologists could not *know* how they would perform. They could only infer: infer from the ambitions and pronouncements of the new military ruler, or *a priori*, from supposed characteristics of the military: their social backgrounds, the nature of their occupation, their social function and the like.[58]

The *a priori* reasonings can be met by *a priori* counter-reasonings. The inference from these reasonings – the rosy dawn of 'modernization' – can, at last, be subjected to some kind of empirical test.

The first category of such *a priori* reasonings comprises the arguments based upon the organizational and functional imperatives of the army in an undeveloped society. Lucian Pye's well-known article, 'Armies in the Process of Political Modernization' can be taken as highly representative of this approach.[59]

The argument ran thus. Armies must be technologically specialized, and able to train officers in personnel management, and consequently, many of them have to be trained in 'individual skills' more advanced than those common in the civilian economy. Secondly, officers have to look outside their society for their models and are therefore extremely sensitive to the needs of modernization and technological advancement. Thirdly, as a result of the above, they become highly conscious of the extent to which their countries are backward and aware of the need for substantial changes in society. Is this not true of other organizations however? No, answers Pye: armies are 'rival' institutions. All others operate within the context of their own society, but the soldier is always looking abroad. Also, since the test for an army is in a future war, it feels it must equip itself ahead of its time and not simply adjust to local day-to-day conditions.

All this is very *a priori*. Is the mere use and maintenance of modern

57. Cf. S. E. Finer, *Comparative Government*, Chapter 10 ('The Quasi-Democracy'), pp. 506–29, for a critical review of some of the literature.

58. Cf. H. Bienen, 'The Background to Contemporary Study of Militaries and Modernization', in H. Bienen (ed.), *The Military and Modernization*, Chicago and New York, 1971, pp. 1–33, for a critical review of such literature.

59. L. Pye, 'Armies in the Process of Political Modernization', in J. J. Johnson (ed.), *The Role of the Military in Under-Developed Countries*, pp. 68–89.

weapons, as opposed to manufacturing them, sufficient to imbue officers with the ambition to 'modernize'? Is even an expressed desire to 'modernize' any more significant than a desire to consume Western goods? Are not politicians and businessmen in contact with advanced societies, as much as officers? Are not businesses 'rival' institutions, like armies?

Irrespective of these objections, even if the assertions were true – and not a shred of evidence is proffered – the statements would only apply to that limited number of countries where the armies are specialized and technological. Most armies in fact are infantry armies and of precious small size too: in Africa, the armed forces of Ghana and Nigeria in the year of the *coups*, 1966, were only about 9,000 apiece. And even armies of great size and (apparently) high technical sophistication turn out in practice to be very backward. As late as 1969 General Uruburu was observing of the Argentine army: 'Our engineers cannot in practice guarantee to get the troops of the army across the river, and our logistical system of arsenals is a historical relic from the end of the last century.'[60]

Another, more curious objection may be made. If technological specialization is the spur to the desire to modernize, it should be higher in the navy than in the army of a state with a sizeable navy like Argentina: and higher still in the air force. Yet the navy (as in both Brazil and Chile) was more conservative than the army;[61] and the air force (despite *a priori* assertions), was in Argentina, at least, more politically uncertain and diffident than the other two services.[62] And how comes it, too, that in Portugal the navy was extremely radical and the air force highly conservative?

A second category of equally *a priori* reasonings comprises what may be called stereotypes of 'The Army Officer'. These include the military's self-image of 'the military virtues' (pp. 9–11) and the familiar 'progressive' intellectual's image of them as Blimps; and neither of these is relevant to modernization. Morris Janowitz, however,[63] emphasizes their 'management' functions. He had already emphasized this in his profile on the American soldier:[64] and has projected it into Third World countries. In some, like Argentina, it seems to apply, but manifestly not in all, and possibly in very few.

---

60. Craig, op. cit., p. 90. Cf. pp. 88–9.   61. ibid., pp. 26–9.   62. ibid., p. 34.
63. Janowitz, op. cit., pp. 40–49.
64. M. Janowitz, *The Professional Soldier*, London, 1960. It would be remembered that when he makes this statement Janowitz is contrasting the managerial skills of the military with political skills (the capacity to manipulate) in which he deems the military defective; his statement should be construed in this context.

Finally, we have the identification, familiar from our previous discussion of class motivation (pp. 230–33 above), of the officer class with the middle class, and the middle class with modernization. This is the almost lyrical theme of Manfred Halpern in his article on Arab officers.[65] According to him this 'new' middle class is impelled, out of its own self-concern, to 'establish modern, integrating institutions which can mobilize the spirit and resources of the entire nation',[66] and the army is its 'principal actor and instrument'.[67] As we have seen, Huntington has generalized this thesis: the middle-class army is radical in the days of the oligarchy which it overthrows to admit other middle-class groups into power: once these are admitted, it is a partisan, supporting or ejecting governments formed by such groups: once it is challenged by the masses it turns conservative, and its *coups* become so many vetoes.

Whether middle-class officers do or do not reflect middle-class values as a whole, has already been discussed. The first point to notice therefore is that the Huntington or even the Halpern hypothesis is incompatible with the Pye hypothesis. Whereas Pye sees the military as the unique modernizing force, the former see the middle class as that force – the military's role being merely to allow them to enter the political arena. The implication of Pye's thesis is that the military should govern, or at least, control; the implication of the alternative thesis seems to be that they should allow the 'middle sectors' to do so. There would in any case be a strong *a priori* case for arguing this. The 'middle class' in question is a rag-bag, ranging from postal workers to entrepreneurs, intellectuals, professionals and so forth. Why must one suppose middle-class officers to be more 'modernizing' than industrialists, or professionals, or intellectuals? If entrepreneurial and management ability is in question, the entrepreneurs would seem better equipped. If ideas, aspirations, imagination are concerned, the professionals and intellectuals are better endowed. The second point is that if Huntington is right, as soon as the masses seek to enter the arena, the military become both repressive and conservative. In short, at this stage they *cease* to be modernizers! (Except, as he notes, in Asian and African countries, where the masses are the conservatives and the middle class the modernizers: so that military repression of mass movements in these countries, e.g., Turkey, serves to perpetuate modernization.)[68]

So much for the *a priori* arguments of the sixties. Now, in the 1970s,

65. Halpern, op. cit.

66. M. Halpern, *The Politics of Social Change in the Middle East*, p. 77.

67. M. Halpern, 'Middle East Armies and the New Middle Class', in J. J. Johnson, op. cit., pp. 278–9.   68. Huntington, op. cit., p. 224.

however, we have some empirical data to go on. From this it is pretty plain that as far as Latin America is concerned, the military have – in general – become a politically and socially conservative force. For instance Dario Cantón analysed the military interventions in Argentina between 1900 and 1966, inquiring whether they were successful or not, and whether they were launched in favour of, or against, a movement or government which at the time was a *popular* 'progressive' one. (Thus we are not called on to judge whether the Radicals of 1900 were 'popular' – only whether they were so regarded at that time.) The result is striking. Not one military intervention favourable to a 'popular' tendency was ever successful. Of the revolts against a 'popular' tendency all succeeded except two, and both of these (in 1951 and June 1955) were against Perón. The army never once intervened to redress an electoral injustice, i.e. to support a winning party which had illegally been declared the loser. It never once intervened to annul fraudulent elections when the fraud was used against a popular party. The most it ever did was to remain neutral where the polls favoured the continuation of the popular party *already* in office.[69]

Another study generalizes for Latin America as a whole, over the 1935–64 period. It shows that in 1935–44 the percentage of 'reformist' *coups* stood at 50 per cent: in 1945–54, at 23 per cent: in 1955–64, at 17 per cent. For the same three periods: the *coups* that were low in violence stood at 81 per cent: then at 68 per cent: and in the 1955–64 period, dropped to 33 per cent. By the same token, the proportion of *coups* that overthrew constitutional governments rose from 12 per cent in the first period, to 32 per cent in the second, to 50 per cent in the final period. Those that took place around election time rose from a proportion of 12 per cent in 1935–44 to 32 per cent in 1945–54 to 58 per cent in 1955–64. In short, over this thirty-year span, the military in general became less reform-minded, more anti-constitutional, and more bloody-minded as each decade went by.[70] But as already noticed, the events since 1964 no longer follow this trend line.

These findings are of course consistent with – indeed they confirm – the argument of Huntington: but they are not relevant to arguments of scholars like Halpern or Pye which relate only to Asia. However, these arguments – or rather assertions – have been utterly shattered by a study embracing no less than seventy-four non-Western, non-communist countries.

This is the study, by Eric Nordlinger, published in December 1970.[71]

69. Canton, op. cit.

70. M. Needler, 'Political Development and Military Intervention in Latin America, *American Political Science Review*, September 1966.

71. Nordlinger, op. cit.

The seventy-four countries in question were ones which had received some kind of foreign aid and assistance from the U.S.A. Nordlinger divided them into three groups: those directly ruled by the military at some time during 1957–62; those where the military was highly influential in that period; and those where their influence was little or nil. He then correlated this military dimension with *seven* indicators of economic and social change, each of which could reasonably be regarded as amenable to governmental manipulation. They were (1) Rate of growth of per capita income 1950–63; (2) Change in degree of industrialization 1950–63; (3) Degree of improvement in agricultural productivity since 1950; (4) Rate of improvement in educational enrolment 1957–61; (5) Gross investment rate 1957–62; (6) A measure reflecting the change in the effectiveness of tax systems 1950–63, and (7) A composite measure – and a crucial one – which is qualitative, and assesses (by posing three questions) how far the government and higher civil servants were committed to economic development. Taking all seven indicators together, it turns out that the political strength of the military is correlated with them to the level of only 0·04. In other words, the performance was the same irrespective of whether the military were in control or not. Agricultural development and the expansion of education were in like case being correlated at only 0·07 and 0·08 respectively. Likewise with changes in tax level – correlated at only 0·04. Investment level showed a slightly negative correlation; i.e. to a slight degree, the greater the military control, the less the investment.

Only in two matters is the correlation large enough to permit of an inference. The pace of industrialization is quite positively correlated to the strength of the military: the correlation is 0·29. This, it is argued, is the one type of modernization that one would expect of the military because of its *corporate* interest in planting industries. On the other hand, the correlation between military rule and 'subjective commitment' to economic development is quite clearly *negative*. It stands at −0·22. The implication (borne out by other evidence in the study) is that the military actually oppose groups and strata that are demanding economic change.

Nordlinger went on to divide the seventy-four countries into geographical regions: Latin America (21 states), Middle East and N. Africa (15), Asia (15) and Tropical Africa. Africa stands apart. There, the stronger the military, the higher the rate of G.N.P. increase (0·45), of industrial growth (0·42), of agricultural production (0·60) and of educational expansion (0·34). But there is no correlation with tax changes (0·07) or investment level (0·06). And likewise, there is no correlation between these economic advances, and the leadership's 'commitment' to development.

(Correlation = 0·08.) It would seem that the military suffer development to occur, rather than purposefully press it.

But when we turn to the regions other than Africa the performance is dismal. In each, leaders are antagonistic to modernization: in each region the correlations are negative. It is −0·16 in the Middle East, and −0·17 in Asia – and in Latin America it is −0·43. The other coefficients are as follows:

	Latin America	Middle East & N. Africa	Asia
Rate G.N.P.	0·01	−0·28	0·03
Change industrialization	0·16	0·03	−0·02
Change ag. and productivity	−0·06	−0·03	−0·39
Expansion education	−0·43	−0·12	−0·31
Change tax level	−0·14	−0·11	−0·07
Investment level	−0·38	−0·32	−0·26
Leaders' commitment	−0·43	−0·16	−0·17
Mean correlation	−0·18	−0·14	−0·17

Altogether, this is a deplorable inventory. With one exception – a very modest correlation between military rule and industrialization, which is confined to Latin America – on no matter was there any significant correlation between military rule and economic social advance; on the contrary, there are sometimes strong indications that the greater the strength of military intervention the *slighter* that advance was likely to be. For Latin America, the more military rule, the less the advance in educational enrolment. In Asia, the more military rule the less the advances in agricultural production, and the less the advance in investment levels. The Middle East and North Africa show the most striking negative correlation of all: the more military rule, the less the advance in G.N.P. per capita. So much for *a priori* reasoning.

To understand what causes military intervention, the forms it may take and the kind of régimes it can throw up, forms part of a strictly academic exercise, and I hope that these additional pages will be of service in this enterprise. To pass moral judgements on military intervention and the régimes it throws up is quite another matter. It is clear, however, that very few military régimes have lasted longer than a decade before overthrow or abdication and that those few that have survived have nearly all been punctuated by further *coups*, successful or not. Almost none have created a viable civil successor-régime. So, from the point of view of the constitutional order, their record is profoundly disappointing. It appears, too, that they are not the armed modernizers, the saviours with a sword that they were deemed to be: Africa partly excepted, military rulers as a category have either been no better at 'modernizing' than civilians, or have been worse.

The great obstacle to seeing them for what they are is simply that they are soldiers. The glittering, martial, heroic and austere aura vests them about (although it would be an interesting exercise to count up how many of today's military rulers have ever heard a shot fired in anger). This heroic image still clings to them and seems to invest the things they do with a more than life-size significance. It would be wiser perhaps to regard them as Walter Scott regarded a politician of his day:

He always puts me in mind of Obadiah's bull, who, although as Father Shandy observed, he never produced a calf, went through the business with such a grave demeanour that he always maintained his credit in the parish.

A CHRONOLOGICAL CHECKLIST OF MILITARY INTERVENTIONS, 1958–73

I HAVE defined interventions as being (a) overt – that is to say that there has been a movement of troops, even though no blood has been shed. (b) Actual – that is to say the events are not alleged *ex post facto* in some kind of trial proceedings. Where this occurs I would classify the events not as 'intervention' but a plot, and such 'plots' are not included in the list. (c) There are one or two cases, e.g. Burma 1958, Pakistan 1958, where the civil government has handed over power to the army in an apparently constitutional way but where I have reason to suspect that significant army pressure was exercised in inducing the civil authorities to act in this fashion. I have included such instances as interventions.

An * denotes an unsuccessful coup.

Where the name of the state is italicized this indicates that it has already been affected by military intervention for some precedent year, commencing from 1958.

1958

Burma
France
Iraq
Pakistan
Sudan
Thailand
Venezuela

1959

*Iraq**
*Sudan**

1960

Congo (K)
Ethiopia*
Laos
Salvador
Turkey

1961

Brazil
Ecuador
*France**
Lebanon*
Salvador
S. Korea
Syria
*Venezuela**

1962

Argentina
Burma
Peru
Syria
*Syria**
*Turkey**
Yemen

1963

Algeria*
Dahomey
Dominican Republic
Ecuador
Guatemala
Honduras
Iraq
*Iraq**
Iraq
*Laos**
Peru
S. Vietnam
Syria
*Syria**
Togo
*Turkey**

1964

Bolivia
Brazil
Gabon*
Sudan
*S. Vietnam**

1965

Algeria
Burundi*
Congo (K)
Dahomey
Dahomey
Indonesia*
*Iraq**
*S. Vietnam**

1966

Argentina
Burundi
C.A.R.
Congo–Brazzaville*
Ecuador
Ghana
Indonesia
*Iraq**
Nigeria
Nigeria
Syria
*Syria**
Upper Volta

1967

*Algeria**
Dahomey
*Ghana**
Greece
Sierra Leone
Togo
Yemen

1968

Congo–Brazzaville
Iraq
Mali
Panama
Peru
Sierra Leon
S. Yemen

1969

Bolivia
*Congo–Brazzaville**
Dahomey
Libya
*Panama** N/S
Somalia
S. Yemen
Sudan

1970

Bolivia
Cambodia
Syria
*Togo**

1971

Argentina
*Bolivia**
Morocco*
*Sierra Leone**
Sudan
Sudan
Thailand
Turkey
Uganda

1972

*Burundi**
*Congo–Brazzaville**
Dahomey
Ecuador
*El Salvador**
Ghana
Malagasy Republic?
*Morocco**

1973	**1974**
Afghanistan	*Upper Volta*
Chile*	*Ethiopia*
Chile	Portugal*
Greece	*Uganda**
Ruanda	Niger
Uruguay	*Portugal*
	*Bolivia**
	Yemen
	Cyprus
	*Bolivia**

CHECKLISTS OF MILITARY INTERVENTIONS IN AFRICA, ASIA AND LATIN AMERICA, BY COUNTRY AFFECTED

ASIA

Burma	1958	1962						
Iraq	1958	1959	1963[1]	1963[2]	1963[3]	1965	1966	1968
Pakistan	1958							
Thailand	1958	1971						
Laos	1960	1963						
Turkey	1960	1962	1963	1971				
Lebanon	1961							
S. Korea	1961							
Syria	1961	1962[1]	1962[2]	1963[1]	1963[2]	1966[1]	1966[2]	1970
Yemen	1962	1967	1974					
S. Vietnam	1963	1964	1965					
Indonesia	1965							
S. Yemen	1968	1969						
Cambodia	1970							
Afghanistan	1973							

AFRICA

Sudan	1958	1959	1964	1969	1971[1]	1971[2]
Ethiopia	1960	1974				
Zaïre	1960	1965				
Algeria	1963	1965	1967			
Dahomey	1963	1965[1]	1965[2]	1967	1969	1972
Togo	1963	1967	1970			
Gabon	1964					
Burundi	1965	1966	1972			
C.A.R.	1966					
Congo–Brazzaville	1966	1968	1969	1972		
Ghana	1966	1967	1972			
Nigeria	1966[1]	1966[2]				
Upper Volta	1966	1974				
Sierra Leone	1967	1968	1971			
Mali	1968					

Libya	1969				
Somalia	1969				
Morocco	1971	1972			
Uganda	1971	1974			
Malagasy Republic	1972				
Ruanda	1973				
Niger	1974				

LATIN AMERICA

Venezuela	1958	1961				
El Salvador	1960	1961	1972			
Brazil	1961	1964				
Ecuador	1961	1963	1966	1972		
Argentina	1962	1966	1971			
Peru	1962	1963	1968			
Dominican Republic	1963					
Guatemala	1963					
Honduras	1963					
Bolivia	1964	1969	1970	1971	1974[1]	1974[2]
Panama	1968	1969				
Chile	1973[1]	1973[2]				
Uruguay	1973					

PROPORTION OF STATES AFFECTED BY MILITARY INTERVENTION 1958–73, BY REGION

		No. Affected by Coups	% Affected by Coups
N. America	2	—	—
L. America + Guyana	21	13	62
Caribbean	3	—	—
Australasia	4	—	—
Europe	28	2	7
Middle East	16	6	37
Asia, S & S.E.	22	9	41
Africa	42	21	50
	138	51	37

RELATIONSHIP OF MILITARY INTERVENTION, 1958–73, TO PER CAPITA INCOME
(*Total States = 126*)

P.C.I. in $ (1953–1963)	*Coup* states	Non-*coup* states	All states	*% Coup* to Total
< 250	41	32	73	57%
250–499	7	17	24	29%
500–999	2	10	12	16%
> 999	1	16	17	6%
	51	75	126	40%

RELATIONSHIP OF MILITARY INTERVENTION, 1958–73, TO PER CAPITA INCOME (USING ANOTHER INCOME CLASSIFICATION)
(*Total States = 123*)

P.C.I. in $ (1963)	*Coup* states	Total states	% *Coup* states
< 100	27	43	63%
100–200	13	26	50%
200–500	9	29	31%
> 500	2	25	4%
	51	123	40%

BIBLIOGRAPHY

THIS bibliography is not intended to be comprehensive. It is, principally, a list of the books and articles cited in the text. To this I have added the titles of certain other works which I found particularly useful for background, or for establishing some specific point mentioned in the text.

For the period since 1958, and also for some episodes prior to that date, I have based my narrative and my inferences on the files of the periodicals cited below.

STANDARD WORKS OF REFERENCE

The Annual Register.
Encyclopaedia Britannica.
Enciclopedia illustrada universel (Madrid).

The Middle East, 1961 ('Europa' publications).
Keesing's Contemporary Archives.
The Statesman's Year Book.

PERIODICALS

Daily Telegraph.
Economist.
New York Times.
Time Magazine.

The Times.
The World Today (Royal Institute of International Affairs, London).

THE MILITARY: ORGANIZATION AND GENERAL CONSIDERATIONS

ANDREZEJEWSKI, Stanislaw. *Military Organization and Society*, London, 1954.

Annals of the American Academy of Political Science. *Military Government*, Vol. 267, 1950.

FERRERO, Guglielmo. *Militarism*, London, 1902.

FREEMAN, F. D. The Army as a Social Structure, *Social Forces*, vol. 27, 1948–9.

HOWARD, Michael (ed.). *Soldiers and Governments: Nine Studies in Civil–Military Relations*, London, 1957.

HUNTINGTON, Samuel Phillips. *The Soldier and the State: The Theory and Practice of Civil–Military Relations*, Harvard, 1957.

IRIBARNE, M. F. La Coordination de la politique exterieure et de la politique militaire (Mimeo), World Congress of the International Political Science Association, 1961.

PAGE, C. H. Bureaucracy's Other Face, *Social Forces*, vol. 25, 1946–7.

SPINDLER, D. G. The Military: A Systematic Analysis, *Social Forces*, vol. 27, 1948–9.

VAGTS, Alfred. *A History of Militarism: Civilian and Military*, London, 1959.

AFRICAN COUNTRIES

APTER, David E. The Role of Traditionalism in the Political Modernization of Ghana and Uganda, *World Politics*, vol. 13, 1960.

AUSTIN, Dennis. Parties in Ghana, 1949–1960 (Mimeo), British Political Studies Association Conference papers.

BRETTON, H. L. Political Problems of Poly-ethnic Societies in West Africa (Mimeo), World Congress, International Political Science Association, 1961.

DAVIES, Hezekiah Oladipo. *Nigeria, The Prospects for Democracy*, London, 1961.

HAILEY, William M. Lord. *An African Survey* (Revised, 1956), London, 1957.

HODGKIN, Thomas Love. *Nationalism in Colonial Africa*, London, 1956.

African Political Parties, London, 1961.

HOLT, P. M. *A Modern History of the Sudan*, London, 1961.

KIMBLE, George H. T. *Tropical Africa*, 2 vols., New York, 1961.

LEGUM, Colin. *Pan-Africanism*, London, 1962; New York, 1962.

NKRUMAH, Kwame. *I Speak of Freedom: A Statement of African Ideology*, London, 1961.

SCHACHTER, Ruth. Single-Party Systems in West Africa, *American Political Science Review*, vol. 45, 1961.

SEGAL, Ronald. *Political Africa: A Who's Who of Personalities and Parties*, London, 1961.

BRITAIN

ALANBROOKE, Alan Francis Brooke, Viscount (ed. A. Bryant). *The Turn of the Tide*, London, 1957.

Triumph in the West, London, 1959.

BANNING, Stephen Thomas (revised P. G. Clark). *Military Law*, Aldershot, 1954.

BEAVERBROOK, William Maxwell Aitken, Lord. *Politicians and the War, 1914–1916*, London, 1928.

Men and Power, 1917–1918, London, 1956.

HANKEY, Maurice Pascal Alers Hankey, Lord. *The Supreme Command*, 2 vols., London, 1961.

HOWARD, Michael. Some Reflections on Defence Organization in Great Britain and the U.S.A. (Mimeo), Round Table on Civil–Military Relations, International Political Science Association, 1959.

Civil–Military Relations in Great Britain and the U.S.A., 1954–1958, *American Political Science Quarterly*, vol. 55, 1960.

ISMAY, Hastings Lionel Ismay, Lord. *Memoirs*, London, 1960.

JOHNSON, Franklyn Arthur. *Defence by Committee: The British Committee of Imperial Defence, 1855–1959*, London, 1960.

LLOYD GEORGE, David. *War Memoirs of David Lloyd George*, London, 1938.

MAGNUS, Sir Philip. *Kitchener*, London, 1961.

MONTGOMERY, Bernard Law, Viscount. *Memoirs*, London, 1958.

BIBLIOGRAPHY

MARDER, A. J. *From the Dreadnought to Scapa Flow*, vol. 1, London, 1961.

RYAN, A. P. *Mutiny at the Curragh*, London, 1956.

THOMAS, Hugh. *The Story of Sandhurst*, London, 1961.

TURNER, Ernest Sackville. *Gallant Gentleman: A Portrait of the British Officer, 1600–1956*, London, 1956.

WILLIAMS, T. D. Aspects of Strategy and Foreign Policy and Their Influence on Civil–Military Relations (Mimeo), Round Table on Civil–Military Relations, International Political Science Association, 1960.

FRANCE

BRACE, Richard and Joan. *Ordeal in Algeria*, Princeton, 1960.

BRINTON, Crane. *A Decade of Revolution, 1789–1799*, New York, 1934.

BROMBERGER, Merry and Serge. *Les Treize Complots du Treize Mai*, Paris, 1959.
  Barricades et Colonels, Paris, 1960.

BRUUN, G. *Europe and the French Imperium, 1799–1814*, New York, 1938.

CHAPMAN, Guy. *The Dreyfus Case*, London, 1955.

CLARKE, Michael K. *Algeria in Turmoil: A History of the Rebellion*, London, 1960.

GOODWIN, Albert. *The French Revolution*, London, 1953.

GIRARDET, Raoul. *La Société militaire dans la France contemporaine*, Paris, 1953.
  Pouvoir civil et pouvoir militaire dans la France contemporaine, *Revue Française de Science Politique*, vol. 10, 1960.

HUGO, Victor. *Napoleon the Small*, London, 1952.

KELLY, George A. The French Army Re-enters Politics, *American Political Science Quarterly*, vol. 56, 1961.

LARTEGUEY, J. *Les Mercenaires*, Parid, n.d.
  Les Centurions, Paris, 1960.
  Les Pretoriens, Paris, 1961.

MACRIDIS, R., and BROWN, B. E. *The De Gaulle Republic*, Illinois, 1960.

PALMER, Robert Boswell. *The Age of the Democratic Revolution: A Political History of Europe and America, 1760–1800*, Princeton, 1959.

STAEL-HOLSTEIN, Anne Louise Germaine, Baronne de. *La Revolution française*, Paris, 1821.

THOMPSON, James Matthew. *The French Revolution* (3rd edition), Oxford, 1947.
  Napoleon Bonaparte: His Rise and Fall, Oxford, 1952.

VANDAL, Albert. *L'Avènement de Napoléon*, 2 vols., Paris, 1905–7.

WERTH, Alexander. *The De Gaulle Revolution*, London, 1960.

WILLIAMS, Philip. Algerian Tragedy, *Encounter*, vol. 88, 1961.
  The French Army, *Encounter*, vol. 99, 1961.

WILLIAMS, Philip, and HARRISON, Martin. *De Gaulle's Republic*, London, 1960.

GERMANY

BENOIST-MÉCHIN, J. G. P. M. *Histoire de l'armée allemande*, Paris, 1936.

COPER, Rudolf. *Failure of a Revolution: Germany in 1918–1919*, London, 1955.

279

CRAIG, Gordon Alexander. *The Politics of the Prussian Army, 1640–1945*, Oxford, 1955.

GORDON, Harold J. *The Reichswehr and the German Republic, 1919–1926*, Princeton, 1957.

GÖRLITZ, Walter. *The German General Staff*, London, 1953.

TAYLOR, Alan J. P. *Bismarck*, London, 1955.

TAYLOR, Telford. *Sword and Swastika*, London, 1952.

WHEELER-BENNETT, John. *The Nemesis of Power: The German Army in Politics*, London, 1953.

The Wooden Titan: Hindenburg, London, 1936.

EASTERN EUROPE AND THE BALKANS

DELLIN, L. A. D. (ed.). *Bulgaria*, New York, 1957.

DJILAS, Milovan. *Land Without Justice: An Autobiography of his Youth*, London, 1958.

FORSTER, Edward Seymour. *A Short History of Modern Greece* (3rd edition), London, 1958.

MIJATOVICH, Chedomil. *A Royal Tragedy, Being the Story of the Assassination of King Alexander and Queen Draga of Servia*, London, 1906.

ROUCEK, Joseph Slabey. *The Politics of the Balkans*, New York, 1939.

Balkan Politics, Stanford, 1948.

SETON-WATSON, Hugh. *Eastern Europe Between the Wars* (2nd edition), Cambridge, 1945.

The East European Revolution, London, 1950.

STAVRIANOS, Leften Stavros. *The Balkans since 1453*, New York, 1958.

PORTUGAL

LIVERMORE, Harold Victor. *A History of Portugal*, Cambridge, 1947.

OLIVEIRA SALAZAR, Antonio de. *El pensamiento de la Revolution Nacional*, Buenos Aires, 1938.

SPAIN

AGESTA, Luis Sanchez. *Historia del constitucionalismo español*, Madrid, 1955.

BORKENAU, Franz. *The Spanish Cockpit*, London, 1937.

BRENAN, Gerald. *The Spanish Labyrinth* (2nd Edition), Cambridge, 1950.

The Face of Spain, London, 1950.

MADARIAGA, Salvador de. *Spain* (2nd edition), London, 1942.

MARVAUD, Angel. *L'Espagne au 2ième siècle; étude politique et économique*, Paris, 1913.

MARX, Karl, and ENGELS, Frederick. *Revolution in Spain*, London, 1939.

BIBLIOGRAPHY

ORTEGA Y GASSET, José. *España invertebrada* (5th edition), Madrid, 1948.
   The Revolt of the Masses, New York, 1932.
PEERS, Edgar Allison. *The Spanish Tragedy, 1930–1936* (3rd edition), London,
   1936.
RAMOS OLIVEIRA, Antonio. *Politics, Economics and Men of Contemporary Spain*,
   London, 1946.
RUIZ VILAPLAŅA, Antonio. *Burgos Justice: A Year's Experience of Nationalist
   Spain*, London, 1938.
THOMAS, Hugh. *The Spanish Civil War*, London, 1961.
WHITAKER, Arthur P. *Spain and the Defence of the West*, New York, 1961.
   Germany and the Spanish Civil War. Documents on German Foreign Policy, Series
   D, Vol. III, H.M.S.O., London, 1951.

JAPAN

COLEGROVE, K. The Japanese Cabinet, *American Political Science Review*, vol. 30,
   1936.
GREW, Joseph E. *Ten Years in Japan*, London, 1944.
KASE, Toshikazu. *Eclipse of the Rising Sun*, London, 1951.
LINEBARGER, Paul Myron (ed.). *Far Eastern Governments and Politics – China and
   Japan*, New York, 1954.
MAXON, Y. C. *Control of Japanese Foreign Policy*, University of California, 1957.
MICHAEL, Franz Henry, and TAYLOR, George Edward. *The Far East in the
   Modern World*, New York, 1956.
MORRIS, Ivan I. *Nationalism and the Right Wing in Japan*, London, 1960.
OKAKURA, Kakuzo. *The Awakening of Japan*, London, 1905.
QUIGLEY, Harold Scott, and TURNER, John Elliott. *The New Japan: Government
   and Politics*, Minneapolis, 1956.
REISCHAUER, Robert Karl. *Japan: Government-Politics*, New York, 1939.
SHIGEMITSU, Mamoru. *Japan and Her Destiny: My Struggle for Peace*, London,
   1958.
STORRY, Richard. *The Double Patriots*, London, 1957.
WAKEFIELD, Harold. *New Paths for Japan*, London, 1948.
YINAGA, C. The Military and the Government in Japan, *American Political Science
   Review*, vol. 35, 1946.
Foreign Relations of the United States, vols. IV and V, 1937. Washington, U.S.
   Department of State. 1954–5.

UNITED STATES OF AMERICA

GAVIN, Lt-Gen. J. M. *War and Peace in the Space Age*, New York, 1958.
HUNTINGTON, Samuel Phillips. Inter-service Competition and the Political Role of
   the Armed Services, *American Political Science Review*, vol. 45, 1960.
   Strategic Decision Making in the U.S.A. (Mimeo), Round Table on Civil–
   Military Relations, International Political Science Association, 1959.

JANOWITZ, M. *The Professional Soldier*, Glencoe, Illinois, 1960.

MILLIS, Walter. *Arms and Men: A Study in American Military History*, New York, 1956.

Arms and the State: Civil–Military Elements in National Policy, New York, 1958.

SAPIN, Burton M., and SNYDER, Richard Carlton. *The Role of the Military in American Foreign Policy*, New York, 1954.

SCHLESINGER, A. M., and ROVERE, Richard. *The General and the President*, London, 1952.

TAYLOR, General Maxwell Davenport. *The Uncertain Trumpet*, New York, 1960.

UNION OF SOCIALIST SOVIET REPUBLICS

BERMAN, H. J., and KERNER, N. *Soviet Military Law and Administration*, Cambridge, Mass., 1955.

BRZEZINSKI, Z. *Political Controls in the Soviet Army*, New York, 1954.

CONQUEST, Robert. *Power and Policy in the U.S.S.R.*, London, 1961.

DINERSTEIN, H. S. *War and the Soviet Union*, London, 1959.

ERICKSON, J. *The Soviet High Command*, London, 1962.

GARTHOFF, Raymond J. *How Russia Makes War*, London, 1954.

Soviet Strategy in the Nuclear Age, London, 1958.

HART, Captain Liddell (ed.). *The Soviet Army*, London, 1956.

INKELES, Alex, and BAUER, Raymond A. *The Soviet Citizen: Daily Life in a Totalitarian Society*, Cambridge, Mass., 1959.

POOL, Ithiel de Sola. *Satellite Generals: A Study of Military Élites in the Soviet Sphere*, Stanford, 1955.

SCHAPIRO, Leonard. *The Communist Party of the Soviet Union*, London, 1959.

The U.S.S.R. Today and Tomorrow, Moscow, 1959.

History of the Communist Party of the Soviet Union, Moscow, 1960.

LATIN AMERICA GENERALLY

ADAMS, Richard Newbold (ed.). *Social Change in Latin America*, New York, 1960.

ALEXANDER, Robert Jackson, and PORTER, C. O. *Communism in Latin America*, New Jersey, 1957.

The Struggle for Democracy in Latin America, New York, 1961.

Annals of the American Academy of Political and Social Science. Latin America's Nationalistic Revolutions, vol. 334, 1961.

BAILEY, Helen Miller, and NASATIR, Abraham Phineas. *Latin America: The Development of Its Civilization*, New Jersey, 1960.

BLANKSTEN, George I. Political Groups in Latin America, *American Political Science Review*, vol. 53, 1959.

BRYCE, James. *South America*, London, 1912.

DAVIS, Harold Eugene (ed.). *Government and Politics in Latin America*, New York, 1958.

FERGUSON, Halcro. *The Balance of Race Redressed*, London, 1961.

BIBLIOGRAPHY

FITZGIBBON, Russell Numke (ed.). *The Constitutions of the Americas, as of January 1st, 1948*, Chicago, 1948.

FITZGIBBON, Russell Numke, and JOHNSON, Kenneth F. Measurement of Latin American Political Change, *American Political Science Review*, vol. 55, 1961.

GARCIA CALDERON, Francisco. *Latin America: Its Rise and Progress*, London, 1913.

GIL, Federico Guillermo, and PIERSON, William Whatley. *Governments of Latin America*, New York, 1957.

HANKE, Lewis Ulysses. *Modern Latin America*, 2 vols., New York, 1959.

JOHNSON, John J. *Political Change in Latin America*, Stanford, 1958.

LIEUWEN, Robert. *Arms and Politics in Latin America*, New York, 1960.

MACDONALD, Austin Faulks. *Latin American Politics and Government*, New York, 1954.

RIPPY, James Fred. *Latin America: A Modern History*, Michigan, 1958.

STOKES, William S. Violence as a Power Factor in Latin American Politics, *Western Political Quarterly*, vol. 5, 1952.

SZULC, T. *Twilight of the Tyrants*, New York, 1962.

UCAZA TIGERINO, Jullio. *Sociologia de la politica Hispano-Americana*, Madrid, 1950.

Argentina

ALEXANDER, Robert Jackson. *The Perón Era*, New York, 1951.

BLANKSTEN, George I. *Perón's Argentina*, Chicago, 1953.

BRUCE, James. *These Perplexing Argentines*, New York, 1953.

JOSEPHS, Ray. *Argentine Diary*, New York, 1944.

KELLY, Sir David. *The Ruling Few*, London, 1952.

PENDLE, George. *Argentina* (2nd edition), London, 1961.

SARMIENTO, D. F. *Don Facundo, or Life in the Argentine Republic*, tr. Mrs H. Mann, New York, 1960.

Bolivia

ALEXANDER, Robert Jackson. *The Bolivian National Revolution*, New Jersey, 1958.

Brazil

DACUNHA, E. *Rebellion in the Backlands* (Os sertoens), Chicago, 1957.

HAMBLOCH, Ernest. *His Majesty the President: A Study of Constitutional Brazil*, London, 1935.

HARRIS, Marvin. *Town and Country in Brazil*, New York, 1956.

LAMBERT, Jacques. *Le Brésil*, Paris, 1953.

MORAZÉ, Charles. *Les Trois ages du Brésil: essai de politique*, Paris, 1954.

Colombia

FLUHARTY, V. L. *Dance of the Millions*, Pittsburgh, 1957.

Cuba

FITZGIBBON, Russell H. *Cuba and the United States,* Wisconsin, 1935.
PHILLIPS, Ruby. *Cuba, Island of Paradox,* New York, 1959.

Guatemala

SCHNEIDER, Ronald M. *Communism in Guatemala, 1944–1954,* New York, 1958.
SILVERT, Kalman Hirsch. *A Study in Government: Guatemala,* New Orleans, 1954.
TAYLOR, P. B. The Guatemalan Affair: A critique of U.S. Foreign Policy, *American Political Science Review,* vol. 51, 1957.

Haiti

BELLEGARDE, Dantes. *La Nation haitienne,* Paris, 1938.
COMHOIRE, J. L. El Campesino Haitiano, y su Gobierno, *Ciencias sociales,* vol. 7, 1956.
LEYBURN, James G. *The Haitian People,* Oxford, 1941.
RODMAN, Shelden. *Haiti, the Black Republic,* New York, 1954.

Mexico

CLINE, Howard F. C. *The United States and Mexico,* Cambridge, Mass., 1953.
Mexico, Revolution to Evolution, Oxford, 1962.
PADGETT, L. U. Mexico's One Party System: A Revaluation, *American Political Science Review,* vol. 51, 1957.
SCOTT, Robert Edwin. *Mexican Government in Transition,* Illinois, 1959.
SIMPSON, L. B. *Many Mexicos* (3rd Edition), California, 1959.
TANNENBAUM, Frank. *Mexico: The Struggle for Peace and Bread,* New York, 1950.

Paraguay

RAINE, Philip. *Paraguay,* New Jersey, 1956.

Venezuela

BÉTANCOURT, Romulo. *Venezuela: Política y petroleo,* Mexico, 1956.
LOTT, R. B. The 1952 Venezuelan Elections, *Western Political Quarterly,* vol. 10, 1957
ROURKE, Thomas (pseud.). *Gomez, Tyrant of the Andes,* New York, 1936.

MIDDLE EASTERN COUNTRIES GENERALLY

BERGER, Morroe. The Military Régimes in the Middle East (Mimeo), The Congress for Cultural Freedom, Seminar, 1960.
FISHER, Sydney Nettleton (ed.). *Social Forces in the Middle East,* Ithaca, New York, 1955.
HOURANI, Albert. The Decline of the West in the Middle East, *International Affairs,* vol. 29, 1953.

BIBLIOGRAPHY

KIRK, George. *Contemporary Arab Politics*, London, 1961.

The Middle Eastern Scene, *Yearbook of World Affairs*, London, 1960.

Political Problems of Selected Poly-ethnic Societies in the Middle East (Mimeo), World Congress, International Political Science Association, 1961.

LAQUEUR, Walter Ze'ev. *Communism and Nationalism in the Middle East*, London, 1956.

(Ed.) *The Middle East in Transition*, London, 1958.

The Soviet Union and the Middle East, London, 1959.

LERNER, Daniel. *The Passing of Traditional Society*, Glencoe, Illinois.

MARLOWE, John. *Arab Nationalism and British Imperialism*, London, 1961.

PARTNER, Peter. *A Short Political Guide to the Arab World*, London, 1960; New York, 1960.

The Middle East (3rd edition), Royal Institute of International Affairs, London, 1958.

Iraq

BIRDWOOD, Christopher Bromhead, Viscount. *Nuri-es-Said: A Study in Arab Leadership*, London, 1959.

CARACTACUS (pseud.). *Revolution in Iraq*, London, 1959.

HARRIS, G. L. (ed.). *Iraq*, New Haven, 1958.

KHADDURI, Majid. *Independent Iraq: A Study in Iraqi Politics*, London, 1960.

Syria and Jordan

PATAI, Raphael. *The Kingdom of Jordan*, Princeton, 1958.

ZIADEH, A. *Syria and Lebanon*, London.

Turkey

LERNER, Daniel, and ROBINSON, Richard D. Swords and Ploughshares: the Turkish Army as a Modernizing Force, *World Politics*, vol. 13, 1960.

LEWIS, Bernard. *The Emergence of Modern Turkey*, London, 1961.

LEWIS, Geoffrey L. *Turkey* (2nd edition), New York, 1960.

RAMSAUER, Ernest E. *The Young Turks: Prelude to the Revolution of 1908*, Princeton, 1957.

RUSTOW, Dankwart A. The Army and the Founding of the Turkish Republic, *World Politics*, vol. 11, 1959.

The United Arab Republic (Southern Region: Egypt)

BARAWY, Rashid El. *The Military Coup in Egypt*, Cairo, 1952.

HARRIS, G. L. (ed.). *Egypt*, New Haven, 1957.

LACOUTURE, Jean and Simonne. *Egypt in Transition*, London, 1958.

NASSER, Gamal Abdel. *Egypt's Liberation: The Philosophy of the Revolution*, Washington, D.C., 1955.

NEGUIB, Mohammed. *Egypt's Destiny*, London, 1955.

PROCTOR, J. H. The Legislative Activity of the Egyptian National Assembly, 1957–1958, *Parliamentary Affairs*, vol. 13, 1959–60.
VATIKIOTIS, P. J. *The Egyptian Army in Politics*, Bloomington, Indiana, 1961.
WHEELOCK, Keith M. *Nasser's New Egypt*, London, 1960.

SOUTH AND SOUTH-EAST ASIA GENERALLY

BRIMMELL, Jack Henry. *Communism in South-East Asia*, London, 1959.
BUTWELL, Richard. *Southeast Asia Today – and Tomorrow*, London, 1962; New York, 1961.
CARNELL, F. G. Political Ideas and Ideologies in South and South-East Asia (Mimeo), British Political Studies Association Conference paper, 1960.
KAHIN, George McTurnan. *Governments and Politics of South-East Asia*, Ithaca, New York, 1959.
MENDE, Tibor. *South-East Asia Between Two Worlds*, London, 1955.
ROSE, Saul. *Socialism in Southern Asia*, London, 1959.
THAYER, Philip W., and PHILLIPS, William T. *Nationalism and Progress in Free Asia*, Baltimore, 1956.

Burma

BUTWELL, R., and VON DER MELIDEN, F. The 1960 General Election in Burma, *Pacific Affairs*, vol. 33, 1960.
FURNIVALL, John Sydenham. *Colonial Policy and Practice: A Comparative Study of Burma and Netherlands India*, Cambridge, 1948.
PYE, Lucian. *Politics, Personality, and Nation-building: Burma's Search for Identity*, Yale, 1962.
TINKER, Hugh. *The Union of Burma* (3rd edition), Oxford, 1961.

India

ZINKIN, Taya. India and Military Dictatorship, *Pacific Affairs*, vol. 32, 1955.

Indonesia

MOSSMAN, James. *Rebels in Paradise: Indonesia's Civil War*, London, 1961.
NASUTION, Abdul Haris. *Fundamentals of Guerrilla Warfare and the Indonesian Defence System, Past and Future*, Djakarta, 1960.
WERTHEIM, W. F. *Indonesian Society in Transition*, New York, 1956.

Korea

ALLEN, R. C. South Korea, The New Régime, *Pacific Affairs*, vol. 24, 1961.

Pakistan

WINT, Guy. The 1958 Revolution in Pakistan, *St Antony's Papers*, no. 8, 1960.

South Vietnam

SCIGLIANO, R. Political Parties in South Vietnam. *Pacific Affairs*, vol. 33, 1960.

Thailand

DARLING, F. C. Marshal Sarit and Absolutist Rule in Thailand, *Pacific Affairs*, vol. 33, 1960.

LANDON, K. P. *Siam in Transition*, Shanghai, 1939.

THE FUTURE OF THE EMERGENT NATIONS GENERALLY

ALMOND, Gabriel A., and COLEMAN, James S. (ed.). *The Politics of the Developing Areas*, Princeton, 1960.

HAYES, Carlton J. H. *The Historical Evolution of Modern Nationalism*, New York, 1949.

Nationalism: A Religion, New York, 1960.

KEDOURIE, Elie. *Nationalism*, London, 1960.

PARKINSON, Francis. Social Dynamics of Under-developed Countries, *Yearbook of World Affairs*, London, 1960.

RUSTOW, Dankwart A. New Horizons for Comparative Politics, *World Politics*, vol. 9, 1957.

SHILS, E. A. Political Developments in New States, *Comparative Studies in Sociology and History*, vol. 2, 1960.

POLITICAL THEORY

HOBBES, Thomas. *The Leviathan*, Everyman ed., London.

LIPSET, Seymour. *Political Man*, London, 1961.

MAINE, Sir Henry Sumner. *Popular Government*, London, 1885.

MARX, Karl, and ENGELS, Frederick. *Selected Works*, 2 vols., London, 1958.

MOSCA, Gaetano (ed. Livingston, Arthur). *The Ruling Class*, New York, 1939.

Histoire des Doctrines Politiques, Paris, 1936.

PARETO, Vilfredo (ed. Livingston, Arthur). *The Mind and Society*, 4 vols., New York, 1935.

ROUSSEAU, Jean Jacques. *The Social Contract*, Everyman ed., London.

TALMON, Jacob Laib. *The Origins of Totalitarian Democracy*, London, 1952.

Political Messianism: The Romantic Phase, London, 1960.

SUPPLEMENTARY BIBLIOGRAPHY

GENERAL WORKS, SYMPOSIA, ETC.

ABRAHAMSSON, B. *Military Professionalization and Political Power*, Beverley Hills, California, 1972.

ANDREWS, W. G., and RA'ANAN, U. *The Politics of the Coup d'État*, New York, 1969.

BIENEN, H. (ed.). *The Military Intervenes: Case Studies in Political Development*, New York, 1968.

BIENEN, H. (ed.). *The Military and Modernisation*, Chicago, 1971.

DOWSE, R. E. The Military and Political Development, (in C. Leys (ed.) *Politics and Change in Developing Countries*, Cambridge, 1969).

FELDBURG, R. L. Political Systems and the Role of the Military, *Sociological Quarterly*, 1970, vol. XI, no. 2, pp. 206–18.

FINER, S. E. The Military Régime (in *Comparative Government*, London, 1970).

GUTTERIDGE, W. F. *Military Institution and Power in New States*, London, 1964.

HAMON, L. *Le Role extra-militaire de l'armée dans le tiers monde*, Paris, 1966.

HOPKINS, K. Civil–Military Relations in Developing Countries, *British Journal of Sociology*, 1966, pp. 165–81.

HUNTINGTON, S. P. *Changing Patterns in Military Politics*, New York, Glencoe, 1962.

HUNTINGTON, S. P. Civil–Military Relations (in *International Encyclopaedia of the Social Sciences*, New York, 1968).

HUNTINGTON, S. P. *Political Order in Changing Societies*, Yale, 1968.

JANOWITZ, M. *The Military in the Political Development of New Nations*, Chicago, 1964.

JOHNSON, J. J. (ed.). *The Role of the Military in Underdeveloped Countries*, Princeton, N.J., 1962.

KELLEHER, C. (ed.) *Political–Military Systems*, London, 1975.

KENNEDY, G. *The Military in the Third World*, London, 1974.

LUCKHAM, A. R. A. Comparative Typology of Civil–Military Relations, *Government & Opposition*, 1971, vol. VI, no. 1.

LUTTWAK, E. *Coup d'État: A Practical Handbook*, London, 1968.

MCWILLIAMS, W. C. (ed.). *Garrison and Government: Politics and the Military in New States*, San Francisco, 1967.

PINCKNEY, R. The Theory and Practice of Military Government, *Political Studies*, vol. XXI, no. 2, June 1973, pp. 152–66.

RAPOPORT, D. C. A Comparative Theory of Military and Political Types (in S. P. Huntington, *Changing Patterns in Military Politics* (op. cit., pp. 71–102).

RIZZO, A. *L'Alternativa in uniforme*, Milan, 1973.

VAN DOORN, J. (ed.). *Armed Forces and Society*, The Hague, 1968.

VAN DOORN, J. (ed.). *Military Profession and Military Régimes*, The Hague, 1969.

AFRICA

BERGHE, P. L. van den. The Military and Political Change in Africa (in C. E. Welch, ed., *Soldier and State in Africa*, Evanston, 1970).

FIRST, R. *The Barrel of a Gun*, London, 1970.

GUTTERIDGE, W. F. *The Military in African Politics*, London, 1968.

KHAKETLA, B. M. *Lesotho, 1970: An African Coup under the Microscope*, California, 1972.

BIBLIOGRAPHY

LEFEVER, E. W. *Spear and Scepter: Army, Police and Politics in Tropical Africa*, Brookings Inst., Washington, D.C., 1970.

LUCKHAM, A. R. *The Nigerian Military*, Cambridge, 1971.

MAZRUI, A. The *Lumpenproletariat* and the *Lumpenmilitariat*: African Soldiers as a New Political Class, *Political Studies*, vol. XXI, no. 1, 1973.

MINERS, N. J. *The Nigerian Army 1965–66*, New York, 1971.

PANTER-BRICK, S. K. (ed.). *Nigeria under Military Rule*, London, 1970.

PINCKNEY, R. *Ghana under Military Rule 1966–1969*, London, 1972.

SKURNIK, W. A. E. *The Military and Politics: Dahomey and Upper Volta* (in C. Welch, ed. q.v.).

WELCH, C. E. (ed.). *Soldier and State in Africa*, Evanston, 1970.

WELCH, C. E. The Roots and Implications of Military Intervention (in C. Welch, ed., q.v.).

ZOLBERG, A. R. Military Rule and Political Development in Tropical Africa (in J. Van Doorn, ed., *Military Profession and Military Régimes*, q.v.).

LATIN AMERICA

ASTIZ, C. A. *Pressure Groups and Power Élites in Peruvian Politics*, Ithaca, New York, 1969.

BELTRAN, V. R. The Army and Structural Changes in 20th Century Argentina (in J. Van Doorn (ed.) *Armed Forces and Society*, q.v.).

BELTRAN, V. R. (ed.). *El papel politico y social de las fuerzas armadas en América Latina* (Caracas, Venezuela, 1970).

CANTON, D. Military Intervention in Argentina (in J. Van Doorn (ed.) *Military Profession and Military Regimes*, q.v.).

CRAIG, A. *The Argentine Armed Forces, 1955–70*, unpublished Ph.D. thesis, University of Manchester, U.K., 1973.

HOROWITZ, I. L. The Military Élites, in S. M. Lipset and A. Solari, eds., *Élites in Latin America*, Oxford, 1967.

IMAZ, J. L. *Los que mandan*, Buenos Aires, 1964.

JOHNSON, J. J. *The Military and Society in Latin America*, Stanford, 1964.

KOSSOK, M. *Potentialities and Limitations of the Change of the Political and Social Function of the Armed Forces in the Developing Countries: The Case of Latin America* (Mimeo: presented to 7th World Congress of Sociology, Varna, Bulgaria, 1970).

MCALISTER, L. N. *The Military in Latin American Sociopolitical Evolution*, Washington, D.C., 1970.

NEEDLER, M. C. *Political Development in Latin America: Instability, Violence and Evolutionary Change*, New York, 1968.

NEEDLER, M. C. Political Development and Military Intervention in Latin America, *American Political Science Review*, vol. 60, September 1966.

NEEDLER, M. C. Political Development and Socio-Economic Development in Latin America, *American Political Science Review*, no. 3, 1968.

289

NUN, J. The Middle-Class Military Coup (in C. Veliz, ed., *The Politics of Conformity in Latin America*, Oxford, 1967).

POTASH, R. A. *The Army and Politics in Argentina, 1928–1945*, Stanford, 1969.

PUTNAM, R. D. Towards Explaining Military Intervention in Latin American Politics (in *World Politics*, vol. XX, 1967–8, pp. 81–110).

STEPAN, A. *The Military in Politics: Changing Patterns in Brazil*, Princeton, 1971.

THE MIDDLE EAST

ABDEL-MALEK, A. *Egypt, Military Society* (tr. C. L. Markmann), New York, 1968.

BE'ERI, E. *Army Officers in Arab Politics and Society*, London, 1970.

DANN, U. *Iraq Under Qassem 1958–1963*, London, 1969.

HADDAD, G. M. *Revolution and Military Rule in the Middle East: The Northern Tier*, New York, 1965.

HALPERN, M. *The Politics of Social Change in the Middle East and North Africa*, Princeton, N.J., 1963.

HUREWITZ, J. C. *Middle East Politics: the Military Dimension*, New York, 1969.

LUTTWAK, E., and HOROWITZ, D. *The Israeli Army*, London, 1975.

PERLMUTTER, A. *Military and Politics in Israel*, London, 1969.

TORREY, G. H. *Syrian Politics and the Military*, Ohio, 1964.

VATIKIOTIS, P. J. *Politics and the Military in Jordan*, London, 1967.

SOUTH AND SOUTH-EAST ASIA

BADGLEY, J. H. Two Styles of Military Rule: Thailand and Burma (*Government & Opposition*, vol. IV, no. 1, 1969).

FALL, B. *The Two Vietnams: A Political and Military Analysis*, London, 1964.

GETTLEMAN, M. F. (ed.). *Vietnam*, London, 1966.

GRANT, B. *Indonesia*, London, 1967.

KAHIN, G. McT. (ed.). *Government and Politics of Southeast Asia*, Ithaca, New York, 1964.

KIM, Se-Jin. *The Politics of Military Revolution in Korea*, N. Carolina, 1971.

LISSAK, M. *The Deceptive Agent of Modernization: Civil–Military Relations in Thailand and Burma* (2 vols. – Mimeo: Department of Sociology, The Hebrew University of Jerusalem, 1973).

POLOMKA, P. *Indonesia Since Sukarno*, London, 1971.

TINKER, H. *Ballot Box and Bayonet*, London, 1964.

U.S.A.

COOK, F. J. *The Warfare State*, N.Y., 1962.

JANOWITZ, M. (ed.). *The New Military: Changing Patterns of Organisation*, New York, 1964.

JUST, W. *Military Men*, London, 1972.

BIBLIOGRAPHY

MOSKOS, C. C. *The American Enlisted Man*, New York, 1970.
RAYMOND, J. *Power at the Pentagon*, London, 1964.
SHEEHAN, N. (ed.). *The Pentagon Papers*, New York, 1971.
STEIN, H. *American Civil–Military Relations*, Alabama, 1963.

EUROPE

AMBLER, J. S. *The French Army in Politics, 1945–1962*, Ohio, 1966.
BAYNES, Lt-Col. J. C. M. *The Soldier in Modern Society*, London, 1972.
BUSQUET, Bragulat, J. *El militar de carrera en España*, Barcelona, 1967.
CHANTEBOUT, B. *L'Organisation Generale de la Defense Nationale depuis la Fin de la Seconde Guerre Mondiale*, Paris, 1967.
COULOUMBIS, T. A. Greece: Five Years after the Coup (*Greek Review of Social Research*, vol. 14, pp. 172–85, Athens, 1972).
FURNESS, E. *De Gaulle and the French Army*, New York, 1964.
GIRARDET, R. (ed.). *La Crise militaire française 1945–1962*, Paris, 1964.
GORCE, P. M. de la: *The French Army: A Military and Political History* (*1890–1962*), New York, 1963.
KOLKOWICZ, R. The Military (in H. G. Skilling and F. Griffiths, eds., *Interest Groups in Soviet Politics*, Princeton, 1971).
KOLKOWICZ, R. *The Soviet Military and the Communist Party*, Princeton, 1967.
KOURVETARIS, G. A. *Professional Self-Images and Political Perspectives in the Greek Military* (Mimeo: American Sociological Association, Washington, D.C., 1970).
LEGG, K. R. *Politics in Modern Greece*, Stanford, 1969.
MOSKOS, C. C. *The Breakdown of Parliamentary Democracy in Greece 1965–1967* (Mimeo: World Congress of Sociology, Varna, Bulgaria, 1970).
PAPANDREOU, A. *Democracy at Gunpoint*, London, 1973.
PAYNE, S. G. *Politics and the Military in Modern Spain*, Stanford, 1967.
PLANCHAIS, J. *Une Histoire politique de l'Armée, Vol. 2, 1940–1967*, Paris, 1967.
SIOTIS, J. *Some Notes on the Military in Greek Politics*, Mimeo: World Congress of Sociology, Varna, Bulgaria, 1970.
TATU, M. *Power in the Kremlin*, London, 1967.
TSOUCALAS, C. *The Greek Tragedy*, 1969.

INDEX OF PERSONS

INDEX OF COUNTRIES

Laos 13, 203, 217

Latin America 3, 37, 49, 54, 103, 118, 140, 190–91, 203, 208, 214, 215, 218, 219, 223, 230, 232, 235, 237, 266
  nationhood and 209
  wars of independence 200, 201, 202, 203, 208–9

Latvia 2 n.

Lebanon 1, 2, 203, 218

Liberia 218

Libya 202, 257

Liechtenstein 2

Lithuania 2

Malaya 202, 208

Mexico 103, 139–40, 149
  re-civilianization of 180–83, 186, 215

Middle East 3, 49, 103, 208, 218, 219, 223

Morocco 202, 223

Nepal 3

Nicaragua 2, 223

Nigeria 208, 215, 226
  military, motivations of: 'the national interest' 234
  role of: 1966 coup 225, 226, 230, 235, 247, 262

Nyasaland 212

Pakistan 2, 33, 173, 202, 203, 210, 211, 215, 218, 221
  level of political culture in 79, 99, 105–6
  military, disengagement of 258
  military, mood of 55–6
    motivations of: 'the national interest' 72–3; class interest 38
    opportunities to intervene 72–3, 105–6
    role of: 1958 Coup 74 and n., 104, 105–6, 219; Ayub Khan dictatorship 12, 71, 219; post-1961 régime 173 n., 218 n.

Panama 2

Paraguay: level of political culture 118–19
  role of military in 119–20; disengagement of 257–8

Persia 70, 201, 203, 210

Peru 2, 13, 54 n., 103
  military: motivations of: corporate interest 48–9

opportunities to intervene 71
  role of: 1948 Coup 48–9, 164, 219; Odría régime 12, 33, 164

Philippines, The 218

Poland 203

Portugal 1, 2, 28, 203, 227–8
  air force 262
  Armed Forces' Movement 228
  military, motivations of: class interest 227
    role of: 1974 coup 227; Spinola régime 248
  navy 262

Prussia 197
  military reforms in 198–9

Rome 187

Ruanda 229

Rumania 69, 150, 201, 203

San Marino 2

Saudi Arabia 3, 80 n., 257

Senegal 212

Serbia 2, 30, 55, 56, 201, 203

Sierra Leone: 1968 coup 226
  military, disengagement of 258

Somalia 212

South-East Asia 3, 49, 103, 117, 201, 204, 218, 219

Spain: level of political culture 68, 79, 99
  military, disengagement of 257–8
  military, mood of 61–2
    motivations of: 'the national interest' 33, 53; class interest 33; regional interest 38; corporate interest 46; individual self-interest 51
    opportunity to intervene 68–9, 72, 100, 138, 147–8
    role of: French Imperial period 197; 19th century 30, 45–6; 'Restoration régime (1874–1916) 46–7; 1916–23 47, 138; Primo de Rivera régime (1923–30) 12, 16, 160; The Republic and Civil War (1930–39) 62, 147–8; Franco régime 12, 149, 158–9, 221
  techniques of intervention 134

Sudan 2, 33, 71, 79, 99, 100, 104, 106, 107, 150, 160, 162–3, 174, 203, 215, 218, 219, 242, 260

Switzerland 79

INDEX OF SUBJECTS

MORE ABOUT PENGUINS
AND PELICANS

Penguinews, which appears every month, contains details of all the new books issued by Penguins as they are published. From time to time it is supplemented by *Penguins in Print*, which is a complete list of all titles available. (There are some five thousand of these.)

A specimen copy of *Penguinews* will be sent to you free on request. For a year's issues (including the complete lists) please send £1·00 if you live in the British Isles or elsewhere. Just write to Dept EP, Penguin Books Ltd, Harmondsworth, Middlesex, enclosing a cheque or postal order, and your name will be added to the mailing list.

In the U.S.A.: For a complete list of books available from Penguin in the United States write to Dept CS, Penguin Books Inc., 7110 Ambassador Road, Baltimore, Maryland 21207.

In Canada: For a complete list of books available from Penguin in Canada write to Penguin Books Canada Ltd, 41 Steelcase Road West, Markham, Ontario.